A WRITER'S READER

THIRD EDITION

Donald Hall

D. L. Emblen
Santa Rosa Junior College

 **LITTLE, BROWN AND COMPANY**
Boston   Toronto

For William R. Booth

Library of Congress Catalog Card No. 81-84224

ISBN 0-316-339873

9 8 7 6 5 4 3 2 1

HAL

*Published simultaneously in Canada
by Little, Brown & Company (Canada) Limited*

Printed in the United States of America

Preface

Reading well precedes writing well. Of all the ancestors claimed by a fine piece of prose, the most important is the prose from which the writer learned his craft. Writers learn craft, not by memorizing rules about restrictive clauses, but by striving to equal a standard formed from reading.

A composition course, then, must be two courses: one in reading, another in writing. If students lack practice in writing, they are usually unpracticed readers as well. Most students lack quality of reading as well as quantity; and if we assert that good models help us, we admit that bad models hurt us. People who read bad prose twelve hours a week — newspapers, popular fiction, textbooks — are as ill-served as people who read nothing at all. Surely most textbooks, from freshman handbooks through the text for Psych 101, encourage the illusion that words merely stand in for ideas, or carry information on their backs — that words exist for the convenience of thinking much as turnpikes exist for the sake of automobiles.

This barbarism underlies the vogue of speed reading, which urges us to scan lines for comprehension, ignoring syntax and metaphor, ignoring image and feeling and sound. If we are to grow and to learn — and surely if we are to write well — we must learn to read slowly and intimately, and to read good writing. We must learn to read actively, even aggressively, without the passivity derived from watching television. The active reader questions as he reads, subjects each author's ideas to skeptical scrutiny, and engages the writer in dialogue as part of the reading process.

For language embodies the human psyche. Learning to read — that privilege so recently extended to the ancestors of most of us — allows us to enter human history. In books we perceive the gesture, the pulse, the heartbeat, the pallor, the eye-movement, the pitch, and the tone of people who lived before us, or who live now in other places, in other skins, in other habits, customs, beliefs, and ideas.

Language *embodies* the human psyche, which includes ideas and the feelings that properly accompany ideas. There is no sleight-of-mind by which the idea may be separated from its body and remain alive. The body of good writing is rhythm and image, metaphor and syntax, order of phrase and order of paragraph.

A NOTE TO THE SECOND EDITION

Many teachers helped us prepare the second edition of *A Writer's Reader* — in letters, in conversations at colleges all over the country, in responses to a Little, Brown survey of users. We thank more people than we can list.

We have added considerable material, far more than we have cut, and we are pleased with what we have come up with. We believe that we have made a representative sampling of good prose. We like some pieces more than others, heaven knows, but we believe that all of them provide something to learn from. We have included a wide variety of American prose, not only contemporary but historical, with high points of our history represented in their own style and syntax. We hope that young Americans will attach themselves to the body of their history by immersion in its significant utterances.

We have numbered paragraphs for ease of reference. Although *A Writer's Reader* is a collection of essays, we have again violated coherence by including fiction, feeling that the contrast afforded by a few short stories among the essays was useful and refreshing. For this edition, we have gone further afield and included several poems, for the same reason. Perhaps we should make an argument for including poems — but let us just say that we enjoy them, and we hope you do too. To satisfy students' curiosity, we have included headnotes to the poems; but we have stopped short of suggesting questions after them, lest we seem to surround a landscape garden with a hundred-foot-high concrete wall.

We have chosen to arrange our essays, stories, and poems alphabetically by author. This arrangement makes for random juxtaposition, irrational sequence, and no sense at all — which is why we chose it. We expect no one to teach these pieces in alphabetical order. (We expect teachers to find their own order — which they would do whatever order we attempted to impose.) In our first edition we struggled to make a stylistic organization, listing some essays as examples of "Sentences," others as examples of "Paragraphs." For the editors themselves, a year after deciding on our organization, it was no longer clear why essay X was to be studied for its sentences, essay Y for its paragraphs. With a rhetorical organization, one runs into another sort of problem. Although an essay may contain Division, or Process Analysis, or an example of Example, the same essay is likely to use three or four other patterns as well. No piece of real prose is ever so pure as our systems of classification. Thematic organizations, which have their attractions, have similar flaws; is E. B. White's theme, in "Once More to the Lake," Mortality? Aging? Youth and Age? or, How I Spent My Summer Vacation?

Our arrangement is more arbitrary than an arrangement by style or rhetoric or theme, and presents itself only to be ignored. At the same time, there are dozens of ways in which these essays (and poems and stories) can be used together. Our Instructor's Manual suggests several combinations. Our Rhetorical Index, printed as an appendix to the text itself, lists single-paragraph examples of rhetorical patterns as well as longer units. We hope that students will find the Rhetorical Index useful. Freshmen who return to their rooms from class, set to write a paper using Comparison and Contrast, sometimes find themselves in need of a concrete example of the assigned pattern to imitate.

Thus, we have tried to supply some useful maps to go with our arbitrary arrangement.

We must admit that we take pleasure in the strange juxtapositions the alphabet imposes. We enjoy beginning our book with Henry Adams, James Agee, Woody Allen, Maya Angelou. . . .

A NOTE TO THE THIRD EDITION

Still more teachers have contributed their experience to making the third edition of *A Writer's Reader*. Although our principles have remained the same, we have made changes in our selections; no one wants to teach the same essays year after year. We have made a new Rhetorical Index for this edition and have added a Thematic Index. Following suggestions from several teachers, we have chosen to represent a few authors by small clusters of their work. Thus, we include three essays by George Orwell; Flannery O'Connor is represented by an essay, a story, and four letters; Langston Hughes contributes an essay, two poems, and two of his "Simple" stories; from Sylvia Plath we print a notebook entry and the poem she later derived from it.

ACKNOWLEDGMENTS

We thank the following users of the first and second editions for their helpful comments: Louise Ackley, Maureen Andrews, Jane Berk, Meredith Berman, Charles E. Bolton, Ed Buckley, Sandra Burns, Jon Burton, Richard Cloyed, Steven Connelly, Randy Conine, Roger Conner, Charles L. Cornwell, Valecia Crisafulli, Garber Davidson, Virginia de Araujo, Elizabeth Failla, Gala Fitzgerald, Frances B. Foreman, Peggy Gledhill, Barbara Hamilton, Walter Harrison, John Huntington, Donald Kansch, Gregory Keeler, Jeff Kluewer, John Larner, Karen LeFerre, Richard H. Lerner, Opal A. Lovett, Nellie McCrory, Sherry McGuire, Andrew Makarushka, Steven J. Masello, Richard Maxwell, Deanne Milan, Molly Moore-Kehler, Barbara Olive, Stephen O'Neil, Beverly Palmer, Ray Peterson, Martha Rainbolt, Harriet Susskind Rosenblum, Terry Shelton, Donald K. Skiles, Thomas Skmetzo, Marilyn Smith, Andrew Solomon, David A. Spurr, Helen Stauffer, Art Suchoki, Kathleen Sullivan, Jane Bamblin Thomas, Darlene Unrue, Sara Varhus, Craig Watson, Richard A. Widmayer, Gary Williams, Suzanne Wilson, George Wymer, and Robert Lee Zimmerman. We thank Charles Christensen, David W. Lynch, and Donna McCormick, at Little, Brown, for their efforts on the book's behalf.

Contents

parents, crowding in at the lighted doors. But once he was inside, the locker room would be bright and hot, and the other guys would be there, laughing it up and towel-slapping, and the tight feeling would leave. Now there were whole days when it didn't leave."

*Henry Adams (1838–1918) entertained notions of a political
career, in keeping with family traditions, but withdrew from
Washington in distaste over the corruption of the Grant administration. For a time, he taught history at Harvard and edited the*
North American Review. *After publishing two anonymous
novels without great success, he undertook and completed the
massive* History of the United States During the Administrations
of Jefferson and Madison. *His best works are* Mont St. Michel and
Chartres *(1904) and his autobiography — written in the third
person and called* The Education of Henry Adams *(1907) — from
which we take this fragment of reminiscence.*

*Hundreds of American writers have recollected visits to grand-
father's house; few were grandson to one president and great-
grandson to another. Adams's contrasts of style — eighteenth
century with nineteenth, Boston with the small town of Quincy,
the Brooks grandfather with the Adams grandfather — culminate
in an anecdote that illuminates the fundamental contrast of
private and public.*

1

HENRY ADAMS
Winter and Summer

Boys are wild animals, rich in the treasures of sense, but the New   1
England boy had a wider range of emotions than boys of more equable
climates. He felt his nature crudely, as it was meant. To the boy Henry
Adams, summer was drunken. Among senses, smell was the strongest
— smell of hot pine-woods and sweet-fern in the scorching summer
noon; of new-mown hay; of ploughed earth; of box hedges; of peaches,
lilacs, syringas; of stables, barns, cow-yards; of salt water and low tide
on the marshes; nothing came amiss. Next to smell came taste, and
the children knew the taste of everything they saw or touched, from

pennyroyal and flagroot to the shell of a pignut and the letters of a spelling book — the taste of A-B, AB, suddenly revived on the boy's tongue sixty years afterwards. Light, line, and color as sensual pleasures, came later and were as crude as the rest. The New England light is glare, and the atmosphere harshens color. The boy was a full man before he ever knew what was meant by atmosphere; his idea of pleasure in light was the blaze of a New England sun. His idea of color was a peony, with the dew of early morning on its petals. The intense blue of the sea, as he saw it a mile or two away, from the Quincy hills; the cumuli in a June afternoon sky; the strong reds and greens and purples of colored prints and children's picture-books, as the American colors then ran; these were ideals. The opposites or antipathies, were the cold grays of November evenings, and the thick, muddy thaws of Boston winter. With such standards, the Bostonian could not but develop a double nature. Life was a double thing. After a January blizzard, the boy who could look with pleasure into the violent snow-glare of the cold white sunshine, with its intense light and shade, scarcely knew what was meant by tone. He could reach it only by education.

2   Winter and summer, then, were two hostile lives, and bred two separate natures. Winter was always the effort to live; summer was tropical license. Whether the children rolled in the grass, or waded in the brook, or swam in the salt ocean, or sailed in the bay, or fished for smelts in the creeks, or netted minnows in the salt-marshes, or took to the pine-woods and the granite quarries, or chased muskrats and hunted snapping-turtles in the swamps, or mushrooms or nuts on the autumn hills, summer and country were always sensual living, while winter was always compulsory learning. Summer was the multiplicity of nature; winter was school.

3   The bearing of the two seasons on the education of Henry Adams was no fancy; it was the most decisive force he ever knew; it ran through life, and made the division between its perplexing, warring, irreconcilable problems, irreducible opposites, with growing emphasis to the last year of study. From earliest childhood the boy was accustomed to feel that, for him, life was double. Winter and summer, town and country, law and liberty, were hostile, and the man who pretended they were not, was in his eyes a schoolmaster — that is, a man employed to tell lies to little boys. Though Quincy was but two hours' walk from Beacon Hill, it belonged in a different world. For two hundred years, every Adams, from father to son, had lived within sight of State Street, and sometimes had lived in it, yet none had ever taken kindly to the town, or been taken kindly by it. The boy inherited his

double nature. He knew as yet nothing about his great-grandfather, who had died a dozen years before his own birth: he took for granted that any great-grandfather of his must have always been good, and his enemies wicked; but he divined his great-grandfather's character from his own. Never for a moment did he connect the two ideas of Boston and John Adams; they were separate and antagonistic; the idea of John Adams went with Quincy. He knew his grandfather John Quincy Adams only as an old man of seventy-five or eighty who was friendly and gentle with him, but except that he heard his grandfather always called "the President," and his grandmother "the Madam," he had no reason to suppose that his Adams grandfather differed in character from his Brooks grandfather who was equally kind and benevolent. He liked the Adams side best, but for no other reason than that it reminded him of the country, the summer, and the absence of restraint. Yet he felt also that Quincy was in a way inferior to Boston, and that socially Boston looked down on Quincy. The reason was clear enough even to a five-year-old child. Quincy had no Boston style. Little enough style had either; a simpler manner of life and thought could hardly exist, short of cave-dwelling. The flint-and-steel with which his grandfather Adams used to light his own fires in the early morning was still on the mantelpiece of his study. The idea of a livery or even a dress for servants, or of an evening toilette, was next to blasphemy. Bathrooms, water-supplies, lighting, heating, and the whole array of domestic comforts, were unknown at Quincy. Boston had already a bathroom, a water-supply, a furnace, and gas. The superiority of Boston was evident, but a child liked it no better for that.

The magnificence of his grandfather Brooks's house in Pearl 4 Street or South Street has long ago disappeared, but perhaps his country house at Medford may still remain to show what impressed the mind of a boy in 1845 with the idea of city splendor. The President's place at Quincy was the larger and older and far the more interesting of the two; but a boy felt at once its inferiority in fashion. It showed plainly enough its want of wealth. It smacked of colonial age, but not of Boston style or plush curtains. To the end of his life he never quite overcame the prejudice thus drawn in with his childish breath. He never could compel himself to care for nineteenth-century style. He was never able to adopt it, any more than his father or grandfather or great-grandfather had done. Not that he felt it as particularly hostile, for he reconciled himself to much that was worse; but because, for some remote reason, he was born an eighteenth-century child. The old house at Quincy was eighteenth-century. What style it had was in its

Queen Anne mahogany panels and its Louis Seize chairs and sofas. The panels belonged to an old colonial Vassall who built the house; the furniture had been brought back from Paris in 1789 or 1801 or 1817, along with porcelain and books and much else of old diplomatic remnants; and neither of the two eighteenth-century styles — neither English Queen Anne nor French Louis Seize — was comfortable for a boy, or for any one else. The dark mahogany had been painted white to suit daily life in winter gloom. Nothing seemed to favor, for a child's objects, the older forms. On the contrary, most boys, as well as grown-up people, preferred the new, with good reason, and the child felt himself distinctly at a disadvantage for the taste.

5   Nor had personal preference any share in his bias. The Brooks grandfather was as amiable and as sympathetic as the Adams grandfather. Both were born in 1767, and both died in 1848. Both were kind to children, and both belonged rather to the eighteenth than to the nineteenth centuries. The child knew no difference between them except that one was associated with winter and the other with summer; one with Boston, the other with Quincy. Even with Medford, the association was hardly easier. Once as a very young boy he was taken to pass a few days with his grandfather Brooks under charge of his aunt, but became so violently homesick that within twenty-four hours he was brought back in disgrace. Yet he could not remember ever being seriously homesick again.

6   The attachment to Quincy was not altogether sentimental or wholly sympathetic. Quincy was not a bed of thornless roses. Even there the curse of Cain set its mark. There as elsewhere a cruel universe combined to crush a child. As though three or four vigorous brothers and sisters, with the best will, were not enough to crush any child, every one else conspired towards an education which he hated. From cradle to grave this problem of running order through chaos, direction through space, discipline through freedom, unity through multiplicity, has always been, and must always be, the task of education, as it is the moral of religion, philosophy, science, art, politics, and economy; but a boy's will is his life, and he dies when it is broken, as the colt dies in harness, taking a new nature in becoming tame. Rarely has the boy felt kindly towards his tamers. Between him and his master has always been war. Henry Adams never knew a boy of his generation to like a master, and the task of remaining on friendly terms with one's own family, in such a relation, was never easy.

7   All the more singular it seemed afterwards to him that his first serious contact with the President should have been a struggle of will,

in which the old man almost necessarily defeated the boy, but instead of leaving, as usual in such defeats, a lifelong sting, left rather an impression of as fair treatment as could be expected from a natural enemy. The boy met seldom with such restraint. He could not have been much more than six years old at the time — seven at the utmost — and his mother had taken him to Quincy for a long stay with the President during the summer. What became of the rest of the family he quite forgot; but he distinctly remembered standing at the house door one summer morning in a passionate outburst of rebellion against going to school. Naturally his mother was the immediate victim of his rage; that is what mothers are for, and boys also; but in this case the boy had his mother at unfair disadvantage, for she was a guest, and had no means of enforcing obedience. Henry showed a certain tactical ability by refusing to start, and he met all efforts at compulsion by successful, though too vehement protest. He was in fair way to win, and was holding his own, with sufficient energy, at the bottom of the long staircase which led up to the door of the President's library, when the door opened, and the old man slowly came down. Putting on his hat, he took the boy's hand without a word, and walked with him, paralyzed by awe, up the road to the town. After the first moments of consternation at this interference in a domestic dispute, the boy reflected that an old gentleman close on eighty would never trouble himself to walk near a mile on a hot summer morning over a shadeless road to take a boy to school, and that it would be strange if a lad imbued with the passion of freedom could not find a corner to dodge around, somewhere before reaching the school door. Then and always, the boy insisted that this reasoning justified his apparent submission; but the old man did not stop, and the boy saw all his strategical points turned, one after another, until he found himself seated inside the school, and obviously the centre of curious if not malevolent criticism. Not till then did the President release his hand and depart.

The point was that this act, contrary to the inalienable rights of boys, and nullifying the social compact, ought to have made him dislike his grandfather for life. He could not recall that it had this effect even for a moment. With a certain maturity of mind, the child must have recognized that the President, though a tool of tyranny, had done his disreputable work with a certain intelligence. He had shown no temper, no irritation, no personal feeling, and had made no display of force. Above all, he had held his tongue. During their long walk he had said nothing; he had uttered no syllable of revolting cant about the duty of obedience and the wickedness of resistance to law; he had

James Agee (1909–1955) was a journalist, critic, poet, and nov-
elist. He was an early critic of film as art, and wrote the script for
The African Queen, *among other movies. A heart attack killed*
him at forty-five, before he had finished his novel A Death in the
Family. *Editors assembled the final manuscript and included as*
a prologue the essay reprinted here. The novel was awarded the
Pulitzer Prize in 1958. His prose evokes lost time; detail is
described with intimate precision, landscape rendered exactly
with a wash of nostalgia.

2

JAMES AGEE

Knoxville: Summer 1915

We are talking now of summer evenings in Knoxville, Tennessee 1
in the time that I lived there so successfully disguised to myself as a
child. It was a little bit mixed sort of block, fairly solidly lower middle
class, with one or two juts apiece on either side of that. The houses
corresponded: middle-sized gracefully fretted wood houses built in the
late nineties and early nineteen hundreds, with small front and side
and more spacious back yards, and trees in the yards, and porches.
These were softwooded trees, poplars, tulip trees, cottonwoods. There
were fences around one or two of the houses, but mainly the yards ran
into each other with only now and then a low hedge that wasn't doing
very well. There were few good friends among the grown people, and
they were not poor enough for the other sort of intimate acquaintance,
but everyone nodded and spoke, and even might talk short times,
trivially, and at the two extremes of the general or the particular, and

ordinarily nextdoor neighbors talked quite a bit when they happened to run into each other, and never paid calls. The men were mostly small businessmen, one or two very modestly executives, one or two worked with their hands, most of them clerical, and most of them between thirty and forty-five.

2   But it is of these evenings, I speak.

3   Supper was at six and was over by half past. There was still daylight, shining softly and with a tarnish, like the lining of a shell; and the carbon lamps lifted at the corners were on in the light, and the locusts were started, and the fire flies were out, and a few frogs were flopping in the dewy grass, by the time the fathers and the children came out. The children ran out first hell bent and yelling those names by which they were known; then the fathers sank out leisurely in crossed suspenders, their collars removed and their necks looking tall and shy. The mothers stayed back in the kitchen washing and drying, putting things away, recrossing their traceless footsteps like the life-time journeys of bees, measuring out the dry cocoa for breakfast. When they came out they had taken off their aprons and their skirts were dampened and they sat in rockers on their porches quietly.

4   It is not of the games children played in the evening that I want to speak now, it is of a contemporaneous atmosphere that has little to do with them: that of the fathers of families, each in his space of lawn, his shirt fishlike pale in the unnatural light and his face nearly anonymous, hosing their lawns. The hoses were attached at spigots that stood out of the brick foundations of the houses. The nozzles were variously set but usually so there was a long sweet stream of spray, the nozzle wet in the hand, the water trickling the right forearm and the peeled-back cuff, and the water whishing out a long loose and low-curved cone, and so gentle a sound. First an insane noise of violence in the nozzle, then the still irregular sound of adjustment, then the smoothing into steadiness and a pitch as accurately tuned to the size and style of stream as any violin. So many qualities of sound out of one hose: so many choral differences out of those several hoses that were in earshot. Out of any one hose, the almost dead silence of the release, and the short still arch of the separate big drops, silent as a held breath, and the only noise the flattering noise on leaves and the slapped grass at the fall of each big drop. That, and the intense hiss with the intense stream; that, and that same intensity not growing less but growing more quiet and delicate with the turn of the nozzle, up to that extreme tender whisper when the water was just a wide bell of film. Chiefly, though, the hoses were set much alike, in a compro-

mise between distance and tenderness of spray (and quite surely a
sense of art behind this compromise, and a quiet deep joy, too real to
recognize itself), and the sounds therefore were pitched much alike;
pointed by the snorting start of a new hose; decorated by some man
playful with the nozzle; left empty, like God by the sparrow's fall,
when any single one of them desists: and all, though near alike, of
various pitch; and in this unison. These sweet pale streamings in the
light lift out their pallors and their voices all together, mothers hushing their children, the hushing unnaturally prolonged, the men gentle
and silent and each snail-like withdrawn into the quietude of what he
singly is doing, the urination of huge children stood loosely military
against an invisible wall, and gentle happy and peaceful, tasting the
mean goodness of their living like the last of their suppers in their
mouths; while the locusts carry on this noise of hoses on their much
higher and sharper key. The noise of the locust is dry, and it seems not
to be rasped or vibrated but urged from him as if through a small
orifice by breath that can never give out. Also there is never one locust
but an illusion of at least a thousand. The noise of each locust is
pitched in some classic locust range out of which none of them varies
more than two full tones: and yet you seem to hear each locust dis-
crete from all the rest, and there is a long, slow pulse in their noise,
like the scarcely defined arch of a long and high set bridge. They are
all around in every tree, so that the noise seems to come from nowhere
and everywhere at once, from the whole shell heaven, shivering in
your flesh and teasing your eardrums, the boldest of all the sounds of
night. And yet it is habitual to summer nights, and is of the great order
of noises, like the noises of the sea and of the blood her precocious
grandchild, which you realize you are hearing only when you catch
yourself listening. Meantime from low in the dark, just outside the
swaying horizons of the hoses, conveying always grass in the damp of
dew and its strong green-black smear of smell, the regular yet spaced
noises of the crickets, each a sweet cold silver noise threenoted, like
the slipping each time of three matched links of a small chain.

But the men by now, one by one, have silenced their hoses and   5
drained and coiled them. Now only two, and now only one, is left, and
you see only ghostlike shirt with the sleeve garters, and sober mystery
of his mild face like the lifted face of large cattle enquiring of your
presence in a pitchdark pool of meadow; and now he too is gone; and
it has become that time of evening when people sit on their porches,
rocking gently and talking gently and watching the street and the
standing up into their sphere of possession of the trees, of bird–hung

havens, hangars. People go by; things go by. A horse, drawing a buggy, breaking his hollow iron music on the asphalt; a loud auto; a quiet auto; people in pairs, not in a hurry, scuffling, switching their weight of aestival body, talking casually, the taste hovering over them of vanilla, strawberry, pasteboard and starched milk, the image upon them of lovers and horsemen, squared with clowns in hueless amber. A street car raising its iron moan; stopping, belling and starting; stertorous; rousing and raising again its iron increasing moan and swimming its gold windows and straw seats on past and past and past, the bleak spark crackling and cursing above it like a small malignant spirit set to dog its tracks; the iron whine rises on rising speed; still risen, faints; halts; the faint stinging bell; rises again, still fainter; fainting, lifting, lifts, faints forgone: forgotten. Now is the night one blue dew.

> Now is the the night one blue dew, my father has drained, he has coiled the hose.
> Low on the length of lawns, a frailing of fire who breathes.
> Content, silver, like peeps of light, each cricket makes his comment over and over in the drowned grass.
> A cold toad thumpily flounders.
> Within the edges of damp shadows of side yards are hovering children nearly sick with joy of fear, who watch the unguarding of a telephone pole.
> Around white carbon corner lamps bugs of all sizes are lifted elliptic, solar systems. Big hardshells bruise themselves, assailant: he is fallen on his back, legs squiggling. '
> Parents on porches: rock and rock: From damp strings morning glories: hang their ancient faces.
> The dry and exalted noise of the locusts from all the air at once enchants my eardrums.

6   On the rough wet grass of the back yard my father and mother have spread quilts. We all lie there, my mother, my father, my uncle, my aunt, and I too am lying there. First we were sitting up, then one of us lay down, and then we all lay down, on our stomachs, or on our sides, or on our backs, and they have kept on talking. They are not talking much, and the talk is quiet, of nothing in particular, of nothing at all in particular, of nothing at all. The stars are wide and alive, they seem each like a smile of great sweetness, and they seem very near. All my people are larger bodies than mine, quiet, with voices gentle and meaningless like the voices of sleeping birds. One is an artist, he is living at home. One is a musician, she is living at home. One is my mother who is good to me. One is my father who is good to me. By

some chance, here they are, all on this earth; and who shall ever tell the sorrow of being on this earth, lying, on quilts, on the grass, in a summer evening, among the sounds of the night. May God bless my people, my uncle, my aunt, my mother, my good father, oh, remember them kindly in their time of trouble; and in the hour of their taking away.

After a little I am taken in and put to bed. Sleep, soft smiling, draws me unto her: and those receive me, who quietly treat me, as one familiar and well beloved in that home: but will not, oh, will not, not now, not ever; but will not ever tell me who I am. 7

___ CONSIDERATIONS _____

1. Agee is famous for the close attention he pays to the senses. In this piece, which one — seeing, hearing, smelling, tasting, touching — is exercised the most?

2. What do you make of Agee's paragraph sense? Compare, for example, Paragraph 2 with Paragraph 4. Would you recommend breaking the latter into smaller units? Where? Why, or why not?

3. The first sentence of Paragraph 1 offers an opportunity for experimentation. Copy it out *without* the following phrases: "so successfully," "disguised," and "to myself." Then replace the phrases, one at a time, considering how each addition changes the dimension, the direction, or the depth of the story begun. Which of the three works the greatest change? Why?

4. How does the first sentence embody a theme important to the whole story? Is that theme sounded elsewhere in the story?

5. Agee's evocation of a summer evening might seem strange to an apartment-dweller in Knoxville in 1981. Would it be possible to write so serenely about a summer evening in the Knoxville — or Detroit, or Minneapolis, or San Francisco — of today?

6. Agee's attempt to recapture and thus understand his childhood — or at least a moment of it — is similar to and different from the efforts of several other writers in this book. Compare and contrast "Knoxville: Summer 1915" with one of these: Henry Adams (pages 1–6); Frank Conroy (pages 105–112); Lillian Hellman (pages 199–205); Langston Hughes (pages 213–215); or E. B. White (pages 459–464).

Woody Allen (b. 1935) is a universal genius, best known for acting in, writing, and directing movies. His films range from What's New, Pussycat? *(1964) through* Love and Death *(1975) and* Annie Hall *(1977) to* Stardust Memories *(1980). He has also published short fiction in* Playboy *and* The New Yorker, *and in 1978 won an O. Henry Award for the best American short story of the previous year. His prose is collected in three volumes,* Getting Even *(1972),* Without Feathers *(1975), and* Side Effects *(1980).*

He began his career as a comedy writer for television shows, then became a comedian himself. His first great successes were Broadway plays, Don't Drink the Water *(1966) and* Play It Again, Sam *(1969). This playlet comes from* Getting Even.

_3

WOODY ALLEN

Death Knocks

1   *(The play takes place in the bedroom of the Nat Ackermans' two-story house, somewhere in Kew Gardens. The carpeting is wall-to-wall. There is a big double bed and a large vanity. The room is elaborately furnished and curtained, and on the walls there are several paintings and a not really attractive barometer. Soft theme music as the curtain rises. Nat Ackerman, a bald, paunchy fifty-seven-year-old dress manufacturer, is lying on the bed finishing off tomorrow's* Daily News. *He wears a bathrobe and slippers, and reads by a bed light clipped to the white headboard of the bed. The time is near*

midnight. Suddenly we hear a noise, and Nat sits up and looks at the window.)

Nat: What the hell is that?

(Climbing awkwardly through the window is a sombre, caped figure. The intruder wears a black hood and skintight black clothes. The hood covers his head but not his face, which is middle-aged and stark white. He is something like Nat in appearance. He huffs audibly and then trips over the windowsill and falls into the room.)

Death *(for it is no one else):* Jesus Christ. I nearly broke my neck.

Nat *(watching with bewilderment):* Who are you? 5

Death: Death.

Nat: Who?

Death: Death. Listen — can I sit down? I nearly broke my neck. I'm shaking like a leaf.

Nat: Who *are* you?

Death: *Death.* You got a glass of water? 10

Nat: Death? What do you mean, Death?

Death: What is wrong with you? You see the black costume and the whitened face?

Nat: Yeah.

Death: Is it Halloween?

Nat: No. 15

Death: Then I'm Death. Now can I get a glass of water — or a Fresca?

Nat: If this is some joke —

Death: What kind of joke? You're fifty-seven? Nat Ackerman? One eighteen Pacific Street? Unless I blew it — where's that call sheet? *(He fumbles through pocket, finally producing a card with an address on it. It seems to check.)*

Nat: What do you want with me?

Death: What do I want? What do you think I want? 20

Nat: You must be kidding. I'm in perfect health.

Death *(unimpressed):* Uh-huh. *(Looking around)* This is a nice place. You do it yourself?

Nat: We had a decorator, but we worked with her.

Death *(looking at picture on the wall):* I love those kids with the big eyes.

Nat: I don't want to go yet. 25

Death: *You* don't want to go? Please don't start in. As it is, I'm nauseous from the climb.

Nat: What climb?

Death: I climbed up the drainpipe. I was trying to make a dramatic entrance. I see the big windows and you're awake reading. I figure it's worth a shot. I'll climb up and enter with a little — you know . . . *(Snaps fingers)* Meanwhile, I get my heel caught on some vines, the drainpipe breaks, and I'm hanging by a thread. Then my cape begins to tear. Look, let's just go. It's been a rough night.

Nat: You broke my drainpipe?

30   Death: Broke. It didn't break. It's a little bent. Didn't you hear anything? I slammed into the ground.

Nat: I was reading.

Death: You must have really been engrossed. *(Lifting newspaper Nat was reading)* "NAB COEDS IN POT ORGY." Can I borrow this?

Nat: I'm not finished. ·

Death: Er — I don't know how to put this to you, pal . . .

35   Nat: Why didn't you just ring downstairs?

Death: I'm telling you, I could have, but how does it look? This way I get a little drama going. Something. Did you read *Faust?*

Nat: What?

Death: And what if you had company? You're sitting there with important people. I'm Death — I should ring the bell and traipse right in the front? Where's your thinking?

Nat: Listen, Mister, it's very late.

40   Death: Yeah. Well, you want to go?

Nat: Go where?

Death: Death. It. The Thing. The Happy Hunting Grounds. *(Looking at his own knee)* Y'know, that's a pretty bad cut. My first job, I'm liable to get gangrene yet.

Nat: Now, wait a minute. I need time. I'm not ready to go.

Death: I'm sorry. I can't help you. I'd like to, but it's the moment.

45   Nat: How can it be the moment? I just merged with Modiste Originals.

Death: What's the difference, a couple of bucks more or less.

Nat: Sure, what do you care? You guys probably have all your expenses paid.

Death: You want to come along now?

Nat *(studying him)*: I'm sorry, but I cannot believe you're Death.

50   Death: Why? What'd you expect — Rock Hudson?

Nat: No, it's not that.

Death: I'm sorry if I disappointed you.

Nat: Don't get upset. I don't know, I always thought you'd be . . . uh . . . taller.

Death: I'm five seven. It's average for my weight.

Nat: You look a little like me.   55

Death: Who should I look like? I'm your death.

Nat: Give me some time. Another day.

Death: I can't. What do you want me to say?

Nat: One more day. Twenty-four hours.

Death: What do you need it for? The radio said rain tomorrow.   60

Nat: Can't we work out something?

Death: Like what?

Nat: You play chess?

Death: No, I don't.

Nat: I once saw a picture of you playing chess.   65

Death: Couldn't be me, because I don't play chess. Gin rummy, maybe.

Nat: You play gin rummy?

Death: Do I play gin rummy? Is Paris a city?

Nat: You're good, huh?

Death: Very good.   70

Nat: I'll tell you what I'll do —

Death: Don't make any deals with me.

Nat: I'll play you gin rummy. If you win, I'll go immediately. If I win, give me some more time. A little bit — one more day.

Death: Who's got time to play gin rummy?

Nat: Come on. If you're so good.   75

Death: Although I feel like a game . . .

Nat: Come on. Be a sport. We'll shoot for a half hour.

Death: I really shouldn't.

Nat: I got the cards right here. Don't make a production.

Death: All right, come on. We'll play a little. It'll relax me.   80

Nat *(getting cards, pad, and pencil):* You won't regret this.

Death: Don't give me a sales talk. Get the cards and give me a Fresca and put out something. For God's sake, a stranger drops in, you don't have potato chips or pretzels.

Nat: There's M&M's downstairs in a dish.

Death: M&M's. What if the President came? He'd get M&M's too?

Nat: You're not the President.   85

Death: Deal.

(Nat deals, turns up a five.)

Nat: You want to play a tenth of a cent a point to make it interesting?

Death: It's not interesting enough for you?

90 Nat: I play better when money's at stake.

Death: Whatever you say, Newt.

Nat: Nat. Nat Ackerman. You don't know my name?

Death: Newt, Nat — I got such a headache.

Nat: You want that five?

95 Death: No.

Nat: So pick.

Death *(surveying his hand as he picks):* Jesus, I got nothing here.

Nat: What's it like?

Death: What's what like?

100 *(Throughout the following, they pick and discard.)*

Nat: Death.

Death: What should it be like? You lay there.

Nat: Is there anything after?

Death: Aha, you're saving twos.

105 Nat: I'm asking. Is there anything after?

Death *(absently):* You'll see.

Nat: Oh, then I will actually see something?

Death: Well, maybe I shouldn't have put it that way. Throw.

Nat: To get an answer from you is a big deal.

110 Death: I'm playing cards.

Nat: All right, play, play.

Death: Meanwhile, I'm giving you one card after another.

Nat: Don't look through the discards.

Death: I'm not looking. I'm straightening them up. What was the knock card?

115 Nat: Four. You ready to knock already?

Death: Who said I'm ready to knock? All I asked was what was the knock card.

Nat: And all I asked was is there anything for me to look forward to.

Death: Play.

Nat: Can't you tell me anything? Where do we go?

120 Death: We? To tell you the truth, *you* fall in a crumpled heap on the floor.

Nat: Oh, I can't wait for that! Is it going to hurt?

Death: Be over in a second.

Nat: Terrific. *(Sighs)* I needed this. A man merges with Modiste Originals . . .

Death: How's four points?
Nat: You're knocking?   125
Death: Four points is good?
Nat: No, I got two.
Death: You're kidding.
Nat: No, you lose.
Death: Holy Christ, and I thought you were saving sixes.   130
　Nat: No. Your deal. Twenty points and two boxes. Shoot. *(Death deals.)* I must fall on the floor, eh? I can't be standing over the sofa when it happens?
Death: No. Play.
Nat: Why not?
Death: Because you fall on the floor! Leave me alone. I'm trying to concentrate.
　Nat: Why must it be on the floor? That's all I'm saying! Why   135
can't the whole thing happen and I'll stand next to the sofa?
Death: I'll try my best. Now can we play?
Nat: That's all I'm saying. You remind me of Moe Lefkowitz. He's also stubborn.
　Death: I remind him of Moe Lefkowitz. I'm one of the most terrifying figures you could possibly imagine, and him I remind of Moe Lefkowitz. What is he, a furrier?
　Nat: You should be such a furrier. He's good for eighty thousand a year. Passementeries. He's got his own factory. Two points.
Death: What?   140
Nat: Two points. I'm knocking. What have you got?
Death: My hand is like a basketball score.
Nat: And it's spades.
Death: If you didn't talk so much.
(They redeal and play on.)   145
　Nat: What'd you mean before when you said this was your first job?
Death: What does it sound like?
Nat: What are you telling me — that nobody ever went before?
Death: Sure they went. But I didn't take them.
Nat: So who did?   150
Death: Others.
Nat: There's others?
Death: Sure. Each one has his own personal way of going.
Nat: I never knew that.

155 Death: Why should you know? Who are you?

Nat: What do you mean who am I? Why — I'm nothing?

Death: Not nothing. You're a dress manufacturer. Where do you come to knowledge of the eternal mysteries?

Nat: What are you talking about? I make a beautiful dollar. I sent two kids through college. One is in advertising, the other's married. I got my own home. I drive a Chrysler. My wife has whatever she wants. Maids, mink coat, vacations. Right now she's at the Eden Roc. Fifty dollars a day because she wants to be near her sister. I'm supposed to join her next week, so what do you think I am — some guy off the street?

Death: All right. Don't be so touchy.

160 Nat: Who's touchy?

Death: How would you like it if I got insulted quickly?

Nat: Did I insult you?

Death: You didn't say you were disappointed in me?

Nat: What do you expect? You want me to throw you a block party?

165 Death: I'm not talking about that. I mean me personally. I'm too short, I'm this, I'm that.

Nat: I said you looked like me. It's like a reflection.

Death: All right, deal, deal.

(They continue to play as music steals in and the lights dim until all is in total darkness. The lights slowly come up again, and now it is later and their game is over. Nat tallies.)

Nat: Sixty-eight . . . one-fifty . . . Well, you lose.

170 Death *(dejectedly looking through the deck):* I knew I shouldn't have thrown that nine. Damn it.

Nat: So I'll see you tomorrow.

Death: What do you mean you'll see me tomorrow?

Nat: I won the extra day. Leave me alone.

Death: You were serious?

175 Nat: We made a deal.

Death: Yeah, but —

Nat: Don't "but" me. I won twenty-four hours. Come back tomorrow.

Death: I didn't know we were actually playing for time.

Nat: That's too bad about you. You should pay attention.

180 Death: Where am I going to go for twenty-four hours?

Nat: What's the difference? The main thing is I won an extra day.

Death: What do you want me to do — walk the streets?

Nat: Check into a hotel and go to a movie. Take a *schvitz.* Don't make a federal case.

Death: Add the score again.

Nat: Plus you owe me twenty-eight dollars.   185

Death: *What?*

Nat: That's right, Buster. Here it is — read it.

Death *(going through pockets):* I have a few singles — not twenty-eight dollars.

Nat: I'll take a check.

Death: From what account?   190

Nat: Look who I'm dealing with.

Death: Sue me. Where do I keep my checking account?

Nat: All right, gimme what you got and we'll call it square.

Death: Listen, I need that money.

Nat: Why should you need money?   195

Death: What are you talking about? You're going to the Beyond.

Nat: So?

Death: So — you know how far that is?

Nat: So?

Death: So where's gas? Where's tolls?   200

Nat: We're going by car!

Death: You'll find out. *(Agitatedly)* Look — I'll be back tomorrow, and you'll give me a chance to win the money back. Otherwise I'm in definite trouble.

Nat: Anything you want. Double or nothing we'll play. I'm liable to win an extra week or a month. The way you play, maybe years.

Death: Meantime I'm stranded.

Nat: See you tomorrow.

Death *(being edged to the doorway):* Where's a good hotel? What   205
am I talking about hotel, I got no money. I'll go sit in Bickford's. *(He picks up the* News.*)*

Nat: Out. Out. That's my paper. *(He takes it back.)*

Death *(exiting):* I couldn't just take him and go. I had to get involved in rummy.

Nat *(calling after him):* And be careful going downstairs. On one of the steps the rug is loose.

(And, on cue, we hear a terrific crash. Nat sighs, then crosses to   210
the bedside table and makes a phone call.)

Nat: Hello, Moe? Me. Listen, I don't know if somebody's playing a joke, or what, but Death was just here. We played a little gin . . . No, *Death*. In person. Or somebody who claims to be Death. But, Moe, he's such a *schlep!*

CURTAIN

_____ **CONSIDERATIONS** _____

1. Death is something most people avoid talking about. Instead they fall back on euphemisms. Make a collection of euphemisms for death and dying and write an essay on the subject.

2. Nat is insulted by the suggestion that he doesn't know anything about death. "I make a beautiful dollar," he protests. "I sent two kids through college . . ." What do you think of the *logic* of his reply?

3. Obviously, dialogue is everything in a play. Study how some of the other writers in this book make use of dialogue in essays and stories. How could you use it in a forthcoming essay?

4. Nat: You want to play a tenth of a cent a point to make it interesting?
   Death: It's not interesting enough for you?

What does this exchange suggest about habitual or superficial vs. real or essential values? Are the same ideas suggested by the hackneyed expression, "The condemned man ate a hearty breakfast"?

5. The Kew Gardens mentioned in the stage-setting for "Death Knocks" is not the site of the Royal Botanical Gardens in London, but a residential section in a suburb of New York City. As you *listen* to the lines of the play, do you hear any clues that the characters are New Yorkers, not Londoners? Can you find other authors in this book who make use of voice in their work?

6. Woody Allen's playlet is a somewhat unusual example of a writer using personification. What are some more common personifications of death — in essays, stories, poems, cartoons, movies? Many other authors in this book use this literary device. Study their examples, then try your hand at personification.

Maya Angelou (b. 1928) told an interviewer, "One would say of my life — born loser — had to be; from a broken family, raped at eight, unwed mother at sixteen . . . it's a fact, but it's not the truth."

When she grew up, Maya Angelou became an actress, a singer, a dancer, a songwriter, a teacher, an editor, and a poet. She sang and danced professionally in Porgy and Bess *with a company that traveled through twenty-two countries of Europe and Asia. She wrote for the* Ghana Times *and she taught modern dance in Rome and in Tel Aviv. Her recent books are* Gather Together in My Name *(1974),* Oh Pray My Wings Are Gonna Fit Me Well *(1975), and* And Still I Rise *(1978).*

In 1969 she wrote her autobiography; I Know Why the Caged Bird Sings *was an immediate success. As she says, "I speak to the black experience, but I am always talking about the human condition." The book recounts her early life, with realism and with joy. This section describes a masterful black con man, skillful at turning white bigotry into black profits.*

4

MAYA ANGELOU
Mr. Red Leg

Our house was a fourteen-room typical San Franciscan post-Earthquake affair. We had a succession of roomers, bringing and taking their different accents, and personalities and foods. Shipyard workers clanked up the stairs (we all slept on the second floor except Mother and Daddy Clidell) in their steel-tipped boots and metal hats, and gave way to much-powdered prostitutes, who giggled through their makeup 1 and hung their wigs on the door-knobs. One couple (they were college graduates) held long adult conversations with me in the big kitchen downstairs, until the husband went off to war. Then the wife who had been so charming and ready to smile changed into a silent shadow that played infrequently along the walls. An older couple lived with us for a year or so. They owned a restaurant and had no personality to enchant or interest a teenager, except that the husband was called Uncle Jim, and the wife Aunt Boy. I never figured that out.

2   The quality of strength lined with tenderness is an unbeatable combination, as are intelligence and necessity when unblunted by formal education. I was prepared to accept Daddy Clidell as one more faceless name added to Mother's roster of conquests. I had trained myself so successfully through the years to display interest, or at least attention, while my mind skipped free on other subjects that I could have lived in his house without ever seeing him and without his becoming the wiser. But his character beckoned and elicited admiration. He was a simple man who had no inferiority complex about his lack of education and, even more amazing, no superiority complex because he had succeeded despite that lack. He would say often, "I been to school three years in my life. In Slaten, Texas, times was hard, and I had to help my daddy on the farm."

3   No recriminations lay hidden under the plain statement, nor was there boasting when he said, "If I'm living a little better now, it's because I treats everybody right."

4   He owned apartment buildings and, later, pool halls, and was famous for being that rarity "a man of honor." He didn't suffer, as many "honest men" do, from the detestable righteousness that diminishes their virtue. He knew cards and men's hearts. So during the age when Mother was exposing us to certain facts of life, like personal hygiene, proper posture, table manners, good restaurants and tipping practices, Daddy Clidell taught me to play poker, blackjack, tonk and high, low, Jick, Jack and the Game. He wore expensive tailored suits and a large yellow diamond stickpin. Except for the jewelry, he was a conservative dresser and carried himself with the unconscious pomp of a man of secure means. Unexpectedly, I resembled him, and when he, Mother and I walked down the street his friends often said, "Clidell, that's sure your daughter. Ain't no way you can deny her."

5   Proud laughter followed those declarations, for he had never had children. Because of his late-arriving but intense paternal sense, I was introduced to the most colorful characters in the Black underground. One afternoon, I was invited into our smoke-filled dining room to

make the acquaintance of Stonewall Jimmy, Just Black, Cool Clyde, Tight Coat and Red Leg. Daddy Clidell explained to me that they were the most successful con men in the world, and they were going to tell me about some games so that I would never be "anybody's mark."

To begin, one man warned me, "There ain't never been a mark yet that didn't want something for nothing." Then they took turns showing me their tricks, how they chose their victims (marks) from the wealthy bigoted whites and in every case how they used the victims' prejudice against them. 6

Some of the tales were funny, a few were pathetic, but all were amusing or gratifying to me, for the Black man, the con man who could act the most stupid, won out every time over the powerful, arrogant white. 7

I remember Mr. Red Leg's story like a favorite melody. 8

"Anything that works against you can also work for you once you understand the Principle of Reverse. 9

"There was a cracker in Tulsa who bilked so many Negroes he could set up a Negro Bilking Company. Naturally he got to thinking, Black Skin means Damn Fool. Just Black and I went to Tulsa to check him out. Come to find out, he's a perfect mark. His momma must have been scared in an Indian massacre in Africa. He hated Negroes only a little more than he despised Indians. And he was greedy. 10

"Black and I studied him and decided he was worth setting up against the store. That means we were ready to put out a few thousand dollars in preparation. We pulled in a white boy from New York, a good con artist, and had him open an office in Tulsa. He was supposed to be a Northern real estate agent trying to buy up valuable land in Oklahoma. We investigated a piece of land near Tulsa that had a toll bridge crossing it. It used to be part of an Indian reservation but had been taken over by the state. 11

"Just Black was laid out as the decoy, and I was going to be the fool. After our friend from New York hired a secretary and had his cards printed, Black approached the mark with a proposition. He told him that he had heard that our mark was the only white man colored people could trust. He named some of the poor fools that had been taken by that crook. It just goes to show you how white folks can be deceived by their own deception. The mark believed Black. 12

"Black told him about his friend who was half Indian and half colored and how some Northern white real estate agent had found out that he was the sole owner of a piece of valuable land and the Northerner wanted to buy it. At first the man acted like he smelled a rat, 13 but from the way he gobbled up the proposition, turns out what he thought he smelled was some nigger money on his top lip.

14   "He asked the whereabouts of the land but Black put him off. He told this cracker that he just wanted to make sure that he would be interested. The mark allowed how he was being interested, so Black said he would tell his friend and they'd get in touch with him. Black met the mark for about three weeks in cars and in alleys and kept putting him off until the white man was almost crazy with anxiety and greed and then accidentally it seemed Black let drop the name of the Northern real estate agent who wanted the property. From that moment on we knew we had the big fish on the line and all we had to do was to pull him in.

15   "We expected him to try to contact our store, which he did. That cracker went to our setup and counted on his whiteness to ally him with Spots, our white boy, but Spots refused to talk about the deal except to say the land had been thoroughly investigated by the biggest real estate concern in the South and that if our mark did not go around raising dust he would make sure that there would be a nice piece of money in it for him. Any obvious inquiries as to the rightful owner-ship of the land could alert the state and they would surely push through a law prohibiting the sale. Spots told the mark he would keep in touch with him. The mark went back to the store three or four times but to no avail, then just before we knew he would crack, Black brought me to see him. That fool was as happy as a sissy in a C.C.C. camp. You would have thought my neck was in a noose and he was about to light the fire under my feet. I never enjoyed taking anybody so much.

16   "Anyhow, I played scary at first but Just Black told me that this was one white man that our people could trust. I said I did not trust no white man because all they wanted was to get a chance to kill a Black man legally and get his wife in the bed. (I'm sorry, Clidell.) The mark assured me that he was the only white man who did not feel like that. Some of his best friends were colored people. In fact, if I didn't know it, the woman who raised him was a colored woman and he still sees her to this day. I let myself be convinced and then the mark began to drag the Northern whites. He told me that they made Negroes sleep in the street in the North and that they had to clean out toilets with their hands in the North and even things worse than that. I was shocked and said, "Then I don't want to sell my land to that white man who offered seventy-five thousand dollars for it.' Just Black said, 'I wouldn't know what to do with that kind of money,' and I said that

all I wanted was to have enough money to buy a home for my old mom, to buy a business and to make one trip to Harlem. The mark asked how much would that cost and I said I reckoned I could do it on fifty thousand dollars.

"The mark told me no Negro was safe with that kind of money. That white folks would take it from him. I said I knew it but I had to have at least forty thousand dollars. He agreed. We shook hands. I said it would do my heart good to see the mean Yankee go down on some of 'our land.' We met the next morning and I signed the deed in his car and he gave me the cash.   17

"Black and I had kept most of our things in a hotel over in Hot Springs, Arkansas. When the deal was closed we walked to our car, drove across the state line and on to Hot Springs.   18

"That's all there was to it."   19

When he finished, more triumphant stories rainbowed around the room riding the shoulders of laughter. By all accounts those storytellers, born Black and male before the turn of the twentieth century, should have been ground into useless dust. Instead they used their intelligence to pry open the door of rejection and not only became wealthy but got some revenge in the bargain.   20

It wasn't possible for me to regard them as criminals or be anything but proud of their achievements.   21

The needs of a society determine its ethics, and in the Black American ghettos the hero is that man who is offered only the crumbs from his country's table but by ingenuity and courage is able to take for himself a Lucullan feast. Hence the janitor who lives in one room but sports a robin's-egg-blue Cadillac is not laughed at but admired, and the domestic who buys forty-dollar shoes is not criticized but is appreciated. We know that they have put to use their full mental and physical powers. Each single gain feeds into the gains of the body collective.   22

Stories of law violations are weighed on a different set of scales in the Black mind than in the white. Petty crimes embarrass the community and many people wistfully wonder why Negros don't rob more banks, embezzle more funds and employ graft in the unions. "We are the victims of the world's most comprehensive robbery. Life demands a balance. It's all right if we do a little robbing now." This belief appeals particularly to one who is unable to compete legally with his fellow citizens.   23

My education and that of my Black associates were quite different from the education of our white schoolmates. In the classroom we   24 all learned past participles, but in the streets and in our homes the Blacks learned to drop *s*'s from plurals and suffixes from past-tense verbs. We were alert to the gap separating the written word from the colloquial. We learned to slide out of one language and into another without being conscious of the effort. At school, in a given situation, we might respond with "That's not unusual." But in the street, meeting the same situation, we easily said, "It be's like that sometimes."

_____ **CONSIDERATIONS** _____

1. Most of Angelou's essay is devoted to Mr. Red Leg telling a story. Notice how close to pure narration that story is. Compare it with the selections in this book by Annie Dillard (pages 135–137), John James Audubon (pages 29–32), or Richard Wright (pages 480–488), and contrast the amount of description and narration in Mr. Red Leg's story to that in one of the others.

2. Compare Angelou's essay with that of Frank Conroy (pages 105–112), who also emphasizes memorable characters. How do the two authors differ in their reasons for devoting so much space to Mr. Red Leg and to Ramos and Ricardo?

3. At the end of her essay, Angelou sets out an important linguistic principle. Paraphrase that idea and provide examples from your own experience or research.

4. "Stories of law violations are weighed on a different set of scales in the Black mind than in the white." Is a similar difference seen in the minds of two generations? Discuss relative justice versus absolute law.

5. Angelou demonstrates her versatility as a writer frequently in this essay by managing two voices. Find examples and discuss.

6. From what you learn of Angelou's upbringing in the essay, compile a *negative* report by a social worker on Angelou's childhood. Are there positive details in the essay that would allow you to refute a negative report?

Matthew Arnold (1822–1888) was the preeminent man of let-ters in Victorian England, famous for his essays on culture and literature, as well as for his poetry. "Dover Beach" laments the decline of religious faith and attempts to transfer devotion from God to a human companion. Although the quandary and the response were products of the Victorian Age, "Dover Beach" still calls to men and women a century after its making.

5

MATTHEW ARNOLD
Dover Beach

The sea is calm to-night.
The tide is full, the moon lies fair
Upon the straits; on the French coast the light
Gleams and is gone; the cliffs of England stand,
Glimmering and vast, out in the tranquil bay.   5
Come to the window, sweet is the night-air!
Only, from the long line of spray
Where the sea meets the moon-blanch'd land,
Listen! You hear the grating roar
Of pebbles which the waves draw back, and fling,   10
At their return, up the high strand,
Begin, and cease, and then again begin,
With tremulous cadence slow, and bring
The eternal note of sadness in.

Sophocles long ago   15
Heard it on the Ægean, and it brought
Into his mind the turbid ebb and flow
Of human misery; we

Find also in the sound a thought,
20 Hearing it by this distant northern sea.

The Sea of Faith
Was once, too, at the full, and round earth's shore
Lay like the folds of a bright girdle furl'd.
But now I only hear
25 Its melancholy, long, withdrawing roar,
Retreating, to the breath
Of the night-wind, down the vast edges drear
And naked shingles° of the world.   pebbled beaches

Ah, love, let us be true
30 To one another! for the world, which seems
To lie before us like a land of dreams,
So various, so beautiful, so new,
Hath really neither joy, nor love, nor light,
Nor certitude, nor peace, nor help for pain;
35 And we are here as on a darkling plain
Swept with confused alarms of struggle and flight,
Where ignorant armies clash by night.

John James Audubon (1785–1851) was born in Haiti and stud-
ied natural history and painting in France. When he was eighteen
he came to the United States to try his fortune, which did not
thrive. He taught drawing, painted portraits, and hunted game
for a living. Birds of America *began to appear in 1827. The fol-*
lowing account of the American passenger pigeon comes from his
Ornithological Biography *(1831–1839). Audubon was a great art-*
ist who combined the exact observation of painter and scientist
with the writer's ability to render sight, sound, and smell.

Audubon reported that these birds were "killed in immense
numbers." Although billions darkened the skies in Audubon's
time, the bird is now extinct; the last passenger pigeon died on
September 1, 1914, in the Cincinnati zoo.

6

JOHN JAMES AUDUBON

The Passenger Pigeon

The multitudes of wild pigeons in our woods are astonishing. 1
Indeed, after having viewed them so often, and under so many circumstances, I even now feel inclined to pause, and assure myself that what
I am going to relate is fact. Yet I have seen it all, and that, too, in the
company of persons who, like myself, were struck with amazement.

In the autumn of 1813 I left my house at Henderson, on the 2
banks of the Ohio, on my way to Louisville. In passing over the Bar-
rens, a few miles beyond Hardensburg, I observed the pigeons flying
from north-east to south-west, in greater numbers than I thought I had
ever seen them before, and feeling an inclination to count the flocks
that might pass within reach of my eye in one hour, I dismounted,
seated myself on an eminence, and began to mark with my pencil,
making a dot for every flock that passed. In a short time, finding the

task which I had undertaken impracticable, as the birds poured in in countless multitudes, I rose, and counting the dots then put down found that one hundred and sixty-three had been made in twenty-one minutes. I travelled on, and still met more the farther I proceeded. The air was literally filled with pigeons; the light of noonday was obscured as by an eclipse; and the continued buzz of wings had a tendency to lull my senses to repose.

3   Whilst waiting for dinner at Young's Inn, at the confluence of Salt River with the Ohio, I saw, at my leisure, immense legions still going by, with a front reaching far beyond the Ohio on the west, and the beech wood forests directly on the east of me. Not a single bird alighted, for not a nut or acorn was that year to be seen in the neighborhood. They consequently flew so high, that different trials to reach them with a capital rifle proved ineffectual; nor did the reports disturb them in the least. I cannot describe to you the extreme beauty of their aerial evolutions, when a hawk chanced to press upon the rear of a flock. At once, like a torrent, and with a noise like thunder, they rushed into a compact mass, pressing upon each other towards the center. In these almost solid masses, they darted forward in undulating and angular lines, descended and swept close over the earth with inconceivable velocity, mounted perpendicularly so as to resemble a vast column, and, when high, were seen whirling and twisting within their continued lines, which then resembled the coils of a gigantic serpent.

4   Before sunset I reached Louisville, distant from Hardensburg fifty-five miles. The pigeons were still passing in undiminished numbers and continued to do so for three days in succession. The people were all in arms. The banks of the Ohio were crowded with men and boys, incessantly shooting at the pilgrims, which there flew lower, as they passed the river. Multitudes were thus destroyed. For a week or more, the population fed on no other flesh than that of pigeons, and talked of nothing but pigeons. The atmosphere, during this time, was strongly impregnated with the peculiar odor which emanates from the species.

5   As soon as the pigeons discover a sufficiency of food to entice them to alight, they fly round in circles, reviewing the country below. During their evolutions, on such occasions, the dense mass which they form exhibits a beautiful appearance, as it changes its direction, now displaying a glistening sheet of azure, when the backs of the birds come simultaneously into view, and anon suddenly presenting a mass of rich, deep purple. Then they pass lower, over the woods, and for a moment are lost among the foliage, but again emerge, and are seen

gliding aloft. They now alight; but the next moment, as if suddenly alarmed, they take to wing, producing by the flappings of their wings a noise like the roar of distant thunder, and sweep through the forests to see if danger is near. Hunger, however, soon brings them to the ground. When alighted, they are seen industriously throwing up the withered leaves in quest of the fallen mast. The rear ranks are continually rising, passing over the main body, and alighting in front, in such rapid succession, that the whole flock seems still on the wing. The quantity of ground thus swept is astonishing; and so completely has it been cleared, that the gleaner who might follow in their rear would find his labor completely lost. Whilst feeding, their avidity is at times so great, that in attempting to swallow a large acorn or nut, they are seen gasping for a long while, as if in the agonies of suffocation.

On such occasions, when the woods are filled with these pigeons,　6 they are killed in immense numbers, although no apparent diminution ensues. About the middle of the day, after their repast is finished, they settle on the trees, to enjoy rest and digest their food. On the ground they walk with ease, as well as on the branches, frequently jerking their beautiful tails, and moving their necks backward and forward in the most graceful manner. As the sun begins to sink beneath the horizon, they depart *en masse* for the roosting-place, which not unfrequently is hundreds of miles distant, as has been ascertained by persons who have kept an account of their arrivals and departures.

Let us now inspect their place of nightly rendezvous. One of　7 these curious roosting-places, on the banks of the Green River, in Kentucky, I repeatedly visited. It was, as is always the case, in a portion of the forest where the trees were of great magnitude, and where there was little underwood. I rode through it upwards of forty miles, and, crossing it in different parts, found its average breadth to be rather more than three miles. My first view of it was about a fortnight subsequent to the period when they had made choice of it, and I arrived there nearly two hours before sunset.

Many trees two feet in diameter, I observed, were broken off at　8 no great distance from the ground; and the branches of many of the largest and tallest had given way, as if the forest had been swept by a tornado. Everything proved to me that the number of birds resorting to this part of the forest must be immense beyond conception. As the period of their arrival approached, their foes anxiously prepared to receive them. Some were furnished with iron pots containing sulphur, others with torches of pine knots, many with poles, and the rest with guns. The sun was lost to our view, yet not a pigeon had arrived. Everything was ready, and all eyes were gazing on the clear sky, which appeared in glimpses amidst the tall trees. Suddenly there burst forth a general cry of, "Here they come!" The noise which they made, though yet distant, reminded me of a hard gale at sea passing through the rigging of a close-reefed vessel. As the birds arrived and passed over me, I felt a current of air that surprised me. Thousands were soon knocked down by the pole-men. The birds continued to pour in. The fires were lighted, and a magnificent, as well as wonderful and almost terrifying, sight presented itself. The pigeons, arriving by thousands, alighted everywhere, one above another, until solid masses, as large as hogsheads, were formed on the branches all around. Here and there the perches gave way under the weight with a crash, and falling to the ground, destroyed hundreds of the birds beneath, forcing down the dense groups with which every stick was loaded. It was a scene of uproar and confusion. I found it quite useless to speak, or even to shout, to those persons who were nearest to me. Even the reports of the guns were seldom heard, and I was made aware of the firing only by seeing the shooters reloading.

9   The uproar continued the whole night; and as I was anxious to know to what distance the sound reached, I sent off a man, accustomed to perambulate the forest, who, returning two hours afterward, informed me he had heard it distinctly when three miles distant from the spot. Towards the approach of day, the noise in some measure subsided, long before objects were distinguishable, the pigeons began to move off in a direction quite different from that in which they had arrived the evening before, and at sunrise all that were able to fly had disappeared. The howlings of the wolves now reached our ears, and the foxes, lynxes, cougars, bears, raccoons, opossums, and polecats were seen sneaking off, whilst eagles, and hawks of different species, accompanied by a crowd of vultures, came to supplant them, and enjoy their share of the spoil.

____ CONSIDERATIONS ____

1. One of the most determined observers of nature in the history of biology, Audubon earned the respect his work still enjoys because he refused to draw conclusions from anything but direct observation. Isolate several examples of that principle in action in "The Passenger Pigeon," then write about the importance of primary sources to a student or researcher in any field.

2. Audubon's descriptions are clear and precise, yet some students find

him difficult to read because of antiquated or archaic expressions. List such words and phrases in "The Passenger Pigeon," and opposite each write an accurate, contemporary equivalent.

3. How many times in this essay does Audubon use the passive construction? For instance, see the end of Paragraph 3: "... these almost solid masses ... were seen whirling and twisting ..." Most modern writing texts urge the beginning writer to avoid the passive. Are Audubon's passive constructions justifiable?

4. In Paragraphs 1 and 4, Audubon expresses the general amazement with which whole towns witnessed the flights of the passenger pigeon. Is that feeling of awe over natural phenomena still common? Can you draw upon anything in your experience to parallel that feeling? See also Annie Dillard's "Strangers to Darkness," Norman Mailer's "A Walk on the Moon," and Loren Eiseley's "How Flowers Changed the World."

5. Henry David Thoreau's journals, with their careful observations, show him to be an important naturalist like Audubon. Were their writing styles similar? See Thoreau's "To Build My House."

6. In what sense, if any, would you call Audubon's essay an environmentalist's view of natural resources? Could an anti-environmentalist make use of it?

James Baldwin (b. 1924) published his first novel, Go Tell It on the Mountain, *when he was still in his twenties. His most recent is* Just Above My Head *(1979). Son of a Harlem minister, he has written three other novels, a book of stories, one play, and several collections of essays. In these pages Baldwin summarizes his life to the age of thirty-one, then concentrates a life's ambition into one sentence.*

_7_

JAMES BALDWIN

Autobiographical Notes

1   I was born in Harlem thirty-one years ago. I began plotting novels at about the time I learned to read. The story of my childhood is the usual bleak fantasy, and we can dismiss it with the restrained observation that I certainly would not consider living it again. In those days my mother was given to the exasperating and mysterious habit of having babies. As they were born, I took them over with one hand and held a book with the other. The children probably suffered, though they have since been kind enough to deny it, and in this way I read *Uncle Tom's Cabin* and *A Tale of Two Cities* over and over and over again; in this way, in fact, I read just about everything I could get my hands on — except the Bible, probably because it was the only book I was encouraged to read. I must also confess that I wrote — a great deal — and my first professional triumph, in any case, the first effort of mine to be seen in print, occurred at the age of twelve or thereabouts, when a short story I had written about the Spanish revolution won some sort of prize in an extremely short-lived church newspaper.

I remember the story was censored by the lady editor, though I don't remember why, and I was outraged.

Also wrote plays, and songs, for one of which I received a letter   2 of congratulations from Mayor La Guardia, and poetry, about which the less said, the better. My mother was delighted by all these goings-on, but my father wasn't, he wanted me to be a preacher. When I was fourteen I became a preacher, and when I was seventeen I stopped. Very shortly thereafter I left home. For God knows how long I struggled with the world of commerce and industry — I guess they would say they struggled with *me* — and when I was about twenty-one I had enough done of a novel to get a Saxton Fellowship. When I was twenty-two the fellowship was over, the novel turned out to be unsalable, and I started waiting on tables in a Village restaurant and writing book reviews — mostly, as it turned out, about the Negro problem, concerning which the color of my skin made me automatically an expert. Did another book, in company with photographer Theodore Pelatowski, about the store-front churches in Harlem. This book met exactly the same fate as my first — fellowship, but no sale. (It was a Rosenwald Fellowship.) By the time I was twenty-four I had decided to stop reviewing books about the Negro problem — which, by this time, was only slightly less horrible in print than it was in life — and I packed my bags and went to France, where I finished, God knows how, *Go Tell It on the Mountain.*

Any writer, I suppose, feels that the world into which he was   3 born is nothing less than a conspiracy against the cultivation of his talent — which attitude certainly has a great deal to support it. On the other hand, it is only because the world looks on his talent with such a frightening indifference that the artist is compelled to make his talent important. So that any writer, looking back over even so short a span of time as I am here forced to assess, finds that the things which hurt him and the things which helped him cannot be divorced from each other; he could be helped in a certain way only because he was hurt in a certain way; and his help is simply to be enabled to move from one conundrum to the next — one is tempted to say that he moves from one disaster to the next. When one begins looking for influences one finds them by the score. I haven't thought much about my own, not enough anyway; I hazard that the King James Bible, the rhetoric of the store-front church, something ironic and violent and perpetually understated in Negro speech — and something of Dickens' love for bravura — have something to do with me today; but I wouldn't stake my life on it. Likewise, innumerable people have helped me in many ways; but finally, I suppose, the most difficult (and most rewarding) thing in my life has been the fact that I was born a Negro and was forced, therefore, to effect some kind of truce with this reality. (Truce, by the way, is the best one can hope for.)

4   One of the difficulties about being a Negro writer (and this is not special pleading, since I don't mean to suggest that he has it worse than anybody else) is that the Negro problem is written about so widely. The bookshelves groan under the weight of information, and everyone therefore considers himself informed. And this information, furthermore, operates usually (generally, popularly) to reinforce traditional attitudes. Of traditional attitudes there are only two — For or Against — and I, personally, find it difficult to say which attitude has caused me the most pain. I am speaking as a writer; from a social point of view I am perfectly aware that the change from ill-will to good-will, however motivated, however imperfect, however expressed, is better than no change at all.

5   But it is part of the business of the writer — as I see it — to examine attitudes, to go beneath the surface, to tap the source. From this point of view the Negro problem is nearly inaccessible. It is not only written about so widely; it is written about so badly. It is quite possible to say that the price a Negro pays for becoming articulate is to find himself, at length, with nothing to be articulate about. ("You taught me language," says Caliban to Prospero, "and my profit on't is I know how to curse.") Consider: the tremendous social activity that this problem generates imposes on whites and Negroes alike the necessity of looking forward, of working to bring about a better day. This is fine, it keeps the waters troubled; it is all, indeed, that has made possible the Negro's progress. Nevertheless, social affairs are not generally speaking the writer's prime concern, whether they ought to be or not; it is absolutely necessary that he establish between himself and these affairs a distance which will allow, at least, for clarity, so that before he can look forward in any meaningful sense, he must first be allowed to take a long look back. In the context of the Negro problem neither whites nor blacks, for excellent reasons of their own, have the faintest desire to look back; but I think that the past is all that makes the present coherent, and further, that the past will remain horrible for exactly as long as we refuse to assess it honestly.

6   I know, in any case, that the most crucial time in my own development came when I was forced to recognize that I was a kind of bastard of the West; when I followed the line of my past I did not find

myself in Europe but in Africa. And this meant that in some subtle way, in a really profound way, I brought to Shakespeare, Bach, Rembrandt, to the stones of Paris, to the cathedral at Chartres and to the Empire State Building, a special attitude. These were not really my creations, they did not contain my history; I might search in them in vain forever for any reflection of myself. I was an interloper; this was not my heritage. At the same time I had no other heritage which I could possibly hope to use — I had certainly been unfitted for the jungle or the tribe. I would have to appropriate these white centuries, I would have to make them mine — I would have to accept my special attitude, my special place in this scheme — otherwise I would have no place in *any* scheme. What was the most difficult was the fact that I was forced to admit something I had always hidden from myself, which the American Negro has had to hide from himself as the price of his public progress; that I hated and feared white people. This did not mean that I loved black people; on the contrary, I despised them, possibly because they failed to produce Rembrandt. In effect, I hated and feared the world. And this meant, not only that I thus gave the world an altogether murderous power over me, but also that in such a self-destroying limbo I could never hope to write.

One writes out of one thing only — one's own experience. Every-   7
thing depends on how relentlessly one forces from this experience the last drop, sweet or bitter, it can possibly give. This is the only real concern of the artist, to recreate out of the disorder of life that order which is art. The difficulty then, for me, of being a Negro writer was the fact that I was, in effect, prohibited from examining my own experience too closely by the tremendous demands and the very real dangers of my social situation.

I don't think the dilemma outlined above is uncommon. I do   8
think, since writers work in the disastrously explicit medium of language, that it goes a little way towards explaining why, out of the enormous resources of Negro speech and life, and despite the example of Negro music, prose written by Negroes has been generally speaking so pallid and so harsh. I have not written about being a Negro at such length because I expect that to be my only subject, but only because it was the gate I had to unlock before I could hope to write about anything else. I don't think that the Negro problem in America can be even discussed coherently without bearing in mind its context; its context being the history, traditions, customs, the moral assumptions and preoccupations of the country; in short, the general social fabric.

Appearances to the contrary, no one in America escapes its effects and everyone in America bears some responsibility for it. I believe this the more firmly because it is the overwhelming tendency to speak of this problem as though it were a thing apart. But in the work of Faulkner, in the general attitude and certain specific passages in Robert Penn Warren, and, most significantly, in the advent of Ralph Ellison, one sees the beginnings — at least — of a more genuinely penetrating search. Mr. Ellison, by the way, is the first Negro novelist I have ever read to utilize in language, and brilliantly, some of the ambiguity and irony of Negro life.

9   About my interests: I don't know if I have any, unless the morbid desire to own a sixteen-millimeter camera and make experimental movies can be so classified. Otherwise, I love to eat and drink — it's my melancholy conviction that I've scarcely ever had enough to eat (this is because it's *impossible* to eat enough if you're worried about the next meal) — and I love to argue with people who do not disagree with me too profoundly, and I love to laugh. I do *not* like bohemia, or bohemians, I do not like people whose principal aim is pleasure, and I do not like people who are *earnest* about anything. I don't like people who like me because I'm a Negro; neither do I like people who find in the same accident grounds for contempt. I love America more than any other country in the world, and, exactly for this reason, I insist on the right to criticize her perpetually. I think all theories are suspect, that the finest principles may have to be modified, or may even be pulverized by the demands of life, and that one must find, therefore, one's own moral center and move through the world hoping that this center will guide one aright. I consider that I have many responsibilities, but none greater than this: to last, as Hemingway says, and get my work done.

10   I want to be an honest man and a good writer.

——— CONSIDERATIONS ———

1. Why didn't the young Baldwin read the Bible? In your education, have you ever been affected by similar feelings?

2. Point out specific features of Baldwin's style that account for its slightly ironic tone. What other authors in this book make use of irony? Why?

3. Baldwin finds it difficult, he says, to distinguish the things that helped him as a writer from those that hurt him. Can you draw any parallels with your experience as a student?

4. Baldwin wrote this essay for a book that appeared in 1955, when he was thirty-one years old and had already published two successful novels. How do those facts affect your response to the last sentence in the essay?

5. Many black writers have argued that the black artist must reject all of white culture. How does Baldwin explain his acceptance of Shakespeare, Bach, Rembrandt, the cathedral at Chartres, and the Empire State Building?

6. Note how many years Baldwin covers in the first half-dozen sentences of Paragraph 2. How do you explain the lack of details about those years? Is this a weakness or a strength of the essay?

Frithjof Bergmann (b. 1930) grew up half-Jewish in Nazi Austria, working on a farm while both parents lived in hiding. He graduated from his Austrian secondary school in 1950 and eighteen months later took his B.A. degree summa cum laude at Lewis and Clark College in Oregon. After receiving his Ph.D. in philosophy from Princeton in 1958, he lived in a New Hampshire cabin for two years, growing his own food, "living like Thoreau." From this solitude he returned to teaching, mostly at the University of Michigan, where he is a professor of philosophy.

8

FRITHJOF BERGMANN
Two Sides of Freedom

1   Our culture has a schizophrenic view of freedom. Two schools of thought concerning liberty are simultaneously alive in it. These schools proceed from utterly different, almost contradictory assumptions to equally different and opposed conclusions — yet they do not argue with each other. The conflict is not brought out into the open. There is no exchange; not much communication. The two go their own separate ways as if there were a gentlemen's agreement to keep quiet.

2   For the first school it is axiomatic that freedom is wonderful: freedom separates man from the beasts, and raises him above nature; it is the *sine qua non* of his distinguished position. Liberty gives a man a unique and incommensurate status which is lost to him when it is forfeited. His claim to it is indisputable for it constitutes and defines his being; it is the essence of his manhood. To gain it is more mandatory than all other conquests; to lose it is final defeat.

This is the more "official" tradition. It views freedom as satisfy-   3
ing, as the natural and obvious object of every man's longing. People,
according to it, want freedom as spontaneously and directly as babies
want milk. All political faiths, no matter how sharply they may disagree on other matters, subscribe to this view — though, in very different fashions. All sides fight for freedom. Every conquest is a
"liberation." Even the Nazis declared that they were for it.

The divergences between the various political canons seem no   4
greater on this score than those between the sectarian creeds of one
religion. All invoke the same ancient text: that freedom is desirable. If
politics occupies in the modern age the place that religion held in the
Middle Ages — if it now furnishes the basic framework of orientation,
the instruments of salvation, and the only ideas that match the power
then possessed by their more theological antecedents — then freedom
holds now in this new framework the place that was formerly occupied by Grace. Only by entering into the Kingdom of Freedom will the
new man be born from the old Adam.

This view of freedom helps to paint the general picture of history,   5
which still orders the world for us in a drama of progress. We think
mankind is attaining ever greater freedom. It was Hegel who first
developed this hope into a system. He depicted history as mankind's
difficult advance towards its own liberation and he placed an immense
and radiant value upon freedom. He did not see in history a gratifying,
steady climb but rather thought it addicted to the exploration of blind
alleys and the paying of monstrous prices. He thought it, in his own
famous phrase, "the slaughterbench on which whole nations are sac-
rificed." Yet he believed that it was, in spite of the carnage and the
waste, somehow justified and redeemed. Why? Because it did lead to
freedom. Freedom sufficed. It merited the cost.

From this school also, we learned to make freedom the final   6
standard of adjudication for the superiority of "our way of life," and of
our institutions, even our superiority as human beings. We are free,
that is why we are better. This is rock bottom. It ends the debate. And
the origin as well as the rationalization of many foreign and domestic
policies follow the same pattern. The last resort to which one takes
recourse is that this or that stratagem promotes freedom. Everyone
knows that this invocation is often hypocritical. But the fact that one
acts the devotee of freedom when one is not, shows only how unques-
tioned and sacrosanct the value of freedom has become. "Give me
liberty or give me death!" might be the emblem of this first tradition.

If one had to choose a single motto for the second tradition, one   7 might pick the phrase "escape from freedom." In that school Sartre and Kierkegaard are prominent, but Dostoyevsky wrote the formulation which has become classical for modern writers. It is The Grand Inquisitor chapter of *The Brothers Karamazov* and we shall look at it more closely.

8   In this chapter Ivan tells Alyosha a parable which is set in the sixteenth century in Spain at the height of the Inquisition: Jesus returns for one day to this earth, the day after the Grand Inquisitor presided over a large-scale execution of heretics, a splendid, spectacular *auto-da-fé* in which almost a hundred misbelievers were burnt at the stake. The crowd recognizes Jesus, and has already burst into Hosannahs, when the Grand Inquisitor, knowing that it is Jesus, orders his guards to arrest him. That night the Grand Inquisitor visits Jesus in the inquisitorial prison, and by far the largest part of the story records the conversation that occurs between them, in which the Grand Inquisitor justifies himself and his Inquisition and even his arrest of Jesus to Jesus himself. The heart of his argument is that Jesus tried to set mankind free, but mankind does not want and cannot bear freedom. He, the Grand Inquisitor, therefore took this terrible gift from them out of compassion and out of mercy. The freedom that Jesus bestowed upon man was an affliction and a scourge. Man suffers from it and cannot sustain it. It makes demands upon him that he cannot meet. He does not possess the dimensions, the stature and the strength to endure it. What mankind really wants, what it craves is mystery and authority. "Man strives for nothing so incessantly and so painfully as to find someone to worship."

9   In essence the Grand Inquisitor poses a dilemma: One can either grant to mankind what it wants, although that dispensation will be degrading, or one can offer noble values, but then one has to be cruel. One has only a choice between a compassion that concedes to mankind the vulgarities for which it hankers — and a will to raise and lift it, which is ultimately brutal. It is impossible to give both happiness and dignity at the same time. Faced with this either/or, the Grand Inquisitor elects to be gentle, and grant all mankind the mystery, the authority, the object of worship, the servitude it wants. He knows that what he does and gives is revolting, but the fact that he renders himself repulsive is a gauge of his compassion. To give only what is still consistent with one's own immaculateness is too sparing. The Grand Inquisitor makes a more strenuous sacrifice and Jesus stands accused, charged with lukewarmness.

10   For this tradition the first basic ground rule is that the options

open to us are split. The terms are: one or the other — but not both. In the novel Ivan's outrage against this basic premise renders him incapable of action. He is too noble to give mankind what it wants, but too sensitive to afflict it with high values. His refusal of this choice holds him in the stocks in which he is tortured. And this same dilemma was faced by a whole line of thinkers, all the way from Plato down to Sartre *(Dirty Hands)*.

From the point of this bifurcation, Liberalism looks like an 11 impossible insistence on having both; it links happiness and freedom, satisfaction and nobility so that there need be no choice. It is amazing that Liberalism usually treats this as completely obvious, that it talks as if there never had been any question. But there is, at the very least, a problem which has to be faced.

The choice which Ivan poses runs directly counter to a structural 12 thought-pattern that had dominant importance during the Enlightenment and that still governs much of our thinking: in essence it holds that the defects of societies and men are in the last accounting due to man's repression, to one or the other of the ways in which man is held down. Liberation, therefore, is *the* answer, and the political question reduces simply to the question of how a maximum of freedom can be won. One operates on the assumption that there is no upper limit to the amount of freedom that each individual wants (and that is good for him), and one believes that the need for limits is entirely external. This means that society should impose only that minimum of restraints required to safeguard other people, and it also means that other people and society are primarily perceived as something that sets limits.

To attack this thought-pattern challenges not just the founda- 13 tions on which Liberalism rests. It threatens the whole spectrum of political discussion, and crosses sharply even the main hope that underpins most revolutions. Take the famous closing lines of Trotsky's *Literature and Revolution*. Once the revolution has been won,

> Man will become immeasurably stronger, wiser and subtler; his body will become more harmonized, his movements more rhythmic, his voice more musical. The forms of life will become dynamically dramatic. The average human type will rise to the heights of an Aristotle, a Goethe, or a Marx. And above this ridge new peaks will rise.

Why did man not attain these peaks before? Because something 14 actively prevented it. Once he is free of hindrances the ascent will happen almost by itself. The capacities were in man all along; they only needed room in which they could unfold.

15   This view of man sees him mainly thwarted. It believes that his nobility only has to be released. In Dostoyevsky's parable we confront a very different vision: one which sees in man both more fragility and more evil.

16   To bring these two traditions into contact with each other settles nothing and our reason for doing so is precisely the reverse: to unsettle a few dogmas about freedom. But the notion that servitude may be granted from compassion may still strike us as a mere hyperbole. We shrug it off. We know that people basically do want freedom.

17   But do they?

18   Dostoyevsky obviously did not mean trivial choices. The Grand Inquisitor says that it is the need for miracles, for mystery and authority that concerns him; it was the hunger for an object of worship that he sought to relieve. But is this hunger so great? One measure of its intensity is the fast rise of the psychoanalytic movement. Even if we set aside the issue of the scientific merit of Freud's ideas (and disregard the fact that many have used them to abrogate responsibility in favor of the mysteries of their own unconscious); even if we consider nothing but the popularity of psychoanalytic treatment, we still get some indication of that appetite. The sheer fact that so many people find it necessary to submit their lives to an inspection, that so many are impelled to display their intimacies for an appraisal, and precisely that they do this in spite of their doubts and reservations is evidence enough of the reality of that need.

19   Or take totalitarianism: We repeat phrases like "people need an identity" and "people want a definition of themselves" in an absent-minded way. Yet the desires are as palpable as those for sex and food. To get some sense of their reality and power one must remember what people are prepared to do — the kind of hunger, suffering and denials they accept for an "insignia," for a "name," a "title" (for a button to pin on their lapel), and also how the whole tone and rhythm of someone's life is changed, how he no longer walks in the same way, because now there is a phrase, or an image, that applies to him.

20   Once one has thought concretely about the "need for an identity," one's picture of how totalitarianism grows may be reversed. Customarily we imagine that two forces pull in opposite directions: the desire for freedom, and the fear of going hungry. We think that these conflict and that freedom sometimes loses out. But often this is

not what actually occurs. When someone joins a severely regimented group, he does not usually do so by a cautiously conducted barter. Two things are not weighed against each other. The urgency is all in one direction. There is a feeling of relief, almost of exultation. Independence was not wanted, freedom was feared.

In some contexts we accept this as a platitudinous fact. When   21 suburbia or fraternities are the topic, no one needs to be reminded that people in general want "to fit in," want "to be part of the group," want "to be accepted," that there is a herd for every lone wolf. And yet these banalities are barred from other contexts. Virtually every political, philosophical or moral discussion of freedom in the abstract assumes the very opposite: that men demand individuality and freedom, that only measures such as repression and brainwashing can begin to curtail these desires, and that men will rebel if freedom is not granted. We have again the same schizophrenic segregation, and here it is reinforced with semantics. Instead of saying bluntly that people do not want freedom, we say that people need a sense of solidarity and of communion, or at worst that they need to "conform." Desires contrary to freedom are given other designations, thus preserving the illusion that the appetite for freedom is unqualified and absolute. This compartmentalization is carried to such extremes that even the theoretical and historical explanations of modern totalitarianism rigidly adhere to it. In the analysis of totalitarian movements the major question usually is: What constrained a people at this point to yield up their freedom and to submit to a more dictatorial rule? But this question is probably malposed. It assumes that there is a natural tendency towards freedom and the "explanation" of totalitarianism becomes in effect a list of the pressures that overrode this tendency. This may be the wrong way round; if men in general do not desire freedom then the important question would be, What at this point weakened the imposition of individuality and freedom and what allowed the natural drive towards conformity to go unchecked?

There is no reason why a man who dreads retirement cannot be   22 said to fear a kind of freedom, or why a middle-aged mother who clings to her children cannot be said to hold on to a kind of servitude. Part of what makes these crises painful is the discovery that the exigencies of a job or of raising children, which so far were experienced as confinements, in fact provided one's life with structure and coherence. The sense of futility, the exasperation at not having anything outside oneself that demands one's service, the whole experience of having to live

"for oneself" — for nothing but the prolongation of one's own existence — these are all the effects of a kind of freedom. Even the most
hyperbolic-seeming dicta suddenly sound straightforward once they
are placed into such circumstances. Sartre has said that "we are condemned to be free," and in one of his plays Orestes says that "freedom
crashed down upon him." If this were said by a man whose life's work
has just been taken from him, we would understand it right away.

23   One last example. Consider how we invoke for our actions the
support and the endorsement of abstractions. We have a penchant for
acting "in the name" of something. If nothing plausible is close to
hand, we reach out for airy, dubious notions; we become the shield-
bearers of Progress, of Enlightenment, of Order, of Good Judgment. It
is as if we need something, even if it has to be a half-discarded fancy,
to which our act can be subordinated; something that will give it the
guise of an instrument that performs a service. It is possible to look at
morality in this perspective and to imagine it as a kind of last recourse:
if all else fails, we still invoke its blank and stony categories and act at
least in the name of Goodness. This whole phenomenon constitutes
still a different stratagem with which we avoid freedom. That we
become so cunning, and palliate the threat of an autonomous bare
action with such disguises, shows how deep our fear of freedom really
is.

_____ **CONSIDERATIONS** _____

1. To see how Bergmann's observations are relevant to our daily lives, it
may be useful to translate some of his general statements into specific examples. For instance, would you consider the last sentence of his second paragraph to be accurately reflected by the common expression, "Better dead than
red"? Carry out similar paraphrases of other statements by Bergmann. Does he
himself provide any such examples?

2. In Paragraphs 7, 8, and 9 Bergmann makes significant use of a parable
from the novel *The Brothers Karamazov*. But Bergmann's deepest concern is
with the reasonableness of our thoughts about freedom. To what extent is it
logical, legitimate, or effective to base a nonfictional argument upon a fictional example?

3. In Paragraph 19 Bergmann says that labels or titles change "the whole
tone and rhythm of someone's life," even to the point of how he walks. Think
of examples from your own experience or from such readings as those by Maya
Angelou, George Orwell, Studs Terkel, John Updike, or Eudora Welty. Build
an essay on those examples.

4. Judging by Bergmann's discussion, would you think it fair to describe the phrase "people need an identity" as a euphemism for "people really don't want freedom"?

5. In Paragraph 21, Bergmann writes, "Desires contrary to freedom are given other designations." Is that another way of saying that we often prefer rationalizations to rationality?

6. Bergmann uses comparison and contrast to organize his material. See also Bruce Catton, "Grant and Lee," and Henry Adams, "Winter and Summer." There are, however, important differences between Bergmann's and Catton's use of the rhetorical form. Study both to discern these differences.

Leonard Bernstein (b. 1918) is soloist, composer, and musical pedagogue as well as conductor. Some of his compositions are Kaddish *(1963) and* Mass *(1971; performed at the opening of the John F. Kennedy Center for the Performing Arts in Washington, D.C.). His musical comedies include* On the Town *(1944) and* West Side Story *(1957). From 1958 to 1969 he was conductor of the New York Philharmonic, sometimes leading the orchestra from the keyboard while he performed as soloist.*

9

LEONARD BERNSTEIN
The Art of Conducting

1   Mendelssohn fathered the "elegant" school, whereas Wagner inspired the "passionate" school of conducting. The ideal modern conductor is a synthesis of the two attitudes, and this synthesis is rarely achieved. In fact, it's practically impossible. Almost any musician can be a conductor, even a pretty good one; but only a rare musician can be a great one.

2   The qualities that distinguish *great* conductors lie far beyond and above . . . [technique]. We now begin to deal with the intangibles, the deep magical aspect of conducting. It is the mystery of relationships — conductor and orchestra bound together by the tiny but powerful split second. How can I describe to you the magic of the moment of beginning a piece of music? There is only one possible fraction of a second that feels exactly right for starting. There is a wait while the orchestra readies itself and collects its powers; while the conductor concentrates his whole will and force toward the work in hand; while

the audience quiets down, and the last cough has died away. There is no slight rustle of a program book; the instruments are poised and — bang! That's it. One second later, it is too late, and the magic has vanished.

This psychological timing is constantly in play throughout the   3
performance of music. It means that a great conductor is one who has great sensitivity to the flow of time; who makes one note move to the next in exactly the right way and at the right instant. For music, as we said, exists in the medium of time. It is time itself that must be carved up, molded, and remolded until it becomes, like a statue, an existing shape and form. This is the hardest to do. For a symphony is not like a statue, which can be viewed all at once, or bit by bit at leisure, in one's own chosen time. With music we are trapped in time. Each note is gone as soon as it has sounded, and it never can be recontemplated or heard again at the particular instant of rightness. It is always too late for a second look.

So the conductor is a kind of sculptor whose element is time   4
instead of marble; and in sculpting it, he must have a superior sense of proportion and relationship. He must judge the largest rhythms, the whole phraseology of a work. He must conquer the form of a piece not only in the sense of form as a mold, but form in its deepest sense, knowing and controlling where the music relaxes, where it begins to accumulate tension, where the greatest tension is reached, where it must ease up to gather strength for the next lap, where it unloads that strength.

These are the intangibles of conducting, the mysteries that no   5
conductor can learn or acquire. If he has a natural faculty for deep perception it will increase and deepen as he matures. If he hasn't he will always remain a pretty good conductor. But even the pretty good conductor must have one more attribute in his personality, without which all the mechanics and knowledge and perception are useless; and that is the power to *communicate* all this to his orchestra — through his arms, face, eyes, fingers, and whatever vibrations may flow from him. If he uses a baton, the baton itself must be a living thing, charged with a kind of electricity, which makes it an instrument of meaning in its tiniest movement. If he does not use a baton, his hands must do the job with equal clarity. But baton or no baton, his gestures must be first and always meaningful in terms of the music.

The chief element in the conductor's technique of communica-   6
tion is the preparation. Everything must be shown to the orchestra

before it happens. Once the player is playing the note, it is too late. So the conductor always has to be at least a beat or two ahead of the orchestra. And he must hear two things at the same time: what the players are doing at any moment, and what they are about to do a moment later. Therefore, the basic trick is in the preparatory upbeat. It is exactly like breathing: the preparation is like an inhalation, and the music sounds as an exhalation. We all have to inhale in order to speak, for example; all verbal expression is exhaled. So it is with music: we inhale on the upbeat and sing out a phrase of music, then inhale again and breathe out the next phrase. A conductor who breathes with the music has gone far in acquiring a technique.

7   But the conductor must not only make his orchestra play; he must make them want to play. He must exalt them, lift them, start their adrenalin pouring, either through cajoling or demanding or raging. But however he does it, he must make the orchestra love the music as he loves it. It is not so much imposing his will on them like a dictator; it is more like projecting his feelings around him so that they reach the last man in the second violin section. And when this happens — when one hundred men share his feelings, exactly, simultaneously, responding as one to each rise and fall of the music, to each point of arrival and departure, to each little inner pulse — then there is a human identity of feeling that has no equal elsewhere. It is the closest thing I know to love itself. On this current of love the conductor can communicate at the deepest levels with his players, and ultimately with his audience. He may shout and rant and curse and insult his players at rehearsal — as some of our greatest conductors are famous for doing — but if there is this love, the conductor and his orchestra will remain knit together through it all and function as one.

8   Well, there is our ideal conductor. And perhaps the chief requirement of all is that he be humble before the composer; that he never interpose himself between the music and the audience; that all his efforts, however strenuous or glamorous, be made in the service of the composer's meaning — the music itself, which, after all, is the whole reason for the conductor's existence.

_____ **CONSIDERATIONS** _____

1. "There is only one possible fraction of a second that feels exactly right for starting." Is this Bernstein describing a symphony conductor, or John

McPhee observing a basketball star leaping to make a jump shot? (See the essay by McPhee elsewhere in this book.) Perhaps *all* performers have something in common. Discuss that possibility, thinking of these two essays.

2. In Paragraph 4, Bernstein emphasizes the conductor's mastery of form. On a smaller scale, you are faced with the same challenge whenever you write an essay. What are some of the forms of writing exemplified in this book? Select one or two and explain the importance of form to their success.

3. Apparently Leonard Bernstein, like Lewis Thomas (see his "Notes on Punctuation"), likes semicolons; every paragraph of this essay has at least one. Consult Thomas on the function of this punctuation mark; then analyze and evaluate Bernstein's use of it.

4. Nearly half of Paragraph 6 consists of an extended simile: "It is exactly like breathing. . . ." Study how Bernstein develops this figure of speech. Some people assume that figurative writing is merely decorative; strike out the last seven lines of the paragraph and write an explanation of the same phenomenon in literal language.

5. At the next concert you attend, either instrumental or choral, study the conductor's communication with orchestra or chorus. Reread Bernstein's Paragraph 5 and write a short report on the concert, emphasizing the communication between conductor and conducted.

6. Have you ever experienced the love Bernstein describes in Paragraph 7? Must you have been a member of a symphonic orchestra to know what he's talking about? Why?

7. A small exercise in inference: How does the conductor — the center of all eyes, those of performers and audience — keep from thinking that he is the reason everyone's there?

You could write a history of any Western language by examining its translations of the Bible. In our language, one translation has not only reflected English, but has helped to create it. The King James Version, in England usually called the Authorized, is a great work of English prose, which has impressed its rhythms and its imagery on the ears of English speakers for nearly four centuries. The sounds of the King James Bible underlie most of the oratory in our past, and much of the poetry. Even today, many people find the voice of this translation the voice of beauty and authority in English prose.

In 1604, a conference of English churchmen undertook to sponsor the new translation, and fifty-four translators — scholars from Oxford and Cambridge and the Anglican center of Winchester — began work. (Some people claim that the King James Bible is the only work of genius ever accomplished by a committee.) The scholars worked quickly, and the translation appeared in 1611, dedicated to James I of England.

Of course no translation satisfies everyone, or satisfies forever. Biblical scholarship steadily exposed mistranslations in the stately rhythms of the King James sentences. As the spoken language changed, Jacobean phrases (the diction already somewhat archaic in 1611) came to seem quaint, and finally obscure. For some the King James Version came to seem exclusive or elitist, a barrier to the clarity of God's Word. Revisions and new translations have been numerous.

The New English Bible had its origin in another conference of churchmen, in 1946, and was finished in 1970. Committees of scholars and literary advisers met regularly to determine accuracy and regulate style. This translation was not a revision of the King James, like so many other versions, but a wholly new translation from the original languages into contemporary English. Widely applauded for its accuracy, in its style the New English Bible has pleased some readers and appalled others.

10

THE HOLY BIBLE
From **Ecclesiastes**

The King James Bible   *The New English Bible*

─────────────── CHAPTER ONE ───────────────

1 The words of the Preacher, the son of David, king in Jerusalem.

2 Vanity of vanities, saith the Preacher; vanity of vanities, all is vanity. 3 What profit hath man of all his labor wherein he laboreth under the sun? 4 One generation goeth, and another generation cometh; but the earth abideth for ever. 5 The sun also ariseth, and the sun goeth down, and hasteth to its place where it ariseth. 6 The wind goeth toward the south, and turneth about unto the north; it turneth about continually in its course, and the wind returneth again to its circuits. 7 All the rivers run into the sea, yet the sea is not full; unto the place whither the rivers go, thither they go again. 8 All things are full of weariness; man cannot utter *it:* the eye is not satisfied with seeing, nor the ear filled with hearing. 9 That which hath been is that which shall be; and that which

The words of the Speaker, the son of David, king in Jerusalem. 1

Emptiness, emptiness, says the Speaker, emptiness, all is empty. 2 What does man gain from all his 3 labour and his toil here under the sun? Generations come and genera- 4 tions go, while the earth endures for ever.

The sun rises and the sun goes 5 down; back it returns to its place and rises there again. The wind blows 6 south, the wind blows north, round and round it goes and returns full circle. All streams run into the sea, yet 7 the sea never overflows; back to the place from which the streams ran they return to run again.

All things are wearisome; no man 8 can speak of them all. Is not the eye surfeited with seeing, and the ear sated with hearing? What has hap- 9 pened will happen again, and what has been done will be done again, and

hath been done is that which shall be done: and there is no new thing under the sun. 10 Is there a thing whereof it may be said, See, this is new? it hath been long ago, in the ages which were before us. 11 There is no remembrance of the former *generations;* neither shall there be any remembrance of the latter *generations* that are to come, among those that shall come after.

12 I the Preacher was king over Israel in Jerusalem. 13 And I applied my heart to seek and to search out by wisdom concerning all that is done under heaven: it is a sore travail that God hath given to the sons of men to be exercised therewith. 14 I have seen all the works that are done under the sun; and, behold, all is vanity and a striving after wind. 15 That which is crooked cannot be made straight; and that which is wanting cannot be numbered. 16 I communed with mine own heart, saying, Lo, I have gotten me great wisdom above all that were before me in Jerusalem; yea, my heart hath had great experience of wisdom and knowledge. 17 And I applied my heart to know wisdom, and to know madness and folly: I perceived that this also was a striving after wind. 18 For in much wisdom is much grief; and he that increaseth knowledge increaseth sorrow.

there is nothing new under the sun. Is 10 there anything of which one can say, 'Look, this is new'? No, it has already existed, long ago before our time. The 11 men of old are not remembered, and those who follow will not be remembered by those who follow them.

I, the Speaker, ruled as king over 12 Israel in Jerusalem; and in wisdom I 13 applied my mind to study and explore all that is done under heaven. It is a sorry business that God has given men to busy themselves with. I have 14 seen all the deeds that are done here under the sun; they are all emptiness and chasing the wind. What is 15 crooked cannot become straight; what is not there cannot be counted. I said to myself, 'I have amassed great 16 wisdom, more than all my predecessors on the throne in Jerusalem; I have become familiar with wisdom and knowledge.' So I applied my 17 mind to understand wisdom and knowledge, madness and folly, and I came to see that this too is chasing the wind. For in much wisdom is 18 much vexation, and the more a man knows, the more he has to suffer.

CHAPTER TWO

1 I said in my heart, Come now, I will prove thee with mirth; therefore enjoy pleasure: and, behold, this also was vanity. 2 I said of laughter, It is mad; and of mirth, What doeth it? 3 I searched in my heart how to cheer

I said to myself, 'Come, I will plunge 1 into pleasures and enjoy myself'; but this too was emptiness. Of laughter I 2 said, 'It is madness!' And of pleasure, 'What is the good of that?' So I sought 3 to stimulate myself with wine, in the

my flesh with wine, my heart yet guiding *me* with wisdom, and how to lay hold on folly, till I might see what it was good for the sons of men that they should do under heaven all the days of their life.

4 I made me great works; I builded me houses; I planted me vineyards; 5 I made me gardens and parks, and I planted trees in them of all kinds of fruit; 6 I made me pools of water, to water therefrom the forest where trees were reared; 7 I bought men-servants and maid-servants, and had servants born in my house; also I had great possessions of herds and flocks, above all that were before me in Jerusalem; 8 I gathered me also silver and gold, and the treasure of kings and of the provinces; I gat me men-singers and women-singers, and the delights of the sons of men, musical instruments, and that of all sorts. 9 So I was great, and increased more than all that were before me in Jerusalem: also my wisdom remained with me. 10 And whatsoever mine eyes desired I kept not from them; I withheld not my heart from any joy; for my heart rejoiced because of all my labor; and this was my portion from all my labor. 11 Then I looked on all the works that my hands had wrought, and on the labor that I had labored to do; and, behold, all was vanity and a striving after wind, and there was no profit under the sun.

12 And I turned myself to behold wisdom, and madness, and folly: for what *can* the man *do* that cometh after the king? *even* that which hath been done long ago. 13 Then I saw that wisdom excelleth folly, as far as light excelleth darkness. 14 The wise man's eyes are in his head, and

hope of finding out what was good for men to do under heaven throughout the brief span of their lives. But my mind was guided by wisdom, not blinded by folly.

I undertook great works; I built 4 myself houses and planted vineyards; I made myself gardens and parks and 5 planted all kinds of fruit-trees in them; I made myself pools of water 6 to irrigate a grove of growing trees; I 7 bought slaves, male and female, and I had my home-born slaves as well; I had possessions, more cattle and flocks than any of my predecessors in Jerusalem; I amassed silver and gold 8 also, the treasure of kings and provinces; I acquired singers, men and women, and all that man delights in. I was great, greater than all my pre- 9 decessors in Jerusalem; and my wisdom stood me in good stead. Whatever my eyes coveted, I refused 10 them nothing, nor did I deny myself any pleasure. Yes indeed, I got pleasure from all my labour, and for all my labour this was my reward. Then 11 I turned and reviewed all my handiwork, all my labour and toil, and I saw that everything was emptiness and chasing the wind, of no profit under the sun.

I set myself to look at wisdom and 12 at madness and folly. Then I per- 13 ceived that wisdom is more profitable than folly, as light is more profitable than darkness: the wise man has eyes 14 in his head, but the fool walks in the dark. Yet I saw also that one and the same fate overtakes them both. So I 15 said to myself, 'I too shall suffer the fate of the fool. To what purpose have I been wise? What is the profit of it? Even this', I said to myself, 'is emptiness. The wise man is remembered 16

the fool walketh in darkness: and yet I perceived that one event happeneth to them all. 15 Then said I in my heart, As it happeneth to the fool, so will it happen even to me; and why was I then more wise? Then said I in my heart, that this also is vanity. 16 For of the wise man, even as of the fool, there is no remembrance for ever; seeing that in the days to come all will have been long forgotten. And how doth the wise man die even as the fool! 17 So I hated life, because the work that is wrought under the sun was grievous unto me; for all is vanity and a striving after wind.

18 And I hated all my labor wherein I labored under the sun, seeing that I must leave it unto the man that shall be after me. 19 And who knoweth whether he will be a wise man or a fool? yet will he have rule over all my labor wherein I have labored, and wherein I have showed myself wise under the sun. This also is vanity. 20 Therefore I turned about to cause my heart to despair concerning all the labor wherein I had labored under the sun. 21 For there is a man whose labor is with wisdom, and with knowledge, and with skillfulness; yet to a man that hath not labored therein shall he leave it for his portion. This also is vanity and a great evil. 22 For what hath a man of all his labor, and of the striving of his heart, wherein he laboreth under the sun? 23 For all his days are *but* sorrows; and his travail is grief; yea, even in the night his heart taketh no rest. This also is vanity.

24 There is nothing better for a man *than* that he should eat and drink, and make his soul enjoy good in his labor. This also I saw, that it is

no longer than the fool, for, as the passing days multiply, all will be forgotten. Alas, wise man and fool die the same death!' So I came to hate life, since everything that was done here under the sun was a trouble to me; for all is emptiness and chasing the wind. So I came to hate all my labour and toil here under the sun, since I should have to leave its fruits to my successor. What sort of a man will he be who succeeds me, who inherits what others have acquired? Who knows whether he will be a wise man or a fool? Yet he will be master of all the fruits of my labour and skill here under the sun. This too is emptiness.

Then I turned and gave myself up to despair, reflecting upon all my labour and toil here under the sun. For anyone who toils with wisdom, knowledge, and skill must leave it all to a man who has spent no labour on it. This too is emptiness and utterly wrong. What reward has a man for all his labour, his scheming, and his toil here under the sun? All his life long his business is pain and vexation to him; even at night his mind knows no rest. This too is emptiness. There is nothing better for a man to do than to eat and drink and enjoy himself in return for his labours. And yet I saw that this comes from the hand of God. For without him who can enjoy his food, or who can be anxious? God gives wisdom and knowledge and joy to the man who pleases him, while to the sinner is given the trouble of gathering and amassing wealth only to hand it over to someone else who pleases God. This too is emptiness and chasing the wind.

from the hand of God.   25 For who can eat, or who can have enjoyment, more than I?   26 For to the man that pleaseth him *God* giveth wisdom, and knowledge, and joy; but to the sinner he giveth travail, to gather and to heap up, that he may give to him that pleaseth God. This also is vanity and a striving after wind.

--------------------- CHAPTER THREE ---------------------

1 For everything there is a season, and a time for every purpose under heaven: 2 a time to be born, and a time to die; a time to plant, and a time to pluck up that which is planted;   3 a time to kill, and a time to heal; a time to break down, and a time to build up;   4 a time to weep, and a time to laugh; a time to mourn, and a time to dance;   5 a time to cast away stones, and a time to gather stones together; a time to embrace, and a time to refrain from embracing;   6 a time to seek, and a time to lose; a time to keep, and a time to cast away;   7 a time to rend, and a time to sew; a time to keep silence, and a time to speak;   8 a time to love, and a time to hate; a time for war, and a time for peace.   9 What profit hath he that worketh in that wherein he laboreth?   10 I have seen the travail which God hath given to the sons of men to be exercised therewith.   11 He hath made everything beautiful in its time: also he hath set eternity in their heart, yet so that man cannot find out the work that God hath done from the beginning even to the end.   12 I know that there is nothing better for them, than to rejoice, and to do good so long as they live.   13 And also that every man should eat and drink,

For everything its season, and for every activity under heaven its time: 1
a time to be born and a time to   2
  die;
a time to plant and a time to
  uproot;
a time to kill and a time to heal;   3
a time to pull down and a time to
  build up;
a time to weep and a time to   4
  laugh;
a time for mourning and a time for
  dancing;
a time to scatter stones and a time   5
  to gather them;
a time to embrace and a time to
  refrain from embracing;
a time to seek and a time to lose;   6
a time to keep and a time to throw
  away;
a time to tear and a time to mend;   7
a time for silence and a time for
  speech;
a time to love and a time to hate;   8
a time for war and a time for
  peace.
What profit does one who works   9
get from all his labour? I have seen   10
the business that God has given men
to keep them busy. He has made   11
everything to suit its time; moreover
he has given men a sense of time past
and future, but no comprehension of

and enjoy good in all his labor, is the gift of God.

God's work from beginning to end. I know that there is nothing good for man except to be happy and live the best life he can while he is alive. Moreover, that a man should eat and drink and enjoy himself, in return for all his labours, is a gift of God. 12 13

_____ CONSIDERATIONS _____

1. When we study sentence structure, we study syntax. Have the editors of the newer translation of Ecclesiastes made syntactic as well as lexical changes? Explain and illustrate.

2. List differences between the two versions of Ecclesiastes, beginning with the new version changing "Preacher" into "Speaker" and "vanity" into "emptiness." Studying your list, can you generalize about the changes?

3. Writers as diverse as James Baldwin, William Faulkner, and Abraham Lincoln — these three collected in this book — have attributed some of their own style to the King James Bible. Such style must generate great power. By comparing the two texts here, determine specific characteristics of the style of the King James Version.

4. Many people have objected to modernized versions of the Bible. Can you reconstruct and explain their objections?

5. In what way might a philosophy of life be built on a line from Ecclesiastes? One of these might be 2:24. How true is the common saying that you can find anything you want to find in the Bible?

6. Compare closely the two versions of 3:1–9. Does the change in *form* create a major difference in *effect?* Explain.

Ambrose Bierce (1842–1914?) was born in a log cabin on Horse Cave Creek in Ohio. He educated himself by reading the books in his father's small library, and as a young man served in the army during the Civil War. Starting as a journalist in California, he made himself an elegant writer of short stories, which were often supernatural or macabre in theme. Because he was writing in the primitive West, in a country still generally primitive, his serious work went generally unrecognized. Melancholy deepened into misanthropy. The definitions in The Devil's Dictionary *(1906) are funny — but the humor is serious, and the wit is bitter.*

In 1913, Bierce put his affairs in order and went to Mexico, which was in the midst of a civil war. He wrote a friend as he left, ". . . if you hear of my being stood up against a Mexican stone wall and shot to rags please know that I think it a pretty good way to depart this life. It beats old age, disease, or falling down a flight of stairs." He was never heard from again.

11

AMBROSE BIERCE

Some Devil's Definitions

Belladonna, n. In Italian a beautiful lady; in English a deadly 1
poison. A striking example of the essential identity of the two tongues.

Bigot, n. One who is obstinately and zealously attached to an 2
opinion that you do not entertain.

Bore, n. A person who talks when you wish him to listen. 3

Brute, n. See HUSBAND. 4

Cabbage, n. A familiar kitchen-garden vegetable about as large 5
and wise as a man's head.

Calamity, n. A more than commonly plain and unmistakable 6 reminder that the affairs of this life are not of our own ordering. Calamities are of two kinds: misfortune to ourselves, and good fortune to others.

7   *Cannibal, n.* A gastronome of the old school who preserves the simple tastes and adheres to the natural diet of the pre-pork period.

8   *Cannon, n.* An instrument employed in the rectification of national boundaries.

9   *Cat, n.* A soft, indestructible automaton provided by nature to be kicked when things go wrong in the domestic circle.

10   *Christian, n.* One who believes that the New Testament is a divinely inspired book admirably suited to the spiritual needs of his neighbor. One who follows the teachings of Christ in so far as they are not inconsistent with a life of sin.

11   *Clairvoyant, n.* A person, commonly a woman, who has the power of seeing that which is invisible to her patron — namely, that he is a blockhead.

12   *Commerce, n.* A kind of transaction in which A plunders from B the goods of C, and for compensation B picks the pocket of D of money belonging to E.

13   *Compromise, n.* Such an adjustment of conflicting interests as gives each adversary the satisfaction of thinking he has got what he ought not to have, and is deprived of nothing except what was justly his due.

14   *Compulsion, n.* The eloquence of power.

15   *Congratulation, n.* The civility of envy.

16   *Conservative, n.* A statesman who is enamored of existing evils, as distinguished from the Liberal, who wishes to replace them with others.

17   *Consul, n.* In American politics, a person who having failed to secure an office from the people is given one by the Administration on condition that he leave the country.

18   *Consult, v. t.* To seek another's approval of a course already decided on.

19   *Corsair, n.* A politician of the seas.

20   *Coward, n.* One who in a perilous emergency thinks with his legs.

21   *Curiosity, n.* An objectionable quality of the female mind. The desire to know whether or not a woman is cursed with curiosity is one of the most active and insatiable passions of the masculine soul.

22   *Cynic, n.* A blackguard whose faulty vision sees things as they

are, not as they ought to be. Hence the custom among the Scythians of plucking out a cynic's eyes to improve his vision.

Dance, v. i. To leap about to the sound of tittering music, preferably with arms about your neighbor's wife or daughter. There are many kinds of dances, but all those requiring the participation of the two sexes have two characteristics in common: they are conspicuously innocent, and warmly loved by the vicious. 23

Debauchee, n. One who has so earnestly pursued pleasure that he has had the misfortune to overtake it. 24

Decalogue, n. A series of commandments, ten in number — just enough to permit an intelligent selection for observance, but not enough to embarrass the choice. 25

Defame, v. t. To lie about another. To tell the truth about another. 26

Dentist, n. A prestidigitator who, putting metal into your mouth, pulls coins out of your pocket. 27

Die, n. The singular of "dice." We seldom hear the word, because there is a prohibitory proverb, "Never say die." 28

Discussion, n. A method of confirming others in their errors. 29

Distance, n. The only thing that the rich are willing for the poor to call theirs, and keep. 30

Duel, n. A formal ceremony preliminary to the reconciliation of two enemies. Great skill is necessary to its satisfactory observance; if awkwardly performed the most unexpected and deplorable consequences sometimes ensue. A long time ago a man lost his life in a duel. 31

Eccentricity, n. A method of distinction so cheap that fools employ it to accentuate their incapacity. 32

Edible, adj. Good to eat, and wholesome to digest, as a worm to a toad, a toad to a snake, a snake to a pig, a pig to a man, and a man to a worm. 33

Education, n. That which discloses to the wise and disguises from the foolish their lack of understanding. 34

Effect, n. The second of two phenomena which always occur together in the same order. The first, called a Cause, is said to generate the other — which is no more sensible than it would be for one who has never seen a dog except in pursuit of a rabbit to declare the rabbit the cause of the dog. 35

36   *Egotist, n.* A person of low taste, more interested in himself than in me.

37   *Erudition, n.* Dust shaken out of a book into an empty skull.

38   *Eulogy, n.* Praise of a person who has either the advantages of wealth and power, or the consideration to be dead.

39   *Female, n.* One of the opposing, or unfair, sex.

40   *Fib, n.* A lie that has not cut its teeth. An habitual liar's nearest approach to truth: the perigee of his eccentric orbit.

41   *Fiddle, n.* An instrument to tickle human ears by friction of a horse's tail on the entrails of a cat.

42   *Friendship, n.* A ship big enough to carry two in fair weather, but only one in foul.

43   *Garter, n.* An elastic band intended to keep a woman from coming out of her stockings and desolating the country.

44   *Ghost, n.* The outward and visible sign of an inward fear.

45   *Glutton, n.* A person who escapes the evils of moderation by committing dyspepsia.

46   *Gout, n.* A physician's name for the rheumatism of a rich patient.

47   *Grammar, n.* A system of pitfalls thoughtfully prepared for the feet of the self-made man, along the path by which he advances to distinction.

48   *Guillotine, n.* A machine which makes a Frenchman shrug his shoulders with good reason.

___ **CONSIDERATIONS** _____

1. To appreciate the humor in some of Bierce's definitions, you may have to look up in your desk dictionary some of his words, such as "gastronome," "zealously," "adversary," "civility," "insatiable," "prestidigitator," "perigee," "dyspepsia." How do you add words to your working vocabulary?

2. *The Devil's Dictionary* was first published in 1906. Judging from the definitions here, would you say that Bierce's book is dated? Which items strike you as most relevant to our times? Which are least relevant? Why?

3. Do you find a consistent tone or attitude in Bierce's dictionary? Explain and provide ample evidence.

4. George Orwell, in "Politics and the English Language" (pages 310–322), is hard on euphemisms. Would Bierce agree with Orwell?

5. Which of these would most appreciate Bierce's brand of humor: Annie Dillard ("Strangers to Darkness"), Frederick Douglass ("Plantation Life"), Flannery O'Connor ("A Good Man Is Hard to Find"), or George Orwell ("A Hanging")?

6. Compose a page of definitions for your own Devil's Dictionary, perhaps concentrating on words currently popular.

Caroline Bird (b. 1915) was born in New York City, taught at Vassar, and now divides her time between Manhattan and Poughkeepsie. She has been an editor and a teacher, as well as the author of Born Female *(1968),* Everything a Woman Needs to Know to Get Paid What She's Worth *(1973), and* The Case against College *(1975). She argues the case against college with a clear vigor, a committed pugnacity; only a skilled debater with a good college education could dispute her.*

12

CAROLINE BIRD
Where College Fails Us

1   The case *for* college has been accepted without question for more than a generation. All high school graduates ought to go, says Conventional Wisdom and statistical evidence, because college will help them earn more money, become "better" people, and learn to be more responsible citizens than those who don't go.

2   But college has never been able to work its magic for everyone. And now that close to half our high school graduates are attending, those who don't fit the pattern are becoming more numerous, and more obvious. College graduates are selling shoes and driving taxis; college students sabotage each other's experiments and forge letters of recommendation in the intense competition for admission to graduate school. Others find no stimulation in their studies, and drop out — often encouraged by college administrators.

3   Some observers say the fault is with the young people them-selves — they are spoiled, stoned, overindulged, and expecting too

From *Signature Magazine*, Diners Club, Inc. © 1975. Reprinted by permission of the author.

much. But that's mass character assassination, and doesn't explain all campus unhappiness. Others blame the state of the world, and they are partly right. We've been told that young people have to go to college because our economy can't absorb an army of untrained eighteen-year-olds. But disillusioned graduates are learning that it can no longer absorb an army of trained twenty-two-year-olds, either.

Some adventuresome educators and campus watchers have 4 openly begun to suggest that college may not be the best, the proper, the only place for every young person after the completion of high school. We may have been looking at all those surveys and statistics upside down, it seems, and through the rosy glow of our own remembered college experiences. Perhaps college doesn't make people intelligent, ambitious, happy, liberal, or quick to learn new things — maybe it's just the other way around, and intelligent, ambitious, happy, liberal, and quick-learning people are merely the ones who have been attracted to college in the first place. And perhaps all those successful college graduates would have been successful whether they had gone to college or not. This is heresy to those of us who have been brought up to believe that if a little schooling is good, more has to be much better. But contrary evidence is beginning to mount up.

The unhappiness and discontent of young people is nothing new, 5 and problems of adolescence are always painfully intense. But while traveling around the country, speaking at colleges, and interviewing students at all kinds of schools — large and small, public and private — I was overwhelmed by the prevailing sadness. It was as visible on campuses in California as in Nebraska and Massachusetts. Too many young people are in college reluctantly, because everyone told them they ought to go, and there didn't seem to be anything better to do. Their elders sell them college because it's good for them. Some never learn to like it, and talk about their time in school as if it were a sentence to be served.

Students tell us the same thing college counselors tell us — they 6 go because of pressure from parents and teachers, and stay because it seems to be an alternative to a far worse fate. It's "better" than the Army or a dead-end job, and it has to be pretty bad before it's any worse than staying at home.

College graduates say that they don't want to work "just" for the 7 money: They want work that matters. They want to help people and save the world. But the numbers are stacked against them. Not only are there not enough jobs in world-saving fields, but in the current slowdown it has become evident that there never were, and probably never will be, enough jobs requiring higher education to go around.[1]

8   Students who tell their advisers they want to help people, for example, are often directed to psychology. This year the Department of Labor estimates that there will be 4,300 new jobs for psychologists, while colleges will award 58,430 bachelor's degrees in psychology.[2]

9   Sociology has become a favorite major on socially conscious campuses, but graduates find that social reform is hardly a paying occupation. Male sociologists from the University of Wisconsin reported as gainfully employed a year after graduation included a legal assistant, sports editor, truck unloader, Peace Corps worker, publications director, and a stockboy — but no sociologist per se. The highest paid worked for the post office.

10   Publishing, writing, and journalism are presumably the vocational goal of a large proportion of the 104,000 majors in Communications and Letters expected to graduate in 1975. The outlook for them is grim. All of the daily newspapers in the country combined are expected to hire a total of 2,600 reporters this year. Radio and television stations may hire a total of 500 announcers, most of them in local radio stations. Nonpublishing organizations will need 1,100 technical writers, and public-relations activities another 4,400. Even if new graduates could get all these jobs (they can't, of course), over 90,000 of them will have to find something less glamorous to do.[3]

11   Other fields most popular with college graduates are also pathetically small. Only 1,900 foresters a year will be needed during this decade, although schools of forestry are expected to continue graduating twice that many.[4] Some will get sub-professional jobs as forestry aides. Schools of architecture are expected to turn out twice as many as will be needed,[5] and while all sorts of people want to design things,

[1] [Editors' Note: Ms. Bird's article appeared in 1975.] According to the Department of Labor Bureau of Statistics, 13.5 million college graduates will enter the labor force from 1978 to 1990; the Bureau predicts only 10.2 million job openings in traditional jobs for college graduates during that period.

[2] 1981 figures: 6,700 new jobs for psychologists, 40,687 bachelor's degrees.

[3] 1980 figures: 130,000 graduates in Communications and Letters versus 2,400 new job openings for reporters and 850 new job openings for radio and television announcers; statistics are not available for technical writers.

[4] Projected figures for the 1980s indicate there will be a need for an average of 1,400 new foresters each year, while schools of forestry are expected to grant an average of 3,000 bachelor's degrees each year.

[5] The ratio for architects has improved according to 1980 forecasts: 4,000 new job openings versus 5,690 graduates in architecture.

the Department of Labor forecasts that there will be jobs for only 400 new industrial designers[6] a year. As for anthropologists, only 400 will be needed every year in the 1970s[7] to take care of all the college courses, public-health research, community surveys, museums, and all the archaeological digs on every continent. (For these jobs graduate work in anthropology is required.)

Many popular occupations may seem to be growing fast without   12 necessarily offering employment to very many. "Recreation work" is always cited as an expanding field, but it will need relatively few workers who require more special training than life guards. "Urban planning" has exploded in the media, so the U.S. Department of Labor doubled its estimate of the number of jobs to be filled every year in the 1970s — to a big, fat 800.[8] A mere 200 oceanographers[9] a year will be able to do all the exploring of "inner space" — and all that exciting underwater diving you see demonstrated on television — for the entire decade of the 1970s.

Whatever college graduates *want* to do, most of them are going   13 to wind up doing what *there is* to do. During the next few years, according to the Labor Department, the biggest demand will be for stenographers and secretaries, followed by retail-trade salesworkers, hospital attendants, bookkeepers, building custodians, registered nurses, foremen, kindergarten and elementary-school teachers, receptionists, cooks, cosmetologists, private-household workers, manufacturing inspectors, and industrial machinery repairmen.[10] These are the jobs which will eventually absorb the surplus archaeologists, urban planners, oceanographers, sociologists, editors, and college professors.

Vocationalism is the new look on campus because of the discour-   14 aging job market faced by the generalists. Students have been opting for medicine and law in droves. If all those who check "doctor" as their career goal succeed in getting their MDs, we'll immediately have

[6] Current projections indicate 550 new job openings for industrial designers each year in the 1980s.

[7] In the 1980s, 350 anthropologists will be needed each year.

[8] This figure remains the same for the 1980s.

[9] In the 1980s only 150.

[10] In the 1980s the order has altered: secretaries and stenographers; retail sales workers; building custodians; cashiers; bookkeeping workers; nursing aides, orderlies, and attendants; cooks and chefs; kingergarten and elementary school teachers; registered nurses; assemblers; waiters and waitresses; guards; foremen; local truck drivers; accountants; licensed practical nurses; typists; carpenters; industrial machine repairers; real estate agents and brokers; construction laborers; engineers; bank clerks; private household workers; receptionists; and wholesale trade sales workers.

ten times the target ratio of doctors for the population of the United States. Law schools are already graduating twice as many new lawyers every year as the Department of Labor thinks we will need, and the oversupply grows annually.[11]

15   Specialists often find themselves at the mercy of shifts in demand, and the narrower the vocational training, the more risky the long-term prospects. Engineers are the classic example of the "Yo-Yo" effect in supply and demand. Today's shortage is apt to produce a big crop of engineering graduates after the need has crested, and teachers face the same squeeze.

16   Worse than that, when the specialists turn up for work, they often find that they have learned a lot of things in classrooms that they will never use, that they will have to learn a lot of things on the job that they were never taught, and that most of what they have learned is less likely to "come in handy later" than to fade from memory. One disillusioned architecture student, who had already designed and built houses, said, "It's the degree you need, not everything you learn getting it."

17   A diploma saves the employer the cost of screening candidates and gives him a predictable product: He can assume that those who have survived the four-year ordeal have learned how to manage themselves. They have learned how to budget their time, meet deadlines, set priorities, cope with impersonal authority, follow instructions, and stick with a task that may be tiresome without direct supervision.

18   The employer is also betting that it will be cheaper and easier to train the college graduate because he has demonstrated his ability to learn. But if the diploma serves only to identify those who are talented in the art of schoolwork, it becomes, in the words of Harvard's Christopher Jencks, "a hell of an expensive aptitude test." It is unfair to the candidates because they themselves must bear the cost of the screening — the cost of college. Candidates without the funds, the academic temperament, or the patience for the four-year obstacle race are ruled out, no matter how well they may perform on the job. But if "everyone" has a diploma, employers will have to find another way to choose employees, and it will become an empty credential.

19   (Screening by diploma may in fact already be illegal. The 1971 ruling of the Supreme Court in *Griggs* v. *Duke Power Co.* contended that an employer cannot demand a qualification which systematically excludes an entire class of applicants, unless that qualification reliably

[11] These figures are similar for the 1980s.

predicts success on the job. The requiring of a high school diploma was outlawed in the *Griggs* case, and this could extend to a college diploma.)

The bill for four years at an Ivy League college is currently climb-   20 ing toward $25,000; at a state university, a degree will cost the student and his family about $10,000 (with taxpayers making up the differ- ence).[12]

Not many families can afford these sums, and when they look   21 for financial aid, they discover that someone else will decide how much they will actually have to pay. The College Scholarship Service, which establishes a family's degree of need for most colleges, is guided by noble principles: uniformity of sacrifice, need rather than merit. But families vary in their willingness to "sacrifice" as much as the bureaucracy of the CSS thinks they ought to. This is particularly true of middle-income parents, whose children account for the bulk of the country's college students. Some have begun to rebel against this attempt to enforce the same values and priorities on all. "In some families, a college education competes with a second car, a color tele- vision, or a trip to Europe — and it's possible that college may lose," one financial-aid officer recently told me.

Quite so. College is worth more to some middle-income families   22 than to others. It is chilling to consider the undercurrent of resent- ment that families who "give up everything" must feel toward their college-age children, or the burden of guilt children must bear every time they goof off or receive less than top grades in their courses.

The decline in return for a college degree within the last genera-   23 tion has been substantial. In the 1950s, a Princeton student could pay his expenses for the school year — eating club and all — on less than $3,000.[13] When he graduated, he entered a job market which provided a comfortable margin over the earnings of his agemates who had not been to college. To be precise, a freshman entering Princeton in 1956, the earliest year for which the Census has attempted to project life- time earnings, could expect to realize a 12.5 percent return on his investment. A freshman entering in 1972, with the cost nearing $6,000 annually, could expect to realize only 9.3 percent, less than might be available in the money market. This calculation was made with the help of a banker and his computer, comparing college as an invest-

[12] According to the National Center for Educational Statistics, the bill for four years at an Ivy League college is now closer to $36,000; the bill at a state university is close to $13,000.

ment in future earnings with other investments available in the boom-ing money market of 1974, and concluded that in strictly financial terms, college is not always the best investment a young person can make.

24   I postulated a young man (the figures are different with a young woman, but the principle is the same) whose rich uncle would give him, in cash, the total cost of four years at Princeton — $34,181.[13] (The total includes what the young man would earn if he went to work instead of to college right after high school.) If he did not spend the money on Princeton, but put it in the savings bank at 7.5 percent interest compounded daily, he would have, at retirement age sixty-four, more than fives times as much as the $199,000 extra he could expect to earn between twenty-two and sixty as a college man rather than a mere high school graduate. And with all that money accumu-lating in the bank, he could invest in something with a higher return than a diploma. At age twenty-eight, when his nest egg had reached $73,113, he could buy a liquor store, which would return him well over 20 percent on his investment, as long as he was willing to mind the store. He might get a bit fidgety sitting there, but he'd have to be dim-witted to lose money on a liquor store, and right now we're talk-ing only about dollars.

25   If the young man went to a public college rather than Princeton, the investment would be lower, and the payoff higher, of course, be-cause other people — the taxpayers — put up part of the capital for him. But the difference in return between an investment in public and private colleges is minimized because the biggest part of the invest-ment in either case is the money a student might earn if he went to work, not to college — in economic terms, his "foregone income." That he bears himself.

26   Rates of return and dollar signs on education are a fascinating brain teaser, and, obviously, there is a certain unreality to the game. But the same unreality extends to the traditional calculations that have always been used to convince taxpayers that college is a worth-while investment.

27   The ultimate defense of college has always been that while it may not teach you anything vocationally useful, it will somehow make you a better person, able to do anything better, and those who make it through the process are initiated into the "fellowship of edu-

---

[13] In 1981, the cost for a year at Princeton is $10,044.

cated men and women." In a study intended to probe what graduates seven years out of college thought their colleges should have done for them, the Carnegie Commission found that most alumni expected the "development of my abilities to think and express myself." But if such respected educational psychologists as Bruner and Piaget are right, specific learning skills have to be acquired very early in life, perhaps even before formal schooling begins.

So, when pressed, liberal-arts defenders speak instead about something more encompassing, and more elusive. "College changed me inside," one graduate told us fervently. The authors of a Carnegie Commission report, who obviously struggled for a definition, concluded that one of the common threads in the perceptions of a liberal education is that it provides "an integrated view of the world which can serve as an inner guide." More simply, alumni say that college should have "helped me to formulate the values and goals of my life." 28

In theory, a student is taught to develop these values and goals himself, but in practice, it doesn't work quite that way. All but the wayward and the saintly take their sense of the good, the true, and the beautiful from the people around them. When we speak of students acquiring "values" in college, we often mean that they will acquire the values — and sometimes that means only the tastes — of their professors. The values of professors may be "higher" than many students will encounter elsewhere, but they may not be relevant to situations in which students find themselves in college and later. 29

Of all the forms in which ideas are disseminated, the college professor lecturing a class is the slowest and most expensive. You don't have to go to college to read the great books or learn about the great ideas of Western Man. Today you can find them everywhere — in paperbacks, in the public libraries, in museums, in public lectures, in adult-education courses, in abridged, summarized, or adapted form in magazines, films, and television. The problem is no longer one of access to broadening ideas; the problem is the other way around: how to choose among the many courses of action proposed to us, how to edit the stimulations that pour into our eyes and ears every waking hour. A college experience that piles option on option and stimulation on stimulation merely adds to the contemporary nightmare. 30

What students and graduates say that they did learn on campus comes under the heading of personal, rather than intellectual, development. Again and again I was told that the real value of college is learning to get along with others, to practice social skills, to "sort out my head," and these have nothing to do with curriculum. 31

32   For whatever impact the academic experience used to have on college students, the sheer size of many undergraduate classes in the 1970s dilutes faculty-student dialogue, and, more often than not, they are taught by teachers who were hired when colleges were faced with a shortage of qualified instructors, during their years of expansion and when the big rise in academic pay attracted the mediocre and the less than dedicated.

33   On the social side, colleges are withdrawing from responsibility for feeding, housing, policing, and protecting students at a time when the environment of college may be the most important service it could render. College officials are reluctant to "intervene" in the personal lives of the students. They no longer expect to take over from parents, but often insist that students — who have, most often, never lived away from home before — take full adult responsibility for their plans, achievements, and behavior.

34   Most college students do not live in the plush, comfortable country-clublike surroundings their parents envisage, or, in some cases, remember. Open dorms, particularly when they are coeducational, are noisy, usually overcrowded, and often messy. Some students desert the institutional "zoos" (their own word for dorms) and move into run-down, overpriced apartments. Bulletin boards in student centers are littered with notices of apartments to share and the drift of conversation suggests that a lot of money is dissipated in scrounging for food and shelter.

35   Taxpayers now provide more than half of the astronomical sums that are spent on higher education. But less than half of today's high school graduates go on, raising a new question of equity: Is it fair to make all the taxpayers pay for the minority who actually go to college? We decided long ago that it is fair for childless adults to pay school taxes because everyone, parents and nonparents alike, profits by a literate population. Does the same reasoning hold true for state-supported higher education? There is no conclusive evidence on either side.

36   Young people cannot be expected to go to college for the general good of mankind. They may be more altruistic than their elders, but no great numbers are going to spend four years at hard intellectual labor, let alone tens of thousands of family dollars, for "the advancement of human capability in society at large," one of the many purposes invoked by the Carnegie Commission report. Nor do any considerable number of them want to go to college to beat the Russians to Jupiter, improve the national defense, increase the Gross Na-

tional Product, lower the crime rate, improve automobile safety, or create a market for the arts — all of which have been suggested at one time or other as benefits taxpayers get for supporting higher education.

One sociologist said that you don't have to have a reason for 37 going to college because it's an institution. His definition of an institution is something everyone subscribes to without question. The burden of proof is not on why you should go to college, but why anyone thinks there might be a reason for not going. The implication — and some educators express it quite frankly — is that an eighteen-year-old high school graduate is still too young and confused to know what he wants to do, let alone what is good for him.

Mother knows best, in other words. 38

It had always been comfortable for students to believe that au- 39 thorities, like Mother, or outside specialists, like educators, could determine what was best for them. However, specialists and authorities no longer enjoy the credibility former generations accorded them. Patients talk back to doctors and are not struck suddenly dead. Clients question the lawyer's bills and sometimes get them reduced. It is no longer self-evident that all adolescents must study a fixed curriculum that was constructed at a time when all educated men could agree on precisely what it was that made them educated.

The same with college. If high school graduates don't want to 40 continue their education, or don't want to continue it right away, they may perceive more clearly than their elders that college is not for them.

College is an ideal place for those young adults who love learning 41 for its own sake, who would rather read than eat, and who like nothing better than writing research papers. But they are a minority, even at the prestigious colleges, which recruit and attract the intellectually oriented.

The rest of our high school graduates need to look at college 42 more closely and critically, to examine it as a consumer product, and decide if the cost in dollars, in time, in continued dependency, and in future returns, is worth the very large investment each student — and his family — must make.

—— CONSIDERATIONS ———————————————

1. To what extent is Bird's essay an attack on the conviction that universal education is the surest way to cure the ills and injustices of the world?

2. In her first paragraph, the author states three popular justifications

for a college education. Examine her essay to see how, for the most part, it is organized around those three reasons.

3. In her final paragraph, Bird urges high school graduates to examine college "as a consumer product." Is that possible? Explain. Read about Richard Wright's struggle to educate himself ("The Library Card," pages 480–488) and try to imagine him examining that experience as "a consumer product."

4. Bird makes extensive use of statistics to prove her first proposition: that college is a poor investment. Does she cite the sources of her figures? Does she use the figures fairly? How can you tell?

5. How many of your college friends have clear ideas of their vocational or educational goals? Do you? What about friends who are not in college?

6. Bird points out, rightly enough, that "you don't have to go to college to read the great books or learn about the great ideas of Western Man." Judging from your experience with self-directed reading programs, how effective is Bird's statement as an argument?

Carol Bly (b. 1930) was born in Minnesota and graduated from Wellesley College. Now living in Minnesota, she works for the National Farmers' Union, makes crossword puzzles to order, and writes. Her short stories have appeared in The New Yorker *and the* American Review. *This essay was originally published in* Preview, *magazine of Minnesota Public Radio, and collected in her 1981 book,* Letters from the Country.

13

CAROL BLY

Getting Tired

The men have left a gigantic 6600 combine a few yards from our grove, at the edge of the stubble. For days it was working around the farm; we heard it on the east, later on the west, and finally we could see it grinding back and forth over the windrows on the south. But now it has been simply squatting at the field's edge, huge, tremendously still, very professional, slightly dangerous.

We all have the correct feelings about this new combine: this isn't the good old farming where man and soil are dusted together all day; this isn't farming a poor man can afford, either, and therefore it further threatens his hold on the American "family farm" operation. We have been sneering at this machine for days, as its transistor radio, amplified well over the engine roar, has been grinding up our silence, spreading a kind of shrill ghetto evening all over the farm.

But now it is parked, and after a while I walk over to it and climb up its neat little John-Deere-green ladder on the left. Entering the big cab up there is like coming up into a large ship's bridge on visitors' day — heady stuff to see the inside workings of a huge operation like the Queen Elizabeth II. On the other hand I feel left out, being only a dumbfounded passenger. The combine cab has huge windows flaring wider at the top; they lean forward over the ground, and the driver sits so high behind the glass in its rubber moldings, it is like a movie-set spaceship. He has obviously come to dominate the field, whether he farms it or not.

4   The value of the 66 is that it can do anything, and to change it from a combine into a cornpicker takes one man about half an hour, whereas most machine conversions on farms take several men a half day. It frees its owner from a lot of monkeying.

5   Monkeying, in city life, is what little boys do to clocks so they never run again. In farming it has two quite different meanings. The first is small side projects. You monkey with poultry, unless you're a major egg handler. Or you monkey with ducks or geese. If you have a very small milk herd, and finally decide that prices plus state regulations don't make your few Holsteins worthwhile, you "quit monkeying with them." There is a hidden dignity in this word: it precludes mention of money. It lets the wife of a very marginal farmer have a conversation with a woman who may be helping her husband run fifteen hundred acres. "How you coming with those geese?" "Oh, we've been real disgusted. We're thinking of quitting monkeying with them." It saves her having to say, "We lost our shirts on those darn geese."

6   The other meaning of monkeying is wrestling with and maintaining machinery, such as changing heads from combining to cornpicking. Farmers who cornpick the old way, in which the corn isn't shelled automatically during picking in the field but must be elevated to the top of a pile by belt and then shelled, put up with some monkeying.

7   Still, cornpicking and plowing is a marvelous time of the year on farms; one of the best autumns I've had recently had a few days of fieldwork in it. We were outside all day, from six in the morning to eight at night — coming in only for noon dinner. We ate our lunches on a messy truck flatbed. (For city people who don't know it: *lunch* isn't a noon meal; it is what you eat out of a black lunch pail at 9 A.M. and 3 P.M. If you offer a farmer a cup of coffee at 3:30 P.M. he or she is likely to say, "No thanks, I've already had lunch.") There were four of us hired to help — a couple to plow, Celia (a skilled farmhand who worked steady for our boss), and me. Lunch was always two sandwiches of white commercial bread with luncheon meat, and one very

generous piece of cake-mix cake carefully wrapped in Saran Wrap. (I never found anyone around here self-conscious about using Saran Wrap when the Dow Chemical Company was also making napalm.)

It was very pleasant on the flatbed, squinting out over the yellow picked cornstalks — each time we stopped for lunch, a larger part of the field had been plowed black. We fell into the easy psychic habit of farmworkers: admiration of the boss. "Ja, I see he's buying one of those big 4010s," someone would say. We always perked up at inside information like that. Or "Ja," as the woman hired steady told us, "he's going to plow the home fields first this time, instead of the other way round." We temporary help were impressed by that, too. Then, with real flair, she brushed a crumb of luncheon meat off her jeans, the way you would make sure to flick a gnat off spotless tennis whites. It is the true feminine touch to brush a crumb off pants that are encrusted with Minnesota Profile A heavy loam, many swipes of SAE 40 oil, and grain dust.

All those days, we never tired of exchanging information on how *he* was making out, what *he* was buying, whom *he* was going to let drive the new tractor, and so on. There is always something to talk about with the other hands, because farming is genuinely absorbing. It has the best quality of work: nothing else seems real. And everyone doing it, even the cheapest helpers like me, can see the layout of the whole — from spring work, to cultivating, to small grain harvest, to cornpicking, to fall plowing.

The second day I was promoted from elevating corncobs at the corn pile to actual plowing. Hour after hour I sat up there on the old Alice, as she was called (an Allis-Chalmers WC that looked rusted from the Flood). You have to sit twisted part way around, checking that the plowshares are scouring clean, turning over and dropping the dead crop and soil, not clogging. For the first two hours I was very political. I thought about what would be good for American farming — stronger marketing organizations, or maybe a law like the Norwegian Odal law, preventing the breaking up of small farms or selling them to business interests. Then the sun got high, and each time I reached the headlands area at the field's end I dumped off something else, now my cap, next my jacket, finally my sweater.

Since the headlands are the last to be plowed, they serve as a field road until the very end. There are usually things parked there — a pickup or a corn trailer — and things dumped — my warmer clothing, our afternoon lunch pails, a broken furrow wheel someone picked up.

By noon I'd dropped all political interest, and was thinking only:

how unlike this all is to Keats's picture of autumn, a "season of mists and mellow fruitfulness." This gigantic expanse of horizon, with everywhere the easy growl of tractors, was simply teeming with extrovert energy. It wouldn't calm down for another week, when whoever was lowest on the totem pole would be sent out to check a field for dropped parts or to drive away the last machines left around.

13   The worst hours for all common labor are the hours after noon dinner. Nothing is inspiring then. That is when people wonder how they ever got stuck in the line of work they've chosen for life. Or they wonder where the cool Indian smoke of secrets and messages began to vanish from their marriage. Instead of plugging along like a cheerful beast working for me, the Allis now smelled particularly gassy. To stay awake I froze my eyes onto an indented circle in the hood around the gas cap. Someone had apparently knocked the screw cap fitting down into the hood, so there was a moat around it. In this moat some overflow gas leapt in tiny waves. Sometimes the gas cap was a castle, this was the moat; sometimes it was a nuclear-fission plant, this was the horrible hot-water waste. Sometimes it was just the gas cap on the old Alice with the spilt gas bouncing on the hot metal.

14   Row after row. I was stupefied. But then around 2:30 the shadows appeared again, and the light, which had been dazing and white, grew fragile. The whole prairie began to gather itself for the cool evening. All of a sudden it was wonderful to be plowing again, and when I came to the field end, the filthy jackets and the busted furrow wheel were just benign mistakes: that is, if it chose to, the jacket could be a church robe, and the old wheel could be something with some pride to it, like a helm. And I felt the same about myself: instead of being someone with a half interest in literature and a half interest in farming doing a half-decent job plowing, I could have been someone desperately needed in Washington or Zurich. I drank my three o'clock coffee joyously, and traded the other plowman a Super-Valu cake-mix lemon cake slice for a Holsum baloney sandwich because it had garlic in it.

15   By seven at night we had been plowing with headlights for an hour. I tried to make up games to keep going, on my second wind, on my third wind, but labor is labor after the whole day of it; the mind refuses to think of ancestors. It refuses to pretend the stalks marching up to the right wheel in the spooky light are men-at-arms, or to imagine a new generation coming along. It doesn't care. Now the Republicans could have announced a local meeting in which they would propose a new farm program whereby every farmer owning less than five hundred acres must take half price for his crop, and every farmer

owning more than a thousand acres shall receive triple price for his crop, and I was so tired I wouldn't have shown up to protest.

A million hours later we sit around in a daze at the dining-room 16
table, and nobody says anything. In low, courteous mutters we ask for the macaroni hotdish down this way, please. Then we get up in ones and twos and go home. Now the farm help are all so tired we *are* a little like the various things left out on the headlands — some tools, a jacket, someone's thermos top — used up for that day. Thoughts won't even stick to us any more.

Such tiredness must be part of farmers' wanting huge machinery 17
like the Deere 6600. That tiredness that feels so good to the occasional laborer and the athlete is disturbing to a man destined to it eight months of every year. But there is a more hidden psychology in the issue of enclosed combines versus open tractors. It is this: one gets too many impressions on the open tractor. A thousand impressions enter as you work up and down the rows: nature's beauty or nature's stubbornness, politics, exhaustion, but mainly the feeling that all this repetition — last year's cornpicking, this year's cornpicking, next year's cornpicking — is taking up your lifetime. The mere repetition reveals your eventual death.

When you sit inside a modern combine, on the other hand, you 18
are so isolated from field, sky, all the real world, that the brain is dulled. You are not sensitized to your own mortality. You aren't sensitive to anything at all.

This must be a common choice of our mechanical era: to hide 19
from life inside our machinery. If we can hide from life in there, some idiotic part of the psyche reasons, we can hide from death in there as well.

___ CONSIDERATIONS _____

1. In Paragraphs 5 and 6, Carol Bly clarifies the slang term, "monkeying." Hers is not a conventional definition; does she make the term understandable to someone who had never heard it before? What are the requirements of a definition? Have you read essays built as extended definitions? See D. H. Lawrence's "Pornography."

2. Compare Paragraphs 9 and 17 on the nature of work. How do you account for the positive view of Paragraph 9 and the negative view of Paragraph 17?

3. Why, in Paragraph 12, does Bly allude to John Keats's famous ode,

"To Autumn" (1819)? Can you appreciate what she is doing if you've never read the poem? How quickly can you find it in your college library? Aside from the collected poems of John Keats, what would be the surest source for the poem?

4. Notice when Bly changes suddenly from past to present tense. Why does she make the shift? Is something gained by the change?

5. Think about Bly's generalizations in her final paragraph. Selecting an appropriate piece of machinery — a car, a computer, a television set — respond to Bly's generalizations.

Ronald Blythe (b. 1922) lives in a seventeenth-century farm-house in rural England. He has written literary criticism and art history, but his best-known works use transcriptions of speech. (See also Studs Terkel, pages 397–402.) Akenfield *(1969) was subtitled* Portrait of an English Village. *In* The View in Winter *(1979), an account of aging, Blythe uses tape-recorded interviews with his own commentary, of which this small essay on sexuality in old age is a sample.*

14

RONALD BLYTHE
Aging and Sexuality

The hope that sexuality itself would wither away and not add its   1
desperate frustrations to agedness has long since been turned into the
quite unfounded assurance that, with age, we naturally become asex-
ual. What evidence we have to the contrary we manipulate to prove
the social desirability of a sexless old age and to advocate the controls
needed to achieve it. We tell the old, if you do not conform to the
negative ideal you will be either ludicrous or indecent, that people
will be frightened of you, or think of you as pitiful, or as a nuisance,
for you are engaging in what is next to impossible or unthinkable.
Thus the wistful legend and the rules of convenience which it has
spawned. These rules and attitudes are among the very last of the
superstitions to be overturned by our society in its urgent quest to
understand the realities of old age. The notion that the aged are
beyond sex or unsexed still governs most public and private systems
to house them and, outside, in such countless ordinary situations as

going to the pub, the cinema, on holiday, etc., the elderly man or woman finds it prudent to conceal any interest in what should take his or her fancy. We approve of this and are grateful to old relatives, friends, neighbours, and even old strangers for this disciplined concealment. But we prefer not to know that among the most important reasons why the old guard their eroticism from the risk of having it mocked or judged is not that they believe it to be shameful or unnatural at their time of life, but to protect from contempt something which has in the past brought them so much love and delight. For all our new caring and planning, to be old today is to be contemptible. Why? Because to be old is to be part of a huge and commonplace problem, a member of a social group so increasingly demanding in its needs as to create another kind of helplessness in the young and middle-aged, causing them to feel guilty and resentful. The reason why old age was venerated in the past was that it was extraordinary. Among the few ways in which an aged individual can escape from being lumped into a mere problematical category is to let his genital primacy remind him of his own distinctive personality, even if at this stage it means little more than living in what has been described as "a kind of afterimage."

2   Proof that overt sexuality in the aged is all part of the sexual legitimacy which accompanies us all from the cradle to the grave, so to speak, lies in its ability to disturb society as it does. We may prohibit it or ridicule it, but when we become involved with it, however peripherally, it is always a bit of a shock to find in it something neither old nor age-defying. As was said at the first symposium of the Boston Society for Gerontologic Psychiatry nearly twenty years ago, when the entire subject began to be demythologised, "The conflicts concerning sexual expression are long-standing. However, many people who during their youth and middle years were able to achieve relative comfort about sexuality became uncomfortable with their erotic desire in a culture that either forbids or denies it its reality."

3   The fact that the idealised sexual standard of our culture emphasises the firm bodies of youth may also cause reactive oedipal conflicts in the aged, it was pointed out by two of the delegates, Dr. Zinberg and Dr. Kaufman. "The passage of the years has not made forbidden sexual interests any easier for the person to tolerate [and] we know full well from our patients that it is not only the children, but also the parents, whose sexual interests and defenses against them are activated by the processes of development. This *ronde* does not stop until

death. The shame experienced by the old man as the result of a forbidden sexual impulse that may or may not be repressed sets up reverberations in his younger physician and family. . . . This rondelay of point and counterpoint is complicated by the cultural attitude which makes it extremely necessary for both sides to deny that it is taking place. When feelings are so urgently repressed, the result is often more rather than less activity."

However, the old are not only expected to continue to repress 4 what they were obliged to repress most of their lives, but also that conventional sexuality which, until they became old, was an acceptable or even a welcome aspect of their personalities. It could include the sexual display manifested in clothes and hair styles, and the playful sensuality which doesn't feel obliged to conceal itself in bodily contacts such as hugs, handshakes, kisses, etc. All this and much more becomes subject to a new discretion when one is old. And not the least tragic part of old age is learning how to provide false evidence in such matters, the tacit lie which says "I feel nothing, I am past all that."

Modern geriatric psychiatry speaks of the aged as being wounded 5 in their narcissism — a poignant term and one which eloquently compresses the whole business of what we once were and what we must inevitably become, should we see our time out. To be sexually prohibited, even if it is only in some ignorant, unwritten and folk-saw sense, is a gratuitous addition to this hurt. The natural checks and balances of old age lie in spiritual sublimations and in the slowly dying organism itself, not in socially convenient taboos. In any case, they are only a surface matter, for the old learn how to prevent too great a wounding of their narcissism by making healthy forays into the past, where they can still encounter the material to make a self-acceptable image. Such an image is bound to have its bright and exciting sexual facets for, as A. L. Vischer says, "It is difficult to renounce a thing when we know its value and the delight that it affords and when our memory of it does not fade but even calls for repetition." He adds that in a period in which youth, physical beauty and the achievement of sexual ecstasy are the standard grist of every popular newspaper, glossy magazine, song, film and advertisement, "It is not surprising that the subject of sexuality is not so easily exhausted by the older generation." There is much in our treatment of the old and our attitudes towards them which are reminiscent of those which dominated thinking about the "intractable" problem of the poor in the nineteenth century. They are not *us,* is what we are often saying (politely and humanely, of course), and there are so *many* of them! Such a situation can only alter when it becomes natural to say that the old *are* us — and to believe it.

_____ CONSIDERATIONS _____

1. Contrary to common journalistic practice, Blythe's essay opens with a lengthy first paragraph so substantial that it may frighten off the timid reader. One way to attack such a solid block of type is to use your pencil and try to break it into smaller paragraphs. When you break up Blythe's paragraph, think of this paragraph as an essay in itself; can you locate the one sentence that expresses the central, controlling idea? Try the same technique with the first paragraph of Thoreau's "To Build My House."

2. Blythe closes with an observation about the prevalence of adversary thinking about the young and the old. He compares this notion with the nineteenth-century attitude toward the poor. Can you do the same with prejudices toward another minority — religious, political, or cultural?

3. Watch how Blythe works his research material into his essay. He does not use footnotes, but he is careful to acknowledge his sources. Find two examples of his subtle attributions of the sources of information.

4. In Paragraph 2, Blythe uses the word "demythologised." Learning a few common Greek and Latin roots, suffixes, and affixes can help your vocabulary. Divide "demythologised" into its four constituent parts; list other words made of the same units; consult a good dictionary to help you understand these interchangeable parts. See also D. H. Lawrence's use of "decreation," in Paragraph 16 of "Pornography."

5. Do you agree with Blythe's implication (Paragraph 3) that our culture is oriented toward youth? How does this orientation affect the problem of aging?

Kenneth E. Boulding (b. 1910) grew up in England and in 1937 moved to the United States, where he has taught at various universities, most recently the University of Colorado. Some of his books are Economic Analysis *(1941),* Economics of Peace *(1945),* Disarmament and the Economy *(1963),* The Meaning of the Twentieth Century *(1964),* Beyond Economics *(1968), and* Collected Papers, Vols. 1–5 *(1971–75).*

15

KENNETH E. BOULDING
Nature and Artifice

My first act of personal freedom is to declare that there is no 1
such thing as "the environment." Every species and every individual member of a species has an environment of its own, and constitutes part of the environment of others. All species taken together, whether chemical like hydrogen atoms or water molecules, biological like mosquitoes or humans, or societal like automobiles or Supreme Court decisions, constitute a world. A world consists of interacting ecosystems of interacting species, under conditions of constantly changing parameters. Evolution is precisely this ecological interaction under constantly changing parameters. It goes on all the time. The universe is a disequilibrium system, and has been so for probably twenty billion years. All species are ultimately endangered. It is a rare biological species, for instance, that lasts more than ten million years. Why, then, do we feel that there is something called "the environment" which is threatened?

Reprinted with permission from the May 1979 issue of *The Center Magazine,* a publication of the Robert Maynard Hutchins Center for the Study of Democratic Institutions, Santa Barbara, California.

2   There are several answers to this question, some of which are better than others. The least satisfactory answer is the view that there is something called "nature" in the absence of the human race, or at least only in the presence of a few highly worthy and privileged members of it, a presence which is wise, beautiful, and good, and which is threatened by the expansion of the human race in both numbers and affluence. I refrain from calling this the "Sierra Club illusion," out of my respect for the Sierra Club, though traces of it can be found in that worthy body. It is an illusion that gives many amiable and virtuous young people part of their charm, but it can also cause trouble if it is taken too seriously. "Doing what comes naturally" is by no means a universal recipe for the good life; and nature, if not, as Tennyson observed, always red in tooth and claw, is highly capable of producing systems which are unfriendly to human values and survival, like Mars, Venus, and the moon.

3   The most sensible answer, which of course is my answer to the question of what we mean by the threatened environment, is that we evaluate the total state of the world by essentially human valuations and are concerned at the prospect of this total state going from bad to worse rather than from bad to better. Environmentalism, then, is seen as an aspect of a larger normative science which seeks to understand the formation and critique of human values. The frank recognition that we are evaluating the world by human valuations gets away from the search for the natural, which is an utter illusion because there isn't anything that is not natural, and directs the search toward the good. Indeed, in my naughtier moments I argue that all good things are artificial and that the great object of human activity is to distort nature toward an artificially constructed good by the standards of human valuations. Human artifacts are outcomes of the same evolutionary process that produced the snail darter, that is, through learned structures which are then transmitted through a learning process. That is just as evolutionary as anything else. Agriculture, housing, clothing, and all economic goods represent such productive distortions of nature.

4   The selective process in the evolution of human artifacts, however, is teleological in the sense that the survival probability of these artifacts depends on their ability to be ranked high on human valuations both present and future. Human valuation involves postulating a goodness function. Some of the variables in the argument are beyond our control, although we still evaluate them: a natural disaster is still

regarded as bad even if unavoidable. Those variables that are subject to human decision, however, tend to be changed in the light of the goodness function itself. We have to face the fact that each person has a different goodness function, and that some social processes are necessary to coordinate these different evaluations. I have argued that there are three major processes of coordination of values. I call them the "three P's" — prices (markets), policemen (politics), and preachments (the moral order). These interact continually in the processes of societal evolution.

Where, in all this evolutionary melee, is the role, and evaluation, of personal freedom? Freedom is a multidimensional concept, not easy to reduce to a measure. I don't know any social indicator of it, or even a single definition. It has at least two major dimensions. One is the dimension of power, that is, how far out from an individual is the boundary which divides that which he or she can do from what is impossible to do? The power of an individual is the area within the fence that surrounds the individual. On the far side of that fence lies the impossible. A powerless individual is surrounded by a very small enclosure; the powerful is in the middle of a large one. A further dimension of power is the ability of the individual to push back the fence by action.

Freedom, however, is more than power; it relates to the nature, and especially to the legitimacy, of the power or possibility of boundary. Particularly where the position of the fence is imposed by others, and more so when the imposition is perceived as illegitimate, there is a sense of unfreedom as well as of impotence. The potentiality for change is also an element in the situation.

Another dimension of freedom is particularly well-represented by the economic dimension; this is the dimension of general scarcity, of what we can afford. Economic power is a function of income opportunities plus a relative price structure. It is not a fixed fence, but a flexible fence of limited length. If we push it out in one direction we will find it pulled in another direction; if we buy A, we cannot afford B, if we buy B, we cannot afford A. This type of flexible restriction may apply in somewhat less degree to political and even moral trade-offs.

The really critical question is why do things so easily go from bad to worse rather than from bad to better, on some reasonably coordinated scale of human values? The next question is, do the social institutions which prevent things from going from bad to worse, or encourage things to go from bad to better, require limitations on the power of individuals which are perceived as illegitimate and therefore as unfreedom?

9   Earth, indeed, is a very unusual place, and considering the very narrow physical range within which biological and societal evolution is possible, it is something of a miracle that it has survived so long on this planet. With the coming of the human race with its unprecedented capacity for producing artifacts and for creating artificial environments like houses and spaceships, the physical limits of evolution have been pushed back to the point where it might now be possible to take the great leap beyond the earth into outer space; that is, we may be on the edge of a transition as profound as the one from the sea to the land.

10   One facet of the benevolent-nature illusion that has a good deal of validity is the principle that the growth of the human race has now produced a situation where we are an increasingly large part of the total system, and hence we cannot regard our own environment as something too large to be affected by our own behavior and our own dynamics. The ten million humans of the Paleolithic era could not much affect the total system of the earth, though we should not underestimate their capacity to muck things up. For instance, they hunted the mammoth and many other large animals to extinction, and that must have had a quite noticeable effect on the biosphere. But they probably did not have any large effect on the soils and the atmosphere.

11   The four to five billion humans of today, and still more the eight billion almost certainly in prospect, have a potential for widespread extinction of other species, for destruction of soils, and for potentially adverse changes in the atmosphere, not to mention radioactivity and nuclear war, which might undermine the habitat of the human species itself. This is a phenomenon by no means unfamiliar to dear old Mother Nature: the oxygen that we breathe today is probably the excrement of the earliest anaerobic forms of life, and it seems to have just about finished them off, although at a slow enough pace so that genetic mutation could produce aerobic organisms that turned out better. The role of ecological catastrophe in evolution is obscure but by no means negligible, though we undoubtedly have a right to be bothered by an impending catastrophe which might include us.

12   Most processes by which things go from bad to worse fall under the general head of "tragedies of the commons" — situations in which what is rational for the individual in the short run turns out to be adverse to the group or society, and therefore also adverse to the indi-

vidual in the longer run. The overgrazing of commons, made famous by Garrett Hardin, is only one of numerous examples. Others are arms races, addictive behavior, economic externalities, failures of the invisible hand of the market, failures of the visible fist of government, failures of the moral dynamic, and so on for a very long list.

In general, there are two broad classes of solutions: one is property, the dividing up of the commons into private property supported by law and legitimated public threat-systems. This is not always possible. The other solution is the development of a sense and institutions of community and a common adminstration of the commons. Each of these may involve restrictions on individual power; if these are perceived as legitimate, however, they will not be regarded as infringements on freedom. The simplest example of the commons of a road intersection is the stop light, which allocates property in the road at regular intervals, interferes with the power to cross the intersection, but is not usually regarded as an infringement of liberty.

There is also need for a constant critique of legitimacy. Restrictions on power may be accepted as legitimate which are in fact destructive and lead to stagnation. The world is divided into doers and stoppers; of these the stoppers tend to be the most preachy and political, the doers the most amoral and economic. Sins of commission certainly need to be stopped, but in so doing we may encourage the sins of omission — leaving undone the things we ought to have done — which are hard to detect, easy to foster and excuse, and often in the long run may be more damaging than the sins of commission.

I cannot resist the temptation to sum up in an old piece of doggerel of mine:

> Freedom is what's inside the fence
> Of morals, money, law, and sense;
> And we are free if this is wide
> (Or nothing's on the other side).
> We come to politics (and sin)
> When your fine freedoms fence me in;
> And so through law we come to be
> Curtailing freedom — to be more free.

____ CONSIDERATIONS _____

1. In discussing such abstractions as "nature" and "freedom," Boulding writes abstractly, thus making it especially important for the reader to under-

stand Boulding's vocabulary. If terms like "parameters" (Paragraph 1), "normative" (Paragraph 3), "teleological" (Paragraph 4), "impotence" (Paragraph 6), "Paleolithic" (Paragraph 10), and "amoral" (Paragraph 14) are not familiar to you, can you truly claim an understanding of his essay?

2. Is it possible to reconcile Boulding's idea that "The universe is a disequilibrium system" and the popular belief in "the balance of nature"?

3. In Paragraphs 6 and 7, and again in his closing verse, Boulding uses the analogy of a fence to help his readers understand the boundaries of freedom. In effect, Boulding creates a metaphor; that is, he uses a concrete object to convey an abstract idea. Note, in other sections of this book, several additional examples of the metaphor. Make use of the same device in your next essay.

4. To what extent can you agree with Boulding (in Paragraph 3) that "there isn't anything that is not natural" and that man-made artifacts — plastic, for example — are as "natural" as anything else? Or do you find yourself subject to what he refrains from calling the "Sierra Club illusion" (Paragraph 2)?

5. Boulding describes "freedom" as a "multidimensional concept," that is, one which defies any simple definition. How successful is he, in Paragraphs 5, 6, and 7, in his attempts to clarify the term?

6. In the final couplet of his closing verse, Boulding presents a paradox, a statement that seems contradictory but is actually true. In what way, if any, is Boulding's paradox well-founded or true?

7. Boulding's allusion to Garrett Hardin (Paragraph 12) refers us to an important essay that the biologist published in 1967 in *Science*. Track down that essay in the periodical section of your college library, summarize Hardin's points, and respond to his argument with an essay of your own.

*Randolph Bourne (1886–1918) contracted spinal tuberculosis
when he was four years old, which left him with a deformed
back. After high school, financially unable to attend college, he
learned that "the bitterest struggles of the handicapped man
come when he tackles the business world." He took a scholarship at Columbia University when he was twenty-three, and
soon began to publish articles in magazines.*

"A Philosophy of Handicap" first appeared in the Atlantic
Monthly, *and was later reprinted in Bourne's first book,* Youth
and Life *(1913). Subsequent books included the posthumous*
Untimely Papers, *edited by James Oppenheim (1919), and* The
History of a Literary Radical and Other Essays, *edited by Van
Wyck Brooks (1920). Bourne died in the influenza epidemic that
followed World War I.*

16

RANDOLPH BOURNE

A Philosophy of Handicap

It would not be thought, ordinarily, that the man whom physical   1
disabilities have made so helpless that he is unable to move around
among his fellows, can bear his lot more happily, even though he
suffer pain, and face life with a more cheerful and contented spirit,
than can the man whose handicaps are merely enough to mark him
out from the rest of his fellows without preventing him from entering
with them into most of their common affairs and experiences. But the
fact is that the former's very helplessness makes him content to rest
and not to strive. I know a young man so helplessly disabled that he
has to be carried about, who is happy in reading a little, playing chess,
taking a course or two in college, and all with the sunniest good will

91

in the world, and a happiness that seems strange and unaccountable to my restlessness. He does not cry for the moon.

2   When the handicapped youth, however, is in full possession of his faculties, and can move about freely, he is perforce drawn into all the currents of life. Particularly if he has his own way in the world to make, his road is apt to be hard and rugged, and he will penetrate to an unusual depth in his interpretation both of the world's attitude toward such misfortunes, and of the attitude toward the world which such misfortunes tend to cultivate in men like him. For he has all the battles of a stronger man to fight, and he is at a double disadvantage in fighting them. He has constantly with him the sense of being obliged to make extra efforts to overcome the bad impression of his physical defects, and he is haunted with a constant feeling of weakness and low vitality which makes effort more difficult and renders him easily faint-hearted and discouraged by failure. He is never confident of himself, because he has grown up in an atmosphere where nobody has been very confident of him; and yet his environment and circumstances call out all sorts of ambitions and energies in him which, from the nature of his case, are bound to be immediately thwarted. This attitude is likely to keep him at a generally low level of accomplishment unless he have an unusually strong will, and a strong will is perhaps the last thing to develop under such circumstances.

3   The handicapped man is always conscious that the world does not expect very much from him. And it takes him a long time to see in this a challenge instead of a firm pressing down to a low level of accomplishment. As a result, he does not expect very much from himself; he is timid in approaching people, and distrustful of his ability to persuade and convince. He becomes extraordinarily sensitive to other people's first impression of him; those who are to be his friends he knows instantly, and further acquaintance adds little to the intimacy and warm friendship that he at once feels for them. On the other hand, those who do not respond to him immediately cannot by any effort either on his part or theirs overcome that first alienation.

4   This sensitiveness has both its good and its bad sides. It makes friendship the most precious thing in the world to him, and he finds that he arrives at a much richer and wider intimacy with his friends than do ordinary men with their light, surface friendships, based on good fellowship or the convenience of the moment. But on the other hand this sensitiveness absolutely unfits him for business and the practice of a profession, where one must be "all things to all men,"

and the professional manner is indispensable to success. For here, where he has to meet a constant stream of men of all sorts and conditions, his sensitiveness to these first impressions will make his case hopeless. Except with those few who by some secret sympathy will seem to respond, his physical deficiencies will stand like a huge barrier between his personality and other men's. The magical good fortune of attractive personal appearance makes its way almost without effort in the world, breaking down all sorts of walls of disapproval and lack of interest. Even the homely person can attract by personal charm.

The doors of the handicapped man are always locked, and the   5
key is on the outside. He may have treasures of charm inside, but they will never be revealed unless the person outside cooperates with him in unlocking the door. A friend becomes, to a much greater degree than with the ordinary man, the indispensable means of discovering one's own personality. One only exists, so to speak, with friends. It is easy to see how hopelessly such a sensitiveness incapacitates a man for business, professional or social life, where the hasty and superficial impression is everything, and disaster is the fate of the man who has not all the treasures of his personality in the front window, where they can be readily inspected and appraised.

It thus takes the handicapped man a long time to get adjusted to   6
his world. Childhood is perhaps the hardest time of all. As a child he is a strange creature in a strange land. It was my own fate to be just strong enough to play about with the other boys, and attempt all their games and "stunts," without being strong enough actually to succeed in any of them. It never used to occur to me that my failures and lack of skill were due to circumstances beyond my control, but I would always impute them, in consequence of my rigid Calvinistic upbringing, I suppose, to some moral weakness of my own. I suffered tortures in trying to learn to skate, to climb trees, to play ball, to conform in general to the ways of the world. I never resigned myself to the inevitable, but overexerted myself constantly in a grim determination to succeed. I was good at my lessons, and through timidity rather than priggishness, I hope, a very well-behaved boy at school; I was devoted, too, to music, and learned to play the piano pretty well. But I despised my reputation for excellence in these things, and instead of adapting myself philosophically to the situation, I strove and have been striving ever since to do the things I could not.

As I look back now it seems perfectly natural that I should have   7
followed the standards of the crowd, and loathed my high marks in

lessons and deportment, and the concerts to which I was sent by my
aunt, and the exhibitions of my musical skill that I had to give before
admiring ladies. Whether or not such an experience is typical of handicapped children, there is tragedy there for those situated as I was. For
had I been a little weaker physically, I should have been thrown back
on reading omnivorously and cultivating my music, with some possible results; while if I had been a little stronger, I could have partici-
pated in the play on an equal footing with the rest. As it was, I simply
tantalized myself, and grew up with a deepening sense of failure, and
a lack of pride in that at which I really excelled.

8   When the world became one of dances and parties and social
evenings and boy-and-girl attachments — the world of youth — I was
to find myself still less adapted to it. And this was the harder to bear
because I was naturally sociable, and all these things appealed tremendously to me. This world of admiration and gayety and smiles and
favors and quick interest and companionship, however, is only for the
well-begotten and the debonair. It was not through any cruelty or
dislike, I think, that I was refused admittance; indeed they were
always very kind about inviting me. But it was more as if a ragged
urchin had been asked to come and look through a window at the light
and warmth of a glittering party; I was truly in the world, but not of
the world. Indeed there were times when one would almost prefer
conscious cruelty to this silent, unconscious, gentle oblivion. And this
is the tragedy, I suppose, of all the ill-favored and unattractive to a
greater or less degree; the world of youth is a world of so many conventions, and the abnormal in any direction is so glaringly and hide-
ously abnormal.

9   Although it took me a long time to understand this, and I continued to attribute my failure mostly to my own character, trying hard to
compensate for my physical deficiencies by my skill and cleverness, I
suffered comparatively few pangs, and got much better adjusted to this
world than the other. For I was older, and I had acquired a lively
interest in all the social politics; I would get so interested in watching
how people behaved, and in sizing them up, that only at rare intervals
would I remember that I was really having no hand in the game. This
interest just in the ways people are human, has become more and
more a positive advantage in my life, and has kept sweet many a
situation that might easily have cost me a pang. Not that a person
with disabilities should be a sort of detective, evil-mindedly using his
social opportunities for spying out and analyzing his friends' foibles,
but that, if he does acquire an interest in people quite apart from their

relation to him, he may go into society with an easy conscience and a
certainty that he will be entertained and possibly entertaining, even
though he cuts a poor enough social figure. He must simply not expect
too much.

Perhaps the bitterest struggles of the handicapped man come 10
when he tackles the business world. If he has to go out for himself to
look for work, without fortune, training, or influence, as I personally
did, his way will indeed be rugged. His disability will work against
him for any position where he must be much in the eyes of men, and
his general insignificance has a subtle influence in convincing those
to whom he applies that he is unfitted for any kind of work. As I have
suggested, his keen sensitiveness to other people's impressions of him
makes him more than usually timid and unable to counteract that
fatal first impression by any display of personal force and will. He
cannot get his personality over across that barrier. The cards seem
stacked against him from the start. With training and influence something might be done, but alone and unaided his case is almost hopeless. The attitude toward him ranges from, "You can't expect us to
create a place for you," to, "How could it enter your head that we
should find any use for you?" He is discounted at the start: it is not
business to make allowances for anybody; and while people are not
cruel or unkind, it is the hopeless finality of the thing that fills one's
heart with despair.

The environment of the big city is perhaps the worst possible 11
that a man in such a situation could have. For the thousands of seeming opportunities lead one restlessly on and on, and keep one's mind
perpetually unsettled and depressed. There is a poignant mental torture that comes with such an experience, — the urgent need, the
repeated failure, or rather the repeated failure even to obtain a chance
to fail, the realization that those at home can ill afford to have you
idle, the growing dread of encountering people — all this is something
that those who have never been through it can never realize. Personally I know of no particular way of escape. One can expect to do little
by one's own unaided efforts. I solved my difficulties by evading them,
by throwing overboard some of my responsibility, and taking the desperate step of entering college on a scholarship. Desultory work is not
nearly so humiliating when one is using one's time to some advantage,
and college furnishes an ideal environment where the things at which
a man handicapped like myself can succeed really count. One's self-
respect can begin to grow like a weed.

For at the bottom of all the difficulties of a man like me is really 12 the fact that his self-respect is so slow in growing up. Accustomed from his childhood to being discounted, his self-respect is naturally not very strong, and it would require pretty constant success in a congenial line of work really to confirm it. If he could only more easily separate the factors that are due to his physical disability from those that are due to his weak will and character, he might more quickly attain self-respect, for he would realize what he is responsible for, and what he is not. But at the beginning he rarely makes allowances for himself; he is his own severest judge. He longs for a "strong will," and yet the experience of having his efforts promptly nipped off at the beginning is the last thing on earth to produce that will.

13   If the handicapped youth is brought into harsh and direct touch with the real world, life proves a much more complex thing to him than to the ordinary man. Many of his inherited platitudes vanish at the first touch. Life appears to him as a grim struggle, where ability does not necessarily mean opportunity and success, nor piety sympathy, and where helplessness cannot count on assistance and kindly interest. Human affairs seem to be running on a wholly irrational plan, and success to be founded on chance as much as on anything. But if he can stand the first shock of disillusionment, he may find himself enormously interested in discovering how they actually do run, and he will want to burrow into the motives of men, and find the reasons for the crass inequalities and injustices of the world he sees around him. He has practically to construct anew a world of his own, and explain a great many things to himself that the ordinary person never dreams of finding unintelligible at all. He will be filled with a profound sympathy for all who are despised and ignored in the world. When he has been through the neglect and struggles of a handicapped and ill-favored man himself, he will begin to understand the feelings of all the horde of the unpresentable and unemployable, the incompetent and the ugly, the queer and crotchety people who make up so large a proportion of human folk.

14   We are perhaps too prone to get our ideas and standards of worth from the successful, without reflecting that the interpretations of life which patriotic legend, copy-book philosophy, and the sayings of the wealthy give us, are pitifully inadequate for those who fall behind in the race. Surely there are enough people to whom the task of making a decent living and maintaining themselves and their families in their social class, or of winning and keeping the respect of their fellows, is a hard and bitter task, to make a philosophy gained through personal disability and failure as just and true a method of appraising the life

around us as the cheap optimism of the ordinary professional man. And certainly a kindlier, for it has no shade of contempt or disparagement about it. . . .

The difference between what the strongest of the strong and the most winning of the attractive can get out of life, and what I can, is after all so slight. Our experiences and enjoyments, both his and mine, are so infinitesimal compared with the great mass of possibilities; and there must be a division of labor. If he takes the world of physical satisfactions and of material success, I can at least occupy the far richer kingdom of mental effort and artistic appreciation. And on the side of what we are to put into life, although I admit that achievement on my part will be harder relatively to encompass than on his, at least I may have the field of artistic creation and intellectual achievement for my own. Indeed, as one gets older, the fact of one's disabilities fades dimmer and dimmer away from consciousness. One's enemy is now one's own weak will, and the struggle is to attain the artistic ideal one has set. 15

But one must have grown up, to get this attitude. And that is the best thing the handicapped man can do. Growing up will have given him one of the greatest satisfactions of his life, and certainly the most durable one. It will mean at least that he is out of the woods. Childhood has nothing to offer him; youth little more. They are things to be gotten through with as soon as possible. For he will not understand, and he will not be understood. He finds himself simply a bundle of chaotic impulses and emotions and ambitions, very few of which, from the nature of the case, can possibly be realized or satisfied. He is bound to be at cross-grains with the world, and he has to look sharp that he does not grow up with a bad temper and a hateful disposition, and become cynical and bitter against those who turn him away. By growing up, his horizon will broaden; he will get a better perspective, and will not take the world so seriously as he used to, nor will failure frighten him so much. He can look back and see how inevitable it all was, and understand how precarious and problematic even the best regulated of human affairs may be. And if he feels that there were times when he should have been able to count upon the help and kindly counsel of relatives and acquaintances who remained dumb and uninterested, he will not put their behavior down as proof of the depravity of human nature, but as due to an unfortunate blindness which it will be his work to avoid in himself by looking out for others when he has the power. 16

When he has grown up, he will find that people of his own age 17 and experience are willing to make those large allowances for what is out of the ordinary, which were impossible for his younger friends, and that grown-up people touch each other on planes other than the purely superficial. With a broadening of his own interests, he will find himself overlapping with other people's personalities at new points, and will discover with rare delight that he is beginning to be understood and appreciated — at least to a greater degree than when he had to keep his real interests hid as something unusual. For he will begin to see in his friends, his music and books, and his interest in people and social betterment, his true life; many of his restless ambitions will fade gradually away, and he will come to recognize all the more clearly some true ambition of his life that is within the range of his capabilities. He will have built up his world, and have sifted out the things that are not going to concern him, and the participation in which will only serve to vex and harass him. He may well come to count his disabilities even as a blessing, for it has made impossible to him at last many things in the pursuit of which he would only fritter away his time and dissipate his interest. He must not think of "resigning himself to his fate"; above all, he must insist on his own personality. For once really grown up, he will find that he has acquired self-respect and personality. Grownup-ness, I think, is not a mere question of age, but of being able to look back and understand and find satisfaction in one's experience, no matter how bitter it may have been.

18   So to all the handicapped and unappreciated, I would say, — Grow up as fast as you can. Cultivate the widest interests you can, and cherish all your friends. Cultivate some artistic talent, for you will find it the most durable of satisfactions, and perhaps one of the surest means of livelihood as well. Achievement is, of course, on the knees of the gods; but you will at least have the thrill of trial, and, after all, not to try is to fail. Taking your disabilities for granted, and assuming constantly that they are being taken for granted, make your social intercourse as broad and as constant as possible. Do not take the world too seriously, nor let too many social conventions oppress you. Keep sweet your sense of humor, and above all do not let any morbid feelings of inferiority creep into your soul. You will find yourself sensitive enough to the sympathy of others, and if you do not find people who like you and are willing to meet you more than halfway, it will be because you have let your disability narrow your vision and shrink up your soul. It will be really your own fault, and not that of your circumstances. In a word, keep looking outward; look out eagerly

for those things that interest you, for people who will interest you and be friends with you, for new interests and opportunities to express yourself. You will find that your disability will come to have little meaning for you, that it will begin to fade quite completely out of your sight; you will wake up some fine morning and find yourself, after all the struggles that seemed so bitter to you, really and truly adjusted to the world.

____ CONSIDERATIONS ____

1. After reading Bourne on common attitudes toward the handicapped, turn to Ronald Blythe, who writes on attitudes toward the aged. Can you discover a parallel between the two essays?

2. The problem Bourne brings up in Paragraph 6 may remind you of any young person who does not excel in the games and pranks of his peers. Recall your own experience for examples, explore the implications of what Bourne calls his "Calvinistic upbringing," and produce an essay on the subject: "Handicapped: the Normal Condition of Youth." Could you make use of Bourne's implication (Paragraph 8) that young people are more conventional than they are likely to admit? Do you find in his last paragraph any remnant of his Calvinist upbringing?

3. Both Bourne (in Paragraph 13) and Bergmann (in his Paragraph 21) make use of the word "platitude" in their discussions of conventional thought. Devote a little time to that word — its parts, its origins, its uses, synonyms and antonyms — in order to study each writer's ideas.

4. "We are perhaps too prone to get our ideas and standards of worth from the successful," writes Bourne in Paragraph 14. If he were alive today, would the mass media, especially TV, bear out his observation?

5. Although Bourne draws upon his own experience of physical and psychological impairments, he uses no anecdotes or detailed examples in his essay. The essay proceeds along a uniform plane of generalization, without the dramatic peaks or valleys found in writers who move between general statement and concrete illustration. Compare Adams, Agee, Bly, Dillard, Ephron, or Momaday. What are the advantages and disadvantages of Bourne's approach?

6. In explaining that the best thing the handicapped man can do is to grow up, Bourne says that "Childhood has nothing to offer him; youth little more" (Paragraph 16). Read the first couple of paragraphs of Henry Adams's "Winter and Summer." Could Bourne have used Adams's memories of boyhood to support his statement?

Bruce Catton (1899–1978) became a historian while working as a newspaper reporter and magazine editor. His books, many on the Civil War, include Mr. Lincoln's Army *(1951) and* A Stillness at Appomattox *(1953). Catton has received both the Pulitzer Prize and the National Book Award.*

_17_

BRUCE CATTON

Grant and Lee: A Study in Contrasts

1   When Ulysses S. Grant and Robert E. Lee met in the parlor of a modest house at Appomattox Court House, Virginia, on April 9, 1865, to work out the terms for the surrender of Lee's Army of Northern Virginia, a great chapter in American life came to a close, and a great new chapter began.

2   These men were bringing the Civil War to its virtual finish. To be sure, other armies had yet to surrender, and for a few days the fugitive Confederate government would struggle desperately and vainly, trying to find some way to go on living now that its chief support was gone. But in effect it was all over when Grant and Lee signed the papers. And the little room where they wrote out the terms was the scene of one of the poignant, dramatic contrasts in American History.

3   They were two strong men, these oddly different generals, and they represented the strengths of two conflicting currents that, through them, had come into final collision.

From *The American Story* ed. Earl Schenk Miers, © 1956 by Broadcast Music, Inc. Used by permission of the copyright holder.

Back of Robert E. Lee was the notion that the old aristocratic 4
concept might somehow survive and be dominant in American life.

Lee was tidewater Virginia, and in his background were family, 5
culture, and tradition . . . the age of chivalry transplanted to a New
World which was making its own legends and its own myths. He
embodied a way of life that had come down through the age of knight-
hood and the English country squire. America was a land that was
beginning all over again, dedicated to nothing much more complicated
than the rather hazy belief that all men had equal rights and should
have an equal chance in the world. In such a land Lee stood for the
feeling that it was somehow of advantage to human society to have a
pronounced inequality in the social structure. There should be a leisure class, backed by ownership of land; in turn, society itself should
be keyed to the land as the chief source of wealth and influence. It
would bring forth (according to this ideal) a class of men with a strong
sense of obligation to the community; men who lived not to gain
advantage for themselves, but to meet the solemn obligations which
had been laid on them by the very fact that they were privileged. From
them the country would get its leadership; to them it could look for
the higher values — of thought, of conduct, of personal deportment
— to give it strength and virtue.

Lee embodied the noblest elements of this aristocratic ideal. 6
Through him, the landed nobility justified itself. For four years, the
Southern states had fought a desperate war to uphold the ideals for
which Lee stood. In the end, it almost seemed as if the Confederacy
fought for Lee; as if he himself was the Confederacy . . . the best thing
that the way of life for which the Confederacy stood could ever have
to offer. He had passed into legend before Appomattox. Thousands of
tired, underfed, poorly clothed Confederate soldiers, long since past
the simple enthusiasm of the early days of the struggle, somehow
considered Lee the symbol of everything for which they had been
willing to die. But they could not quite put this feeling into words. If
the Lost Cause, sanctified by so much heroism and so many deaths,
had a living justification, its justification was General Lee.

Grant, the son of a tanner on the Western frontier, was every- 7
thing Lee was not. He had come up the hard way and embodied nothing in particular except the eternal toughness and sinewy fiber of the
men who grew up beyond the mountains. He was one of a body of
men who owed reverence and obeisance to no one, who were self-
reliant to a fault, who cared hardly anything for the past but who had
a sharp eye for the future.

8   These frontier men were the precise opposites of the tidewater aristocrats. Back of them, in the great surge that had taken people over the Alleghenies and into the opening Western country, there was a deep, implicit dissatisfaction with a past that had settled into grooves. They stood for democracy, not from any reasoned conclusion about the proper ordering of human society, but simply because they had grown up in the middle of democracy and knew how it worked. Their society might have privileges, but they would be privileges each man had won for himself. Forms and patterns meant nothing. No man was born to anything except perhaps to a chance to show how far he could rise. Life was competition.

9   Yet along with this feeling had come a deep sense of belonging to a national community. The Westerner who developed a farm, opened a shop, or set up in business as a trader, could hope to prosper only as his own community prospered — and his community ran from the Atlantic to the Pacific and from Canada down to Mexico. If the land was settled, with towns and highways and accessible markets, he could better himself. He saw his fate in terms of the nation's own destiny. As its horizons expanded, so did his. He had, in other words, an acute dollars-and-cents stake in the continued growth and development of his country.

10   And that, perhaps, is where the contrast between Grant and Lee becomes most striking. The Virginia aristocrat, inevitably, saw himself in relation to his own region. He lived in a static society which could endure almost anything except change. Instinctively, his first loyalty would go to the locality in which that society existed. He would fight to the limit of endurance to defend it, because in defending it he was defending everything that gave his own life its deepest meaning.

11   The Westerner, on the other hand, would fight with an equal tenacity for the broader concept of society. He fought so because everything he lived by was tied to growth, expansion, and a constantly widening horizon. What he lived by would survive or fall with the nation itself. He could not possibly stand by unmoved in the face of an attempt to destroy the Union. He would combat it with everything he had, because he could only see it as an effort to cut the ground out from under his feet.

12   So Grant and Lee were in complete contrast, representing two diametrically opposed elements in American life. Grant was the modern man emerging; beyond him, ready to come on the stage, was the great age of steel and machinery, of crowded cities and a restless bur-

geoning vitality. Lee might have ridden down from the old age of chivalry, lance in hand, silken banner fluttering over his head. Each man was the perfect champion of his cause, drawing both his strengths and his weaknesses from the people he led.

Yet it was not all contrast, after all. Different as they were — in   13
background, in personality, in underlying aspiration — these two great soldiers had much in common. Under everything else, they were marvelous fighters. Furthermore, their fighting qualities were really very much alike.

Each man had, to begin with, the great virtue of utter tenacity   14
and fidelity. Grant fought his way down the Mississippi Valley in spite of acute personal discouragement and profound military handicaps. Lee hung on in the trenches at Petersburg after hope itself had died. In each man there was an indomitable quality . . . the born fighter's refusal to give up as long as he can still remain on his feet and lift his two fists.

Daring and resourcefulness they had, too; the ability to think   15
faster and move faster than the enemy. These were the qualities which gave Lee the dazzling campaigns of Second Manassas and Chancellorsville and won Vicksburg for Grant.

Lastly, and perhaps greatest of all, there was the ability, at the   16
end, to turn quickly from war to peace once the fighting was over. Out of the way these two men behaved at Appomattox came the possibility of a peace of reconciliation. It was a possibility not wholly realized, in the years to come, but which did, in the end, help the two sections to become one nation again . . . after a war whose bitterness might have seemed to make such a reunion wholly impossible. No part of either man's life became him more than the part he played in their brief meeting in the McLean house at Appomattox. Their behavior there put all succeeding generations of Americans in their debt. Two great Americans, Grant and Lee — very different, yet under everything very much alike. Their encounter at Appomattox was one of the great moments of American history.

_____ **CONSIDERATIONS** _____

1. Bruce Catton's "Grant and Lee" is a classic example of the comparison-contrast essay, both in subject matter and organization. Select equally different figures of your own time and write about them, following Catton's organizational method.

2. After studying the contrast Catton offers in Paragraphs 10 and 11, consider an essay on similar trends in modern American life — adherents of no-growth against those who argue for expansion. Compare the "stoppers" and the "doers" described by Kenneth E. Boulding in Paragraph 14 of his essay.

3. "Two great Americans, Grant and Lee," writes Catton in his last paragraph. Do you find evidence that Catton favored either?

4. In Paragraph 6, Catton describes Lee as a "symbol." A symbol of what? How can you recognize a symbol when you see one? Why would anyone fight for a symbol?

5. Nowhere in his essay does Catton describe physical appearances. A half hour's research in your college library should give you enough description to add at least a paragraph to Catton's essay. Where, in that essay, would you insert such an addition? Do you find that physical description contributes to or confuses the contrast of their natures that Catton presents?

6. Judging by the proportions of this essay, decide whether Catton found the differences between the two men more interesting than their similarities.

Frank Conroy (b. 1936) grew up in various towns along the eastern seaboard, and attended Haverford College. He plays the jazz piano and teaches writing at various American colleges. He writes about his early life in the only book he has published to date, Stop-Time *(1967). His prose has the qualities that make the best reminiscence: details feel exact and bright, though miniature with distance, like the landscape crafted for background to model trains.*

18

FRANK CONROY

A Yo-Yo Going Down

The common yo-yo is crudely made, with a thick shank between two widely spaced wooden disks. The string is knotted or stapled to the shank. With such an instrument nothing can be done except the simple up-down movement. My yo-yo, on the other hand, was a perfectly balanced construction of hard wood, slightly weighted, flat, with only a sixteenth of an inch between the halves. The string was not attached to the shank, but looped over it in such a way as to allow the wooden part to spin freely on its own axis. The gyroscopic effect thus created kept the yo-yo stable in all attitudes. 1

I started at the beginning of the book and quickly mastered the novice, intermediate, and advanced stages, practicing all day every day in the woods across the street from my house. Hour after hour of practice, never moving to the next trick until the one at hand was mastered. 2

3   The string was tied to my middle finger, just behind the nail. As I threw — with your palm up, make a fist; throw down your hand, fingers unfolding, as if you were casting grain — a short bit of string would tighten across the sensitive pad of flesh at the tip of my finger. That was the critical area. After a number of weeks I could interpret the condition of the string, the presence of any imperfections on the shank, but most importantly the exact amount of spin or inertial energy left in the yo-yo at any given moment — all from that bit of string on my fingertip. As the throwing motion became more and more natural I found I could make the yo-yo "sleep" for an astonishing length of time — fourteen or fifteen seconds — and still have enough spin left to bring it back to my hand. Gradually the basic moves became reflexes. Sleeping, twirling, swinging, and precise aim. Without thinking, without even looking, I could run through trick after trick involving various combinations of the elemental skills, switching from one to the other in a smooth continuous flow. On particularly good days I would hum a tune under my breath and do it all in time to the music.

4   Flicking the yo-yo expressed something. The sudden, potentially comic extension of one's arm to twice its length. The precise neatness of it, intrinsically soothing, as if relieving an inner tension too slight to be noticeable, the way a man might hitch up his pants simply to enact a reassuring gesture. It felt good. The comfortable weight in one's hand, the smooth, rapid descent down the string, ending with a barely audible snap as the yo-yo hung balanced, spinning, pregnant with force and the slave of one's fingertip. That it was vaguely masturbatory seems inescapable. I doubt that half the pubescent boys in American could have been captured by any other means, as, in the heat of the fad, half of them were. A single Loop-the-Loop might represent, in some mysterious way, the act of masturbation, but to break down the entire repertoire into the three stages of throw, trick, and return representing erection, climax, and detumescence seems immoderate.

5   The greatest pleasure in yo-yoing was an abstract pleasure — watching the dramatization of simple physical laws, and realizing they would never fail if a trick was done correctly. The geometric purity of it! The string wasn't just a string, it was a tool in the enactment of theorems. It was a line, an idea. And the top was an entirely different sort of idea, a gyroscope, capable of storing energy and of interacting with the line. I remember the first time I did a particularly lovely trick, one in which the sleeping yo-yo is swung from right to left while the string is interrupted by an extended index finger. Momentum car-

ries the yo-yo in a circular path around the finger, but instead of completing the arc the yo-yo falls on the taut string between the performer's hands, where it continues to spin in an upright position. My pleasure at that moment was as much from the beauty of the experiment as from pride. Snapping apart my hands I sent the yo-yo into the air above my head, bouncing it off nothing, back into my palm.

I practiced the yo-yo because it pleased me to do so, without the slightest application of will power. It wasn't ambition that drove me, but the nature of yo-yoing. The yo-yo represented my first organized attempt to control the outside world. It fascinated me because I could see my progress in clearly defined stages, and because the intimacy of it, the almost spooky closeness I began to feel with the instrument in my hand, seemed to ensure that nothing irrelevant would interfere. I was, in the language of jazz, "up tight" with my yo-yo, and finally free, in one small area at least, of the paralyzing sloppiness of life in general. 6

The first significant problem arose in the attempt to do fifty consecutive Loop-the-Loops. After ten or fifteen the yo-yo invariably started to lean and the throws became less clean, resulting in loss of control. I almost skipped the whole thing because fifty seemed excessive. Ten made the point. But there it was, written out in the book. To qualify as an expert you had to do fifty, so fifty I would do. 7

It took me two days, and I wouldn't have spent a moment more. All those Loop-the-Loops were hard on the strings. Time after time the shank cut them and the yo-yo went sailing off into the air. It was irritating, not only because of the expense (strings were a nickel each, and fabricating your own was unsatisfactory), but because a random element had been introduced. About the only unforeseeable disaster in yo-yoing was to have your string break, and here was a trick designed to do exactly that. Twenty-five would have been enough. If you could do twenty-five clean Loop-the-Loops you could do fifty or a hundred. I supposed they were simply trying to sell strings and went back to the more interesting tricks. 8

The witty nonsense of Eating Spaghetti, the surprise of The Twirl, the complex neatness of Cannonball, Backwards Round the World, or Halfway Round the World — I could do them all, without false starts or sloppy endings. I could do every trick in the book. Perfectly. 9

The day was marked on the kitchen calendar (God Gave Us Bluebell Natural Bottled Gas). I got on my bike and rode into town. Pedal- 10 ing along the highway I worked out with the yo-yo to break in a new string. The twins were appearing at the dime store.

11   I could hear the crowd before I turned the corner. Kids were coming on bikes and on foot from every corner of town, rushing down the streets like madmen. Three or four policemen were busy keeping the street clear directly in front of the store, and in a small open space around the doors some of the more adept kids were running through their tricks, showing off to the general audience or stopping to compare notes with their peers. Standing at the edge with my yo-yo safe in my pocket, it didn't take me long to see I had them all covered. A boy in a sailor hat could do some of the harder tricks, but he missed too often to be a serious threat. I went inside.

12   As Ramos and Ricardo performed I watched their hands carefully, noticing little differences in style, and technique. Ricardo was a shade classier, I thought, although Ramos held an edge in the showy two-handed stuff. When they were through we went outside for the contest.

13   "Everybody in the alley!" Ramos shouted, his head bobbing an inch or two above the others. "Contest starting now in the alley!" A hundred excited children followed the twins into an alley beside the dime store and lined up against the wall.

14   "Attention all kids!" Ramos yelled, facing us from the middle of the street like a drill sergeant. "To qualify for contest you got to Rock the Cradle. You got to rock yo-yo in cradle four time. Four time! Okay? Three time no good. Okay. Everybody happy?" There were murmurs of disappointment and some of the kids stepped out of line. The rest of us closed ranks. Yo-yos flicked nervously as we waited. "Winner receive grand prize. Special Black Beauty Prize Yo-Yo with Diamonds," said Ramos, gesturing to his brother who smiled and held up the prize, turning it in the air so we could see the four stones set on each side. ("The crowd gasped . . ." I want to write. Of course they didn't. They didn't make a sound, but the impact of the diamond yo-yo was obvious.) We'd never seen anything like it. One imagined how the stones would gleam as it revolved, and how much prettier the tricks would be. The ultimate yo-yo! The only one in town! Who knew what feats were possible with such an instrument? All around me a fierce, nervous resolve was settling into the contestants, suddenly skittish as racehorses.

15   "Ricardo will show trick with Grand Prize Yo-Yo. Rock the Cradle four time!"

16   "One!" cried Ramos.

"Two!" the kids joined in.   17

"Three!" It was really beautiful. He did it so slowly you would   18
have thought he had all the time in the world. I counted seconds under
my breath to see how long he made it sleep.

"Four!" said the crowd.   19

"Thirteen" I said to myself as the yo-yo snapped back into his   20
hand. Thirteen seconds. Excellent time for that particular trick.

"Attention all kids!" Ramos announced. "Contest start now at   21
head of line."

The first boy did a sloppy job of gathering his string but managed   22
to rock the cradle quickly four times.

"Okay." Ramos tapped him on the shoulder and moved to the   23
next boy, who fumbled. "Out." Ricard followed, doing an occasional
Loop-the-Loop with the diamond yo-yo. "Out . . . out . . . okay," said
Ramos as he worked down the line.

There was something about the man's inexorable advance that   24
unnerved me. His decisions were fast, and there was no appeal. To my
surprise I felt my palms begin to sweat. Closer and closer he came, his
voice growing louder, and then suddenly he was standing in front of
me. Amazed, I stared at him. It was as if he'd appeared out of thin air.

"What happen boy, you swarrow bubble gum?"   25

The laughter jolted me out of it. Blushing, I threw down my yo-   26
yo and executed a slow Rock the Cradle, counting the four passes and
hesitating a moment at the end so as not to appear rushed.

"Okay." He tapped my shoulder. "Good."   27

I wiped my hands on my blue jeans and watched him move down   28
the line. "Out . . . out . . . out." He had a large mole on the back of his
neck.

Seven boys qualified. Coming back, Ramos called out, "Next   29
trick Backward Round the World! Okay? Go!"

The first two boys missed, but the third was the kid in the sailor   30
hat. Glancing quickly to see that no one was behind him, he hunched
up his shoulder, threw, and just barely made the catch. There was
some loose string in his hand, but not enough to disqualify him.

Number four missed, as did number five, and it was my turn. I   31
stepped forward, threw the yo-yo almost straight up over my head, and
as it began to fall pulled very gentle to add some speed. It zipped neatly
behind my legs and there was nothing more to do. My head turned to
one side, I stood absolutely still and watched the yo-yo come in over
my shoulder and slap into my hand. I added a Loop-the-Loop just to
show the tightness of the string.

32   "Did you see that?" I heard someone say.

33   Number seven missed, so it was between myself and the boy in the sailor hat. His hair was bleached by the sun and combed up over his forehead in a pompadour, held from behind by the white hat. He was a year or two older than me. Blinking his blue eyes nervously, he adjusted the tension of his string.

34   "Next trick Cannonball! Cannonball! You go first this time," Ramos said to me.

35   Kids had gathered in a circle around us, those in front quiet and attentive, those in back jumping up and down to get a view. "Move back for room," Ricardo said, pushing them back. "More room, please."

36   I stepped into the center and paused, looking down at the ground. It was a difficult trick. The yo-yo had to land exactly on the string and there was a chance I'd miss the first time. I knew I wouldn't miss twice. "Can I have one practice?"

37   Ramos and Ricardo consulted in their mother tongue, and then Ramos held up his hands. "Attention all kids! Each boy have one practice before trick."

38   The crowd was then silent, watching me. I took a deep breath and threw, following the fall of the yo-yo with my eyes, turning slightly, matador-fashion, as it passed me. My finger caught the string, the yo-yo came up and over, and missed. Without pausing I threw again. "Second time," I yelled, so there would be no misunderstanding. The circle had been too big. This time I made it small, sacrificing beauty for security. The yo-yo fell where it belonged and spun for a moment. (A moment I don't rush, my arms widespread, my eyes locked on the spinning toy. The Trick! There it is, brief and magic, right before your eyes! My hands are frozen in the middle of a deaf-and-dumb sentence, holding the whole airy, tenuous statement aloft for everyone to see.) With a quick snap I broke up the trick and made my catch.

39   Ramos nodded. "Okay. Very good. Now next boy."

40   Sailor-hat stepped forward, wiping his nose with the back of his hand. He threw once to clear the string.

41   "One practice," said Ramos.

42   He nodded.

43   "C'mon Bobby," someone said. "You can do it."

44   Bobby threw the yo-yo out to the side, made his move, and missed. "Damn," he whispered. (He said "dahyum.") The second time

he got halfway through the trick before his yo-yo ran out of gas and fell impotently off the string. He picked it up and walked away, winding slowly.

Ramos came over and held my hand in the air. "The winner!" he   45
yelled. "Grand prize Black Beauty Diamond Yo-Yo will now be awarded."

Ricardo stood in front of me. "Take off old yo-yo." I loosened the   46
knot and slipped it off. "Put out hand." I held out my hand and he looped the new string on my finger, just behind the nail, where the mark was. "You like Black Beauty," he said, smiling as he stepped back. "Diamond make pretty colors in the sun."

"Thank you," I said.   47

"Very good with yo-yo. Later we have contest for whole town.   48
Winner go to Miami for State Championship. Maybe you win. Okay?"

"Okay." I nodded. "Thank you."   49

A few kids came up to look at Black Beauty. I threw it once or   50
twice to get the feel. It seemed a bit heavier than my old one. Ramos and Ricardo were surrounded as the kids called out their favorite tricks.

"Do Pickpocket! Pickpocket!"   51

"Do the Double Cannonball!"   52

"Ramos! Ramos! Do the Turkish Army!"   53

Smiling, waving their hands to ward off the barrage of requests,   54
the twins worked their way through the crowd toward the mouth of the alley. I watched them moving away and was immediately struck by a wave of fierce and irrational panic. "Wait," I yelled, pushing through after them. "Wait!"

I caught them on the street.   55

"No more today," Ricardo said, and then paused when he saw it   56
was me. "Okay. The champ. What's wrong? Yo-yo no good?"

"No. It's fine."   57

"Good. You take care of it."   58

"I wanted to ask when the contest is. The one where you get to   59
go to Miami."

"Later. After school begins." They began to move away. "We   60
have to go home now."

"Just one more thing," I said, walking after them. "What is the   61
hardest trick you know?"

Ricardo laughed. "Hardest trick is killing flies in air."   62

"No, no. I mean a real trick."   63

64   They stopped and looked at me. "There is a very hard trick," Ricardo said. "I don't do it, but Ramos does. Because you won the contest he will show you. But only once, so watch carefully."

65   We stepped into the lobby of the Sunset Theater. Ramos cleared his string. "Watch," he said, and threw. The trick started out like a Cannonball, and then unexpectedly folded up, opened again, and as I watched breathlessly the entire complex web spun around in the air, propelled by Ramos' two hands making slow circles like a swimmer. The end was like the end of a Cannonball.

66   "That's beautiful," I said, genuinely awed. "What's it called?"

67   "The Universe."

68   "The Universe," I repeated.

69   "Because it goes around and around," said Ramos, "like the planets."

_____ **CONSIDERATIONS** _____

1. List the several ways in which Conroy says one can get pleasure from the yo-yo.

2. How much of performance is play? Would you use the word performance for the work of a painter, an opera singer, a tennis star, a poet? Are professional athletes paid to play? What is the difference between work and play?

3. One respected writer says that "play is the direct opposite of seriousness," yet writers like Conroy are serious in recalling their childhood play. Can you resolve this apparent contradiction?

4. Conroy's essay might be divided into two major sections. Where would you draw the dividing line? Describe the two sections in terms of the author's intention. In the second section, the author makes constant use of dialogue; in the first, there is none. Why?

5. "I practiced the yo-yo because it pleased me to do so, without the slightest application of will power." Consider the relevance or irrelevance of will power to pleasure. Are they mutually exclusive?

6. In Paragraph 14, Conroy interrupts his narrative with a parenthetical remark about himself as the writer: "('The crowd gasped . . . ' I want to write. Of course they didn't. They didn't make a sound, but the impact of the diamond yo-yo was obvious.)" Are such glimpses of the writer conscious of himself writing useful or merely distracting? Discuss.

*Robert Gorham Davis (b. 1908) recently retired as professor of
English at Columbia University. He has published books about
John Dos Passos and C. P. Snow, successful textbooks, short
stories, and literary essays. Not a philosopher but a literary man,
he writes here about logic as we know it in daily life — or, more
likely, as we do not know it well enough.*

19

ROBERT GORHAM DAVIS
Logic and Logical Fallacies

Expression does not exist apart from thought, and cannot be ana- 1
lyzed or profitably discussed apart from thought. Just as clear and
effective organization is essential to good writing, so consistent thinking and coherence of mind underlie consistent writing and coherence
of style. The faults and errors which [fall] under the headings of style
and structure are closely bound up with orderly thought, as the student can hardly fail to notice. But some direct suggestions on the
modes of consistent thinking and of analyzing and criticizing arguments and assertions ought also to prove useful. The following pages
accordingly present some notes on logic and common logical fallacies.

UNDEFINED TERMS

The first requirement for logical discourse is knowing what the 2
words you use actually mean. Words are not like paper money or

counters in a game. Except for technical terms in some of the sciences, they do not have a fixed face value. Their meanings are fluid and changing, influenced by many considerations of context and reference, circumstance and association. This is just as true of common words such as *fast* as it is of literary terms such as *romantic*. Moreover, if there is to be communication, words must have approximately the same meaning for the reader that they have for the writer. A speech in an unknown language means nothing to the hearer. When an adult speaks to a small child or an expert to a layman, communication may be seriously limited by lack of a mature vocabulary or ignorance of technical terms. Many arguments are meaningless because the speakers are using important words in quite different senses.

3   Because we learn most words — or guess at them — from the contexts in which we first encounter them, our sense of them is often incomplete or wrong. Readers sometimes visualize the Assyrian who comes down like the wolf on the fold as an enormous man dressed in cohorts (some kind of fancy armor, possibly) gleaming in purple and gold. "A rift in the lute" suggests vaguely a cracked mandolin. Failure to ascertain the literal meaning of figurative language is a frequent reason for mixed metaphors. We are surprised to find that the "devil" in "the devil to pay" and "the devil and the deep blue sea" is not Old Nick, but part of a ship. Unless terms mean the same thing to both writer and reader, proper understanding is impossible.

ABSTRACTIONS

4   The most serious logical difficulties occur with abstract terms. An abstraction is a word which stands for a quality found in a number of different objects or events from which it has been "abstracted" or taken away. We may, for instance, talk of the "whiteness" of paper or cotton or snow without considering qualities of cold or inflammability or usefulness which these materials happen also to possess. Usually, however, our minds carry over other qualities by association. See, for instance, the chapter called "The Whiteness of the Whale" in *Moby Dick*.

5   In much theoretic discussion the process of abstraction is carried so far that although vague associations and connotations persist, the original objects or events from which the qualities have been abstracted are lost sight of completely. Instead of thinking of words like *sincerity* and *Americanism* as symbols standing for qualities that

have to be abstracted with great care from examples and test cases, we come to think of them as real things in themselves. We assume that Americanism is Americanism just as a bicycle is a bicycle, and that everyone knows what it means. We forget that before the question, "Is Father Coughlin sincere?" can mean anything, we have to agree on the criteria of sincerity.

When we try to define such words and find examples, we discover   6 that almost no one agrees on their meaning. The word *church* may refer to anything from a building on the corner of Spring Street to the whole tradition of institutionalized Christianity. *Germany* may mean a geographical section of Europe, a people, a governing group, a cultural tradition, or a military power. Abstractions such as *freedom, courage, race, beauty, truth, justice, nature, honor, humanism, democracy,* should never be used in a theme unless their meaning is defined or indicated clearly by the context. Freedom for whom? To do what? Under what circumstances? Abstract terms have merely emotional value unless they are strictly defined by asking questions of this kind. The study of a word such as *nature* in a good unabridged dictionary will show that even the dictionary, indispensable though it is, cannot determine for us the sense in which a word is being used in any given instance. Once the student understands the importance of definition, he will no longer be betrayed into fruitless arguments over such questions as whether free verse is "poetry" or whether you can change "human nature."

NAME-CALLING

It is a common unfairness in controversy to place what the writer   7 dislikes or opposes in a generally odious category. The humanist dismisses what he dislikes by calling it *romantic;* the liberal, by calling it *fascist;* the conservative, by calling it *communistic.* These terms tell the reader nothing. What is *piety* to some will be *bigotry* to others. *Non-Catholics* would rather be called *Protestants* than *heretics.* What is *right-thinking* except a designation for those who agree with the writer? Labor leaders become *outside agitators;* industrial organizations, *forces of reaction;* the Child Labor Amendment, the *youth control bill;* prison reform, *coddling;* progressive education, *fads and frills.* Such terms are intended to block thought by an appeal to prejudice and associative habits. Three steps are necessary before such epithets have real meaning. First, they must be defined; second, it must be shown that the object to which they are applied actually possesses these qualities; third, it must be shown that the possession of such qualities in this particular situation is necessarily undesirable. Unless a person is alert and critical both in choosing and in interpreting words, he may be alienated from ideas with which he would be in sympathy if he had not been frightened by a mere name.

GENERALIZATION

8   Similar to the abuse of abstract terms and epithets is the habit of presenting personal opinions in the guise of universal laws. The student often seems to feel that the broader the terms in which he states an opinion, the more effective he will be. Ordinarily the reverse is true. An enthusiasm for Thomas Wolfe should lead to a specific critical analysis of Wolfe's novels that will enable the writer to explain his enthusiasm to others; it should not be turned into the argument that Wolfe is "the greatest American novelist," particularly if the writer's knowledge of American novelists is somewhat limited. The same questions of *who* and *when* and *why* and under what *circumstances* which are used to check abstract terms should be applied to generalizations. Consider how contradictory proverbial wisdom is when detached from particular circumstances. "Look before you leap," but "he who hesitates is lost."

9   Superlatives and the words *right* and *wrong, true* and *untrue, never* and *always* must be used with caution in matters of opinion. When a student says flatly that X is true, he often is really saying that he or his family or the author of a book he has just been reading, persons of certain tastes and background and experience, *think* that X is true. Unless these people are identified and their reasons for thinking so explained, the assertion is worthless. Because many freshmen are taking survey courses in which they read a single work by an author or see an historical event through the eyes of a single historian whose bias they may not be able to measure, they must guard against this error.

SAMPLING

10   Assertions of a general nature are frequently open to question because they are based on insufficient evidence. Some persons are quite ready, after meeting one Armenian or reading one medieval

romance, to generalize about Armenians and medieval romances. One ought, of course, to examine objectively as many examples as possible before making a generalization, but the number is less important than the representativeness of the examples chosen. The Literary Digest Presidential Poll, sent to hundreds of thousands of people selected from telephone directories, was far less accurate than the Gallup Poll which questioned far fewer voters, but selected them carefully and proportionately from all different social groups.[1] The "typical" college student, as portrayed by moving pictures and cartoons, is very different from the "representative" college student as determined statistically. We cannot let uncontrolled experience do our sampling for us; instances and examples which impress themselves upon our minds do so usually because they are exceptional. In propaganda and arguments extreme cases are customarily treated as if they were characteristic.

If one is permitted arbitrarily to select some examples and ignore others, it is possible to find convincing evidence for almost any theory, no matter how fantastic. The fact that the mind tends naturally to remember those instances which confirm its opinions imposes a duty upon the writer, unless he wishes to encourage prejudice and superstition, to look carefully for exceptions to all generalizations which he is tempted to make. We forget the premonitions which are not followed by disaster and the times when our hunches failed to select the winner in a race. Patent medicine advertisements print the letters of those who survived their cure, and not of those who died during it. All Americans did not gamble on the stock exchange in the twenties, and all Vermonters are not thin-lipped and shrewd. Of course the search for negative examples can be carried too far. Outside of mathematics or the laboratory, few generalizations can be made airtight, and most are not intended to be. But quibbling is so easy that resort to it is very common, and the knowledge that people can and will quibble over generalizations is another reason for making assertions as limited and explicitly conditional as possible.

FALSE ANALOGY

Illustration, comparison, analogy are most valuable in making an essay clear and interesting. It must not be supposed, however, that they prove anything or have much argumentative weight. The rule

11

12

[1] On the basis of its misconducted poll, a magazine called *The Literary Digest* predicted a landslide for Landon over Roosevelt in 1936. — ED.

that what is true of one thing in one set of circumstances is not necessarily true of another thing in another set of circumstances seems almost too obvious to need stating. Yet constantly nations and businesses are discussed as if they were human beings with human habits and feelings; human bodies are discussed as if they were machines; the universe, as if it were a clock. It is assumed that what held true for seventeenth century New England or the thirteen Atlantic colonies also holds true for an industrial nation of 130,000,000 people. Carlyle dismissed the arguments for representative democracy by saying that if a captain had to take a vote among his crew every time he wanted to do something, he would never get around Cape Horn. This analogy calmly ignores the distinction between the law-making and the executive branches of constitutional democracies. Moreover, voters may be considered much more like the stockholders of a merchant line than its hired sailors. Such arguments introduce assumptions in a metaphorical guise in which they are not readily detected or easily criticized. In place of analysis they attempt to identify their position with some familiar symbol which will evoke a predictable, emotional response in the reader. The revival during the 1932 presidential campaign of Lincoln's remark, "Don't swap horses in the middle of the stream," was not merely a picturesque way of saying keep Hoover in the White House. It made a number of assumptions about the nature of depressions and the function of government. This propagandist technique can be seen most clearly in political cartoons.

DEGREE

13   Often differences in degree are more important than differences in kind. By legal and social standards there is more difference between an habitual drunkard and a man who drinks temperately, than between a temperate drinker and a total abstainer. In fact differences of degree produce what are regarded as differences of kind. At known temperatures ice turns to water and water boils. At an indeterminate point affection becomes love and a man who needs a shave becomes a man with a beard. The fact that no men or systems are perfect makes rejoinders and counter-accusations very easy if differences in degree are ignored. Newspapers in totalitarian states, answering American accusations of brutality and suppression, refer to lynchings and gangsterism here. Before a disinterested judge could evaluate these mutual accusations, he would have to settle the question of the degree to

which violent suppression and lynching are respectively prevalent in the countries under consideration. On the other hand, differences in degree may be merely apparent. Lincoln Steffens pointed out that newspapers can create a "crime wave" any time they wish, simply by emphasizing all the minor assaults and thefts commonly ignored or given an inch or two on a back page. The great reported increases in insanity may be due to the fact that in a more urban and institutionalized society cases of insanity more frequently come to the attention of authorities and hence are recorded in statistics.

CAUSATION

The most common way of deciding that one thing causes another 14 thing is the simple principle: *post hoc, ergo propter hoc,* "After this, therefore because of this." Rome fell after the introduction of Christianity; therefore Christianity was responsible for the fall of Rome. Such reasoning illustrates another kind of faulty generalization. But even if one could find ten cases in which a nation "fell" after the introduction of Christianity, it still would not be at all certain that Christianity caused the fall. Day, it has frequently been pointed out, follows night in every observable instance, and yet night cannot be called the cause of day. Usually a combination of causes produces a result. Sitting in a draught may cause a cold, but only given a certain physical condition in the person sitting there. In such instances one may distinguish between necessary and sufficient conditions. Air is a necessary condition for the maintenance of plant life, but air alone is not sufficient to produce plant life. And often different causes at different times may produce the same result. This relation is known as plurality of causes. If, after sitting in a stuffy theatre on Monday, and then again after eating in a stuffy restaurant on Thursday, a man suffered from headaches, he might say, generalizing, that bad air gave him headaches. But actually the headache on Monday may have been caused by eye-strain and on Thursday by indigestion. To isolate the causative factor it is necessary that all other conditions be precisely the same. Such isolation is possible, except in very simple instances, only in the laboratory or with scientific methods. If a picture falls from the wall every time a truck passes, we can quite certainly say that the truck's passing is the cause. But with anything as complex and conditional as a nation's economy or human character, the determination of cause is not easy or certain. A psychiatrist often sees a patient for an hour daily for a year or more before he feels that he understands his psychosis.

15   Ordinarily when we speak of cause we mean the proximate or immediate cause. The plants were killed by frost; we had indigestion from eating lobster salad. But any single cause is one in an unbroken series. When a man is murdered, is his death caused by the loss of blood from the wound, or by the firing of the pistol, or by the malice aforethought of the murderer? Was the World War "caused" by the assassination at Sarajevo? Were the Navigation Acts or the ideas of John Locke more important in "causing" the American Revolution? A complete statement of cause would comprise the sum total of the conditions which preceded an event, conditions stretching back indefinitely into the past. Historical events are so interrelated that the isolation of a causative sequence is dependent chiefly on the particular preoccupations of the historian. An economic determinist can "explain" history entirely in terms of economic developments; an idealist, entirely in terms of the development of ideas.

SYLLOGISTIC REASONING

16   The formal syllogism of the type,

> All men are mortal
> John is a man
> Therefore John is mortal,

is not so highly regarded today as in some earlier periods. It merely fixes an individual as a member of a class, and then assumes that the individual has the given characteristics of the class. Once we have decided who John is, and what "man" and "mortal" mean, and have canvassed all men, including John, to make sure that they are mortal, the conclusion naturally follows. It can be seen that the chief difficulties arise in trying to establish acceptable premises. Faults in the premises are known as "material" fallacies, and are usually more serious than the "formal" fallacies, which are logical defects in drawing a conclusion from the premises. But although directly syllogistic reasoning is not much practiced, buried syllogisms can be found in all argument, and it is often a useful clarification to outline your own or another writer's essay in syllogistic form. The two most frequent defects in the syllogism itself are the undistributed and the ambiguous middle. The middle term is the one that appears in each of the premises and not in the conclusion. In the syllogism,

> All good citizens vote
> John votes
> Therefore John is a good citizen,

the middle term is not "good citizens," but "votes." Even though it were true that all good citizens vote, nothing prevents bad citizens from voting also, and John may be one of the bad citizens. To distribute the middle term "votes" one might say (but only if that is what one meant),

> All voters are good citizens
> John is a voter
> Therefore John is a good citizen.

The ambiguous middle term is even more common. It represents 17 a problem in definition, while the undistributed middle is a problem in generalization. All acts which benefit others are virtuous, losing money at poker benefits others, therefore losing at poker is a virtuous act. Here the middle term "act which benefits others" is obviously used very loosely and ambiguously.

NON SEQUITUR

This phrase, meaning "it does not follow," is used to characterize 18 the kind of humor found in pictures in which the Marx Brothers perform. It is an amusing illogicality because it usually expresses, beneath its apparent incongruity, an imaginative, associative, or personal truth. "My ancestors came over on the Mayflower; therefore I am naturally opposed to labor unions." It is not logically necessary that those whose ancestors came over on the Mayflower should be opposed to unions; but it may happen to be true as a personal fact in a given case. Contemporary psychologists have effectively shown us that there is often such a wide difference between the true and the purported reasons for an attitude that, in rationalizing our behavior, we are often quite unconscious of the motives that actually influence us. A fanatical antivivisectionist, for instance, may have temperamental impulses toward cruelty which he is suppressing and compensating for by a reasoned opposition to any kind of permitted suffering.

We may expect, then, to come upon many conclusions which are psychologically interesting in themselves, but have nothing to do with the given premises.

IGNORATIO ELENCHI

19   This means, in idiomatic English, "arguing off the point," or ignoring the question at issue. A man trying to show that monarchy is the best form of government for the British Empire may devote most of his attention to the character of George V and the affection his people felt for him. In ordinary conversational argument it is almost impossible for disputants to keep to the point. Constantly turning up are tempting side-issues through which one can discomfit an opponent or force him to irrelevant admissions that seem to weaken his case.

BEGGING THE QUESTION;
ARGUING IN A CIRCLE

20   The first of these terms means to assume in the premises what you are pretending to prove in the course of your argument. The function of logic is to demonstrate that because one thing or group of things is true, another must be true as a consequence. But in begging the question you simply say in varying language that what is assumed to be true is assumed to be true. An argument which asserts that we shall enjoy immortality because we have souls which are immaterial and indestructible establishes nothing, because the idea of immortality is already contained in the assumption about the soul. It is the premise which needs to be demonstrated, not the conclusion. Arguing in a circle is another form of this fallacy. It proves the premise by the conclusion and the conclusion by the premise. The conscience forbids an act because it is wrong; the act is wrong because the conscience forbids it.

ARGUMENTS *AD HOMINEM*
AND *AD POPULUM*

21   It is very difficult for men to be persuaded by reason when their interest or prestige is at stake. If one wishes to preach the significance

of physiognomy, it is well to choose a hearer with a high forehead and a determined jaw. The arguments in favor of repealing the protective tariff on corn or wheat in England were more readily entertained by manufacturers than by landowners. The cotton manufacturers in New England who were doing a profitable trade with the South were the last to be moved by descriptions of the evils of slavery. Because interest and desire are so deeply seated in human nature, arguments are frequently mingled with attempts to appeal to emotion, arouse fear, play upon pride, attack the characters of proponents of an opposite view, show that their practice is inconsistent with their principles; all matters which have, strictly speaking, nothing to do with the truth or falsity, the general desirability or undesirability, of some particular measure. If men are desperate enough they will listen to arguments proper only to an insane asylum but which seem to promise them relief.

After reading these suggestions, which are largely negative, the 22 student may feel that any original assertion he can make will probably contain one or several logical faults. This assumption is not true. Even if it were, we know from reading newspapers and magazines that worldly fame is not dimmed by the constant and, one suspects, conscious practice of illogicality. But generalizations are not made only by charlatans and sophists. Intelligent and scrupulous writers also have a great many fresh and provocative observations and conclusions to express and are expressing them influentially. What is intelligence but the ability to see the connection between things, to discern causes, to relate the particular to the general, to define and discriminate and compare? Any man who thinks and feels and observes closely will not want for something to express.

And in his expression a proponent will find that a due regard for 23 logic does not limit but rather increases the force of his argument. When statements are not trite, they are usually controversial. Men arrive at truth dialectically; error is weeded out in the course of discussion, argument, attack, and counterattack. Not only can a writer who understands logic show the weaknesses of arguments he disagrees with, but also, by anticipating the kind of attack likely to be made on his own ideas, he can so arrange them, properly modified with qualifications and exceptions, that the anticipated attack is made much less effective. Thus, fortunately, we do not have to depend on the spirit of fairness and love of truth to lead men to logic; it has the strong support of argumentative necessity and of the universal desire to make ideas prevail.

_____ CONSIDERATIONS _____

1. Davis's first sentence goes far toward explaining why freshman composition classes commonly include a unit on logic, which some would insist is more properly a part of Philosophy I than of English I. To learn Davis's logic in practice, apply Davis's notions about undefined terms and abstractions to the argumentative essays in this book: Frithjof Bergmann, The Holy Bible, Caroline Bird, Ronald Blythe, Kenneth E. Boulding, D. H. Lawrence, H. L. Mencken, Flannery O'Connor, George Orwell, Plato, Don Sharp, Gore Vidal, Virginia Woolf. Do any of these writers use undefined terms or abstractions illogically?

2. Under "Generalization," in Paragraph 8, Davis defines a function of literary criticism and suggests what questions to ask to make such criticism useful to yourself and others. Try out his advice on an essay, short story, or poem in this book that has troubled or pleased you.

3. How clearly and consistently can you discriminate between matters of fact and matters of opinion? Discuss some examples found in your reading.

4. Have you ever been tempted by the *post hoc, ergo propter hoc* fallacy? (See Paragraph 14.) Can you find an example of it in the newspaper, on television, in the conversation of your friends, in any of the readings in this book, in your papers, or in your instructor's remarks?

5. Study Davis's explanation of syllogistic reasoning, Paragraph 16. Try to reduce the major argument of any of the authors noted in question 1 to a syllogism or a series of syllogisms.

Emily Dickinson (1830–1886) was little known as a poet in her lifetime, but is now acknowledged as among the greatest American poets. She lived her entire life in Amherst, Massachusetts, and spent her later years as a virtual recluse in the Dickinsons' brick homestead on Main Street. She was always close to her family, and kept contact with the outside world through a huge correspondence.

She published little poetry in her lifetime. After her death more than a thousand poems were discovered neatly arranged in the bureau of the upstairs bedroom where she wrote. In 1955, a definitive edition of The Poems of Emily Dickinson *was published, containing 1,775 poems and fragments.*

20

EMILY DICKINSON
There's a certain Slant of light

There's a certain Slant of light,
Winter Afternoons—
That oppresses, like the Heft
Of Cathedral Tunes—

Heavenly Hurt, it gives us—   5
We can find no scar,
But internal difference,
Where the Meanings, are—

None may teach it—Any—
10   'Tis the Seal Despair—
An imperial affliction
Sent us of the Air—

When it comes, the Landscape listens—
Shadows—hold their breath—
15   When it goes, 'tis like the Distance
On the look of Death—

Joan Didion (b. 1934) worked as an editor in New York for some years, and then returned to her native California where she supports herself by writing. She has collaborated on screenplays, including Panic in Needle Park *(1971) and* A Star Is Born *(1976). Best known for her novels —* Play It As It Lays *appeared in 1971,* A Book of Common Prayer *in 1977 — she is also admired for her nonfiction, collected in* Slouching Towards Bethlehem *(1969), from which we take this essay, and* The White Album *(1979). Students who keep journals or notebooks, or who practice daily writing, may learn a thing or two from Joan Didion.*

21

JOAN DIDION

On Keeping a Notebook

" 'That woman Estelle,' " the note reads, " 'is partly the reason   1
why George Sharp and I are separated today.' *Dirty crepe-de-Chine wrapper, hotel bar, Wilmington RR, 9:45* A.M. August Monday morning."

Since the note is in my notebook, it presumably has some mean-   2
ing to me. I study it for a long while. At first I have only the most general notion of what I was doing on an August Monday morning in the bar of the hotel across from the Pennsylvania Railroad station in Wilmington, Delaware (waiting for a train? missing one? 1960? 1961? why Wilmington?), but I do remember being there. The woman in the dirty crepe-de-Chine wrapper had come down from her room for a beer, and the bartender had heard before the reason why George Sharp and she were separated today. "Sure," he said, and went on mopping

the floor. "You told me." At the other end of the bar is a girl. She is talking, pointedly, not to the man beside her but to a cat lying in the triangle of sunlight cast through the open door. She is wearing a plaid silk dress from Peck & Peck, and the hem is coming down.

3   Here is what it is: the girl has been on the Eastern Shore, and now she is going back to the city, leaving the man beside her, and all she can see ahead are the viscous summer sidewalks and the 3 A.M. long-distance calls that will make her lie awake and then sleep drugged through all the steaming mornings left in August (1960? 1961?). Because she must go directly from the train to lunch in New York, she wishes that she had a safety pin for the hem of the plaid silk dress, and she also wishes that she could forget about the hem and the lunch and stay in the cool bar that smells of disinfectant and malt and make friends with the woman in the crepe-de-Chine wrapper. She is afflicted by a little self-pity, and she wants to compare Estelles. That is what that was all about.

4   Why did I write it down? In order to remember, of course, but exactly what was it I wanted to remember? How much of it actually happened? Did any of it? Why do I keep a notebook at all? It is easy to deceive oneself on all those scores. The impulse to write things down is a peculiarly compulsive one, inexplicable to those who do not share it, useful only accidentally, only secondarily, in the way that any compulsion tries to justify itself. I suppose that it begins or does not begin in the cradle. Although I have felt compelled to write things down since I was five years old, I doubt that my daughter ever will, for she is a singularly blessed and accepting child, delighted with life exactly as life presents itself to her, unafraid to go to sleep and unafraid to wake up. Keepers of private notebooks are a different breed altogether, lonely and resistant rearrangers of things, anxious malcontents, children afflicted apparently at birth with some presentiment of loss.

5   My first notebook was a Big Five tablet, given to me by my mother with the sensible suggestion that I stop whining and learn to amuse myself by writing down my thoughts. She returned the tablet to me a few years ago; the first entry is an account of a woman who believed herself to be freezing to death in the Arctic night, only to find, when day broke, that she had stumbled onto the Sahara Desert, where she would die of the heat before lunch. I have no idea what turn of a five-year-old's mind could have prompted so insistently "ironic" and exotic a story, but it does reveal a certain predilection for the extreme which has dogged me into adult life; perhaps if I were analyt-

ically inclined I would find it a truer story than any I might have told about Donald Johnson's birthday party or the day my cousin Brenda put Kitty Litter in the aquarium.

So the point of my keeping a notebook has never been, nor is it   6 now, to have an accurate factual record of what I have been doing or thinking. That would be a different impulse entirely, an instinct for reality which I sometimes envy but do not possess. At no point have I ever been able successfully to keep a diary; my approach to daily life ranges from the grossly negligent to the merely absent, and on those few occasions when I have tried dutifully to record a day's events, boredom has so overcome me that the results are mysterious at best. What is this business about "shopping, typing piece, dinner with E, depressed"? Shopping for what? Typing what piece? Who is E? Was this "E" depressed, or was I depressed? Who cares?

In fact I have abandoned altogether that kind of pointless entry;   7 instead I tell what some would call lies. "That's simply not true," the members of my family frequently tell me when they come up against my memory of a shared event. "The party was *not* for you, the spider was *not* a black widow, *it wasn't that way at all.*" Very likely they are right, for not only have I always had trouble distinguishing between what happened and what merely might have happened, but I remain unconvinced that the distinction, for my purposes, matters. The cracked crab that I recall having for lunch the day my father came home from Detroit in 1945 must certainly be embroidery, worked into the day's pattern to lend verisimilitude; I was ten years old and would not now remember the cracked crab. The day's events did not turn on cracked crab. And yet it is precisely that fictitious crab that makes me see the afternoon all over again, a home movie run all too often, the father bearing gifts, the child weeping, an exercise in family love and guilt. Or that is what it was to me. Similarly, perhaps it never did snow that August in Vermont; perhaps there never were flurries in the night wind, and maybe no one else felt the ground hardening and summer already dead even as we pretended to bask in it, but that was how it felt to me, and it might as well have snowed, could have snowed, did snow.

How it felt to me: that is getting closer to the truth about a   8 notebook. I sometimes delude myself about why I keep a notebook, imagine that some thrifty virtue derives from preserving everything observed. See enough and write it down, I tell myself, and then some morning when the world seems drained of wonder, some day when I am only going through the motions of doing what I am supposed to do, which is write — on that bankrupt morning I will simply open my notebook and there it will all be, a forgotten account with accumulated interest, paid passage back to the world out there: dialogue overheard in hotels and elevators and at the hat-check counter in Pavillon (one middle-aged man shows his hat check to another and says, "That's my old football number"); impressions of Bettina Aptheker and Benjamin Sonnenberg and Teddy ("Mr. Acapulco") Stauffer; careful *aperçus* about tennis bums and failed fashion models and Greek shipping heiresses, one of whom taught me a significant lesson (a lesson I could have learned from F. Scott Fitzgerald, but perhaps we must meet the very rich for ourselves) by asking, when I arrived to interview her in her orchid-filled sitting room on the second day of a paralyzing New York blizzard, whether it was snowing outside.

9   I imagine, in other words, that the notebook is about other people. But of course it is not. I have no real business with what one stranger said to another at the hat-check counter in Pavillon; in fact I suspect that the line "That's my old football number" touched not my own imagination at all, but merely some memory of something once read, probably "The Eighty-Yard Run." Nor is my concern with a woman in a dirty crepe-de-Chine wrapper in a Wilmington bar. My stake is always, of course, in the unmentioned girl in the plaid silk dress. *Remember what it was to be me:* that is always the point.

10   It is a difficult point to admit. We are brought up in the ethic that others, any others, all others, are by definition more interesting than ourselves; taught to be diffident, just this side of self-effacing. ("You're the least important person in the room and don't forget it," Jessica Mitford's governess would hiss in her ear on the advent of any social occasion; I copied that into my notebook because it is only recently that I have been able to enter a room without hearing some such phrase in my inner ear.) Only the very young and the very old may recount their dreams at breakfast, dwell upon self, interrupt with memories of beach picnics and favorite Liberty lawn dresses and the rainbow trout in a creek near Colorado Springs. The rest of us are expected, rightly, to affect absorption in other people's favorite dresses, other people's trout.

11   And so we do. But our notebooks give us away, for however dutifully we record what we see around us, the common denominator of all we see is always, transparently, shamelessly, the implacable "I." We are not talking here about the kind of notebook that is patently for

public consumption, a structural conceit for binding together a series of graceful *pensées:* we are talking about something private, about bits of the mind's string too short to use, an indiscriminate and erratic assemblage with meaning only for its maker.

And sometimes even the maker has difficulty with the meaning. 12 There does not seem to be, for example, any point in my knowing for the rest of my life that, during 1964, 720 tons of soot fell on every square mile of New York City, yet there it is in my notebook, labeled "FACT." Nor do I really need to remember that Ambrose Bierce liked to spell Leland Stanford's[1] name "£eland $tanford" or that "smart women almost always wear black in Cuba," a fashion hint without much potential for practical application. And does not the relevance of these notes seem marginal at best?:

> In the basement museum of the Inyo County Courthouse in Independence, California, sign pinned to a mandarin coat: "This MAN-DARIN COAT was often worn by Mrs. Minnie S. Brooks when giving lectures on her TEAPOT COLLECTION."

> Redhead getting out of car in front of Beverly Wilshire Hotel, chinchilla stole, Vuitton bags with tags reading:
> > MRS LOU FOX
> > HOTEL SAHARA
> > VEGAS

Well perhaps not entirely marginal. As a matter of fact, Mrs. 13 Minnie S. Brooks and her MANDARIN COAT pull me back into my own childhood, for although I never knew Mrs. Brooks and did not visit Inyo County until I was thirty, I grew up in just such a world, in houses cluttered with Indian relics and bits of gold ore and ambergris and the souvenirs my Aunt Mercy Farnsworth brought back from the Orient. It is a long way from that world to Mrs. Lou Fox's world, where we all live now, and is it not just as well to remember that? Might not Mrs. Minnie S. Brooks help me to remember what I am? Might not Mrs. Lou Fox help me to remember what I am not?

But sometimes the point is harder to discern. What exactly did I 14 have in mind when I noted down that it cost the father of someone I know $650 a month to light the place on the Hudson in which he lived before the Crash? What use was I planning to make of this line by Jimmy Hoffa: "I may have my faults, but being wrong ain't one of

---

[1] Railroad magnate (1834–1893) who founded the university. — ED.

them"? And although I think it interesting to know where the girls who travel with the Syndicate have their hair done when they find themselves on the West Coast, will I ever make suitable use of it? Might I not be better off just passing it on to John O'Hara? What is a recipe for sauerkraut doing in my notebook? What kind of magpie keeps this notebook? *"He was born the night the Titanic went down."* That seems a nice enough line, and I even recall who said it, but is it not really a better line in life than it could ever be in fiction?

15   But of course that is exactly it: not that I should ever use the line, but that I should remember the woman who said it and the afternoon I heard it. We were on her terrace by the sea, and we were finishing the wine left from lunch, trying to get what sun there was, a California winter sun. The woman whose husband was born the night the *Titanic* went down wanted to rent her house, wanted to go back to her children in Paris. I remember wishing that I could afford the house, which cost $1,000 a month. "Someday you will," she said lazily. "Someday it all comes." There in the sun on her terrace it seemed easy to believe in someday, but later I had a low-grade afternoon hangover and ran over a black snake on the way to the supermarket and was flooded with inexplicable fear when I heard the checkout clerk explaining to the man ahead of me why she was finally divorcing her husband. "He left me no choice," she said over and over as she punched the register. "He has a little seven-month-old baby by her, he left me no choice." I would like to believe that my dread then was for the human condition, but of course it was for me, because I wanted a baby and did not then have one and because I wanted to own the house that cost $1,000 a month to rent and because I had a hangover.

16   It all comes back. Perhaps it is difficult to see the value in having one's self back in that kind of mood, but I do see it; I think we are well advised to keep on nodding terms with the people we used to be, whether we find them attractive company or not. Otherwise they turn up unannounced and surprise us, come hammering on the mind's door at 4 A.M. of a bad night and demand to know who deserted them, who betrayed them, who is going to make amends. We forget all too soon the things we thought we could never forget. We forget the loves and the betrayals alike, forget what we whispered and what we screamed, forget who we were. I have already lost touch with a couple of people I used to be; one of them, a seventeen-year-old, presents little threat, although it would be of some interest to me to know again what it feels like to sit on a river levee drinking vodka-and-orange-juice and

listening to Les Paul and Mary Ford and their echoes sing "How High the Moon" on the car radio. (You see I still have the scenes, but I no longer perceive myself among those present, no longer could even improvise the dialogue.) The other one, a twenty-three-year-old, bothers me more. She was always a good deal of trouble, and I suspect she will reappear when I least want to see her, skirts too long, shy to the point of aggravation, always the injured party, full of recriminations and little hurts and stories I do not want to hear again, at once saddening me and angering me with her vulnerability and ignorance, an apparition all the more insistent for being so long banished.

It is a good idea, then, to keep in touch, and I suppose that keep-   17
ing in touch is what notebooks are all about. And we are all on our own when it comes to keeping those lines open to ourselves: your notebook will never help me, nor mine you. *"So what's new in the whiskey business?"* What could that possibly mean to you? To me it means a blonde in a Pucci bathing suit sitting with a couple of fat men by the pool at the Beverly Hills Hotel. Another man approaches, and they all regard one another in silence for a while. "So what's new in the whiskey business?" one of the fat men finally says by way of welcome, and the blonde stands up, arches one foot and dips it in the pool, looking all the while at the cabaña where Baby Pignatari is talking on the telephone. That is all there is to that, except that several years later I saw the blonde coming out of Saks Fifth Avenue in New York with her California complexion and a voluminous mink coat. In the harsh wind that day she looked old and irrevocably tired to me, and even the skins in the mink coat were not worked the way they were doing them that year, not the way she would have wanted them done, and there is the point of the story. For a while after that I did not like to look in the mirror, and my eyes would skim the newspapers and pick out only the deaths, the cancer victims, the premature coronaries, the suicides, and I stopped riding the Lexington Avenue IRT because I noticed for the first time that all the strangers I had seen for years — the man with the seeing-eye dog, the spinster who read the classified pages every day, the fat girl who always got off with me at Grand Central — looked older than they once had.

It all comes back. Even that recipe for sauerkraut: even that   18
brings it back. I was on Fire Island when I first made that sauerkraut, and it was raining, and we drank a lot of bourbon and ate the sauerkraut and went to bed at ten, and I listened to the rain and the Atlantic and felt safe. I made the sauerkraut again last night and it did not make me feel any safer, but that is, as they say, another story.

22

ANNIE DILLARD

Strangers to Darkness

Where Tinker Creek flows under the sycamore log bridge to the   1
tear-shaped island, it is slow and shallow, fringed thinly in cattail
marsh. At this spot an astonishing bloom of life supports vast breeding
populations of insects, fish, reptiles, birds, and mammals. On windless
summer evenings I stalk along the creek bank or straddle the sycamore log in absolute stillness, watching for muskrats. The night I
stayed too late I was hunched on the log staring spellbound at spreading, reflected stains of lilac on the water. A cloud in the sky suddenly
lighted as if turned on by a switch; its reflection just as suddenly
materialized on the water upstream, flat and floating, so that I
couldn't see the creek bottom, or life in the water under the cloud.
Downstream, away from the cloud on the water, water turtles smooth
as beans were gliding down with the current in a series of easy, weight-

less push-offs, as men bound on the moon. I didn't know whether to trace the progress of one turtle I was sure of, risking sticking my face in one of the bridge's spider webs made invisible by the gathering dark, or take a chance on seeing the carp, or scan the mudbank in hope of seeing a muskrat, or follow the last of the swallows who caught at my heart and trailed it after them like streamers as they appeared from directly below, under the log, flying upstream with their tails forked, so fast.

2 But shadows spread and deepened and stayed. After thousands of years we're still strangers to darkness, fearful aliens in an enemy camp with our arms crossed over our chests. I stirred. A land turtle on the bank, startled, hissed the air from its lungs and withdrew to its shell. An uneasy pink here, an unfathomable blue there, gave great suggestion of lurking beings. Things were going on. I couldn't see whether that rustle I heard was a distant rattlesnake, slit-eyed, or a nearby sparrow kicking in the dry flood debris slung at the foot of a willow. Tremendous action roiled the water everywhere I looked, big action, inexplicable. A tremor welled up beside a gaping muskrat burrow in the bank and I caught my breath, but no muskrat appeared. The ripples continued to fan upstream with a steady, powerful thrust. Night was knitting an eyeless mask over my face, and I still sat transfixed. A distant airplane, a delta wing out of nightmare, made a gliding shadow on the creek's bottom that looked like a stingray cruising upstream. At once a black fin slit the pink cloud on the water, shearing it in two. The two halves merged together and seemed to dissolve before my eyes. Darkness pooled in the cleft of the creek and rose, as water collects in a well. Untamed, dreaming lights flickered over the sky. I saw hints of hulking underwater shadows, two pale splashes out of the water, and round ripples rolling close together from a blackened center.

3 At last I stared upstream where only the deepest violet remained of the cloud, a cloud so high its underbelly still glowed, its feeble color reflected from a hidden sky lighted in turn by a sun halfway to China. And out of that violet, a sudden enormous black body arced over the water. Head and tail, if there was a head and tail, were both submerged in cloud. I saw only one ebony fling, a headlong dive to darkness; then the water closed, and the lights went out.

4 I walked home in a shivering daze, up hill and down. Later I lay openmouthed in bed, my arms flung wide at my sides to steady the whirling darkness. At this latitude I'm spinning 836 miles an hour round the earth's axis; I feel my sweeping fall as a breakneck arc like

the dive of dolphins, and the hollow rushing of wind raises the hairs on my neck and the side of my face. In orbit around the sun I'm moving 64,800 miles an hour. The solar system as a whole, like a merry-go-round unhinged, spins, bobs, and blinks at the speed of 43,200 miles an hour along a course set east of Hercules. Someone has piped, and we are dancing a tarantella until the sweat pours. I open my eyes and I see dark, muscled forms curl out of water, with flapping gills and flattened eyes. I close my eyes and I see stars, deep stars giving way to deeper stars, deeper stars bowing to deepest stars at the crown of an infinite cone.

____ CONSIDERATIONS _____

1. Like exposition and argument, description and narration are encountered together more often than they are encountered separately. Still, there are real differences between describing something and following a sequence of actions. To see this difference, compare and contrast Dillard's descriptive writing with a clearly narrative selection in this book: John James Audubon, Martin Gansberg, Lillian Hellman, Norman Mailer, George Orwell ("Shooting an Elephant"), James C. Rettie, Eudora Welty ("A Worn Path"), or Thomas Wolfe.

2. Telling what she saw that night along Tinker Creek, Dillard uses many literal and figurative images; list them and discuss their differences. In your own essays, do you use phrases that appeal to the senses?

3. Toward the end of this short selection, Dillard suddenly injects facts — the speed of the earth's rotation, for instance. How does this information contribute to her attempt to evoke wonder in us?

4. "Night was knitting an eyeless mask over my face. . . ." Many might describe such language as fancy, flowery, or indirect, and protest that the writer should "just come out and say what she means." Discuss these complaints, thinking of what Dillard intends to accomplish.

5. Dillard describes the effects of one evening on one small creek in one rural neighborhood. Why, then, does she refer to China and the solar system?

Frederick Douglass (1817–1895) was born a slave in Maryland, escaped to Massachusetts in 1838, lectured against slavery, and wrote out of his experience. "Plantation Life" *comes from* A Narrative of the Life of Frederick Douglass, an American Slave, Written by Himself *(1845). During the Civil War he organized two regiments of black troops in Massachusetts; in the Reconstruction period he worked for the government.*

23

FREDERICK DOUGLASS

Plantation Life

1   My master's family consisted of two sons, Andrew and Richard; one daughter, Lucretia, and her husband, Captain Thomas Auld. They lived in one house, upon the home plantation of Colonel Edward Lloyd. My master was Colonel Lloyd's clerk and superintendent. He was what might be called the overseer of the overseers. I spent two years of childhood on this plantation in my old master's family. . . . As I received my first impressions of slavery on this plantation, I will give some description of it, and of slavery as it there existed. The plantation is about twelve miles north of Easton, in Talbot county, and is situated on the border of Miles River. The principal products raised upon it were tobacco, corn, and wheat. These were raised in great abundance; so that, with the products of this and the other farms belonging to him, he was able to keep in almost constant employment a large sloop, in carrying them to market at Baltimore. This sloop was named Sally Lloyd, in honor of one of the colonel's daughters. My master's son-in-law, Captain Auld, was master of the vessel; she was otherwise manned by the colonel's own slaves. Their names were Peter, Isaac, Rich, and Jake. These were esteemed very highly by the other slaves, and looked upon as the privileged ones of the plantation; for it was no small affair, in the eyes of the slaves, to be allowed to see Baltimore.

Colonel Lloyd kept from three to four hundred slaves on his 2
home plantation, and owned a large number more on the neighboring
farms belonging to him. The names of the farms nearest to the home
plantation were Wye Town and New Design. "Wye Town" was under
the overseership of a man named Noah Willis. New Design was under the overseership of a Mr. Townsend. The overseers of these, and
all the rest of the farms, numbering over twenty, received advice and
direction from the managers of the home plantation. This was the
great business place. It was the seat of government for the whole
twenty farms. All disputes among the overseers were settled here. If a
slave was convicted of any high misdemeanor, became unmanageable,
or evinced a determination to run away, he was brought immediately
here, severely whipped, put on board the sloop, carried to Baltimore,
and sold to Austin Woolfolk, or some other slave-trader, as a warning
to the slaves remaining.

Here, too, the slaves of all the other farms received their monthly 3
allowance of food, and their yearly clothing. The men and women
slaves received, as their monthly allowance of food, eight pounds of
pork, or its equivalent in fish, and one bushel of corn meal. Their
yearly clothing consisted of two coarse linen shirts, one pair of linen
trousers, like the shirts, one jacket, one pair of trousers for winter,
made of coarse negro cloth, one pair of stockings, and one pair of
shoes; the whole of which could not have cost more than seven dollars. The allowance of the slave children was given to their mothers,
or the old women having the care of them. The children unable to
work in the field had neither shoes, stockings, jackets, nor trousers,
given to them; their clothing consisted of two coarse linen shirts per
year. When these failed them, they went naked until the next allowance-day. Children from seven to ten years old, of both sexes, almost
naked, might be seen at all seasons of the year.

There were no beds given the slaves, unless one coarse blanket 4
be considered such, and none but the men and women had these. This,
however, is not considered a very great privation. They find less difficulty from the want of beds, than from the want of time to sleep; for
when their day's work in the field is done, the most of them having
their washing, mending, and cooking to do, and having few or none of
the ordinary facilities for doing either of these, very many of their
sleeping hours are consumed in preparing for the field the coming day;
and when this is done, old and young, male and female, married and
single, drop down side by side, on one common bed, — the cold, damp
floor, — each covering himself or herself with their miserable blankets; and here they sleep till they are summoned to the field by the

driver's horn. At the sound of this, all must rise, and be off to the field. There must be no halting; every one must be at his or her post; and woe betides them who hear not this morning summons to the field; for if they are not awakened by the sense of hearing, they are by the sense of feeling: no age nor sex finds any favor. Mr. Severe, the overseer, used to stand by the door of the quarter, armed with a large hickory stick and heavy cowskin, ready to whip any one who was so unfortunate as not to hear, or, from any other cause, was prevented from being ready to start for the field at the sound of the horn.

5   Mr. Severe was rightly named: he was a cruel man. I have seen him whip a woman, causing the blood to run half an hour at the time; and this, too, in the midst of her crying children, pleading for their mother's release. He seemed to take pleasure in manifesting his fiendish barbarity. Added to his cruelty, he was a profane swearer. It was enough to chill the blood and stiffen the hair of an ordinary man to hear him talk. Scarce a sentence escaped him but that was commenced or concluded by some horrid oath. The field was the place to witness his cruelty and profanity. His presence made it both the field of blood and of blasphemy. From the rising till the going down of the sun, he was cursing, raving, cutting, and slashing among the slaves of the field, in the most frightful manner. His career was short. He died very soon after I went to Colonel Lloyd's; and he died as he lived, uttering, with his dying groans, bitter curses and horrid oaths. His death was regarded by the slaves as the result of a merciful providence.

6   Mr. Severe's place was filled by a Mr. Hopkins. He was a very different man. He was less cruel, less profane, and made less noise, than Mr. Severe. His course was characterized by no extraordinary demonstrations of cruelty. He whipped, but seemed to take no pleasure in it. He was called by the slaves a good overseer.

7   The home plantation of Colonel Lloyd wore the appearance of a country village. All the mechanical operations for all the farms were performed here. The shoemaking and mending, the blacksmithing, cartwrighting, coopering, weaving, and grain-grinding, were all performed by the slaves on the home plantation. The whole place wore a business-like aspect very unlike the neighboring farms. The number of houses, too, conspired to give it advantage over the neighboring farms. It was called by the slaves the *Great House Farm*. Few privileges were esteemed higher, by the slaves of the out-farms, than that of being selected to do errands at the Great House Farm. It was associated in their minds with greatness. A representative could not be prouder of his election to a seat in the American Congress, than a

slave on one of the out-farms would be of his election to do errands at the Great House Farm. They regarded it as evidence of great confidence reposed in them by their overseers; and it was on this account, as well as a constant desire to be out of the field from under the driver's lash, that they esteemed it a high privilege, one worth careful living for. He was called the smartest and most trusty fellow, who had this honor conferred upon him the most frequently. The competitors for this office sought as diligently to please their overseers, as the office-seekers in the political parties seek to please and deceive the people. The same traits of character might be seen in Colonel Lloyd's slaves, as are seen in the slaves of the political parties.

The slaves selected to go to the Great House Farm, for the 8 monthly allowance for themselves and their fellow-slaves, were peculiarly enthusiastic. While on their way, they would make the dense old woods, for miles around, reverberate with their wild songs, revealing at once the highest joy and the deepest sadness. They would compose and sing as they went along, consulting neither time nor tune. The thought that came up, came out — if not in the word, in the sound; — and as frequently in the one as in the other. They would sometimes sing the most pathetic sentiment in the most rapturous tone, and the most rapturous sentiment in the most pathetic tone. Into all of their songs they would manage to weave something of the Great House Farm. Especially would they do this, when leaving home. They would then sing most exultingly the following words: —

> I am going away to the Great House Farm!
> O, yea! O, yea! O!

This they would sing, as a chorus, to words which to many would seem unmeaning jargon, but which, nevertheless, were full of meaning to themselves. I have sometimes thought that the mere hearing of those songs would do more to impress some minds with the horrible character of slavery, than the reading of whole volumes of philosophy on the subject could do.

I did not, when a slave, understand the deep meaning of those 9 rude and apparently incoherent songs. I was myself within the circle; so that I neither saw nor heard as those without might see and hear. They told a tale of woe which was then altogether beyond my feeble comprehension; they were tones loud, long, and deep; they breathed the prayer and complaint of souls boiling over with the bitterest anguish. Every tone was a testimony against slavery, and a prayer to God for deliverance from chains. The hearing of those wild notes always depressed my spirit, and filled me with ineffable sadness. I have frequently found myself in tears while hearing them. The mere recurrence of those songs, even now, afflicts me; and while I am writing these lines, an expression of feeling has already found its way down my cheek. To those songs I trace my first glimmering conception of the dehumanizing character of slavery. I can never get rid of that conception. Those songs still follow me, to deepen my hatred of slavery, and quicken my sympathies for my brethren in bonds. If any one wishes to be impressed with the soul-killing effects of slavery, let him go to Colonel Lloyd's plantation, and, on allowance-day, place himself in the deep pine woods, and there let him, in silence, analyze the sounds that shall pass through the chambers of his soul, — and if he is not thus impressed, it will only be because "there is no flesh in his obdurate heart."

10   I have often been utterly astonished, since I came to the north, to find persons who could speak of the singing, among slaves, as evidence of their contentment and happiness. It is impossible to conceive of a greater mistake. Slaves sing most when they are most unhappy. The songs of the slave represent the sorrows of his heart; and he is relieved by them, only as an aching heart is relieved by its tears. At least, such is my experience. I have often sung to drown my sorrow, but seldom to express my happiness. Crying for joy, and singing for joy, were alike uncommon to me while in the jaws of slavery. The singing of a man cast away upon a desolate island might be as appropriately considered as evidence of contentment and happiness, as the singing of a slave; the songs of the one and of the other are prompted by the same emotion.

_____ **CONSIDERATIONS** _____

1. Is there anything to suggest, at the end of Paragraph 7, that Douglass had a talent for satire?

2. In Paragraphs 2 and 7, Douglass sketches the operations of the home plantation and its relationship to the outlying farms owned by the same man. Does the arrangement sound feudal? How did the plantation system differ from feudalism?

3. "I was myself within the circle; so that I neither saw nor heard as those without might see and hear," writes Douglass in Paragraph 9. Is a fish aware that its medium is water? Can a freshman writer understand what he is doing with his own language?

4. What single phenomenon, according to Douglass, taught him the most moving and enduring lesson about the dehumanizing character of slavery? In what way did that lesson surprise those who had not had Douglass's experience?

5. Paragraph 5 offers a good example of Douglass's typical sentence structure: a linear series of independent clauses, with little or no subordination, all of which produces a blunt, stop-and-go effect. Without losing any of the information provided, rewrite the paragraph, reducing the number of sentences from twelve to six. Do this by converting some of the sentences to phrases, modifying clauses, or, in some cases, single-word modifiers.

Loren Eiseley (1907–1977) was an anthropologist who taught at the University of Pennsylvania, and a writer of unusual ability, author of two books of poems and numerous collections of prose including The Night Country *(1971) and* All the Strange Hours *(1975). Eiseley was a scientist-poet, a human brooder over the natural world, determined never to distort the real world by his brooding dream, an objective anthropologist with a talent for subjective response.*

24

LOREN EISELEY
How Flowers Changed the World

1   If it had been possible to observe the Earth from the far side of the solar system over the long course of geological epochs, the watchers might have been able to discern a subtle change in the light emanating from our planet. That world of long ago would, like the red deserts of Mars, have reflected light from vast drifts of stone and gravel, the sands of wandering wastes, the blackness of naked basalt, the yellow dust of endlessly moving storms. Only the ceaseless marching of the clouds and the intermittent flashes from the restless surface of the sea would have told a different story, but still essentially a barren one. Then, as the millennia rolled away and age followed age, a new and greener light would, by degrees, have come to twinkle across those endless miles.

2   This is the only difference those far watchers, by the use of subtle instruments, might have perceived in the whole history of the planet

Earth. Yet that slowly growing green twinkle would have contained the epic march of life from the tidal oozes upward across the raw and unclothed continents. Out of the vast chemical bath of the sea — not from the deeps, but from the element-rich, light-exposed platforms of the continental shelves — wandering fingers of green had crept upward along the meanderings of river systems and fringed the gravels of forgotten lakes.

In those first ages plants clung of necessity to swamps and water- 3 courses. Their reproductive processes demanded direct access to water. Beyond the primitive ferns and mosses that enclosed the borders of swamps and streams the rocks still lay vast and bare, the winds still swirled the dust of a naked planet. The grass cover that holds our world secure in place was still millions of years in the future. The green marchers had gained a soggy foothold upon the land, but that was all. They did not reproduce by seeds but by microscopic swimming sperm that had to wriggle their way through water to fertilize the female cell. Such plants in their higher forms had clever adaptations for the use of rain water in their sexual phases, and survived with increasing success in a wet land environment. They now seem part of man's normal environment. The truth is, however, that there is nothing very "normal" about nature. Once upon a time there were no flowers at all.

A little while ago — about one hundred million years, as the 4 geologist estimates time in the history of our four-billion-year-old planet — flowers were not to be found anywhere on the five continents. Wherever one might have looked, from the poles to the equator, one would have seen only the cold dark monotonous green of a world whose plant life possessed no other color.

Somewhere, just a short time before the close of the Age of Rep- 5 tiles, there occurred a soundless, violent explosion. It lasted millions of years, but it was an explosion, nevertheless. It marked the emergence of the angiosperms — the flowering plants. Even the great evolutionist, Charles Darwin, called them "an abominable mystery," because they appeared so suddenly and spread so fast.

Flowers changed the face of the planet. Without them, the world 6 we know — even man himself — would never have existed. Francis Thompson, the English poet, once wrote that one could not pluck a flower without troubling a star. Intuitively he had sensed like a naturalist the enormous interlinked complexity of life. Today we know that the appearance of the flowers contained also the equally mystifying emergence of man.

7   If we were to go back into the Age of Reptiles, its drowned swamps and birdless forest would reveal to us a warmer but, on the whole, a sleepier world than that of today. Here and there, it is true, the serpent heads of bottom-feeding dinosaurs might be upreared in suspicion of their huge flesh-eating compatriots. Tyrannosaurs, enormous bipedal caricatures of men, would stalk mindlessly across the sites of future cities and go their slow way down into the dark of geologic time.

8   In all that world of living things nothing saw save with the intense concentration of the hunt, nothing moved except with the grave sleepwalking intentness of the instinct-driven brain. Judged by modern standards, it was a world in slow motion, a cold-blooded world whose occupants were most active at noonday but torpid on chill nights, their brains damped by a slower metabolism than any known to even the most primitive of warm-blooded animals today.

9   A high metabolic rate and the maintenance of a constant body temperature are supreme achievements in the evolution of life. They enable an animal to escape, within broad limits, from the overheating or the chilling of its immediate surroundings, and at the same time to maintain a peak mental efficiency. Creatures without a high metabolic rate are slaves to weather. Insects in the first frosts of autumn all run down like little clocks. Yet if you pick one up and breathe warmly upon it, it will begin to move about once more.

10   In a sheltered spot such creatures may sleep away the winter, but they are hopelessly immobilized. Though a few warm-blooded mammals, such as the woodchuck of our day, have evolved a way of reducing their metabolic rate in order to undergo winter hibernation, it is a survival mechanism with drawbacks, for it leaves the animal helplessly exposed if enemies discover him during his period of suspended animation. Thus bear or woodchuck, big animal or small, must seek, in this time of descending sleep, a safe refuge in some hidden den or burrow. Hibernation is, therefore, primarily a winter refuge of small, easily concealed animals rather than of large ones.

11   A high metabolic rate, however, means a heavy intake of energy in order to sustain body warmth and efficiency. It is for this reason that even some of these later warm-blooded mammals existing in our day have learned to descend into a slower, unconscious rate of living during the winter months when food may be difficult to obtain. On a slightly higher plane they are following the procedure of the cold-blooded frog sleeping in the mud at the bottom of a frozen pond.

12   The agile brain of the warm-blooded birds and mammals demands a high oxygen consumption and food in concentrated forms,

or the creatures cannot long sustain themselves. It was the rise of the flowering plants that provided that energy and changed the nature of the living world. Their appearance parallels in a quite surprising manner the rise of the birds and mammals.

Slowly, toward the dawn of the Age of Reptiles, something over two hundred and fifty million years ago, the little naked sperm cells wriggling their way through dew and raindrops had given way to a kind of pollen carried by the wind. Our present-day pine forests represent plants of a pollen-disseminating variety. Once fertilization was no longer dependent on exterior water, the march over drier regions could be extended. Instead of spores simple primitive seeds carrying some nourishment for the young plant had developed, but true flowers were still scores of millions of years away. After a long period of hesitant evolutionary groping, they exploded upon the world with truly revolutionary violence. 13

The event occurred in Cretaceous times in the close of the Age of Reptiles. Before the coming of the flowering plants our own ancestral stock, the warm-blooded mammals, consisted of a few mousy little creatures hidden in trees and underbrush. A few lizard-like birds with carnivorous teeth flapped awkwardly on ili-aimed flights among archaic shrubbery. None of these insignificant creatures gave evidence of any remarkable talents. The mammals in particular had been around for some millions of years, but had remained well lost in the shadow of the mighty reptiles. Truth to tell, man was still, like the genie in the bottle, encased in the body of a creature about the size of a rat. 14

As for the birds, their reptilian cousins the Pterodactyls, flew farther and better. There was just one thing about the birds that paralleled the physiology of the mammals. They, too, had evolved warm blood and its accompanying temperature control. Nevertheless, if one had been seen stripped of his feathers, he would still have seemed a slightly uncanny and unsightly lizard. 15

Neither the birds nor the mammals, however, were quite what they seemed. They were waiting for the Age of Flowers. They were waiting for what flowers, and with them the true encased seed, would bring. Fish-eating, gigantic leather-winged reptiles, twenty-eight feet from wing tip to wing tip, hovered over the coasts that one day would be swarming with gulls. 16

Inland the monotonous green of the pine and spruce forests with their primitive wooden cone flowers stretched everywhere. No grass hindered the fall of the naked seeds to earth. Great sequoias towered to the skies. The world of that time has a certain appeal but it is a 17 giant's world, a world moving slowly like the reptiles who stalked magnificently among the boles of its trees.

18   The trees themselves are ancient, slow-growing and immense, like the redwood groves that have survived to our day on the California coast. All is stiff, formal, upright and green, monotonously green. There is no grass as yet; there are no wide plains rolling in the sun, no tiny daisies dotting the meadows underfoot. There is little versatility about this scene; it is, in truth, a giant's world.

19   A few nights ago it was brought home vividly to me that the world has changed since that far epoch. I was awakened out of sleep by an unknown sound in my living room. Not a small sound — not a creaking timber or a mouse's scurry — but a sharp, rending explosion as though an unwary foot had been put down upon a wine glass. I had come instantly out of sleep and lay tense, unbreathing. I listened for another step. There was none.

20   Unable to stand the suspense any longer, I turned on the light and passed from room to room glancing uneasily behind chairs and into closets. Nothing seemed disturbed, and I stood puzzled in the center of the living room floor. Then a small button-shaped object upon the rug caught my eye. It was hard and polished and glistening. Scattered over the length of the room were several more shining up at me like wary little eyes. A pine cone that had been lying in a dish had been blown the length of the coffee table. The dish itself could hardly have been the source of the explosion. Beside it I found two ribbonlike strips of a velvety-green. I tried to place the two strips together to make a pod. They twisted resolutely away from each other and would no longer fit.

21   I relaxed in a chair, then, for I had reached a solution of the midnight disturbance. The twisted strips were wistaria pods that I had brought in a day or two previously and placed in the dish. They had chosen midnight to explode and distribute their multiplying fund of life down the length of the room. A plant, a fixed, rooted thing, immobilized in a single spot, had devised a way of propelling its offspring across open space. Immediately there passed before my eyes the million airy troopers of the milkweed pod and the clutching hooks of the sandburs. Seeds on the coyote's tail, seeds on the hunter's coat, thistledown mounting on the winds — all were somehow triumphing over life's limitations. Yet the ability to do this had not been with them at the beginning. It was the product of endless effort and experiment.

22   The seeds on my carpet were not going to lie stiffly where they

had dropped like their antiquated cousins, the naked seeds on the pine-cone scales. They were travelers. Struck by the thought, I went out next day and collected several other varieties. I line them up now in a row on my desk — so many little capsules of life, winged, hooked or spiked. Every one is an angiosperm, a product of the true flowering plants. Contained in these little boxes is the secret of that far-off Cretaceous explosion of a hundred million years ago that changed the face of the planet. And somewhere in here, I think, as I poke seriously at one particularly resistant seedcase of a wild grass, was once man himself.

____ CONSIDERATIONS ____

1. Much of Eiseley's popularity among nonscientists comes from figures of speech like those found in nearly every paragraph of "How Flowers Changed the World." Locate several attractive ones and consider these questions: To what extent are figures of speech merely decorative? To what extent can figures of speech communicate what the literal cannot?

2. Eiseley asserts in Paragraph 3 that "there is nothing very 'normal' about nature." What does he mean? Is it in any way related to Kenneth E. Boulding's remark (Paragraph 3, "Nature and Artifice") that "there isn't anything that is not natural"?

3. In Paragraph 6, Eiseley indirectly quotes a line from the English poet Francis Thompson, compressing into ten words the grand concept of ecology. In what way is this concept related to Alice Morgan's similarly compressed statement, "most experiences are hard to conclude"?

4. The organization of Eiseley's essay is interesting. In Paragraphs 7 through 10, he seems to interrupt his explanation of the emergence and importance of flowers with a fairly lengthy passage that does not mention flowers. And again, after describing (in Paragraph 5) the appearance of flowers as a "soundless, violent explosion," Eiseley says nothing about this dramatic event until the end of Paragraph 13, where he merely mentions the revolution and then seems to forget it again through Paragraphs 14, 15, 16, 17, and 18. How do you account for these apparent violations of conventional organization?

5. Explain Eiseley's strategy in Paragraph 19, where he breaks away from his general evolutionary history to explain a noise he heard one night in his own home.

Nora Ephron (b. 1941), daughter of two screen writers, grew up in Hollywood wanting to come to New York and become a writer. She did. She began by working for Newsweek, *and soon was contributing articles to* New York *and a monthly column to* Esquire. *Most of her writing is about women, and manages to be funny and serious, profound and irreverent — and on occasion outrageous. Her latest book, on the media, is* Scribble Scribble *(1978). She has also collected her essays in* Wallflower at the Orgy *(1970) and* Crazy Salad *(1975), from which we take this essay on growing up flat-chested.*

25

NORA EPHRON

A Few Words about Breasts: Shaping Up Absurd

1   I have to begin with a few words about androgyny. In grammar school, in the fifth and sixth grades, we were all tyrannized by a rigid set of rules that supposedly determined whether we were boys or girls. The episode in *Huckleberry Finn* where Huck is disguised as a girl and gives himself away by the way he threads a needle and catches a ball — that kind of thing. We learned that the way you sat, crossed your legs, held a cigarette and looked at your nails, your wristwatch, the way you did these things instinctively was absolute proof of your sex. Now obviously most children did not take this literally, but I did. I thought that just one slip, just one incorrect cross of my legs or flick of an imaginary cigarette ash would turn me from whatever I was into the other thing; that would be all it took, really. Even though I was

outwardly a girl and had many of the trappings generally associated with the field of girldom — a girl's name, for example, and dresses, my own telephone, an autograph book — I spent the early years of my adolescence absolutely certain that I might at any point gum it up. I did not feel at all like a girl. I was boyish. I was athletic, ambitious, outspoken, competitive, noisy, rambunctious. I had scabs on my knees and my socks slid into my loafers and I could throw a football. I wanted desperately not to be that way, not to be a mixture of both things but instead just one, a girl, a definite indisputable girl. As soft and as pink as a nursery. And nothing would do that for me, I felt, but breasts.

I was about six months younger than everyone in my class, and so for about six months after it began, for six months after my friends had begun to develop — that was the word we used, develop — I was not particularly worried. I would sit in the bathtub and look down at my breasts and know that any day now, any second now, they would start growing like everyone else's. They didn't. "I want to buy a bra," I said to my mother one night. "What for?" she said. My mother was really hateful about bras, and by the time my third sister had gotten to the point where she was ready to want one, my mother had worked the whole business into a comedy routine. "Why not use a Band-Aid instead?" she would say. It was a source of great pride to my mother that she had never even had to wear a brassiere until she had her fourth child, and then only because her gynecologist made her. It was incomprehensible to me that anyone would ever be proud of something like that. It was the 1950's, for God's sake. Jane Russell. Cashmere sweaters. Couldn't my mother see that? *"I am too old to wear an undershirt."* Screaming. Weeping. Shouting. "Then don't wear an undershirt," said my mother. "But I want to buy a bra." "What for?"

I suppose that for most girls, breasts, brassieres, that entire thing, has more trauma, more to do with the coming of adolescence, of becoming a woman, than anything else. Certainly more than getting your period, although that too was traumatic, symbolic. But you could *see* breasts; they were there; they were visible. Whereas a girl could claim to have her period for months before she actually got it and nobody would ever know the difference. Which is exactly what I did. All you had to do was make a great fuss over having enough nickels for the Kotex machine and walk around clutching your stomach and moaning for three to five days a month about The Curse and you could convince anybody. There is a school of thought somewhere in the women's lib/women's mag/gynecology establishment that claims that menstrual cramps are purely psychological, and I lean toward it. Not that I didn't have them finally. Agonizing cramps, heating-pad cramps, go-down-to-the-school-nurse-and-lie-on-the-cot cramps. But unlike any pain I have ever suffered, I adored the pain of cramps, welcomed it, wallowed in it, bragged about it. "I can't go. I have cramps." "I can't do that. I have cramps." And most of all, gigglingly, blushingly: "I can't swim. I have cramps." Nobody ever used the hard-core word. Menstruation. God, what an awful word. Never that. "I have cramps."

4   The morning I first got my period, I went into my mother's bedroom to tell her. And my mother, my utterly-hateful-about-bras mother, burst into tears. It was really a lovely moment, and I remember it so clearly not just because it was one of the two times I ever saw my mother cry on my account (the other was when I was caught being a six-year-old kleptomaniac), but also because the incident did not mean to me what it meant to her. Her little girl, her firstborn, had finally become a woman. That was what she was crying about. My reaction to the event, however, was that I might well be a woman in some scientific, textbook sense (and could at least stop faking every month and stop wasting all those nickels). But in another sense — in a visible sense — I was as androgynous and as liable to tip over into boyhood as ever.

5   I started with a 28AA bra. I don't think they made them any smaller in those days, although I gather that now you can buy bras for five year olds that don't have any cups whatsoever in them; trainer bras they are called. My first brassiere came from Robinson's Department Store in Beverly Hills. I went there alone, shaking, positive they would look me over and smile and tell me to come back next year. An actual fitter took me into the dressing room and stood over me while I took off my blouse and tried the first one on. The little puffs stood out on my chest. "Lean over," said the fitter (to this day I am not sure what fitters in bra departments do except to tell you to lean over). I leaned over, with the fleeing hope that my breasts would miraculously fall out of my body and into the puffs. Nothing.

6   "Don't worry about it," said my friend Libby some months later, when things had not improved. "You'll get them after you're married."

7   "What are you talking about?" I said.

8   "When you get married," Libby explained, "your husband will touch your breasts and rub them and kiss them and they'll grow."

9   That was the killer. Necking I could deal with. Intercourse I

could deal with. But it had never crossed my mind that a man was going to touch my breasts, that breasts had something to do with all that, petting, my God they never mentioned petting in my little sex manual about the fertilization of the ovum. I became dizzy. For I knew instantly — as naïve as I had been only a moment before — that only part of what she was saying was true: the touching, rubbing, kissing part, not the growing part. And I knew that no one would ever want to marry me. I had no breasts. I would never have breasts.

My best friend in school was Diana Raskob. She lived a block 10 from me in a house full of wonders. English muffins, for instance. The Raskobs were the first people in Beverly Hills to have English muffins for breakfast. They also had an apricot tree in the back, and a badminton court, and a subscription to *Seventeen* magazine, and hundreds of games like Sorry and Parcheesi and Treasure Hunt and Anagrams. Diana and I spent three or four afternoons a week in their den reading and playing and eating. Diana's mother's kitchen was full of the most colossal assortment of junk food I have ever been exposed to. My house was full of apples and peaches and milk and homemade chocolate-chip cookies — which were nice, and good for you, but-not-right-before-dinner-or-you'll-spoil-your-appetite. Diana's house had nothing in it that was good for you, and what's more, you could stuff it in right up until dinner and nobody cared. Bar-B-Q potato chips (they were the first in them, too), giant bottles of ginger ale, fresh popcorn with melted butter, hot fudge sauce on Baskin-Robbins jamoca ice cream, powdered-sugar doughnuts from Van de Kamps. Diana and I had been best friends since we were seven; we were about equally popular in school (which is to say, not particularly), we had about the same success with boys (extremely intermittent) and we looked much the same. Dark. Tall. Gangly.

It is September, just before school begins. I am eleven years old, 11 about to enter the seventh grade, and Diana and I have not seen each other all summer. I have been to camp and she has been somewhere like Banff with her parents. We are meeting, as we often do, on the street midway between our two houses and we will walk back to Diana's and eat junk and talk about what has happened to each of us that summer. I am walking down Walden Drive in my jeans and my father's shirt hanging out and my old red loafers with the socks falling into them and coming toward me is . . . I take a deep breath . . . a young woman. Diana. Her hair is curled and she has a waist and hips and a bust and she is wearing a straight skirt, an article of clothing I have been repeatedly told I will be unable to wear until I have the hips to hold it up. My jaw drops, and suddenly I am crying, crying hysterically, can't catch my breath sobbing. My best friend has betrayed me. She has gone ahead without me and done it. She has shaped up.

12   Here are some things I did to help:
13   Bought a Mark Eden Bust Developer.
14   Slept on my back for four years.
15   Splashed cold water on them every night because some French actress said in *Life* magazine that that was what *she* did for her perfect bustline.
16   Ultimately, I resigned myself to a bad toss and began to wear padded bras. I think about them now, think about all those years in high school I went around in them, my three padded bras, every single one of them with different sized breasts. Each time I changed bras I changed sizes: one week nice perky but not too obtrusive breasts, the next medium-sized slightly pointed ones, the next week knockers, true knockers; all the time, whatever size I was, carrying around this rubberized appendage on my chest that occasionally crashed into a wall and was poked inward and had to be poked outward — I think about all that and wonder how anyone kept a straight face through it. My parents, who normally had no restraints about needling me — why did they say nothing as they watched my chest go up and down? My friends, who would periodically inspect my breasts for signs of growth and reassure me — why didn't they at least counsel consistency?
17   And the bathing suits. I die when I think about the bathing suits. That was the era when you could lay an uninhabited bathing suit on the beach and someone would make a pass at it. I would put one on, an absurd swimsuit with its enormous bust built into it, the bones from the suit stabbing me in the rib cage and leaving little red welts on my body, and there I would be, my chest plunging straight downward absolutely vertically from my collarbone to the top of my suit and then suddenly, wham, out came all that padding and material and wiring absolutely horizontally.

18   Buster Klepper was the first boy who ever touched them. He was my boyfriend my senior year of high school. There is a picture of him in my high-school yearbook that makes him look quite attractive in a Jewish, horn-rimmed glasses sort of way, but the picture does not

show the pimples, which were air-brushed out, or the dumbness. Well, that isn't really fair. He wasn't dumb. He just wasn't terribly bright. His mother refused to accept it, refused to accept the relentlessly average report cards, refused to deal with her son's inevitable destiny in some junior college or other. "He was tested," she would say to me, apropos of nothing, "and it came out 145. That's near-genius." Had the word underachiever been coined, she probably would have lobbed that one at me, too. Anyway, Buster was really very sweet — which is, I know, damning with faint praise, but there it is. I was the editor of the front page of the high-school newspaper and he was editor of the back page; we had to work together, side by side, in the print shop, and that was how it started. On our first date, we went to see *April Love* starring Pat Boone. Then we started going together. Buster had a green coupe, a 1950 Ford with an engine he had handchromed until it shone, dazzled, reflected the image of anyone who looked into it, anyone usually being Buster polishing it or the gas-station attendants he constantly asked to check the oil in order for them to be overwhelmed by the sparkle on the valves. The car also had a boot stretched over the back seat for reasons I never understood; hanging from the rearview mirror, as was the custom, was a pair of angora dice. A previous girl friend named Solange who was famous throughout Beverly Hills High School for having no pigment in her right eyebrow had knitted them for him. Buster and I would ride around town, the two of us seated to the left of the steering wheel. I would shift gears. It was nice.

There was necking. Terrific necking. First in the car, overlooking   19 Los Angeles from what is now the Trousdale Estates. Then on the bed of his parents' cabana at Ocean House. Incredibly wonderful, frustrating necking, I loved it, really, but no further than necking, please don't, please, because there I was absolutely terrified of the general implications of going-a-step-further with a near-dummy and also terrified of his finding out there was next to nothing there (which he knew, of course; he wasn't that dumb).

I broke up with him at one point. I think we were apart for about   20 two weeks. At the end of that time I drove down to see a friend at a boarding school in Palos Verdes Estates and a disc jockey played *April Love* on the radio four times during the trip. I took it as a sign. I drove straight back to Griffith Park to a golf tournament Buster was playing in (he was the sixth-seeded teen-age golf player in Southern California) and presented myself back to him on the green of the 18th hole. It was all very dramatic. That night we went to a drive-in and I let him get his hand under my protuberances and onto my breasts. He really didn't seem to mind at all.

21   *"Do you want to marry my son?" the woman asked me.*

22   *"Yes," I said.*

23   *I was nineteen years old, a virgin, going with this woman's son, this big strange woman who was married to a Lutheran minister in New Hampshire and pretended she was Gentile and had this son, by her first husband, this total fool of a son who ran the hero-sandwich concession at Harvard Business School and whom for one moment one December in New Hampshire I said — as much out of politeness as anything else — that I wanted to marry.*

24   *"Fine," she said. "Now, here's what you do. Always make sure you're on top of him so you won't seem so small. My bust is very large, you see, so I always lie on my back to make it look smaller, but you'll have to be on top most of the time."*

25   *I nodded. "Thank you," I said.*

26   *"I have a book for you to read," she went on. "Take it with you when you leave. Keep it." She went to the bookshelf, found it, and gave it to me. It was a book on frigidity.*

27   *"Thank you," I said.*

28   That is a true story. Everything in this article is a true story, but I feel I have to point out that that story in particular is true. It happened on December 30, 1960. I think about it often. When it first happened, I naturally assumed that the woman's son, my boyfriend, was responsible. I invented a scenario where he had had a little heart-to-heart with his mother and had confessed that his only objection to me was that my breasts were small; his mother then took it upon herself to help out. Now I think I was wrong about the incident. The mother was acting on her own, I think: that was her way of being cruel and competitive under the guise of being helpful and maternal. You have small breasts, she was saying; therefore you will never make him as happy as I have. Or you have small breasts; therefore you will doubtless have sexual problems. Or you have small breasts; therefore you are less woman than I am. She was, as it happens, only the first of what seems to me to be a never-ending string of women who have made competitive remarks to me about breast size. "I would love to wear a dress like that," my friend Emily says to me, "but my bust is too big." Like that. Why do women say these things to me? Do I attract these remarks the way other women attract married men or alcoholics or homosexuals? This summer, for example. I am at a party

in East Hampton and I am introduced to a woman from Washington. She is a minor celebrity, very pretty and Southern and blonde and outspoken and I am flattered because she has read something I have written. We are talking animatedly, we have been talking no more than five minutes, when a man comes up to join us. "Look at the two of us," the woman says to the man, indicating me and her. "The two of us together couldn't fill an A cup." Why does she say that? It isn't even true, dammit, so why? Is she even more addled than I am on this subject? Does she honestly believe there is something wrong with her size breasts, which, it seems to me, now that I look hard at them, are just right. Do I unconsciously bring out competitiveness in women? In that form? What did I do to deserve it?

As for men.   29

There were men who minded and let me know they minded.   30 There were men who did not mind. In any case, I always minded.

And even now, now that I have been countlessly reassured that   31 my figure is a good one, now that I am grown up enough to understand that most of my feelings have very little to do with the reality of my shape, I am nonetheless obsessed by breasts. I cannot help it. I grew up in the terrible Fifties — with rigid stereotypical sex roles, the insistence that men be men and dress like men and women be women and dress like women, the intolerance of androgyny — and I cannot shake it, cannot shake my feelings of inadequacy. Well, that time is gone, right? All those exaggerated examples of breast worship are gone, right? Those women were freaks, right? I know all that. And yet, here I am, stuck with the psychological remains of it all, stuck with my own peculiar version of breast worship. You probably think I am crazy to go on like this: here I have set out to write a confession that is meant to hit you with the shock of recognition and instead you are sitting there thinking I am thoroughly warped. Well, what can I tell you? If I had had them, I would have been a completely different person. I honestly believe that.

After I went into therapy, a process that made it possible for me   32 to tell total strangers at cocktail parties that breasts were the hang-up of my life, I was often told that I was insane to have been bothered by my condition. I was also frequently told, by close friends, that I was extremely boring on the subject. And my girl friends, the ones with nice big breasts, would go on endlessly about how their lives had been far more miserable than mine. Their bra straps were snapped in class. They couldn't sleep on their stomachs. They were stared at whenever the word "mountain" cropped up in geography. And *Evangeline*, good

God what they went through every time someone had to stand up and recite the Prologue to Longfellow's *Evangeline*: *". . . stand like druids of eld . . . / With beards that rest on their bosoms."* It was much worse for them, they tell me. They had a terrible time of it, they assure me. I don't know how lucky I was, they say.

33   I have thought about their remarks, tried to put myself in their place, considered their point of view. I think they are full of shit.

_____ **CONSIDERATIONS** _____

1. Nora Ephron's account offends some readers and attracts others for the same reason — the frank and casual exploration of a subject that generations have believed unmentionable. This problem is worth investigating: Are there, in fact, subjects that should not be discussed in the popular press? Are there words a writer must not use? Why? And who should make the list of things not to be talked about?

2. Imagine an argument about Ephron's article between a feminist and an antifeminist. What ammunition could each find in the article? Write the dialogue as you hear it.

3. Ephron reports that from a very early age she worried that she might not be "a girl, a definite indisputable girl." Is this anxiety as uncommon as she thought it was? Is worry about one's sex an exclusively female problem?

4. Are our ideas about masculinity and femininity changing? How are such ideas determined? How important are they in shaping personality and in channeling thoughts?

5. Ephron's article is a good example of the very informal essay. What does she do that makes it so informal? Consider both diction and sentence structure.

6. How can one smile at others' problems — or at one's own disappointments, for that matter? How can Ephron see humor now in what she thought of as tragic then?

William Faulkner (1897–1962) was a great novelist, born in Mississippi, who supported himself much of his life by screenwriting and by writing short fiction for magazines. He received the Nobel Prize for literature in 1950. Among his novels are The Sound and the Fury *(1929),* As I Lay Dying *(1930),* Light in August *(1932), and a comic series:* The Hamlet *(1940),* The Town *(1957), and* The Mansion *(1960). "A Rose for Emily" is an expert piece of magazine fiction; remarkably, it also makes an emblem for the disease and decease of a society.*

26

WILLIAM FAULKNER
A Rose for Emily

I

When Miss Emily Grierson died, our whole town went to her funeral: the men through a sort of respectful affection for a fallen monument, the women mostly out of curiosity to see the inside of her house, which no one save an old manservant — a combined gardener and cook — had seen in at least ten years.

It was a big, squarish frame house that had once been white, decorated with cupolas and spires and scrolled balconies in the heavily lightsome style of the seventies, set on what had once been our most select street. But garages and cotton gins had encroached and obliterated even the august names of that neighborhood; only Miss Emily's house was left, lifting its stubborn and coquettish decay above the cotton wagons and the gasoline pumps — an eyesore among eyesores. And now Miss Emily had gone to join the representatives of those august names where they lay in the cedar-bemused cemetery among the ranked and anonymous graves of Union and Confederate soldiers who fell at the battle of Jefferson.

3   Alive, Miss Emily had been a tradition, a duty, and a care; a sort of hereditary obligation upon the town, dating from that day in 1894 when Colonel Sartoris, the mayor — he who fathered the edict that no Negro woman should appear on the streets without an apron — remitted her taxes, the dispensation dating from the death of her father on into perpetuity. Not that Miss Emily would have accepted charity. Colonal Sartoris invented an involved tale to the effect that Miss Emily's father had loaned money to the town, which the town, as a matter of business, preferred this way of repaying. Only a man of Colonel Sartoris' generation and thought could have invented it, and only a woman could have believed it.

4   When the next generation, with its more modern ideas, became mayors and aldermen, this arrangement created some little dissatisfaction. On the first of the year they mailed her a tax notice. February came, and there was no reply. They wrote her a formal letter, asking her to call at the sheriff's office at her convenience. A week later the mayor wrote her himself, offering to call or to send his car for her, and received in reply a note on paper of an archaic shape, in a thin, flowing calligraphy in faded ink, to the effect that she no longer went out at all. The tax notice was also enclosed, without comment.

5   They called a special meeting of the Board of Aldermen. A deputation waited upon her, knocked at the door through which no visitor had passed since she ceased giving china-painting lessons eight or ten years earlier. They were admitted by the old Negro into a dim hall from which a staircase mounted into still more shadow. It smelled of dust and disuse — a close, dank smell. The Negro led them into the parlor. It was furnished in heavy, leather-covered furniture. When the Negro opened the blinds of one window, a faint dust rose sluggishly about their thighs, spinning with slow motes in the single sun-ray. On a tarnished gilt easel before the fireplace stood a crayon portrait of Miss Emily's father.

6   They rose when she entered — a small, fat woman in black, with a thin gold chain descending to her waist and vanishing into her belt, leaning on an ebony cane with a tarnished gold head. Her skeleton was small and spare; perhaps that was why what would have been merely plumpness in another was obesity in her. She looked bloated, like a body long submerged in motionless water, and of that pallid hue. Her eyes, lost in the fatty ridges of her face, looked like two small

pieces of coal pressed into a lump of dough as they moved from one face to another while the visitors stated their errand.

She did not ask them to sit. She just stood in the door and lis- 7
tened quietly until the spokesman came to a stumbling halt. Then they could hear the invisible watch ticking at the end of the gold chain.

Her voice was dry and cold. "I have no taxes in Jefferson. Colonel 8
Sartoris explained it to me. Perhaps one of you can gain access to the city records and satisfy yourselves."

"But we have. We are the city authorities, Miss Emily. Didn't 9
you get a notice from the sheriff, signed by him?"

"I received a paper, yes," Miss Emily said. "Perhaps he considers 10
himself the sheriff. . . . I have no taxes in Jefferson."

"But there is nothing on the books to show that, you see. We 11
must go by the —"

"See Colonel Sartoris. I have no taxes in Jefferson." 12

"But, Miss Emily —" 13

"See Colonel Sartoris." (Colonel Sartoris had been dead almost 14
ten years.) "I have no taxes in Jefferson. Tobe!" The Negro appeared. "Show these gentlemen out."

II

So she vanquished them, horse and foot, just as she had van- 15
quished their fathers thirty years before about the smell. That was two years after her father's death and a short time after her sweetheart — the one we believed would marry her — had deserted her. After her father's death she went out very little; after her sweetheart went away, people hardly saw her at all. A few of the ladies had the temerity to call, but were not received, and the only sign of life about the place was the Negro man — a young man then — going in and out with a market basket.

"Just as if a man — any man — could keep a kitchen properly," 16
the ladies said; so they were not surprised when the smell developed. It was another link between the gross, teeming world and the high and mighty Griersons.

A neighbor, a woman, complained to the mayor, Judge Stevens, 17
eighty years old.

"But what will you have me do about it, madam?" he said. 18

"Why, send her word to stop it," the woman said. "Isn't there a 19
law?"

"I'm sure that won't be necessary," Judge Stevens said. "It's prob- 20 ably just a snake or a rat that nigger of hers killed in the yard. I'll speak to him about it."

21   The next day he received two more complaints, one from a man who came in diffident deprecation. "We really must do something about it, Judge. I'd be the last one in the world to bother Miss Emily, but we've got to do something." That night the Board of Aldermen met — three gray-beards and one younger man, a member of the rising generation.

22   "It's simple enough," he said. "Send her word to have her place cleaned up. Give her a certain time to do it in, and if she don't . . ."

23   "Dammit, sir," Judge Stevens said, "will you accuse a lady to her face of smelling bad?"

24   So the next night, after midnight, four men crossed Miss Emily's lawn and slunk about the house like burglars, sniffing along the base of the brickwork and at the cellar openings while one of them performed a regular sowing motion with his hand out of a sack slung from his shoulder. They broke open the cellar door and sprinkled lime there, and in all the out-buildings. As they recrossed the lawn, a window that had been dark was lighted and Miss Emily sat in it, the light behind her, and her upright torso motionless as that of an idol. They crept quietly across the lawn and into the shadow of the locusts that lined the street. After a week or two the smell went away.

25   That was when people had begun to feel really sorry for her. People in our town remembering how old lady Wyatt, her great-aunt, had gone completely crazy at last, believed that the Griersons held themselves a little too high for what they really were. None of the young men were quite good enough for Miss Emily and such. We had long thought of them as a tableau; Miss Emily a slender figure in white in the background, her father a spraddled silhouette in the foreground, his back to her and clutching a horsewhip, the two of them framed by the back-flung front door. So when she got to be thirty and was still single, we were not pleased exactly, but vindicated; even with insanity in the family she wouldn't have turned down all of her chances if they had really materialized.

26   When her father died, it got about that the house was all that was left to her; and in a way, people were glad. At last they could pity Miss Emily. Being left alone, and a pauper, she had become humanized. Now she too would know the old thrill and the old despair of a penny more or less.

27   The day after his death all the ladies prepared to call at the house and offer condolence and aid, as is our custom. Miss Emily met them at the door, dressed as usual and with no trace of grief on her face. She

told them that her father was not dead. She did that for three days, with the ministers calling on her, and the doctors, trying to persuade her to let them dispose of the body. Just as they were about to resort to law and force, she broke down, and they buried her father quickly.

We did not say she was crazy then. We believed she had to do   28
that. We remembered all the young men her father had driven away, and we knew that with nothing left, she would have to cling to that which had robbed her, as people will.

III

She was sick for a long time. When we saw her again, her hair   29
was cut short, making her look like a girl, with a vague resemblance to those angels in colored church windows — sort of tragic and serene.

The town had just let the contracts for paving the sidewalks, and   30
in the summer after her father's death they began to work. The construction company came with niggers and mules and machinery, and a foreman named Homer Barron, a Yankee — a big, dark, ready man, with a big voice and eyes lighter than his face. The little boys would follow in groups to hear him cuss the niggers, and the niggers singing in time to the rise and fall of picks. Pretty soon he knew everybody in town. Whenever you heard a lot of laughing anywhere about the square, Homer Barron would be in the center of the group. Presently we began to see him and Miss Emily on Sunday afternoons driving in the yellow-wheeled buggy and the matched team of bays from the livery stable.

At first we were glad that Miss Emily would have an interest,   31
because the ladies all said, "Of course a Grierson would not think seriously of a Northerner, a day laborer." But there were still others, older people, who said that even grief could not cause a real lady to forget *noblesse oblige* — without calling it *noblesse oblige*. They just said, "Poor Emily. Her kinsfolk should come to her." She had some kin in Alabama; but years ago her father had fallen out with them over the estate of old lady Wyatt, the crazy woman, and there was no communication between the two families. They had not even been represented at the funeral.

And as soon as the old people said, "Poor Emily," the whispering   32
began. "Do you suppose it's really so?" they said to one another. "Of course it is. What else could . . ." This behind their hands; rustling of craned silk and satin behind jalousies closed upon the sun of Sunday afternoon as the thin, swift clop-clop-clop of the matched team passed: "Poor Emily."

She carried her head high enough — even when we believed that   33 she was fallen. It was as if she demanded more than ever the recognition of her dignity as the last Grierson; as if it had wanted that touch of earthiness to reaffirm her imperviousness. Like when she bought the rat poison, the arsenic. That was over a year after they had begun to say "Poor Emily," and while the two female cousins were visiting her.

34   "I want some poison," she said to the druggist. She was over thirty then, still a slight woman, though thinner than usual, with cold, haughty black eyes in a face the flesh of which was strained across the temples and about the eyesockets as you imagine a lighthouse-keeper's face ought to look. "I want some poison," she said.

35   "Yes, Miss Emily. What kind? For rats and such? I'd recom — "

36   "I want the best you have. I don't care what kind."

37   The druggist named several. "They'll kill anything up to an elephant. But what you want is — "

38   "Arsenic," Miss Emily said. "Is that a good one?"

39   "Is . . . arsenic? Yes ma'am. But what you want — "

40   "I want arsenic."

41   The druggist looked down at her. She looked back at him, erect, her face like a strained flag. "Why, of course," the druggist said. "If that's what you want. But the law requires you to tell what you are going to use it for."

42   Miss Emily just stared at him, her head tilted back in order to look him eye for eye, until he looked away and went and got the arsenic and wrapped it up. The Negro delivery boy brought her the package; the druggist didn't come back. When she opened the package at home there was written on the box, under the skull and bones: "For rats."

IV

43   So the next day we all said, "She will kill herself"; and we said it would be the best thing. When she had first begun to be seen with Homer Barron, we had said, "She will marry him." Then we said, "She will persuade him yet," because Homer himself had remarked — he liked men, and it was known that he drank with the younger men in the Elk's Club — that he was not a marrying man. Later we said, "Poor Emily," behind the jalousies as they passed on Sunday afternoon in the glittering buggy, Miss Emily with her head high and Homer Barron with his hat cocked and a cigar in his teeth, reins and whip in a yellow glove.

44   Then some of the ladies began to say that it was a disgrace to the

town and a bad example to the young people. The men did not want to interfere, but at last the ladies forced the Baptist minister — Miss Emily's people were Episcopal — to call upon her. He would never divulge what happened during that interview, but he refused to go back again. The next Sunday they again drove about the streets and the following day the minister's wife wrote to Miss Emily's relations in Alabama.

So she had blood-kin under her roof again and we sat back to   45
watch developments. At first nothing happened. Then we were sure that they were to be married. We learned that Miss Emily had been to the jeweler's and ordered a man's toilet set in silver, with the letters H.B. on each piece. Two days later we learned that she had bought a complete outfit of men's clothing, including a nightshirt, and we said, "They are married." We were really glad. We were glad because the two female cousins were even more Grierson than Miss Emily had ever been.

So we were surprised when Homer Barron — the streets had been   46
finished some time since — was gone. We were a little disappointed that there was not a public blowing-off, but we believed that he had gone on to prepare for Miss Emily's coming, or to give a chance to get rid of the cousins. (By that time it was a cabal, and we were all Miss Emily's allies to help circumvent the cousins.) Sure enough, after another week they departed. And, as we had expected all along, within three days Homer Barron was back in town. A neighbor saw the Negro man admit him at the kitchen door at dusk one evening.

And that was the last we saw of Homer Barron. And of Miss   47
Emily for some time. The Negro man went in and out with the market basket, but the front door remained closed. Now and then we would see her at a window for a moment, as the men did that night when they sprinkled the lime, but for almost six months she did not appear on the streets. Then we knew that this was to be expected too; as if that quality of her father which had thwarted her woman's life so many times had been too virulent and too furious to die.

When we next saw Miss Emily, she had grown fat and her hair   48
was turning gray. During the next few years it grew grayer and grayer until it attained an even pepper-and-salt iron-gray, when it ceased turning. Up to the day of her death at seventy-four it was still that vigorous iron-gray, like the hair of an active man.

From that time on her front door remained closed, save for a   49
period of six or seven years, when she was about forty, during which she gave lessons in china-painting. She fitted up a studio in one of the

downstairs rooms, where the daughters and granddaughters of Colonel Sartoris' contemporaries were sent to her with the same regularity and in the same spirit that they were sent on Sundays with a twenty-five cent piece for the collection plate. Meanwhile her taxes had been remitted.

50   Then the newer generation became the backbone and the spirit of the town, and the painting pupils grew up and fell away and did not send their children to her with boxes of color and tedious brushes and pictures cut from the ladies' magazines. The front door closed upon the last one and remained closed for good. When the town got free postal delivery Miss Emily alone refused to let them fasten the metal numbers above her door and attach a mailbox to it. She would not listen to them.

51   Daily, monthly, yearly we watched the Negro grow grayer and more stooped, going in and out with the market basket. Each December we sent her a tax notice, which would be returned by the post office a week later, unclaimed. Now and then we would see her in one of the downstairs windows — she had evidently shut up the top floor of the house — like the carven torso of an idol in a niche, looking or not looking at us, we could never tell which. Thus she passed from generation to generation — dear, inescapable, impervious, tranquil, and perverse.

52   And so she died. Fell ill in the house filled with dust and shadows, with only a doddering Negro man to wait on her. We did not even know she was sick; we had long since given up trying to get any information from the Negro. He talked to no one, probably not even to her, for his voice had grown harsh and rusty, as if from disuse.

53   She died in one of the downstairs rooms, in a heavy walnut bed with a curtain, her gray head propped on a pillow yellow and moldy with age and lack of sunlight.

V

54   The Negro met the first of the ladies at the front door and let them in, with their hushed, sibilant voices and their quick, curious glances, and then he disappeared. He walked right through the house and out the back and was not seen again.

55   The two female cousins came at once. They held the funeral on the second day, with the town coming to look at Miss Emily beneath a mass of bought flowers, with the crayon face of her father musing profoundly above the bier and the ladies sibilant and macabre; and the very old men — some in their brushed Confederate uniforms — on the

porch and the lawn, talking of Miss Emily as if she had been a contemporary of theirs, believing that they had danced with her and courted her perhaps, confusing time with its mathematical progression, as the old do, to whom all the past is not a diminishing road, but, instead, a huge meadow which no winter ever quite touches, divided from them now by the narrow bottleneck of the most recent decade of years.

Already we knew that there was one room in the region above   56
stairs which no one had seen in forty years, and which would have to be forced. They waited until Miss Emily was decently in the ground before they opened it.

The violence of breaking down the door seemed to fill this room   57
with pervading dust. A thin, acrid pall as of the tomb seemed to lie everywhere upon this room decked and furnished as for a bridal: upon the valance curtains of faded rose color, upon the rose-shaded lights, upon the dressing table, upon the delicate array of crystal and the man's toilet things backed with tarnished silver, silver so tarnished that the monogram was obscured. Among them lay a collar and tie, as if they had just been removed, which, lifted, left upon the surface a pale crescent in the dust. Upon a chair hung the suit, carefully folded; beneath it the two mute shoes and the discarded socks.

The man himself lay in the bed.   58

For a long while we just stood there, looking down at the pro-   59
found and fleshless grin. The body had apparently once lain in the attitude of an embrace, but now the long sleep that outlasts love, that conquers even the grimace of love, had cuckolded him. What was left of him, rotted beneath what was left of the nightshirt, had become inextricable from the bed in which he lay; and upon him and upon the pillow beside him lay that even coating of the patient and biding dust.

Then we noticed that in the second pillow was the indentation   60
of a head. One of us lifted something from it, and leaning forward, that faint and invisible dust dry and acrid in the nostrils, we saw a long strand of iron-gray hair.

_____ **CONSIDERATIONS** _____

1. The art of narration, some say, is the successful management of a significant sequence of actions through time. But "through time" does not necessarily imply chronological order. Identify the major events of Faulkner's story according to when they actually happened, then arrange them in the

order in which they are given by the author. Try the same technique with the story by Eudora Welty (pages 445–453).

2. Faulkner uses the terms "Negro" and "nigger" to refer to nonwhite persons in the story. Does he intend distinction between the two words? If he were writing the story today, instead of in 1930, might he substitute the word "black"? Why? Can you think of parallel terms used to designate other minority peoples, say, Jews, Catholics, Italians, or Japanese? Of what significance is the variety of such terms?

3. In what ways, if any, is Emily Grierson presented as a sympathetic character? Why?

4. In Part III, Faulkner puts considerable emphasis on the phrase *noblesse oblige.* Look up the meaning of that phrase, then comment on the author's use of it.

5. Who is the "we" in the story? Does "we" play any significant part? Is the "we" anything like the "us" Blythe refers to at the end of Paragraph 5 of his essay "Aging and Sexuality"?

6. Obviously, death is an important feature in this story. Could Faulkner also have had in mind the death of a particular society or a way of life? Does the story invite you to think of symbols?

Jules Feiffer (b. 1929) is a writer, cartoonist, and playwright who first came to public attention through his cartoons in the Village Voice. *A versatile artist, he has written successful novels, including* Harry, the Rat with Women *(1963); plays, like* Little Murders *(1967); and a book on* The Great Comic Book Heroes *(1965), from which we take this appreciation of the greatest of them all.*

27

JULES FEIFFER

Superman

The advent of the super-hero was a bizarre comeuppance for the American dream. Horatio Alger could no longer make it on his own. He needed "Shazam!" Here was fantasy with a cynically realistic base: once the odds were appraised honestly it was apparent you had to be super to get on in this world.

The particular brilliance of Superman lay not only in the fact that he was the first of the super-heroes, but in the concept of his alter ego. What made Superman different from the legion of imitators to follow was not that when he took off his clothes he could beat up everybody — they all did that. What made Superman extraordinary was his point of origin: Clark Kent.

Remember, Kent was not Superman's true identity as Bruce Wayne was the Batman's or (on radio) Lamont Cranston the Shadow's. Just the opposite. Clark Kent was the fiction. Previous heroes — the Shadow, the Green Hornet, The Lone Ranger — were not only more vulnerable; they were fakes. I don't mean to criticize; it's just a statement of fact. The Shadow had to cloud men's minds to be in business. The Green Hornet had to go through the fetishist fol-de-rol of donning costume, floppy hat, black mask, gas gun, menacing automobile, and insect sound effects before he was even ready to go out in the street. The Lone Ranger needed an accoutremental white horse, an Indian, and an establishing cry of Hi-Yo Silver to separate him from all those other masked men running around the West in days of yesteryear.

4   But Superman had only to wake up in the morning to be Superman. In his case, Clark Kent was the put-on. The fellow with the eyeglasses and the acne and the walk girls laughed at wasn't real, didn't exist, was a sacrificial disguise, an act of discreet martyrdom. *Had they but known!*

5   And for what purpose? Did Superman become Clark Kent in order to lead a normal life, have friends, be known as a nice guy, meet girls? Hardly. There's too much of the hair shirt in the role, too much devotion to the imprimatur of impotence — an insight, perhaps, into the fantasy life of the Man of Steel. Superman as a secret masochist? Field for study there. For if it was otherwise, if the point, the only point, was to lead a "normal life," why not a more typical identity? How can one be a cowardly star reporter, subject to fainting spells in time of crisis, and not expect to raise serious questions?

6   The truth may be that Kent existed not for the purposes of the story but for the reader. He is Superman's opinion of the rest of us, a pointed caricature of what we, the noncriminal element, were really like. His fake identity was our real one. That's why we loved him so. For if that wasn't really us, if there were no Clark Kents, only lots of glasses and cheap suits which, when removed, revealed all of us in our true identities — what a hell of an improved world it would have been!

7   In drawing style, both in figure and costume, Superman was a simplified parody of Flash Gordon. But if Alex Raymond was the Dior for Superman, Joe Shuster set the fashion from then on. Everybody else's super-costumes were copies from his shop. Shuster represented the best of old-style comic book drawing. His work was direct, unprettied — crude and vigorous; as easy to read as a diagram. No creamy lines, no glossy illustrative effects, no touch of that bloodless prefabrication that passes for professionalism these days. Slickness, thank God, was beyond his means. He could not draw well, but he drew single-mindedly — no one could ghost that style. It was the man. When assistants began "improving" the appearance of the strip it promptly went downhill. It looked as though it were being drawn in a bank.

But, oh, those early drawings! Superman running up the sides of   8
dams, leaping over anything that stood in his way (No one drew sky-
scrapers like Shuster. Impressionistic shafts, Superman poised over
them, his leaping leg tucked under his ass, his landing leg tautly
pointed earthward), cleaning and jerking two-ton get-away cars and
pounding them into the sides of cliffs — and all this done lightly,
unportentously, still with that early Slam Bradley exuberance. What
matter that the stories quickly lost interest; that once you've made a
man super you've plotted him out of believable conflicts; that even
super-villains, super-mad scientists and, yes, super-orientals were dull
and lifeless next to the overwhelming image of that which Clark Kent
became when he took off his clothes. So what if the stories were
boring, the villains blah? This was the Superman Show — a touring
road company backing up a great star. Everything was a stage wait
until he came on. Then it was all worth-while.

Besides, for the alert reader there were other fields of interest. It   9
seems that among Lois Lane, Clark Kent, and Superman there existed
a schizoid and chaste *ménage à trois*. Clark Kent loved but felt
abashed with Lois Lane; Superman saved Lois Lane when she was in
trouble, found her a pest the rest of the time. Since Superman and
Clark Kent were the same person this behavior demands explanation.
It can't be that Kent wanted Lois to respect him for himself, since
himself was Superman. Then, it appears, he wanted Lois to respect
him for his fake self, to love him when he acted the coward, to be
there when he pretended he needed her. She never was — so, of course,
he loved her. A typical American romance. Superman never needed
her, never needed anybody — in any event, Lois chased *him* — so, of
course, he didn't love her. He had contempt for her. Another typical
American romance.

Love is really the pursuit of a desired object, not pursuit by it.   10
Once you've caught the object there is no longer any reason to love it,
to have it hanging around. There must be other desirable objects out
there, somewhere. So Clark Kent acted as the control for Superman.
What Kent wanted was just that which Superman didn't want to be
bothered with. Kent wanted Lois, Superman didn't — thus marking
the difference between a sissy and a man. A sissy wanted girls who
scorned him; a man scorned girls who wanted him. Our cultural opposite of the man who didn't make out with women has never been the
man who did — but rather the man who could if he wanted to, but
still didn't. The ideal of masculine strength, whether Gary Cooper's,
Lil Abner's, or Superman's, was for one to be so virile and handsome,

to be in such a position of strength, that he need never go near girls. Except to help them. And then get the hell out. Real rapport was not for women. It was for villains. That's why they got hit so hard.

_____ CONSIDERATIONS _____

1. Study Feiffer's diction in his essay, particularly such word choices as "bizarre comeuppance" (Paragraph 1), "fetishist fol-de-rol" and "accoutremental white horse" (Paragraph 3), "imprimatur of impotence" (Paragraph 5), and "a schizoid and chaste *ménage à trois*" (Paragraph 9). Do such combinations attract or repel you as a reader? What does Feiffer accomplish with such combinations of words?

2. In Paragraphs 9 and 10, Feiffer describes what he calls a "typical American romance," and then defines "love." Write a short essay setting forth your agreement or disagreement with his understanding of that all-engrossing subject.

3. To what extent is the popularity of such comic book heroes as Superman dependent upon a macho view of the sex roles?

4. One of the attractions of Superman, and many other "super-heroes," is his appeal to our fondness for fantasy, particularly that common form of fantasy in which we cast ourselves in favorable roles. Write an essay in which you compare and contrast your own favorite fantasy of this sort with the public one produced by Joe Shuster, creator of Superman.

F. Scott Fitzgerald (1896–1940) was born in St. Paul, Minnesota, graduated from Princeton, and became a best-selling novelist with his first book, This Side of Paradise *(1920), when he was only twenty-four. He married a brilliant, disturbed woman named Zelda Sayre, and lived an extravagant life in the Europe of the twenties, supported mostly by facile short stories that he wrote for money. In 1925, despite dissipation of body and talent, Fitzgerald published his masterpiece,* The Great Gatsby. *As the twenties sank into the depressed thirties, Zelda began to spend much time in asylums. Fitzgerald drank heavily, and his writing gradually lost its public.* Tender Is the Night *(1934), a fine novel, found few readers. To support himself and his ailing wife, Fitzgerald turned to Hollywood. He was not a successful script-writer, and Hollywood regarded him with condescension as a has-been. Before his heart failed in 1940, he had begun a Hollywood novel,* The Last Tycoon, *published as a fragment the year after his death. It has moments of the old greatness.*

Like many writers, Fitzgerald kept notebooks. Not quite a journal, these notebooks assemble the raw material of fiction — conversations overheard, a hint of story, an observation of character, a turn of phrase, or a piece of description. These brief selections sample the notes Fitzgerald kept, his own private storehouse, to be raided for his work.

28

F. SCOTT FITZGERALD
Journal Entries

1   Family quarrels are bitter things. They don't go according to any rules. They're not like aches or wounds; they're more like splits in the skin that won't heal because there's not enough material.

2   The absent-minded gentleman on the train started to get off at the wrong station. As he walked back to his seat he assumed a mirthless smile and said aloud as though he were talking to himself: "I thought this was Great Neck."

3   "When I hear people bragging about their social position and who they are, and all that, I just sit back and laugh. Because I happen to be descended directly from Charlemagne. What do you think of that?" Josephine blushed for him.

4   Suddenly her face resumed that expression which can only come from studying moving picture magazines over and over, and only be described as one long blond wish toward something — a wish that you'd have a wedlock with the youth of Shirley Temple, the earning power of Clark Gable; the love of Clark Gable and the talent of Charles Laughton — and with a bright smile the girl was gone.

5   "The time I fell off a closet shelf."
"You what?"
"I fell off a shelf — and he put it in the paper."

"Well, what were you doing?"
"I just happened to be up on a shelf and I fell off."
"Oh, don't say it."
"I've stopped giving any further explanations. Anyhow, father said it was news."

Three frail dock lights glittered dimly upon innumerable fishing 6
boats heaped like shells along the beach. Farther out in the water there were other lights where a fleet of slender yachts rode the tide with slow dignity, and farther still a full ripe moon made the water bosom into a polished dancing floor.

She wanted to crawl into his pocket and be safe forever. 7

She turned her slender smile full upon Lew for a moment, and 8
then aimed it a little aside, like a pocket torch that might dazzle him.

There was once a moving picture magnate who was shipwrecked 9
on a desert island with nothing but two dozen cans of film.

Story of a man trying to live down his crazy past and encounter- 10
ing it everywhere.

Just when somebody's taken him up and making a big fuss over 11
him, he pours the soup down his hostess' back, kisses the serving maid and passes out in the dog kennel. But he's done it too often. He's run through about everybody, until there's no one left.

"She's really radiunt," she said, "really radiunt." 12

Beginning of a story, *Incorrigible*. 13
Father: Who do you admire?
Son: Andy Gump. Who do you think I admire — George Washington? Grow up!

In Virginia the Italian children say: 14
"Lincoln threw blacks out; now they're back."
"The white people fit the Yankees."
"Yankees *are* white people."
"Not I ever hear tell of."

___ **CONSIDERATIONS** _____

1. Like other serious writers — Nathaniel Hawthorne, Katherine Mansfield, Albert Camus, Henry James, Cesare Pavese, Thomas Hardy, Gerard Manley Hopkins, Feodor Dostoevki — Fitzgerald kept a running logbook of observations, ideas, phrases, questions, and notes, some of which were later developed into stories, poems, plays, or novels. Compare these excerpts from Fitzgerald's notebooks with entries by two or three other writers. Describe and discuss the differences and similarities you find.

2. Select an item from Fitzgerald's notebook and build a short essay around it. Which items seem most useful for this purpose? Why?

3. In excerpt 4, Fitzgerald describes a girl's face as "one long blond wish toward something." Explain this peculiar description of a face. Is it effective or not? Why?

4. Imagine a context in which the descriptive passage "Three frail dock lights . . ." would be appropriate. Explain.

5. In excerpt 10, Fitzgerald puts in one short sentence an idea for a story. Sketch the main elements of the story. Has it already been done? Discuss.

6. Compare and contrast the journals of Fitzgerald and Thomas Wolfe (pages 467–473). How do the two journals reveal different approaches to writing?

Frances Fitzgerald (Lanahan) (b. 1921) is the daughter of Zelda and F. Scott Fitzgerald, known when she was a child as Scottie. She wrote this introduction to her father's letters in 1965.

29

FRANCES FITZGERALD (LANAHAN)
Introduction to *Letters to His Daughter*

In my next incarnation, I may not choose again to be the daughter of a Famous Author. The pay is good, and there are fringe benefits, but the working conditions are too hazardous. People who live entirely by the fertility of their imaginations are fascinating, brilliant, and often charming, but they should be sat next to at dinner parties, not lived with. Imagine depending for your happiness upon a Bernard Shaw or a Somerset Maugham, not to mention such contemporary stars as Norman Mailer! I have the impression that the only people quite as insufferable as writers are painters.

I have much puzzled over the why of this, and have compiled a few tentative answers. First, I suppose it is impossible to form the habit of inventing people, building them up, tearing them down, and moving them around like paper dolls, without doing somewhat the same thing with live ones. Good writers are essentially muckrakers, exposing the scandalous condition of the human soul. It is their job to strip veneers from situations and personalities. The rest of us accept our fellow beings at face value, and swallow what we can't accept.

Writers can't: they have to prod, poke, question, test, doubt, and challenge, which requires a constant flow of fresh victims and fresh experience.

3   Second, there is nothing anybody else can do to help a writer. A company president can take on an executive assistant; a lawyer can hire a clerk; even a housewife can unload up to seventy or eighty per cent of her duties. The poor writer can turn to no one but himself until his work is finished, when he can take it to an editor who will show him how to start all over, by himself.

4   He can never say, "Here, Mary — you know this subject as well as I do — be a dear and finish this paragraph for me, will you?"

5   Third, successful writers, like all successful people, are spoiled and indulged by everybody with whom they come in contact. They are, at the same time, spared the rod of discipline imposed by other occupations. A Senator must face the press, greet thousands of constituents, sit through vistaless Saharas of banquets without the oasis of an entertaining word or a glass of wine. An actress must turn up at the theater or the movie set, take care of her looks, memorize her lines. The poor writer is free to do whatever he chooses; if he chooses to get drunk, who can fire him? Between himself and doom stands no one but his creditor.

6   Revered and pampered, he must sit down at his desk each day alone, without rules or guidelines, exactly as if he had previously accomplished nothing. Small wonder he is not all sweetness and light when he emerges, often unvictoriously, from the battle.

7   So the fact that my father became a difficult parent does not surprise or offend me. He gave me a golden childhood, which is as much as any of us can ask for. I can remember nothing but happiness and delight in his company until the world began to be too much for him, when I was about eleven years old. But from the time the first of the letters in this collection was written, when I first went off to camp, until he died in 1940, appropriately closing the pre-World War II era as he appropriately timed his whole life to coincide with the nation's, I can remember almost nothing but the troubles which were reflected in our relations — my mother's hopeless illness, his own bad health and lack of money, and, hardest of all I think, his literary eclipse.

8   During the last five years of my father's life, he couldn't have bought a book of his in any bookstore; he probably couldn't even have asked for one without getting a blank stare from the saleslady. I am

not sentimental by nature, but once a few years ago when I walked into the bookshop of a remote town and saw a whole shelf of F. Scott Fitzgerald sitting there as naturally as if it had been the works of Shakespeare, I burst into tears. A sick wife, poverty, bad luck — we all have to contend with some of these things, and Daddy had helped bring on a good bit of it himself. But the writing part wasn't fair; God had played one of those trump cards which can defeat even the most valiant of us.

So much has been said about him that, to paraphrase Dorothy 9 Parker, if all the reams of paper about F. Scott Fitzgerald were stretched across the Atlantic, I wouldn't be a bit surprised. Edmund Wilson, Arthur Mizener, Sheilah Graham, Andrew Turnbull, Malcolm Cowley, Vance Bourjaily, Arnold Gingrich, Dan Piper, Matthew Bruccoli, John Kuehl, Glenway Wescott, Morley Callaghan, Burke Wilkinson, not to mention Mr. Hemingway with his piercing jabs at the prone body, or the dozens of others who have written Ph.D. theses and articles in magazines large and small, or Budd Schulberg who made a fortune with his photographic description of my father's lowest moment, have all put it far better than I could. The only thing new I can add is a little bit about me.

I was not a perspicacious teenager, and in fact was probably more 10 self-preoccupied than most. But even I dimly perceived, even then, that my father was not only a genius but a great man in his way, despite his partly self-inflicted torments and his gigantic sins. I knew that he was kind, generous, honorable, and loyal, and I admired him and loved him. But self-preservation being the strongest instinct any of us have, especially when we are young, I also knew that there was only one way for me to survive his tragedy, and that was to ignore it. Looking back, I wish I'd been a less exasperating daughter, more thoughtful, more assiduous and more considerate. I hate knowing how much I must have added to his troubles, which is probably why I haven't written about him, in a personal way, long before this.

I was busy surviving, and what I couldn't ignore in the way of 11 objectionable behavior, such as an inkwell flying past my ear, I would put up in the emotional attic as soon as possible. After the ghastly tea-dance, for example, the preparation for which is mentioned in these letters, my friend Peaches Finney and I went back to her house in a state of semi-hysteria. Her parents, who were about the nicest and most considerate people I've ever known, fed us eggs and consolation. Within two hours we were dressed and curled, and deposited by them at the door of the next Christmas party. Meredith Boyce, then the best sixteen-year-old dancer in Baltimore, actually stopped dancing long enough to ask me to sit down.

12   "How can you seem so *cheerful?*" he asked. He was a very good friend; in fact I flattered myself that we had a case of puppy love. "After what happened this afternoon?"

13   "Nothing happened this afternoon," I said.

14   "Are you being brave? Smiling through the tears?"

15   "Not at all. It just never happened, that's all."

16   He told me much later that he had been shocked by my detachment that evening. I asked him why.

17   "Because kids should care more about their parents," he said. "He was so drunk, and so pitiful, and you acted as if he wasn't there."

18   "Meredith, I *had* to," I said. "Don't you see that if I'd allowed myself to care, I couldn't have stood it?"

19   He was unconvinced — he probably still is — and in one way he was right. The trouble with the ostrich approach is that if you use it long enough, it becomes a habit. There are comic-strip jokes about the husband-wife situation in which neither one hears the other until somebody yells "FIRE!" I developed an immunity against my father, so that when he bawled me out for something, I simply didn't hear it.

20   So these gorgeous letters, these absolute pearls of wisdom and literary style, would arrive at Vassar and I'd simply examine them for checks and news, then stick them in my lower right-hand drawer. I'm proud of myself for saving them; I knew they were great letters, and my motives were certainly not acquisitive, because Daddy was an impecunious and obscure author then, with no prospect in sight of *The Great Gatsby* being translated into twenty-seven languages. I saved them the way you save *War and Peace* to read, or Florence to spend some time in later.

21   But at the time I didn't want to be told what to read, how to read it, what courses to take, whether to try out for the college paper, what girls to room with, what football games to go to, how to feel about the Spanish Civil War, whether or not to drink, whether or not to "throw myself away" (if only Daddy had had a daughter at Vassar *now*, what glorious prose he could have composed on this subject!), not to write music for our campus productions, not to put a peroxide streak in my hair, not to go to a debutante party in New York, whether or not to try my hand at social work, and so on and on until I half expected, at the age of eighteen, to be lectured to on when to take a bath.

22   The thing he disapproved of most was a weekend I never took;

Andrew Turnbull asked me what I actually did — I think I went down for a surreptitious visit to the Harold Obers in Scarsdale, who were my substitute parents. There must have been twenty telegrams from California before I got back to college Sunday night.

The thing he approved of most was my going to Harvard Summer   23
School, the year he died. It does have an intellectual-sounding ring, and I'm glad I gave him a sense of accomplishment. In all of my some forty years now, I don't think I've ever done anything so utterly, ridiculously frivolous. I met up with a group of charming people who had flunked out of Harvard for one reason or another, and had such a good time I never took the exams. I spent more time in Cambridge night clubs, wasting time, than I've ever had a chance to do before or since. You'll be relieved to hear that Daddy never learned the full extent of what he doubtless would have considered his daughter's slothfulness and wanton preparation for a life of sin.

Malcolm Cowley said in a review in *The New York Times* once   24
that "Fitzgerald wasn't writing those letters to his daughter at Vassar; he was writing them to himself at Princeton." This is the point, really. I was an imaginary daughter, as fictional as one of his early heroines. He made me sound far more popular and glamorous than I was — I was actually only vaguely pretty, and only danced with by friends, of which fortunately I had a number — but he wanted me so desperately to be so that in these letters, I sound like my contemporary glamor queen, Brenda Frazier. He also made me sound more wicked and hell-bent on pleasure than I could possibly have been. It's true that I preferred boys, Fred Astaire, and fun to the sheer hard labor of working. I *still* prefer boys, Fred Astaire, and fun to the sheer hard labor of working. Doesn't almost everybody?

There's a moral to all of this, and I'm about to get it off my chest.   25

To college students (including my own two): "Don't ignore any   26
good advice, unless it comes from your own parents. Somebody else's parents might very well be right."

To parents (poor struggling creatures): "Don't drop your pearls   27
before swine, at least without making sure the swine are going to put them in the lower right-hand drawer."

Listen carefully to my father, now. Because what he offers is good   28
advice, and I'm sure if he hadn't been my own father that I loved and "hated" simultaneously, I would have profited by it and be the best

educated, most attractive, most successful, most faultless woman on earth today.

_____ CONSIDERATIONS _____

1. In the first part of her essay — say, through Paragraph 7 — Lanahan uses a traditional method of organizing her material. Do you recognize it? Study that section; then apply the method in your next essay.

2. Lanahan says, in Paragraph 3, "there is nothing anybody else can do to help a writer." Writing is lonely work dependent on a writer's self-discipline. What motivates that kind of discipline? Are some motivations more productive than others?

3. In Paragraph 9, Lanahan refers to the enormous body of material written about her famous father. You can sample that criticism, interpretation, and biography by looking into the *Fitzgerald/Hemingway Annual*, which has appeared each year since 1969.

4. Lanahan's memories of her father produce a mixture of emotions, including remorse, sadness, and a sense of what she calls the "tragedy" of his life. Yet through most of her essay she preserves a lightness of tone. Locate passages or phrases or word-choices that illustrate this lightness. Does the tone diminish or heighten her seriousness?

5. In one of his letters to his daughter, Fitzgerald said he did not believe a person could write "succinct prose" without first attempting an "iambic pentameter sonnet" and reading Browning's short dramatic monologues. You might try writing poetry yourself as a means of developing your prose style.

6. Imagine yourself at the age of forty or fifty. Keeping in mind what Lanahan says in Paragraphs 21, 26, 27, and 28, compose a letter to your son or daughter just entering college.

30

F. SCOTT FITZGERALD
Letters to His Daughter

La Paix, Rodgers' Forge
Towson, Maryland

AUGUST 8, 1933

Dear Pie:

I feel very strongly about you doing [your] duty. Would you give 1
me a little more documentation about your reading in French? I am
glad you are happy — but I never believe much in happiness. I never
believe in misery either. Those are things you see on the stage or the
screen or the printed page, they never really happen to you in life.

All I believe in in life is the rewards for virtue (according to your 2
talents) and the *punishments* for not fulfilling your duties, which are
double costly. If there is such a volume in the camp library, will you
ask Mrs. Tyson to let you look up a sonnet of Shakespeare's in which
the line occurs *"Lilies that fester smell far worse than weeds."*

Have had no thoughts today, life seems composed of getting up a 3
Saturday Evening Post story. I think of you, and always pleasantly;
but if you call me "Pappy" again I am going to take the White Cat out
and beat his bottom *hard, six times for every time you are imperti-
nent.* Do you react to that?

4   I will arrange the camp bill.
        Halfwit, I will conclude.
5   Things to worry about:
        Worry about courage
        Worry about cleanliness
        Worry about efficiency
        Worry about horsemanship
        Worry about . . .
6   Things not to worry about:
        Don't worry about popular opinion
        Don't worry about dolls
        Don't worry about the past
        Don't worry about the future
        Don't worry about growing up
        Don't worry about anybody getting ahead of you
        Don't worry about triumph
        Don't worry about failure unless it comes through your own fault
        Don't worry about mosquitoes
        Don't worry about flies
        Don't worry about insects in general
        Don't worry about parents
        Don't worry about boys
        Don't worry about disappointments
        Don't worry about pleasures
        Don't worry about satisfactions
7   Things to think about:
        What am I really aiming at?
        How good am I really in comparison to my contemporaries in
    regard to:
        (a) Scholarship
        (b) Do I really understand about people and am I able to get along
    with them?
        (c) Am I trying to make my body a useful instrument or am I
    neglecting it?

                                        With dearest love,
                                            [*Daddy*]

8   P.S. My come-back to your calling me Pappy is christening you by the
    word Egg, which implies that you belong to a very rudimentary state
    of life and that I could break you up and crack you open at my will

and I think it would be a word that would hang on if I ever told it to your contemporaries. "Egg Fitzgerald." How would you like that to go through life with — "Eggie Fitzgerald" or "Bad Egg Fitzgerald" or any form that might occur to fertile minds? Try it once more and I swear to God I will hang it on you and it will be up to you to shake it off. Why borrow trouble?

Love anyhow.

OCTOBER 20, 1936

Don't be a bit discouraged about your story not being tops. At the same time, I am not going to encourage you about it, because, after all, if you want to get into the big time, you have to have your own fences to jump and learn from experience. Nobody ever became a writer just by wanting to be one. If you have anything to say, anything you feel nobody has ever said before, you have got to feel it so desperately that you will find some way to say it that nobody has ever found before, so that the thing you have to say and the way of saying it blend as one matter — as indissolubly as if they were conceived together.

Let me preach again for a moment: I mean that what you have felt and thought will, by itself, invent a new style, so that when people talk about style they are always a little astonished at the newness of it, because they think that it is only *style* that they are talking about, when what they are talking about is the attempt to express a new idea with such force that it will have the originality of the thought. It is an awfully lonesome business, and, as you know, I never wanted you to go into it, but if you are going into it at all I want you to go into it knowing the sort of things that took me years to learn.

Why are you whining about such matters as study hall, etc., when you deliberately picked this school[1] as the place you wanted to go above all places? Of course it is hard. Nothing any good isn't hard, and you know you have never been brought up soft, or are you quitting on me suddenly? Darling, you know I love you, and I expect you to live up absolutely to what I laid out for you in the beginning.

Scott

Ethel Walker's

Grove Park Inn
Asheville, North Carolina

NOVEMBER 17, 1936

Dearest Pie:

1   I got a School Letter saying that Thanksgiving Day is best, and it is better for me that way. There is no particular advantage in going out two or three times rather than one, without particular objectives; the idea is to go out once and have a good time. I'll be delighted to meet whoever you want, and our engagement is on Thanksgiving Day.

2   (This is a parenthesis: I got the little charms that you sent me for my birthday, the bells dangling and the mule, and appreciated your thought of me — you little donkey!)

3   Park Avenue girls are hard, aren't they? Usually the daughters of "up-and-coming" men and, in a way, the inevitable offspring of that type. It's the "Yankee push" to its last degree, a sublimation of the sort of Jay Gould who began by peddling bad buttons to a county and ended, with the same system of peddler's morals, by peddling five dollar railroads to a nation.

4   Don't mistake me. I think of myself always as a northerner — and I think of you the same way. Nevertheless, we are all of one nation and you will find all the lassitude and laziness there that you despise, enough to fill Savannah and Charleston, just as down here you will find the same "go getter" principle in the Carolinas.

5   I don't know whether you will stay there another year — it all depends on your marks and your work, and I can't give you the particular view of life that I have (which as you know is a tragic one), without dulling your enthusiasm. A whole lot of people have found life a whole lot of fun. I have not found it so. But, I had a hell of a lot of fun when I was in my twenties and thirties; and I feel that it is your duty to accept the sadness, the tragedy of the world we live in, with a certain *esprit*.

6   Now, insofar as your course is concerned, there is no question of your dropping mathematics and taking the easiest way to go into Vassar, and being one of the girls fitted for nothing except to reflect other people without having any particular character of your own. I want you to take mathematics up to the limit of what the school offers. I want you to take physics and I want you to take chemistry. I don't care about your English courses or your French courses at present. If you don't know two languages and the ways that men chose to express their thoughts in those languages by this time, then you don't sound

like my daughter. You are an only child, but that doesn't give you any right to impose on that fact.

I want you to know certain basic scientific principles, and I feel that it is impossible to learn them unless you have gone as far into mathematics as coordinate geometry. *I don't want you to give up mathematics next year.* I learned about writing from doing something that I didn't have any taste for. If you don't carry your mathematics such as coordinate geometry (conic sections), you will have strayed far afield from what I had planned for you. I don't insist on the calculus, but it is certainly nothing to be decided by what is easiest. You are going into Vassar with mathematical credits and a certain side of your life there is going to be scientific. 7

Honey, I wish I could see you. It would be so much easier to go over these important matters without friction, but at a distance it seems rather tough that you are inclined to slide into the subjects that are easy for you, like modern languages. 8

No more until I see you Thanksgiving. 9

With dearest love,
F. Scott Fitz

P.S. Sorry you are on bounds — feel as if I had been the same for six months. However I have bought an ancient Packard roadster and get out more now. I always allow for your exuberance but I hope this doesn't come from a feud with any special teacher, or from any indiscretion of speech, a fault you should be beginning to control. 10

_____ **CONSIDERATIONS** _____

Letter of August 8, 1933

1. "I never believe much in happiness. I never believe in misery either," writes Fitzgerald in Paragraph 1. What, then, does that leave him?

2. In Paragraph 2, Fitzgerald urges his daughter to find a particular sonnet. He gives her the last line as a clue. Find the line in *Familiar Quotations*, by John Bartlett, 15th Edition (Little, Brown and Company, new edition 1981). Use Bartlett to identify the sonnet, find it in your college library, read it, and explain its relevance in Fitzgerald's letter.

3. See if you can sort out the items in the long list of "Things to worry about" and "Things not to worry about." Ignore those two subheadings of

Fitzgerald's and make up your own categories. Which items do you find most difficult to classify? Which items would be hardest to explain to a fourteen-year-old? Why?

4. Notice Fitzgerald's P.S. on a possible nickname for his daughter. Recall nicknames within your own family or circle of friends. Use some of this experience to illustrate an essay on the importance of nicknames. Where does the word "nickname" come from?

Letter of October 20, 1936

1. In the last sentence of Paragraph 1, Fitzgerald sets forth an ideal that few writers achieve. Alexander Pope, writing about poetry in 1709, expressed the same ideal in this single line: "The sound must seem an echo to the sense." Can you find any writers in this book who approach that ideal?

2. "Nobody ever became a writer just by wanting to be one," writes Fitzgerald in Paragraph 1. Would the sentence make just as much sense if you substituted for "writer" any of these: accountant, dancer, botanist, potter, historian, translator, engineer, salesman, philosopher, lover, general, senator, chef, airline pilot?

3. How popular do you think Fitzgerald's remark, "Nothing any good isn't hard," would be today? Do the following rephrasings say the same thing? "Anything any good is hard." "Nothing that isn't hard is any good." "Anything that isn't hard is good." "Nothing that's hard is any good."

4. Fitzgerald says he will not encourage his daughter about her story. Does he provide an adequate explanation of his refusal? Can you find illustrations of that explanation in your own experience?

Letter of November 17, 1936

1. Judging by Paragraphs 6 and 7, father and daughter were apparently not in complete agreement about her program of studies. Speculate on why Fitzgerald, a writer of fiction, would be so insistent that she get a thorough grounding in mathematics and scientific principles. What other author in this book might agree with him?

2. What evidence do you find in this letter that Fitzgerald had a definite plan for his daughter's education? Discuss the wisdom of parental planning of such matters and of the offspring's acceptance of such planning.

3. Who was the Jay Gould that Fitzgerald alludes to in Paragraph 3? Find out a little about him as a means of understanding why Fitzgerald makes the reference in this context.

4. Compare Fitzgerald's statement in the last sentence of Paragraph 5 with Lillian Hellman's remarks in the last paragraph of her essay "Runaway." Imagine the young Lillian receiving a letter from her father like this one of Fitzgerald's. Combine all this in an essay on the ideal father-daughter (or father-son) relationship.

Benjamin Franklin (1706–1790) invented practically every-thing, though perhaps we go too far when we credit him with inventing electricity. Self-educated, intellectual, practical, energetic, mischievous, he founded the American post office, he invented the Franklin stove, he represented the colonies in England before the Revolution, he represented the new republic in France after the Revolution, and he fathered a number of ille-gitimate children.

A solid stylist in his writing, he undertook subjects scientific and moral and philosophical; he wrote an autobiography, and he wrote a book about chess. When he was young he founded a successful printing business in Philadelphia, and created Poor Richard as a font of pithy wisdom in the annual almanacs he published. Here follows a brief selection of Poor Richard's say-ings, cynical and energetic and as American as their author.

31

BENJAMIN FRANKLIN
From Poor Richard's Almanack

He's a Fool that makes
his Doctor his Heir.   1

A countryman between two Lawyers,
is like a fish between two cats.   2

There are no ugly loves, nor handsome Prisons.   3

Keep your eyes wide open before marriage,
half shut afterwards.   4

5 When there's Marriage without love,
   There will be Love without marriage.

6 The greatest monarch on the proudest throne
   is oblig'd to sit upon his own arse.

7 Laws too gentle are seldom obeyed,
   too severe, seldom executed.

8 Lend money to an enemy, and thou'lt gain him,
   to a friend and thou'lt lose him.

9 There are three faithful friends —
   An old wife, an old dog,
   and ready money.

10 Learn of the skillful:
   He that teaches himself
   hath a fool for a master.

11 Necessity never made a good bargain.

12 Eat to live and not live to eat.

13 Drink does not drown Care, but waters it,
   and makes it grow fast.

14 Early to bed and early to rise
   Makes a man healthy, wealthy, and wise.

15 Each year one vicious habit rooted out,
   In time might make the worst man
   good throughout.

16 Pardoning the bad is injuring the good.

17 All would live long
   but none would be old.

18 Hunger never saw bad bread.

Beware of meat twice boil'd. 19
And of an old foe reconcil'd.

Fish and visitors stink in three days. 20

He that lives upon hope, dies fasting. 21

None preaches better than the ant, 22
and she says nothing.

Who has deceiv'd thee as oft as thy self? 23

Beware of him that is slow to anger: 24
He is angry for something, and will not be pleased for nothing.

Suspicion may be no great fault, 25
but showing it may be a great one.

There are three things extreamly hard, 26
steel, a diamond, and to know one's self.

Most people return small favours, 27
acknowledge middling ones,
and repay great ones with ingratitude.

Mankind are very odd creatures; 28
one half censure that they practise,
the other half practise what they censure,
the rest always say and do as they ought.

Take heed of the vinegar of sweet wine 29
and the anger of good-nature.

The wolf sheds his coat once a year, 30
his disposition never.

There was never a good knife made of bad steel. 31

Silence is not always a sign of wisdom 32
but babbling is ever a mark of folly.

33 When you speak to a man, look on his eyes;
when he speaks to thee, look on his mouth.

34 Strange! That a man who has wit enough
to write a satire
Should have folly enough to publish it.

——— CONSIDERATIONS ———————————————————

1. Compare and contrast Poor Richard's sayings with "Some Devil's Definitions" offered by Ambrose Bierce on pages 59–62. What are some similarities and differences?

2. Poor Richard specialized in epigrams. Look up that term in a literary dictionary or handbook and read examples by other authors. What do you consider to be the attributes of a successful epigram? Try your hand at this peculiar, concentrated literary form.

3. How does the English epigram differ from the Japanese *haiku*, a seventeen-syllable poem usually written in three short lines? Are these poetic forms useful to a student of prose composition?

4. Select one of Poor Richard's sayings, and, using it as a thesis statement, build an essay around it.

5. Which of Poor Richard's statements surprises you the most as coming from that grand figure, Benjamin Franklin? Why? Consider how our previous impressions of a writer influence our expectations as we read.

6. Study one of the argumentative essays in this text — for example, one by Caroline Bird, Kenneth E. Boulding, D. H. Lawrence, or Gore Vidal. Summarize the writer's main point in a single, complete sentence. Then, after looking over Poor Richard's sayings again, polish and shape that sentence until it looks and sounds like an epigram.

Robert Frost (1874–1963) was born in California and became the great poet of New England. He published many books of poems, and won the Pulitzer Prize three times. A popular figure, Frost was admired as a gentle, affectionate, avuncular figure given to country sayings. The private Frost was another man — guilty, jealous, generous, bitter, sophisticated, occasionally triumphant, and always complicated.

When President John F. Kennedy was inaugurated in January 1961, he asked Frost to read a poem as part of the ceremony — the first American poet so honored. Frost wrote some lines for the occasion, later published as "For John F. Kennedy His Inauguration," but when he tried to read them at the inauguration, the glare of sun on white paper blinded him; although Vice-President Lyndon Johnson shaded the paper with his hat, Frost was unable to deliver the special lines. Instead, he recited from memory this sonnet on nationality that he had written years before — it was first published in 1942 — but as he repeated it for President Kennedy's inauguration, he changed the next to last word to "will."

32

ROBERT FROST

The Gift Outright

The land was ours before we were the land's.
She was our land more than a hundred years
Before we were her people. She was ours
In Massachusetts, in Virginia,
5   But we were England's, still colonials,
Possessing what we still were unpossessed by,
Possessed by what we now no more possessed.
Something we were withholding made us weak
Until we found out that it was ourselves
10 We were withholding from our land of living,
And forthwith found salvation in surrender.
Such as we were we gave ourselves outright
(The deed of gift was many deeds of war)
To the land vaguely realizing westward,
15 But still unstoried, artless, unenhanced,
Such as she was, such as she would become.

Martin Gansberg (b. 1920) has edited and reported for The
New York Times *for forty years. This story, written in 1964, has
been widely reprinted. Largely because of Gansberg's account,
the murder of Kitty Genovese has become a well-known example
of citizen apathy. When Gansberg returned to the neighborhood
fifteen years afterward, revisiting the place of the murder with a
television crew, the people had not changed: still, no one wanted
to get involved.*

33

MARTIN GANSBERG

38 Who Saw Murder Didn't Call the Police

For more than half an hour 38 respectable, law-abiding citizens   1
in Queens watched a killer stalk and stab a woman in three separate
attacks in Kew Gardens.

Twice their chatter and the sudden glow of their bedroom lights   2
interrupted him and frightened him off. Each time he returned, sought
her out, and stabbed her again. Not one person telephoned the police
during the assault; one witness called after the woman was dead.

That was two weeks ago today.   3

Still shocked is Assistant Chief Inspector Frederick M. Lussen,   4
in charge of the borough's detectives and a veteran of 25 years of
homicide investigations. He can give a matter-of-fact recitation on
many murders. But the Kew Gardens slaying baffles him — not
because it is a murder, but because the "good people" failed to call the
police.

5   "As we have reconstructed the crime," he said, "the assailant had three chances to kill this woman during a 35-minute period. He returned twice to complete the job. If we had been called when he first attacked, the woman might not be dead now."

6   This is what the police say happened beginning at 3:20 A.M. in the staid, middle-class, tree-lined Austin Street area:

7   Twenty-eight-year-old Catherine Genovese, who was called Kitty by almost everyone in the neighborhood, was returning home from her job as manager of a bar in Hollis. She parked her red Fiat in a lot adjacent to the Kew Gardens Long Island Rail Road Station, facing Mowbray Place. Like many residents of the neighborhood, she had parked there day after day since her arrival from Connecticut a year ago, although the railroad frowns on the practice.

8   She turned off the lights of her car, locked the door, and started to walk the 100 feet to the entrance of her apartment at 82–70 Austin Street, which is in a Tudor building, with stores in the first floor and apartments on the second.

9   The entrance to the apartment is in the rear of the building because the front is rented to retail stores. At night the quiet neighborhood is shrouded in the slumbering darkness that marks most residential areas.

10   Miss Genovese noticed a man at the far end of the lot, near a seven-story apartment house at 82–40 Austin Street. She halted. Then, nervously, she headed up Austin Street toward Lefferts Boulevard, where there is a call box to the 102nd Police Precinct in nearby Richmond Hill.

11   She got as far as a street light in front of a bookstore before the man grabbed her. She screamed. Lights went on in the 10-story apartment house at 82–67 Austin Street, which faces the bookstore. Windows slid open and voices punctuated the early-morning stillness.

12   Miss Genovese screamed: "Oh, my God, he stabbed me! Please help me! Please help me!"

13   From one of the upper windows in the apartment house, a man called down: "Let that girl alone!"

14   The assailant looked up at him, shrugged and walked down Austin Street toward a white sedan parked a short distance away. Miss Genovese struggled to her feet.

15   Lights went out. The killer returned to Miss Genovese, now trying to make her way around the side of the building by the parking lot to get to her apartment. The assailant stabbed her again.

"I'm dying!" she shrieked. "I'm dying!" 16

Windows were opened again, and lights went on in many apart- 17
ments. The assailant got into his car and drove away. Miss Genovese
staggered to her feet. A city bus, O–10, the Lefferts Boulevard line to
Kennedy International Airport, passed. It was 3:35 A.M.

The assailant returned. By then, Miss Genovese had crawled to 18
the back of the building, where the freshly painted brown doors to the
apartment house held out hope for safety. The killer tried the first
door; she wasn't there. At the second door, 82–62 Austin Street, he
saw her slumped on the floor at the foot of the stairs. He stabbed her
a third time — fatally.

It was 3:50 by the time the police received their first call, from a 19
man who was a neighbor of Miss Genovese. In two minutes they were
at the scene. The neighbor, a 70-year-old woman, and another woman
were the only persons on the street. Nobody else came forward.

The man explained that he had called the police after much 20
deliberation. He had phoned a friend in Nassau County for advice and
then he had crossed the roof of the building to the apartment of the
elderly woman to get her to make the call.

"I didn't want to get involved," he sheepishly told the police. 21

Six days later, the police arrested Winston Moseley, a 29-year-old 22
business-machine operator, and charged him with homicide. Moseley
had no previous record. He is married, has two children and owns a
home at 133–19 Sutter Avenue, South Ozone Park, Queens. On
Wednesday, a court committed him to Kings County Hospital for
phychiatric observation.

When questioned by the police, Moseley also said that he had 23
slain Mrs. Annie May Johnson, 24, of 146–12 133d Avenue, Jamaica,
on Feb. 29 and Barbara Kralik, 15, of 174–17 140th Avenue, Springfield
Gardens, last July. In the Kralik case, the police are holding Alvin L.
Mitchell, who is said to have confessed that slaying.

The police stressed how simple it would have been to have gotten 24
in touch with them. "A phone call," said one of the detectives, "would
have done it." The police may be reached by dialing "O" for operator
or SPring 7–3100.

Today witnesses from the neighborhood, which is made up of 25
one-family homes in the $35,000 to $60,000 range with the exception
of the two apartment houses near the railroad station, find it difficult
to explain why they didn't call the police.

A housewife, knowingly if quite casually, said, "We thought it 26
was a lover's quarrel." A husband and wife both said, "Frankly, we

were afraid." They seemed aware of the fact that events might have been different. A distraught woman, wiping her hands in her apron, said, "I didn't want my husband to get involved."

27   One couple, now willing to talk about that night, said they heard the first screams. The husband looked thoughtfully at the bookstore where the killer first grabbed Miss Genovese.

28   "We went to the window to see what was happening," he said, "but the light from our bedroom made it difficult to see the street." The wife, still apprehensive, added: "I put out the light and we were able to see better."

29   Asked why they hadn't called the police, she shrugged and replied: "I don't know."

30   A man peeked out from a slight opening in the doorway to his apartment and rattled off an account of the killer's second attack. Why hadn't he called the police at the time? "I was tired," he said without emotion. "I went back to bed."

31   It was 4:25 A.M. when the ambulance arrived to take the body of Miss Genovese. It drove off. "Then," a solemn police detective said, "the people came out."

_____ **CONSIDERATIONS** _____

1. Obviously — though not overtly — Gansberg's newspaper account is a condemnation of the failure of ordinary citizens to feel social responsibility. Explain how the writer makes his purpose obvious without openly stating it. Compare his method with Orwell's use of implication in "A Hanging."

2. In Paragraph 7, Gansberg tells us that Catherine Genovese was called Kitty and that she drove a red Fiat. Are these essential details? If not, why does this writer use them?

3. Newspapers use short paragraphs for visual relief. If you were making this story into a paper, how might you change the paragraphing?

4. Is Gansberg's opening sentence a distortion of the facts? Read his account carefully before you answer; then explain and support your answer with reference to other parts of the story.

5. Gansberg's newspaper report was published nearly twenty years ago. Are similar incidents more common now than then? Were they more common then than in the 1940s, 1920s, 1900s? In what way does the coverage by newspapers and television affect your impressions? What sources could you use to find the facts?

Lillian Hellman (b. 1905) is a playwright, born in New Orleans, who grew up in New Orleans and New York City. She graduated from New York University, and went to work in publishing. The Children's Hour *(1934), her first great success on Broadway, was followed by her most famous play,* The Little Foxes *(1939), and* Watch on the Rhine *(1941). She also wrote the book for Leonard Bernstein's musical,* Candide.

Hellman's recent writings have been autobiographical, and include Pentimento *(1973),* Scoundrel Time *(1977), and* An Unfinished Woman, *which won the National Book Award in 1970. These narratives were collected into one volume with new commentary by the author:* Three *(1979). In 1980 she published* Maybe: A Story.

The anecdote below, which is from An Unfinished Woman, *tells of a climactic episode in the transition from childhood to adolescence, and shows the rebelliousness, strong feeling, and independence that become themes of the autobiography.*

_34_

LILLIAN HELLMAN

Runaway

It was that night that I disappeared, and that night that Fizzy said 1
I was disgusting mean, and Mr. Stillman said I would forever pain my
mother and father, and my father turned on both of them and said he
would handle his family affairs himself without comments from
strangers. But he said it too late. He had come home very angry with
me: the jeweler, after my father's complaints about his unreliability,
had found the lock of hair in the back of the watch. What started out

to be a mild reproof on my father's part soon turned angry when I wouldn't explain about the hair. (My father was often angry when I was most like him.) He was so angry that he forgot that he was attacking me in front of the Stillmans, my old rival Fizzy, and the delighted Mrs. Dreyfus, a new, rich boarder who only that afternoon had complained about my bad manners. My mother left the room when my father grew angry with me. Hannah, passing through, put up her hand as if to stop my father and then, frightened of the look he gave her, went out to the porch. I sat on the couch, astonished at the pain in my head. I tried to get up from the couch, but one ankle turned and I sat down again, knowing for the first time the rampage that could be caused in me by anger. The room began to have other forms, the people were no longer men and women, my head was not my own. I told myself that my head had gone somewhere and I have little memory of anything after my Aunt Jenny came into the room and said to my father, "Don't you remember?" I have never known what she meant, but I knew that soon after I was moving up the staircase, that I slipped and fell a few steps, that when I woke up hours later in my bed, I found a piece of angel cake — an old love, an old custom — left by my mother on my pillow. The headache was worse and I vomited out of the window. Then I dressed, took my red purse, and walked a long way down St. Charles Avenue. A St. Charles Avenue mansion had on its back lawn a famous doll's-house, an elaborate copy of the mansion itself, built years before for the small daughter of the house. As I passed this showpiece, I saw a policeman and moved swiftly back to the doll palace and crawled inside. If I had known about the fantasies of the frightened, that ridiculous small house would not have been so terrible for me. I was surrounded by ornate, carved reproductions of the mansion furniture, scaled for children, bisque figurines in miniature, a working toilet seat of gold leaf in suitable size, small draperies of damask with a sign that said "From the damask of Marie Antoinette," a miniature samovar with small bronze cups, and a tiny Madame Récamier couch on which I spent the night, my legs on the floor. I must have slept, because I woke from a nightmare and knocked over a bisque figurine. The noise frightened me, and since it was now almost light, in one of those lovely mist mornings of late spring when every flower in New Orleans seems to melt and mix with the air, I crawled out. Most of that day I spent walking, although I had a long session in the ladies' room of the railroad station. I had four dollars and two bits, but that wasn't much when you meant it to last forever and when you knew it would not be easy for a fourteen-year-old girl to find work in a city where too many people knew her. Three times I stood in line at the railroad ticket windows to ask where I could go for four dollars, but each time the question seemed too dangerous and I knew no other way of asking.

Toward evening, I moved to the French Quarter, feeling sad and   2
envious as people went home to dinner. I bought a few Tootsie Rolls and a half loaf of bread and went to the St. Louis Cathedral in Jackson Square. (It was that night that I composed the prayer that was to become, in the next five years, an obsession, mumbled over and over through the days and nights: "God forgive me, Papa forgive me, Mama forgive me, Sophronia, Jenny, Hannah, and all others, through this time and that time, in life and in death." When I was nineteen, my father, who had made several attempts through the years to find out what my lip movements meant as I repeated the prayer, said, "How much would you take to stop that? Name it and you've got it." I suppose I was sick of the nonsense by that time because I said, "A leather coat and a feather fan," and the next day he bought them for me.) After my loaf of bread, I went looking for a bottle of soda pop and discovered, for the first time, the whorehouse section around Bourbon Street. The women were ranged in the doorways of the cribs, making the first early evening offers to sailors, who were the only men in the streets. I wanted to stick around and see how things like that worked, but the second or third time I circled the block, one of the girls called out to me. I couldn't understand the words, but the voice was angry enough to make me run toward the French Market.

The Market was empty except for two old men. One of them   3
called to me as I went past, and I turned to see that he had opened his pants and was shaking what my circle called "his thing." I flew across the street into the coffee stand, forgetting that the owner had known me since I was a small child when my Aunt Jenny would rest from her marketing tour with a cup of fine, strong coffee.

He said, in the patois, *"Que faites, ma 'fant? Je suis fermé."*   4

I said, *"Rien. My tante attend"* — Could I have a doughnut?   5

He brought me two doughnuts, saying one was *lagniappe*, but I   6
took my doughnuts outside when he said, *"Mais où est vo' tante à c' heure?"*

I fell asleep with my doughnuts behind a shrub in Jackson Square.   7
The night was damp and hot and through the sleep were many voices and, much later, there was music from somewhere near the river.

When all sounds had ended, I woke, turned my head, and knew I was being watched. Two rats were sitting a few feet from me. I urinated on my dress, crawled backwards to stand up, screamed as I ran up the steps of St. Louis Cathedral and pounded on the doors. I don't know when I stopped screaming or how I got to the railroad station, but I stood against the wall trying to tear off my dress and only knew I was doing it when two women stopped to stare at me. I began to have cramps in my stomach of a kind I had never known before. I went into the ladies' room and sat bent in a chair, whimpering with pain. After a while the cramps stopped, but I had an intimation, when I looked into the mirror, of something happening to me: my face was blotched, and there seemed to be circles and twirls I had never seen before, the straight blonde hair was damp with sweat, and a paste of green from the shrub had made lines on my jaw. I had gotten older.

8   Sometime during that early morning I half washed my dress, threw away my pants, put cold water on my hair. Later in the morning a cleaning woman appeared, and after a while began to ask questions that frightened me. When she put down her mop and went out of the room, I ran out of the station. I walked, I guess, for many hours, but when I saw a man on Canal Street who worked in Hannah's office, I realized that the sections of New Orleans that were known to me were dangerous for me.

9   Years before, when I was a small child, Sophronia and I would go to pick up, or try on, pretty embroidered dresses that were made for me by a colored dressmaker called Bibettera. A block up from Bibettera's there had been a large ruin of a house with a sign, ROOMS — CLEAN — CHEAP, and cheerful people seemed always to be moving in and out of the house. The door of the house was painted a bright pink. I liked that and would discuss with Sophronia why we didn't live in a house with a pink door.

10   Bibettera was long since dead, so I knew I was safe in this Negro neighborhood. I went up and down the block several times, praying that things would work and I could take my cramps to bed. I knocked on the pink door. It was answered immediately by a small young man.

11   I said, "Hello." He said nothing.

12   I said, "I would like to rent a room, please."

13   He closed the door but I waited, thinking he had gone to get the lady of the house. After a long time, a middle-aged woman put her head out of a second-floor window and said, "What you at?"

14   I said, "I would like to rent a room, please. My mama is a widow

and has gone to work across the river. She gave me money and said to come here until she called for me."

"Who your mama?" 15

"Er. My mama." 16

"What you at? Speak out." 17

"I told you. I have money . . ." But as I tried to open my purse, 18
the voice grew angry.

"This a nigger house. Get you off. *Vite.*" 19

I said, in a whisper, "I know. I'm part nigger." 20

The small young man opened the front door. He was laughing. 21
"You part mischief. Get the hell out of here."

I said, "Please" — and then, "I'm related to Sophronia Mason. 22
She told me to come. Ask her."

Sophronia and her family were respected figures in New Orleans 23
Negro circles, and because I had some vague memory of her stately
bow to somebody as she passed this house, I believed they knew her.
If they told her about me I would be in trouble, but phones were not
usual then in poor neighborhoods, and I had no other place to go.

The woman opened the door. Slowly I went into the hall. 24

I said, "I won't stay long. I have four dollars and Sophronia will 25
give more if . . ."

The woman pointed up the stairs. She opened the door of a small 26
room. "Washbasin place down the hall. Toilet place behind the
kitchen. Two-fifty and no fuss, no bother."

I said, "Yes, ma'am, yes ma'am," but as she started to close the 27
door, the young man appeared.

"Where your bag?" 28

"Bag?" 29

"Nobody put up here without no bag." 30

"Oh. You mean the bag with my clothes? It's at the station. I'll 31
go and get it later . . ." I stopped because I knew I was about to say I'm
sick, I'm in pain, I'm frightened.

He said, "I say you lie. I say you trouble. I say you get out." 32

I said, "And I say you shut up." 33

Years later, I was to understand why the command worked, and 34
to be sorry that it did, but that day I was very happy when he turned
and closed the door. I was asleep within minutes.

Toward evening, I went down the stairs, saw nobody, walked a 35
few blocks and bought myself an oyster loaf. But the first bite made
me feel sick, so I took my loaf back to the house. This time, as I

climbed the steps, there were three women in the parlor, and they stopped talking when they saw me. I went back to sleep immediately, dizzy and nauseated.

36   I woke to a high, hot sun and my father standing at the foot of the bed staring at the oyster loaf.

37   He said, "Get up now and get dressed."

38   I was crying as I said, "Thank you, Papa, but I can't."

39   From the hall, Sophronia said, "Get along up now. *Vite.* The morning is late."

40   My father left the room. I dressed and came into the hall carrying my oyster loaf. Sophronia was standing at the head of the stairs. She pointed out, meaning my father was on the street.

41   I said, "He humiliated me. He did. I won't . . ."

42   She said, "Get you going or I will never see you whenever again."

43   I ran past her to the street. I stood with my father until Sophronia joined us, and then we walked slowly, without speaking, to the street-car line. Sophronia bowed to us, but she refused my father's hand when he attempted to help her into the car. I ran to the car meaning to ask her to take me with her, but the car moved and she raised her hand as if to stop me. My father and I walked again for a long time.

44   He pointed to a trash can sitting in front of a house. "Please put that oyster loaf in the can."

45   At Vanalli's restaurant, he took my arm. "Hungry?"

46   I said, "No, thank you, Papa."

47   But we went through the door. It was, in those days, a New Orleans custom to have an early black coffee, go to the office, and after a few hours have a large breakfast at a restaurant. Vanalli's was crowded, the headwaiter was so sorry, but after my father took him aside, a very small table was put up for us — too small for my large father, who was accommodating himself to it in a manner most unlike him.

48   He said, "Jack, my rumpled daughter would like cold crayfish, a nice piece of pompano, a separate bowl of Béarnaise sauce, don't ask me why, French fried potatoes . . ."

49   I said, "Thank you, Papa, but I am not hungry. I don't want to be here."

50   My father waved the waiter away and we sat in silence until the crayfish came. My hand reached out instinctively and then drew back.

51   My father said, "Your mother and I have had an awful time."

52   I said, "I'm sorry about that. But I don't want to go home, Papa."

He said, angrily, "Yes, you do. But you want me to apologize 53
first. I do apologize but you should not have made me say it."

After a while I mumbled, "God forgive me, Papa forgive me, 54
Mama forgive me, Sophronia, Jenny, Hannah . . ."

"Eat your crayfish." 55

I ate everything he had ordered and then a small steak. I suppose 56
I had been mumbling throughout my breakfast.

My father said, "You're talking to yourself. I can't hear you. What 57
are you saying?"

"God forgive me, Papa forgive me, Mama forgive me, Sophronia, 58
Jenny . . ."

My father said, "Where do we start your training as the first 59
Jewish nun on Prytania Street?"

When I finished laughing, I liked him again. I said, "Papa, I'll tell 60
you a secret. I've had very bad cramps and I am beginning to bleed. I'm
changing life."

He stared at me for a while. Then he said, "Well, it's not the way 61
it's usually described, but it's accurate, I guess. Let's go home now to
your mother."

We were never, as long as my mother and father lived, to men- 62
tion that time again. But it was of great importance to them and I've
thought about it all my life. From that day on I knew my power over
my parents. That was not to be too important: I was ashamed of it and
did not abuse it too much. But I found out something more useful and
more dangerous: if you are willing to take the punishment, you are
halfway through the battle. That the issue may be trivial, the battle
ugly, is another point.

———— **CONSIDERATIONS** ————————————————————

1. Hellman's recollection of running away at fourteen is complicated by
her refusal to tell it in strict chronology. Instead, she interrupts the narrative
with flashbacks and episodes of later years. How can one justify such interrup-
tions?

2. On page 203, as she is trying to talk her way into the rooming house
in the black district, Hellman tells a young man to shut up and then adds,
"Years later, I was to understand why the command worked, and to be sorry
that it did." What did she later understand?

3. What was the "power over my parents" that Hellman learned from
her runaway experience? Do you have such a power?

4. Accounts of childhood escapades often suffer as the author idealizes or glamorizes them. Does Hellman successfully resist the temptation? What is your evidence?

5. The bases the fourteen-year-old runaway touched in her flight were actually part of a familiar world: a doll's house, a cathedral, a market, a railroad station. How then does Hellman give her flight more than a touch of horror?

6. In what specific ways did her first menstrual period heighten and distort some of the things that happened — or seemed to happen — to the fourteen-year-old runaway? Discuss the ways in which physiological and psychological conditions seem to feed upon each other.

Ernest Hemingway (1899–1961) was an ambulance driver and a soldier in World War I, and made use of these experiences in his novel. A Farewell to Arms *(1929). One of the Lost Generation of expatriate American writers who lived in Paris in the twenties — a time described in his memoir,* A Moveable Feast *(1964) — he was a great prose stylist and innovator, who received a Nobel Prize for literature in 1954. Other Hemingway novels include* The Sun Also Rises *(1926),* To Have and Have Not *(1937), and* For Whom the Bell Tolls *(1940). His Selected Letters, edited by Carlos Baker, appeared in 1981.*

Many critics prefer Hemingway's short stories to his novels, and his early stories — "Hills Like White Elephants" among them — to his later ones. This early prose is plain, simple, and clean. This story is dialogue virtually without narrative or description or interpretation; yet when we have finished it we have met two people whom we will not easily forget.

35

ERNEST HEMINGWAY
Hills Like White Elephants

The hills across the valley of the Ebro were long and white. On this side there was no shade and no trees and the station was between two lines of rails in the sun. Close against the side of the station there was the warm shadow of the building and a curtain, made of strings of bamboo beads, hung across the open door into the bar, to keep out 5 flies. The American and the girl with him sat at a table in the shade, outside the building. It was very hot and the express from Barcelona would come in forty minutes. It stopped at this junction for two minutes and went on to Madrid.

10   "What should we drink?" the girl asked. She had taken off her hat and put it on the table.

"It's pretty hot," the man said.

"Let's drink beer."

"Dos cervezas," the man said into the curtain.

15   "Big ones?" a woman asked from the doorway.

"Yes. Two big ones."

The woman brought two glasses of beer and two felt pads. She put the felt pads and the beer glasses on the table and looked at the man and the girl. The girl was looking off at the line of hills. They

20 were white in the sun and the country was brown and dry.

"They look like white elephants," she said.

"I've never seen one." The man drank his beer.

"No, you wouldn't have."

"I might have," the man said. "Just because you say I wouldn't

25 have doesn't prove anything."

The girl looked at the bead curtain. "They've painted something on it," she said. "What does it say?"

"Anis del Toro. It's a drink."

"Could we try it?"

30   The man called "Listen" through the curtain.

The woman came out from the bar.

"Four reales."

"We want two Anis del Toros."

"With water?"

35   "Do you want it with water?"

"I don't know," the girl said. "Is it good with water?"

"It's all right."

"You want them with water?" asked the woman.

"Yes, with water."

40   "It tastes like licorice," the girl said and put the glass down.

"That's the way with everything."

"Yes," said the girl. "Everything tastes of licorice. Especially all the things you've waited so long for, like absinthe."

"Oh, cut it out."

45   "You started it," the girl said. "I was being amused. I was having a fine time."

"Well, let's try and have a fine time."

"All right. I was trying. I said the mountains looked like white elephants. Wasn't that bright?"

"That was bright."

"I wanted to try this new drink. That's all we do, isn't it — look at things and try new drinks?"

"I guess so."

The girl looked across at the hills.

"They're lovely hills," she said. "They don't really look like white elephants. I just meant the colouring of their skin through the trees."

"Should we have another drink?"

"All right."

The warm wind blew the bead curtain against the table.

"The beer's nice and cool," the man said.

"It's lovely," the girl said.

"It's really an awfully simple operation, Jig," the man said. "It's not really an operation at all."

The girl looked at the ground the table legs rested on.

"I know you wouldn't mind it, Jig. It's really not anything. It's just to let the air in."

The girl did not say anything.

"I'll go with you and I'll stay with you all the time. They just let the air in and then it's all perfectly natural."

"Then what will we do afterwards?"

"We'll be fine afterwards. Just like we were before."

"What makes you think so?"

"That's the only thing that bothers us. It's the only thing that's made us unhappy."

The girl looked at the bead curtain, put her hand out and took hold of two of the strings of beads.

"And you think then we'll be all right and be happy."

"I know we will. You don't have to be afraid. I've known lots of people that have done it."

"So have I," said the girl. "And afterward they were all so happy."

"Well," the man said, "if you don't want to you don't have to. I wouldn't have you do it if you didn't want to. But I know it's perfectly simple."

"And you really want to?"

"I think it's the best thing to do. But I don't want you to do it if you don't really want to."

"And if I do it you'll be happy and things will be like they were and you'll love me?"

"I love you now. You know I love you."

90   "I know. But if I do it, then it will be nice again if I say things are like white elephants, and you'll like it?"

"I'll love it. I love it now but I just can't think about it. You know how I get when I worry."

"If I do it you won't ever worry?"

95   "I won't worry about that because it's perfectly simple."

"Then I'll do it. Because I don't care about me."

"What do you mean?"

"I don't care about me."

"Well, I care about you."

100   "Oh, yes. But I don't care about me. And I'll do it and then everything will be fine."

"I don't want you to do it if you feel that way."

The girl stood up and walked to the end of the station. Across, on the other side, were fields of grain and trees along the banks of the

105   Ebro. Far away, beyond the river, were mountains. The shadow of a cloud moved across the field of grain and she saw the river through the trees.

"And we could have all this," she said. "And we could have everything and every day we make it more impossible."

110   "What did you say?"

"I said we could have everything."

"We can have everything."

"No, we can't."

"We can have the whole world."

115   "No, we can't."

"We can go everywhere."

"No, we can't. It isn't ours any more."

"It's ours."

"No, it isn't. And once they take it away, you never get it back."

120   "But they haven't taken it away."

"We'll wait and see."

"Come on back in the shade," he said. "You mustn't feel that way."

"I don't feel any way," the girl said. "I just know things."

125   "I don't want you to do anything that you don't want to do — "

"Nor that isn't good for me," she said. "I know. Could we have another beer?"

"All right. But you've got to realize — "

"I realize," the girl said. "Can't we maybe stop talking?"

They sat down at the table and the girl looked across at the hills 130
on the dry side of the valley and the man looked at her and at the
table.

"You've got to realize," he said, "that I don't want you to do it if
you don't want to. I'm perfectly willing to go through with it if it
means anything to you." 135

"Doesn't it mean anything to you? We could get along."

"Of course it does. But I don't want anybody but you. I don't
want anyone else. And I know it's perfectly simple."

"Yes, you know it's perfectly simple."

"It's all right for you to say that, but I do know it." 140

"Would you do something for me now?"

"I'd do anything for you."

"Would you please please please please please please please stop
talking?"

He did not say anything but looked at the bags against the wall 145
of the station. There were labels on them from all the hotels where
they had spent nights.

"But I don't want you to," he said, "I don't care anything about
it."

"I'll scream," the girl said. 150

The woman came out through the curtains with two glasses of
beer and put them down on the damp felt pads. "The train comes in
five minutes," she said.

"What did she say?" asked the girl.

"That the train is coming in five minutes." 155

The girl smiled brightly at the woman, to thank her.

"I'd better take the bags over to the other side of the station," the
man said. She smiled at him.

"All right. Then come back and we'll finish the beer."

He picked up the two heavy bags and carried them around the 160
station to the other tracks. He looked up the tracks but could not see
the train. Coming back, he walked through the bar-room, where people waiting for the train were drinking. He drank an Anis at the bar
and looked at the people. They were all waiting reasonably for the
train. He went out through the bead curtain. She was sitting at the 165
table and smiled at him.

"Do you feel better?" he asked.

"I feel fine," she said. "There's nothing wrong with me. I feel
fine."

___ CONSIDERATIONS _____

1. Nearly all of Hemingway's story is dialogue, often without identifying phrases such as "he said" or "she said." Does the lack of these phrases make it difficult to decide which character is speaking? What, if anything, does Hemingway do to make up for missing dialogue tags? Compare his practice with the way other short story writers in this book handle dialogue.

2. If you have ever questioned the common statement that writers must pay careful attention to *every* word they use, spend a little time examining the way Hemingway uses "it," beginning where the couple start talking about the operation. Try to determine the various possible antecedents for that neutral pronoun in each context where it occurs. Such an effort may help you discover one reason why Hemingway's spare, almost skeletal style is so powerful.

3. Try to put the central conflict of this story in your own words. Imagine yourself the writer suddenly getting the idea for this story and quickly writing a sentence or two to record the idea in your journal. See F. Scott Fitzgerald's journal, pages 174–175, for example.

4. Why is Hemingway *not* explicit about the kind of operation the two characters are discussing? Is he simply trying to mystify the reader? Does this consideration help you understand other stories or poems that seem difficult at first?

5. Although Hemingway's description of locale is limited to a few brief passages, he presents a distinct place. How does that place contribute to your understanding the point of the story?

6. Why does Hemingway refuse to describe the two characters? From what the story offers, what do you know about them?

7. Hemingway's story was written in the 1920s. Have the questions he raises about the operation been resolved since then?

Langston Hughes (1902–1967) was a poet, novelist, playwright, and essayist who wrote with wit and energy; he was a leader in the emergence of black American literature in the twentieth century. More than twenty of his books remain in print, including Selected Poems; *his autobiography,* I Wonder as I Wander; *and* The Langston Hughes Reader. *He argues as well as he sings the blues — and he can tell a story.*

36

LANGSTON HUGHES

Salvation

I was saved from sin when I was going on thirteen. But not really   1
saved. It happened like this. There was a big revival at my Auntie
Reed's church. Every night for weeks there had been much preaching,
singing, praying, and shouting, and some very hardened sinners had
been brought to Christ, and the membership of the church had grown
by leaps and bounds. Then just before the revival ended, they held a
special meeting for children, "to bring the young lambs to the fold."
My aunt spoke of it for days ahead. That night I was escorted to the
front row and placed on the mourners' bench with all the other young
sinners, who had not yet been brought to Jesus.

My aunt told me that when you were saved you saw a light, and   2
something happened to you inside! And Jesus came into your life! And
God was with you from then on! She said you could see and hear and
feel Jesus in your soul. I believed her. I had heard a great many old
people say the same thing and it seemed to me they ought to know.

So I sat there calmly in the hot, crowded church, waiting for Jesus to come to me.

3 The preacher preached a wonderful rhythmical sermon, all moans and shouts and lonely cries and dire pictures of hell, and then he sang a song about the ninety and nine safe in the fold, but one little lamb was left out in the cold. Then he said: "Won't you come? Won't you come to Jesus? Young lambs, won't you come?" And he held out his arms to all us young sinners there on the mourners' bench. And the little girls cried. And some of them jumped up and went to Jesus right away. But most of us just sat there.

4 A great many old people came and knelt around us and prayed, old women with jet-black faces and braided hair, old men with work-gnarled hands. And the church sang a song about the lower lights are burning, some poor sinners to be saved. And the whole building rocked with prayer and song.

5 Still I kept waiting to *see* Jesus.

6 Finally all the young people had gone to the altar and were saved, but one boy and me. He was a rounder's son named Westley. Westley and I were surrounded by sisters and deacons praying. It was very hot in the church, and getting late now. Finally Westley said to me in a whisper: "God damn! I'm tired o' sitting here. Let's get up and be saved." So he got up and was saved.

7 Then I was left all alone on the mourners' bench. My aunt came and knelt at my knees and cried, while prayers and songs swirled all around me in the little church. The whole congregation prayed for me alone, in a mighty wail of moans and voices. And I kept waiting serenely for Jesus, waiting, waiting — but he didn't come. I wanted to see him, but nothing happened to me. Nothing! I wanted something to happen to me, but nothing happened.

8 I heard the songs and the minister saying: "Why don't you come? My dear child, why don't you come to Jesus? Jesus is waiting for you. He wants you. Why don't you come? Sister Reed, what is this child's name?"

9 "Langston," my aunt sobbed.

10 "Langston, why don't you come? Why don't you come and be saved? Oh, Lamb of God! Why don't you come?"

11 Now it was really getting late. I began to be ashamed of myself, holding everything up so long. I began to wonder what God thought about Westley, who certainly hadn't seen Jesus either, but who was now sitting proudly on the platform, swinging his knickerbockered legs and grinning down at me, surrounded by deacons and old women on their knees praying. God had not struck Westley dead for taking his

name in vain or for lying in the temple. So I decided that maybe to save further trouble, I'd better lie, too, and say that Jesus had come, and get up and be saved.

So I got up. 12

Suddenly the whole room broke into a sea of shouting, as they 13 saw me rise. Waves of rejoicing swept the place. Women leaped in the air. My aunt threw her arms around me. The minister took me by the hand and led me to the platform.

When things quieted down, in a hushed silence, punctuated by a 14 few ecstatic "Amens," all the new young lambs were blessed in the name of God. Then joyous singing filled the room.

That night, for the last time in my life but one — for I was a big 15 boy twelve years old — I cried. I cried, in bed alone, and couldn't stop. I buried my head under the quilts, but my aunt heard me. She woke up and told my uncle I was crying because the Holy Ghost had come into my life, and because I had seen Jesus. But I was really crying because I couldn't bear to tell her that I had lied, that I had deceived everybody in the church, and I hadn't seen Jesus, and that now I didn't believe there was a Jesus any more, since he didn't come to help me.

_____ CONSIDERATIONS _____

1. Hughes tells this critical episode of his childhood in a simple, straightforward, unelaborated fashion, almost as though he were still a child telling the story as it happened. Why is it necessary to say "*almost* as though he were still a child"? Compare this account with Randolph Bourne's account of events in his childhood (pages 91–99). Do the two writers remember differently? How would you go about recounting a critical moment in your childhood? Where does simple childhood memory stop and adult judgment take over?

2. Hughes's disillusionment is an example of what people call "an initiation story." Compare it with the Ernest Hemingway short story (pages 207–211), or John Updike's story (pages 432–440), or the autobiographical essay by Lillian Hellman (pages 199–205). Discuss the *degrees* of awareness noticeable among these varied characters.

3. Why was it so important to the congregation of Auntie Reed's church that everyone, children included, acknowledge that they were saved?

4. Why did Westley finally proclaim that he had been saved?

5. In his final paragraph, Hughes writes, "That night, for the last time in my life but one . . . I cried." He does not tell us, in this account, what that other time was. Read a little more of his life, or simply use your imagination, and write a brief account of the other time.

Langston Hughes's poetry took many forms, and much of it resembled song. If you repeat the first two lines of each stanza of these poems, you will discover the classic form of the blues.

37

LANGSTON HUGHES
Two Poems

BAD LUCK CARD

Cause you don't love me
Is awful, awful hard.
Gypsy done showed me
4   My bad luck card.

There ain't no good left
In this world for me
Gypsy done told me —
8   Unlucky as can be.

I don't know what
Po' weary me can do.
Gypsy says I'd kill my self
12   If I was you.

HOMECOMING

I went back in the alley
And I opened up my door.
All her clothes was gone:
She wasn't home no more.   4

I pulled back the covers.
I made down the bed.
A *whole* lot of room
Was the only thing I had.   8

Langston Hughes's "Simple" stories carry ideas, humor, pain, and wisdom. Hughes draws on folk material — as he does in his poems — and shapes and controls it. In his introduction to a collection of stories about Simple, Hughes wrote: "It is impossible to live in Harlem and not know at least a hundred Simples."

38

LANGSTON HUGHES
Two Tales of Simple

FEET LIVE THEIR OWN LIFE

1   "If you want to know about my life," said Simple as he blew the foam from the top of the newly filled glass the bartender put before him, "don't look at my face, don't look at my hands. Look at my feet and see if you can tell how long I been standing on them."

2   "I cannot see your feet through your shoes," I said.

3   "You do not need to see through my shoes," said Simple. "Can't you tell by the shoes I wear — not pointed, not rocking-chair, not French-toed, not nothing but big, long, broad, and flat — that I been standing on these feet a long time and carrying some heavy burdens? They ain't flat from standing at no bar, neither, because I always sets at a bar. Can't you tell that? You know I do not hang out in a bar unless it has stools, don't you?"

4   "That I have observed," I said, "but I did not connect it with your past life."

5   "Everything I do is connected up with my past life," said Simple.

"From Virginia to Joyce, from my wife to Zarita, from my mother's milk to this glass of beer, everything is connected up."

"I trust you will connect up with that dollar I just loaned you when you get paid," I said. "And who is Virginia? You never told me about her." 6

"Virginia is where I was borned," said Simple. "I *would* be borned in a state named after that woman. From that day on, women never give me no peace." 7

"You, I fear, are boasting. If the women were running after you as much as you run after them, you would not be able to sit here on this bar stool in peace. I don't see any women coming to call you out to go home, as some of these fellows' wives do around here." 8

"Joyce better not come in no bar looking for me," said Simple. "That is why me and my wife busted up — one reason. I do not like to be called out of no bar by a female. It's a man's perogative to just set and drink sometimes." 9

"How do you connect that prerogative with your past?" I asked. 10

"When I was a wee small child," said Simple, "I had no place to set and think in, being as how I was raised up with three brothers, two sisters, seven cousins, one married aunt, a common-law uncle, and the minister's grandchild — and the house only had four rooms. I never had no place just to set and think. Neither to set and drink — not even much my milk before some hongry child snatched it out of my hand. I were not the youngest, neither a girl, nor the cutest. I don't know why, but I don't think nobody liked me much. Which is why I was afraid to like anybody for a long time myself. When I did like somebody, I was full-grown and then I picked out the wrong woman because I had no practice in liking anybody before that. We did not get along." 11

"Is that when you took to drink?" 12

"Drink took to me," said Simple. "Whiskey just naturally likes me but beer likes me better. By the time I got married I had got to the point where a cold bottle was almost as good as a warm bed, especially when the bottle could not talk and the bed-warmer could. I do not like a woman to talk to me too much — I mean about me. Which is why I like Joyce. Joyce most in generally talks about herself." 13

"I am still looking at your feet," I said, "and I swear they do not reveal your life to me. Your feet are no open book." 14

"You have eyes but you see not," said Simple. "These feet have stood on every rock from the Rock of Ages to 135th and Lenox. These feet have supported everything from a cotton bale to a hongry woman. 15

These feet have walked ten thousand miles working for white folks and another ten thousand keeping up with colored. These feet have stood at altars, crap tables, free lunches, bars, graves, kitchen doors, betting windows, hospital clinics, WPA desks, social security railings, and in all kinds of lines from soup lines to the draft. If I just had four feet, I could have stood in more places longer. As it is, I done wore out seven hundred pairs of shoes, eighty-nine tennis shoes, twelve summer sandals, also six loafers. The socks that these feet have bought could build a knitting mill. The corns I've cut away would dull a German razor. The bunions I forgot would make you ache from now till Judgment Day. If anybody was to write the history of my life, they should start with my feet."

16   "Your feet are not all that extraordinay," I said. "Besides, everything you are saying is general. Tell me specifically some one thing your feet have done that makes them different from any other feet in the world, just one."

17   "Do you see that window in that white man's store across the street?" asked Simple. "Well, this right foot of mine broke out that window in the Harlem riots right smack in the middle. Didn't no other foot in the world break that window but mine. And this left foot carried me off running as soon as my right foot came down. Nobody else's feet saved me from the cops that night but these *two* feet right here. Don't tell me these feet ain't had a life of their own."

18   "For shame," I said, "going around kicking out windows. Why?"

19   "Why?" said Simple. "You have to ask my great-great-grandpa why. He must of been simple — else why did he let them capture him in Africa and sell him for a slave to breed my great-grandpa in slavery to breed my grandpa in slavery to breed my pa to breed me to look at that window and say, 'It ain't mine! Bam-mmm-mm-m!' and kick it out?"

20   "This bar glass is not yours either," I said. "Why don't you smash it?"

21   "It's got my beer in it," said Simple.

22   Just then Zarita came in wearing her Thursday-night rabbit-skin coat. She didn't stop at the bar, being dressed up, but went straight back to a booth. Simple's hand went up, his beer went down, and the glass back to its wet spot on the bar.

23   "Excuse me a minute," he said, sliding off the stool.

24   Just to give him a pause, the dozens, that old verbal game of maligning a friend's female relatives, came to mind. "Wait," I said.

"You have told me about what to ask your great-great-grandpa. But I want to know what to ask your great-great-*grandma*."

"I don't play the dozens that far back," said Simple, following   25
Zarita into the smoky juke-box blue of the back room.

TEMPTATION

"When the Lord said, 'Let there be light,' and there was light,   1
what I want to know is where was us colored people?"

"What do you mean, 'Where were we colored people?' " I said.   2

"We must *not* of been there," said Simple, "because we are still   3
dark. Either He did not include me or else I were not there."

"The Lord was not referring to people when He said, 'Let there   4
be light.' He was referring to the elements, the atmosphere, the air."

"He must have included some people," said Simple, because   5
white people are light, in fact, *white*, whilst I am dark. How come? I
say, we were not there."

"Then where do you think we were?"   6

"Late as usual," said Simple, "old C. P. Time. We must have   7
been down the road a piece and did not get back on time."

"There was no C. P. Time in those days," I said. "In fact, no   8
people were created — so there couldn't be any Colored People's
Time. The Lord God had not yet breathed the breath of life into anyone."

"No?" said Simple.   9

"No," said I, "because it wasn't until Genesis 2 and 7 that God   10
'formed man of the dust of the earth and breathed into his nostrils the
breath of life and man became a living soul.' His name was Adam.
Then He took one of Adam's ribs and made a woman."

"Then trouble began," said Simple. "Thank God, they was both   11
white."

"How do you know Adam and Eve were white?" I asked.   12

"When I was a kid I seen them on the Sunday school cards," said   13
Simple. "Ever since I been seeing a Sunday School card, they was
white. That is why I want to know where was us Negroes when the
Lord said, 'Let there be light'?"

"Oh, man, you have a color complex so bad you want to trace it   14
back to the Bible."

"No, I don't. I just want to know how come Adam and Eve was   15 white. If they had started out black, this world might not be in the fix it is today. Eve might not of paid that serpent no attention. I never did know a Negro yet that liked a snake."

16   "That snake is a symbol," I said, "a symbol of temptation and sin. And that symbol would be the same, no matter what the race."

17   "I am not talking about no symbol," said Simple. "I am talking about the day when Eve took that apple and Adam et. From then on the human race has been in trouble. There ain't a colored woman living what would take no apple from a snake — and she better not give no snake-apples to her husband!"

18   "Adam and Eve are symbols, too," I said.

19   "You are simple yourself," said Simple. "But I just wish we colored folks had been somewhere around at the start. I do not know where we was when Eden was a garden, but we sure didn't get in on none of the crops. If we had, we would not be so poor today. White folks started out ahead and they are still ahead. Look at me!"

20   "I am looking," I said.

21   "Made in the image of God," said Simple, "but I never did see anybody like me on a Sunday school card."

22   "Probably nobody looked like you in Biblical days," I said. "The American Negro did not exist in B.C. You're a product of Caucasia and Africa, Harlem and Dixie. You've been conditioned entirely by our environment, our modern times."

23   "Times have been hard," said Simple, "but still I am a child of God."

24   "In the cosmic sense, we are all children of God."

25   "I have been baptized," said Simple, "also anointed with oil. When I were a child I come through at the mourners' bench. I was converted. I have listened to Daddy Grace and et with Father Divine, moaned with Elder Lawson and prayed with Adam Powell. Also I have been to the Episcopalians with Joyce. But if a snake were to come up to me and offer *me* an apple, I would say, 'Varmint, be on your way! No fruit today! Bud, you got the wrong stud now, so get along somehow, be off down the road because you're lower than a toad!' Then that serpent would respect me as a wise man — and this world would not be where it is — all on account of an apple. That apple has turned into an atom now."

26   "To hear you talk, if you had been in the Garden of Eden, the world would still be a Paradise," I said. "Man would not have fallen into sin."

27   "Not *this* man," said Simple. "I would have stayed in that garden

making grape wine, singing like Crosby, and feeling fine! I would not be scuffling out in this rough world, neither would I be in Harlem. If I was Adam I would just stay in Eden in that garden with no rent to pay, no landladies to dodge, no time clock to punch — and *my* picture on a Sunday school card, I'd be a *real gone guy* even if I didn't have but one name — Adam — and no initials."

"You would be *real gone* all right. But you were not there. So, my dear fellow, I trust you will not let your rather late arrival on our contemporary stage distort your perspective."   28

"No," said Simple.   29

____ **CONSIDERATIONS** _____

Feet Live Their Own Life

1. In order to get across the extent of his experience, Simple presents some statistics: "I done wore out seven hundred pairs of shoes, eighty-nine tennis shoes, twelve summer sandals . . ." Is that the same technique James C. Rettie uses to imagine a film that would cover 757 million years in a one-year showing? Try concocting statistics of repetitious events or things in your own life as a means of conveying an abstract idea or feeling.

2. "Everything I do is connected up with my past life," says Simple. What sobering truth is expressed by this casual remark? Compare it with Francis Thompson's idea in Paragraph 6 of Loren Eiseley's "How Flowers Changed the World."

3. Compare Hughes's use of dialect with Flannery O'Connor's in "A Good Man Is Hard to Find." Why does an author use dialect? What are the problems with dialect?

4. "Your feet are not all that extraordinary," says Simple's companion. Try exercising your powers of observation on a pair of shoes — not your own — and write the biography revealed.

Temptation

1. What is "C. P. Time"? What has that to do with the burden of Simple's complaints in this story?

2. Discuss the terms "Negro," "colored," "Afro-American," and "black" as changing usage reflects attitudes of whites to blacks and of blacks to themselves. Has a similar concern about labels been true of any other group of people — Englishmen, Britishers, Britons, Anglo-Saxons, for example?

3. In the paragraph beginning "I have been baptized," Simple quickly sketches several stages of influential teachings in his life. Read Hughes's essay "Salvation," and place the boy of that piece in the appropriate stage mentioned by Simple. If Simple had had Hughes's experience as a child, how might he have reacted to subsequent attempts to influence his beliefs?

4. "The apple has turned into an atom now," says Simple. He doesn't explain, but what inferences might you draw from his statement?

Thomas Jefferson (1743–1826) was the third president of the United States, and perhaps more truly the Father of his Country than George Washington was; or maybe we would only like to think so, for such paternity flatters the offspring. Jefferson was a politician, philosopher, architect, inventor, and writer. With an energy equal to his curiosity, he acted to improve the world: he wrote the Declaration of Independence; he wrote a life of Jesus; and he founded the University of Virginia, whose original buildings he designed. An arch-republican, fearful of Alexander Hamilton's monarchical reverence for authority, Jefferson withheld support from the Constitution until he saw the Bill of Rights added to it.

We take this text from Garry Wills's Inventing America *(1978); by juxtaposition, Wills demonstrates the revision of a classic.*

39

THOMAS JEFFERSON

The Declarations of Jefferson and of the Congress

I will state the form of the declaration as originally reported. The parts struck out by Congress shall be distinguished by a black line drawn under them; & those inserted by them shall be placed in the margin or in a concurrent column:

1   A Declaration by the representatives of the United states of America, in [General] Congress assembled.

2   When in the course of human events it becomes necessary for one people to dissolve the political bands which have connected them with another, and to assume among the powers of the earth

Taken from Jefferson's Notes and Proceedings — *Papers*, 1:315–319.

the separate & equal station to which the laws of nature and of nature's god entitle them, a decent respect to the opinions of mankind requires that they should declare the causes which impel them to the separation.

We hold these truths to be self evident: that all men are created   3

certain   equal; that they are endowed by their creator with ∧ [inherent and] inalienable rights; that among these are life, liberty & the pursuit of happiness: that to secure these rights, governments are instituted among men, deriving their just powers from the consent of the governed; that whenever any form of government becomes destructive of these ends, it is the right of the people to alter or to abolish it, & to institute new government, laying it's foundation on such principles, & organising it's powers in such form, as to them shall seem most likely to effect their safety & happiness.

M.?.   Prudence indeed will dictate that governments long established should not be changed for light & transient causes; and accordingly all experience hath shewn that mankind are more disposed to suffer while evils are sufferable than to right themselves by abolishing the forms to which they are accustomed. But when a long train of abuses & usurpations [begun at a distinguished period and] pursuing invariably the same object, evinces a design to reduce them under absolute despotism it is their right, it is their duty to throw off such government, & to provide new guards for their future security. Such has been the patient sufferance of these colonies;

alter   & such is now the necessity which constrains them to ∧ [expunge] their former systems of government. The history of the present

repeated   king of Great Britain is a history of ∧ [unremitting] injuries &
m.p   usurpations, [among which appears no solitary fact to contradict

all having   the uniform tenor of the rest but all have] ∧ in direct object the establishment of an absolute tyranny over these states. To prove this let facts be submitted to a candid world [for the truth of which we pledge a faith yet unsullied by falsehood.]

He has refused his assent to laws the most wholesome & neces-   4
sary for the public good.

He has forbidden his governors to pass laws of immediate &   5
pressing importance, unless suspended in their operation till his assent should be obtained; & when so suspended, he has utterly neglected to attend to them.

He has refused to pass other laws for the accommodation of large   6
districts of people, unless those people would relinquish the right of representation in the legislature, a right inestimable to them, & formidable to tyrants only.

He has called together legislative bodies at places unusual,   7
uncomfortable, and distant from the depository of their public records, for the sole purpose of fatiguing them into compliance with his measures.

8   He has dissolved representative houses repeatedly [& contin-
ually] for opposing with manly firmness his invasions on the rights
of the people.

9   He has refused for a long time after such dissolutions to cause
others to be elected, whereby the legislative powers, incapable of
annihilation, have returned to the people at large for their exercise,
the state remaining in the mean time exposed to all the dangers of
invasion from without & convulsions within.

10   He has endeavored to prevent the population of these states; for
that purpose obstructing the laws for naturalization of foreigners,
refusing to pass others to encourage their migrations hither, &
raising the conditions of new appropriations of lands.

11   He has ∧ [suffered] the administration of justice [totally to cease   obstructed
in some of these states] ∧ refusing his assent to laws for establish-   by
ing judiciary powers.

12   He has made [our] judges dependant on his will alone, for the
tenure of their offices, & the amount & paiment of their salaries.

13   He has erected a multitude of new offices [by a self assumed
power] and sent hither swarms of new officers to harrass our people
and eat out their substance.

14   He has kept among us in times of peace standing armies [and
ships of war] without the consent of our legislatures.

15   He has affected to render the military independant of, & superior
to the civil power.

16   He has combined with others to subject us to a jurisdiction foreign to our constitutions & unacknoleged by our laws, giving his
assent to their acts of pretended legislation for quartering large
bodies of armed troops among us; for protecting them by a mock-
trial from punishment for any murders which they should commit
on the inhabitants of these states; for cutting off our trade with all
parts of the world; for imposing taxes on us without our consent;
for depriving us ∧ of the benefits of trial by jury; for transporting   in many cases
us beyond seas to be tried for pretended offences; for abolishing
the free system of English laws in a neighboring province, establishing therein an arbitrary government, and enlarging it's boundaries, so as to render it at once an example and fit instrument for
introducing the same absolute rule into these ∧ [states]; for taking   colonies
away our charters, abolishing our most valuable laws, and altering
fundamentally the forms of our governments; for suspending our
own legislatures, & declaring themselves invested with power to
legislate for us in all cases whatsoever.

17   He has abdicated government here ∧ [withdrawing his governors,   by declaring
and declaring us out of his allegiance & protection.]   us out of his
                                                                            protection &
18   He has plundered our seas, ravaged our coasts, burnt our towns,   waging war
& destroyed the lives of our people.   against us.

19   He is at this time transporting large armies of foreign merce-

scarcely paralleled in the most barbarous ages, & totally

naries to compleat the works of death, desolation & tyranny already begun with circumstances of cruelty and perfidy ∧ unworthy the head of a civilized nation.

He has constrained our fellow citizens taken captive on the high 20 seas to bear arms against their country, to become the executioners of their friends & brethren, or to fall themselves by their hands.

excited domestic insurrections amongst us, & has

He has ∧ endeavored to bring on the inhabitants of our frontiers 21 the merciless Indian savages, whose known rule of warfare is an undistinguished destruction of all ages, sexes, & conditions [of existence.]

[He has incited treasonable insurrections of our fellow-citizens, 22 with the allurements of forfeiture & confiscation of our property.

He has waged cruel war against human nature itself, violating 23 it's most sacred rights of life and liberty in the persons of a distant people who never offended him, captivating & carrying them into slavery in another hemisphere or to incur miserable death in their transportation thither. This piratical warfare, the opprobrium of *infidel* powers, is the warfare of the *Christian* king of Great Britain. Determined to keep open a market where *Men* should be bought & sold, he has prostituted his negative for suppressing every legislative attempt to prohibit or to restrain this execrable commerce. And that this assemblage of horrors might want no fact of distinguished die, he is now exciting those very people to rise in arms among us, and to purchase that liberty of which he has deprived them, by murdering the people on whom he also obtruded them: thus paying off former crimes committed against the *Liberties* of one people, with crimes which he urges them to commit against the *lives* of another.]

free

In every stage of these oppressions we have petitioned for redress 24 in the most humble terms: our repeated petitions have been answered only by repeated injuries. A prince whose character is thus marked by every act which may define a tyrant is unfit to be the ruler of a ∧ people [who mean to be free. Future ages will scarcely believe that the hardiness of one man adventured, within the short compass of twelve years only, to lay a foundation so broad & so undisguised for tyranny over a people fostered & fixed in principles of freedom.]

an unwarrantable us

Nor have we been wanting in attentions to our British brethren. 25 We have warned them from time to time of attempts by their legislature to extend ∧ [a] jurisdiction over ∧ [these our states.] We have reminded them of the circumstances of our emigration & settlement here, [no one of which could warrant so strange a pretension: that these were effected at the expence of our own blood & treasure, unassisted by the wealth or the strength of Great Britain: that in constituting indeed our several forms of government, we had adopted one common king, thereby laying a foundation for perpetual league & amity with them: but that submission to their parliament was no part of our constitution, nor ever in idea, if history may be credited: and,] we ∧ appealed to their native justice and magnanimity ∧ [as well as to] the ties of our common kindred to disavow these usurpations which ∧ [were likely to] interrupt our connection and correspondence. They too have been deaf to the voice of justice & of consanguinity, [and when occasions have been given them, by the regular course of their laws, of removing from their councils the disturbers of our harmony, they have, by their free election, re-established them in power. At this very time too they are permitting their chief magistrate to send over not only souldiers of our common blood, but Scotch & foreign mercenaries to invade & destroy us. These facts have given the last stab to agonizing affection, and manly spirit bids us to renounce for ever these unfeeling brethren. We must endeavor to forget our former love for them, and to hold them as we hold the rest of mankind enemies in war, in peace friends. We might have been a free and a great people together; but a communication of grandeur & of freedom it seems is below their dignity. Be it so, since they will have it. The road to happiness & to glory is open to us too. We will tread it apart from them, and] ∧ acquiesce in the necessity which denounces our [eternal] separation ∧ !

[right margin notes:] have / and we have / conjured them / by / would inevi-/tably

[right margin notes:] we must / therefore / and hold them / as we hold the / rest of mankind, / enemies in war, / in peace friends.

26 We therefore the representatives of the United states of America in General Congress assembled do in the name, & by the authority of the good people of these [states reject & renounce all allegiance & subjection to the kings of Great Britain & all others who may hereafter claim by, through or under them: we utterly dissolve all political connection which may heretofore have subsisted between us & the people or parliament of Great Britain: & finally we do assert & declare these colonies to be free & independant states,] & that as free & independent states, they have full power to levy war, conclude peace, contract alli-

We therefore the representatives of the United states of America in General Congress assembled, appealing to the supreme judge of the world for the rectitude of our intentions, do in the name, & by the authority of the good people of these colonies, solemnly publish & declare that these United colonies are & of right ought to be free & independant states; that they are absolved from all allegiance to the British crown, and that all political connection between them & the state of Great Britain is, & ought to be, totally dissolved; & that as free & independant states they have full power to levy war, conclude peace, contract alliances,

ances, establish commerce, & to do all other acts & things which independant states may

27 of right do. And for the support of this declaration we mutually pledge to each other our lives, our fortunes & our sacred honour.

establish commerce & to do all other acts & things which independant states may of right do.

And for the support of this declaration, with a firm reliance on the protection of divine providence we mutually pledge to each other our lives, our fortunes & our sacred honour.

_____ **CONSIDERATIONS** _____

1. What part of the original declaration deleted by Congress most surprises you? Why?

2. Make a careful study of the first eight or ten changes imposed by Congress on Jefferson's original declaration. Why do you think each was made? Would any of them have made good examples for George Orwell to use in his "Politics and the English Language"?

3. Garry Wills says in his book, *Inventing America,* that the declaration is easy to misunderstand because it "is written in the lost language of the Enlightenment." What was the Enlightenment? How does the language of that period differ from that of today? Perhaps the declaration should be rewritten in modern English? Compare the two versions of Ecclesiastes (pages 53–58) before you come to a conclusion.

4. If you conclude that the declaration should be rewritten, try your hand at it. Try, say, rewriting the famous third paragraph: "We hold these truths . . ." Can you be sure you're not writing a parody?

5. How is the declaration organized? Does it break down into distinct parts? If so, what is the function of those parts?

6. For a more thorough exploration of the before-and-after versions of the declaration and of the political and literary motives for the changes, see Carl Becker's *The Declaration of Independence.*

D. H. Lawrence (1885–1930) was born in Nottinghamshire, in England, son of a coal-miner father brutalized by work and poverty, and a schoolteacher mother who encouraged his writing. The family was poor and Lawrence was sickly, but he studied to become certified as a teacher, and wrote poetry and fiction when he could. In 1911 he published his first novel, The White Peacock, *and quit his post as a teacher. The next year, he met Frieda von Richthofen Weekley, German wife of a Professor Weekley, and cousin of the Baron Manfred von Richthofen who was to become the Red Baron of World War I. Lawrence and Frieda fell in love, and Frieda left her husband and children to run away with Lawrence; they remained together, tempestuous and difficult and devoted, until his death.*

His first book of poems appeared in 1913, as did the first of his great novels, Sons and Lovers. *Lawrence and Frieda, who were able to marry in 1914, traveled in Germany and Italy, and settled in England when the war started.* The Prussian Officer, *a book of stories, appeared in 1914, followed by* The Rainbow *(1915). That novel's second half,* Women in Love, *was not published until 1920 because publishers feared the response to its relative explicitness about sexual feeling.*

Living by his wits, Lawrence published innumerable stories, essays, novels, poems, criticism, and travel books. He and Frieda traveled continually. After World War I, they took off for Italy; two of his travel books are about that country. A journey to Australia resulted in a novel called Kangaroo *(1923). In the New World, he delighted in Mexico (*The Plumed Serpent, *1926) and New Mexico. During the last years before his death from tuberculosis, he wrote* Lady Chatterley's Lover, *which was suppressed, and his best poetry.*

In Lawrence's novels, his relative explicitness seems mild enough today, but we must remember that he published his first novel before World War I — when Queen Victoria had been dead only ten years. As might be expected, D. H. Lawrence was called a pornographer.

40

D. H. LAWRENCE
Pornography

1   What is pornography to one man is the laughter of genius to another.

2   The word itself, we are told, means "pertaining to harlots" — the graph of the harlot. But nowadays, what is a harlot? If she was a woman who took money from a man in return for going to bed with him — really, most wives sold themselves, in the past, and plenty of harlots gave themselves, when they felt like it, for nothing. If a woman hasn't got a tiny streak of harlot in her, she's a dry stick as a rule. And probably most harlots had somewhere a streak of womanly generosity. Why be so cut and dried? The law is a dreary thing, and its judgments have nothing to do with life. . . .

3   One essay on pornography, I remember, comes to the conclusion that pornography in art is that which is calculated to arouse sexual desire, or sexual excitement. And stress is laid on the fact, whether the author or artist *intended* to arouse sexual feelings. It is the old vexed question of intention, become so dull today, when we know how strong and influential our unconscious intentions are. And why a man should be held guilty of his conscious intentions, and innocent of his unconscious intentions, I don't know, since every man is more made up of unconscious intentions than of conscious ones. I am what I am, not merely what I think I am.

4   However! We take it, I assume, that *pornography* is something base, something unpleasant. In short, we don't like it. And why don't we like it? Because it arouses sexual feelings?

5   I think not. No matter how hard we may pretend otherwise, most

of us rather like a moderate rousing of our sex. It warms us, stimulates us like sunshine on a grey day. After a century or two of Puritanism, this is still true of most people. Only the mob-habit of condemning any form of sex is too strong to let us admit it naturally. And there are, of course, many people who are genuinely repelled by the simplest and most natural stirrings of sexual feeling. But these people are perverts who have fallen into hatred of their fellow-men; thwarted, disappointed, unfulfilled people, of whom, alas, our civilisation contains so many. And they nearly always enjoy some unsimple and unnatural form of sex excitement, secretly.

Even quite advanced art critics would try to make us believe that 6 any picture or book which had "sex appeal" was *ipso facto* a bad book or picture. This is just canting hypocrisy. Half the great poems, pictures, music, stories, of the whole world are great by virtue of the beauty of their sex appeal. Titian or Renoir, the Song of Solomon or *Jane Eyre*, Mozart or "Annie Laurie," the loveliness is all interwoven with sex appeal, sex stimulus, call it what you will. Even Michelangelo, who rather hated sex, can't help filling the Cornucopia with phallic acorns. Sex is a very powerful, beneficial and necessary stimulus in human life, and we are all grateful when we feel its warm, natural flow through us, like a form of sunshine. . . .

Then what is pornography, after all this? It isn't sex appeal or sex 7 stimulus in art. It isn't even a deliberate intention on the part of the artist to arouse or excite sexual feelings. There's nothing wrong with sexual feelings in themselves, so long as they are straightforward and not sneaking or sly. The right sort of sex stimulus is invaluable to human daily life. Without it the world grows grey. I would give everybody the gay Renaissance stories to read, they would help to shake off a lot of grey self-importance, which is our modern civilised disease.

But even I would censor genuine pornography, rigorously. It 8 would not be very difficult. In the first place, genuine pornography is almost always underworld, it doesn't come into the open. In the second, you can recognise it by the insult it offers, invariably, to sex and to the human spirit.

Pornography is the attempt to insult sex, to do dirt on it. This is 9 unpardonable. Take the very lowest instance, the picture postcard sold underhand, by the underworld, in most cities. What I have seen of them have been of an ugliness to make you cry. The insult to the human body, the insult to a vital human relationship! Ugly and cheap they make the human nudity, ugly and degraded they make the sexual act, trivial and cheap and nasty.

10   It is the same with the books they sell in the underworld. They are either so ugly they make you ill, or so fatuous you can't imagine anybody but a cretin or a moron reading them, or writing them.

11   It is the same with the dirty limericks that people tell after dinner, or the dirty stories one hears commercial travellers telling each other in a smoke-room. Occasionally there is a really funny one, that redeems a great deal. But usually they are just ugly and repellent, and the so-called "humour" is just a trick of doing dirt on sex.

12   Now the human nudity of a great many modern people is just ugly and degraded, and the sexual act between modern people is just the same, merely ugly and degrading. But this is nothing to be proud of. It is the castastrophe of our civilisation. I am sure no other civilisation, not even the Roman, has showed such a vast proportion of ignominious and degraded nudity, and ugly, squalid dirty sex. Because no other civilisation has driven sex into the underworld, and nudity to the W.C.

13   The intelligent young, thank heaven, seem determined to alter in these two respects. They are rescuing their young nudity from the stuffy, pornographical hole-and-corner underworld of their elders, and they refuse to sneak about the sexual relation. This is a change the elderly grey ones of course deplore, but it is in fact a very great change for the better, and a real revolution.

14   But it is amazing how strong is the will in ordinary, vulgar people, to do dirt on sex. It was one of my fond illusions, when I was young, that the ordinary healthy-seeming sort of men in railway carriages, or the smoke-room of an hotel or a pullman, were healthy in their feelings and had a wholesome rough devil-may-care attitude towards sex. All wrong! All wrong! Experience teaches that common individuals of this sort have a disgusting attitude towards sex, a disgusting contempt of it, a disgusting desire to insult it. If such fellows have intercourse with a woman, they triumphantly feel that they have done her dirt, and now she is lower, cheaper, more contemptible than she was before.

15   It is individuals of this sort that tell dirty stories, carry indecent picture postcards, and know the indecent books. This is the great pornographical class — the really common men-in-the-street and women-in-the-street. They have as great a hate and contempt of sex as the greyest Puritan, and when an appeal is made to them, they are always on the side of the angels. They insist that a film-heroine shall be a neuter, a sexless thing of washed-out purity. They insist that real sex-feeling shall only be shown by the villain or villainess, low lust.

They find a Titian or a Renoir really indecent, and they don't want their wives and daughters to see it.

Why? Because they have the grey disease of sex-hatred, coupled 16 with the yellow disease of dirt-lust. The sex functions and the excrementory functions in the human body work so close together, yet they are, so to speak, utterly different in direction. Sex is a creative flow, the excrementory flow is towards dissolution, de-creation, if we may use such a word. In the really healthy human being the distinction between the two is instant, our profoundest instincts are perhaps our instincts of opposition between the two flows.

But in the degraded human being the deep instincts have gone 17 dead, and then the two flows become identical. *This* is the secret of really vulgar and of pornographical people: the sex flow and the excrement flow is the same to them. It happens when the psyche deteriorates, and the profound controlling instincts collapse. Then sex is dirt and dirt is sex, and sexual excitement becomes a playing with dirt, and any sign of sex in a woman becomes a show of her dirt. This is the condition of the common, vulgar human being whose name is legion, and who lifts his voice and it is the *Vox populi, vox Dei*. And this is the source of all pornography.

———— **CONSIDERATIONS** ——————————————————————————

1. How much help can you get from your dictionary in understanding terms like "pornography," "obscenity," "lascivious," "lewd"? Why do their definitions seem to take you in circles rather than in a straight line toward some absolute meaning? Are you frustrated by all definitions?

2. "The law is a dreary thing," writes Lawrence in Paragraph 2, "and its judgments have nothing to do with life." Does the language of law give us this impression? Why does law seem removed from life? Are there advantages in this removal?

3. In Paragraph 3, Lawrence mentions the "old, vexed question of intention." Can we use intention to resolve any matter open to interpretation — in literature, for example? How could we possibly establish Shakespeare's intentions when he wrote the sonnet "That Time of Year Thou Mayst in Me Behold"?

4. Throughout his essay, Lawrence scatters generalizations as freely as one might scatter grass seed across a needy lawn; see the last sentence of Paragraph 5, and the third sentence of Paragraph 6. Most teachers claim that such sweeping remarks weaken rather than strengthen an argument. After

studying the whole of Lawrence's essay, can you find any redeeming feature in his tendency to generalize?

5. Compare Lawrence on "the mob-habit of condemning any form of sex" (Paragraph 5) with comparable statements by Blythe in his essay "Old Age and Sexuality." Do you think the two writers would agree with each other? Why?

6. Lawrence's diction is a problem for young American readers when he uses terms more familiar to British readers, or terms that have since changed their meanings dramatically, or terms that have double meanings. Find three examples of terms offering difficulty, and analyze the difficulty in each.

Abraham Lincoln (1809–1865) was our sixteenth president, and a consensus of historians ranks him our greatest president — a ranking generally supported by the American people. He grew up self-educated, nurturing his mind on five special books: the King James Version of the Bible, Shakespeare, Parson Weems's Life of Washington, *John Bunyan's* Pilgrim's Progress, *and Daniel Defoe's* Robinson Crusoe. *His speeches and letters are models of a formal, rhythmic, studied English prose. None of his utterances is so known — so parodied, so quoted, so misquoted — as the speech he gave at Gettysburg.*

41

ABRAHAM LINCOLN

The Gettysburg Address

Four score and seven years ago our fathers brought forth on this continent, a new nation, conceived in Liberty, and dedicated to the proposition that all men are created equal.   1

Now we are engaged in a great civil war, testing whether that nation, or any nation so conceived and so dedicated, can long endure. We are met on a great battle-field of that war. We have come to dedicate a portion of that field, as a final resting place for those who here gave their lives that that nation might live. It is altogether fitting and proper that we should do this.   2

But, in a larger sense, we can not dedicate — we can not consecrate — we can not hallow — this ground. The brave men, living and dead, who struggled here, have consecrated it, far above our poor power to add or detract. The world will little note, nor long remember what we say here, but it can never forget what they did here. It is for us the living, rather, to be dedicated here to the unfinished work which they who fought here have thus far so nobly advanced. It is   3 rather for us to be here dedicated to the great task remaining before us — that from these honored dead we take increased devotion to that cause for which they gave the last full measure of devotion — that we here highly resolve that these dead shall not have died in vain — that this nation, under God, shall have a new birth of freedom — and that government of the people, by the people, for the people, shall not perish from the earth.

___ CONSIDERATIONS _____

1. Lincoln's Gettysburg Address was not subjected to the intense study, criticism, and revision that Congress gave Thomas Jefferson's Declaration of Independence (pages 225–230), but neither did Lincoln give his short speech off the top of his head. He reworked the composition before he delivered it. One of the changes occurred in the last sentence of Paragraph 2, which in an earlier version read, "This we may, in all propriety do." What do you think of his decision to change that sentence?

2. Commentators have noted that Lincoln made telling use of repeated sentence structure. Locate a good example in the address, then compose two sentences of your own, on any subject, but built in the same way.

3. Shortly after Lincoln delivered the address, the *Chicago Times* criticized his phrase, "a new birth of freedom" and called it a misrepresentation of the motives of the men slain at Gettysburg. The *Times* argued that the soldiers had died to maintain the government, the Constitution, and the union — not to advance Lincoln's "odious abolition doctrines." Can an objective reading of the address help you determine whether the *Times* attack had any substance?

4. Note how Lincoln's first reference to place is the word "continent"; his second is to "nation"; his third to "battle-field"; and his fourth to "a portion of that field." What do you make of this progressive narrowing of the field of vision? Can you see a use for such a device in your own writing?

5. Lincoln begins Paragraph 3 with a sentence in which he moves from "dedicate" to "consecrate" to "hallow." Are these words synonyms? If so, why does he say the same thing three times? If they have different meanings, is there any significance in the order in which Lincoln arranges them? Consult a good dictionary or collection of synonyms.

John McPhee (b. 1931) was born in Princeton, New Jersey, where he graduated from college, and where he still lives. His writing, largely for The New Yorker, *has taken him far afield, to Florida for a book about oranges, to Maine for a book about birchbark canoes, and all over the country for encounters with the American wilderness. In 1977 he published a report on Alaska called* Coming into the Country. *His latest book is* Basin and Range *(1981), an account of geology and geologists.*

Here we print an excerpt from McPhee's first book, A Sense of Where You Are *(1965), which told of a Princeton University undergraduate named Bill Bradley — one of the best college basketball players of his day, later a Rhodes Scholar at Oxford University, still later a forward on the champion New York Knickerbockers, and, later still, a senator of the United States elected in 1978.*

42

JOHN McPHEE
Ancestors of the Jump Shot

Bradley is not an innovator. Actually, basketball has had only a few innovators in its history — players like Hank Luisetti, of Stanford, whose introduction in 1936 of the running one-hander did as much to open up the game for scoring as the forward pass did for football; and Joe Fulks, of the old Philadelphia Warriors, whose twisting two-handed heaves, made while he was leaping like a salmon, were the beginnings of the jump shot, which seems to be basketball's ultimate weapon. Most basketball players appropriate fragments of other players' styles, and thus develop their own. This is what Bradley has done, but one of the things that set him apart from nearly everyone else is that the process has been conscious rather than osmotic. His jump shot, for example, has had two principal influences. One is Jerry West, who has one of the best jumpers in basketball. At a summer basketball camp in Missouri some years ago, West told Bradley that he always gives an extra hard bounce to the last dribble before a jump shot, since this seems to catapult him to added height. Bradley has been doing that ever since. Terry Dischinger, of the Detroit Pistons, has told Bradley that he always slams his foot to the floor on the last step before a jump shot, because this stops his momentum and thus prevents drift. Drifting while aloft is the mark of a sloppy jump shot.

2　　Bradley's graceful hook shot is a masterpiece of eclecticism. It consists of the high-lifted knee of the Los Angeles Lakers' Darrall Imhoff, the arms of Bill Russell, of the Boston Celtics, who extends his idle hand far under his shooting arm and thus magically stabilizes the shot, and the general corporeal form of Kentucky's Cotton Nash, a rookie this year with the Lakers. Bradley carries his analyses of shots further than merely identifying them with pieces of other people. "There are five parts to the hook shot," he explains to anyone who asks. As he continues, he picks up a ball and stands about eighteen feet from a basket. "Crouch," he says, crouching, and goes on to demonstrate the other moves. "Turn your head to look for the basket, step, kick, follow through with your arms." Once, as he was explaining this to me, the ball curled around the rim and failed to go in.

3　　"What happened then?" I asked him.

4　　"I didn't kick high enough," he said.

5　　"Do you always know exactly why you've missed a shot?"

6　　"Yes," he said, missing another one.

7　　"What happened that time?"

8　　"I was talking to you. I didn't concentrate. The secret of shooting is concentration."

9　　His set shot is borrowed from Ed Macauley, who was a St. Louis University All-American in the late forties and was later a star member of the Boston Celtics and the St. Louis Hawks. Macauley runs the basketball camp Bradley first went to when he was fifteen. In describing the set shot, Bradley is probably quoting a Macauley lecture. "Crouch like Groucho Marx," he says. "Go off your feet a few inches. You shoot with your legs. Your arms merely guide the ball." Bradley says that he has more confidence in his set shot than in any other. However, he seldom uses it, because he seldom has to. A set shot is a long shot, usually a twenty-footer, and Bradley, with his speed and footwork, can almost always take some other kind of shot, closer to the basket. He will take set shots when they are given to him, though. Two seasons ago, Davidson lost to Princeton, using a compact zone defense that ignored the remoter areas of the court. In one brief sequence, Bradley sent up seven set shots, missing only one. The missed one happened to rebound in Bradley's direction, and he leaped up, caught it with one hand, and scored.

Even his lay-up shot has an ancestral form; he is full of admira- 10 tion for "the way Cliff Hagan pops up anywhere within six feet of the basket," and he tries to do the same. Hagan is a former Kentucky star who now plays for the St. Louis Hawks. Because opposing teams always do everything they can to stop Bradley, he gets an unusual number of foul shots. When he was in high school, he used to imitate Bob Pettit, of the St. Louis Hawks, and Bill Sharman of the Boston Celtics, but now his free throw is more or less his own. With his left foot back about eighteen inches — "wherever it feels comfortable," he says — he shoots with a deep-bending rhythm of knees and arms, one-handed, his left hand acting as a kind of gantry for the ball until the moment of release. What is most interesting, though, is that he concentrates his attention on one of the tiny steel eyelets that are welded under the rim of the basket to hold the net to the hoop — on the center eyelet, of course — before he lets fly. One night, he scored over twenty points on free throws alone; Cornell hacked at him so heavily that he was given twenty-one free throws, and he made all twenty-one, finishing the game with a total of thirty-seven points.

When Bradley, working out alone, practices his set shots, hook 11 shots, and jump shots, he moves systematically from one place to another. around the basket, his distance from it being appropriate to the shot, and he does not permit himself to move on until he has made at least ten shots out of thirteen from each location. He applies this standard to every kind of shot, with either hand, from any distance. Many basketball players, including resonably good ones, could spend five years in a gym and not make ten out of thirteen left-handed hook shots, but that is part of Bradley's daily routine. He talks to himself while he is shooting, usually reminding himself to concentrate but sometimes talking to himself the way every high-school j.v. basketball player has done since the dim twenties — more or less imitating a radio announcer, and saying, as he gathers himself up for a shot, "It's pandemonium in Dillon Gymnasium. The clock is running out. He's up with a jumper. Swish!"

12   Last summer, the floor of the Princeton gym was being resurfaced, so Bradley had to put in several practice sessions at the Lawrenceville School. His first afternoon at Lawrenceville, he began by shooting fourteen-foot jump shots from the right side. He got off to a bad start, and he kept missing them. Six in a row hit the back rim of the basket and bounced out. He stopped, looking discomfited, and seemed to be making an adjustment in his mind. Then he went up for another jump shot from the same spot and hit it cleanly. Four more shots went in without a miss, and then he paused and said, "You want to know something? That basket is about an inch and a half low." Some weeks later, I went back to Lawrenceville with a steel tape, borrowed a stepladder, and measured the height of the basket. It was nine feet ten and seven-eighths inches above the floor, or one and one-eighth inches too low.

_____ CONSIDERATIONS _____

1. McPhee treats Bradley's technique as seriously as any student or critic treats that of a famous musician, author, painter, or sculptor. See, for example, Leonard Bernstein on "The Art of Conducting." Is it nonsense to write about the throwing of a basketball as though it were an art?

2. McPhee likes to borrow phrases from one field and apply them to another. Find at least three examples of this borrowing and evaluate their appropriateness or effectiveness.

3. Compare this McPhee piece and John Updike's short story, "Ace in the Hole."

4. To describe the movements of Bradley's jump shot requires close observation. Go to your college gym or playing field, select a move by a player, make detailed notes, and write a paragraph in which you reproduce in words what that player does with his or her body.

5. Does McPhee avoid the jargon known only to people in basketball? Is his vocabulary obscure, if you do not know the sport? List any special basketball terms McPhee uses, circle those you don't know, and decide how successful he is in making those terms clear to you.

Norman Mailer (b. 1923) grew up in Brooklyn and went to Harvard. As an undergraduate he was already publishing short stories, and his first book was a novel about World War II called The Naked and the Dead *(1948). He has published four novels since —* Barbary Shore *(1951),* The Deer Park *(1955),* An American Dream *(1965), and* Why Are We in Vietnam? *(1967) — but more and more of his writing has been nonfiction.*

He is an eminent practitioner of the New Journalism, nonfiction that employs many devices we used to associate only with fiction — lively description, dialogue, subjective exposition of character, and a tone that combines informality with energy. Early essays appeared in Advertisements for Myself *(1959), along with stories and parts of abandoned novels. In* The Presidential Papers *(1963) he began to go more fully into politics, a subject that returned in* Cannibals and Christians *(1966) and books about the protest movement (*The Armies of the Night, *1968) and about the political campaigns of 1968 and 1972 (*Miami and the Siege of Chicago, *1968;* St. George and the Godfather, *1972). More recently, he is author of books about Marilyn Monroe and Muhammad Ali. In 1979 he published his "true life novel" about the murderer Gary Gilmore,* The Executioner's Song.

Perhaps the best of his nonfiction books is Of a Fire on the Moon *(1971), his account of the first journey to the moon. This book uses some observation and personal experience. Mailer interviewed Werner Von Braun, he watched the Apollo take off. He has used much diligent research in engineering and the sciences, perhaps drawing on memories of his studies for the Bachelor of Science degree in aeronautical engineering that he took at Harvard in 1943. But Mailer's personal style often disguises Mailer's hard work. His novelist's ear for language allows him to describe with brilliance such matters as the difficulty of wedging a bulky space suit through a narrow hatch. Here, he narrates and explains the moments of man's first steps on the moon.*

43

NORMAN MAILER

A Walk on the Moon

1   It was not until nine-forty at night, Houston time, that they got the hatch open at last. In the heat of running almost two hours late, ensconced in the armor of a man-sized spaceship, could they still have felt an instant of awe as they looked out that open hatch at a panorama of theater: the sky is black, but the ground is brightly lit, bright as footlights on the floor of a dark theater. A black and midnight sky, yet on the moon ground, "you could almost go out in your shirt-sleeves and get a suntan," Aldrin would say. "I remember thinking, 'Gee, if I didn't know where I was, I could believe that somebody had created this environment somewhere out in the West and given us another simulation to work in.' " Everywhere on that pitted flat were shadows dark as the sky above, shadows dark as mine shafts.

2   What a struggle to push out from that congested cabin, now twice congested in their bulky-wham suits, no feeling of obstacle against their flesh, their sense of touch dead and numb, spaceman body manipulated out into the moon world like an upright piano turned by movers on the corner of the stairs.

3   "You're lined up on the platform. Put your left foot to the right a little bit. Okay, that's good. Roll left."

4   Armstrong was finally on the porch. Could it be with any sense of an alien atmosphere receiving the fifteen-layer encapsulations of the pack and suit on his back? Slowly, he climbed down the ladder. Archetypal, he must have felt, a boy descending the rungs in the wall of an abandoned well, or was it Jack down the stalk? And there he was on the bottom, on the footpad of the leg of the Lem, a metal plate

perhaps three feet across. Inches away was the soil of the moon. But first he jumped up again to the lowest rung of the ladder. A couple of hours later, at the end of the EVA, conceivably exhausted, the jump from the ground to the rung, three feet up, might be difficult in that stiff and heavy space suit, so he tested it now. "It takes," said Armstrong, "a pretty good little jump."

Now, with television working, and some fraction of the world 5 peering at the murky image of this instant, poised between the end of one history and the beginning of another, he said quietly, "I'm at the foot of the ladder. The Lem footpads are only depressed in the surface about one or two inches, although the surface appears to be very very fine-grained as you get close to it. It's almost like a powder." One of Armstrong's rare confessions of uneasiness is focused later on this moment. "I don't recall any particular emotion or feeling other than a little caution, a desire to be sure it was safe to put my weight on that surface outside Eagle's footpad."

Did his foot tingle in the heavy lunar overshoe? "I'm going to 6 step off the Lem now."

Did something in him shudder at the touch of the new ground? 7 Or did he draw a sweet strength from the balls of his feet? Nobody was necessarily going ever to know.

"That's one small step for a man," said Armstrong, "one giant 8 leap for mankind." He had joined the ranks of the forever quoted. Patrick Henry, Henry Stanley and Admiral Dewey moved over for him.

Now he was out there, one foot on the moon, then the other foot 9 on the moon, the powder like velvet underfoot. With one hand still on the ladder, he comments, "The surface is fine and powdery. I can . . . I can pick it up loosely with my toe." And as he releases his catch, the grains fall back slowly to the soil, a fan of feathers gliding to the floor. "It does adhere in fine layers like powdered charcoal to the sole and sides of my boots. I only go in a small fraction of an inch. Maybe an eighth of an inch. But I can see the footprints of my boots and the treads in the fine sand particles."

Capcom: "Neil, this is Houston. We're copying." 10

Yes, they would copy. He was like a man who goes into a 11 wrecked building to defuse a new kind of bomb. He talks into a microphone as he works, for if a mistake is made, and the bomb goes off, it will be easier for the next man if every detail of his activities has been mentioned as he performed them. Now, he released his grip on the ladder and pushed off for a few steps on the moon, odd loping steps, almost thrust into motion like a horse trotting up a steep slope. It could have been a moment equivalent to the first steps he took as an infant for there was nothing to hold onto and he did not dare to fall — the ground was too hot, the rocks might tear his suit. Yet if he stumbled, he could easily go over for he could not raise his arms above his head nor reach to his knees, his arms in the pressure bladder stood out before him like sausages; so, if he tottered, the weight of the pack could twist him around, or drop him. They had tried to shape up simulations of lunar gravity while weighted in scuba suits at the bottom of a pool, but water was not a vacuum through which to move; so they had also flown in planes carrying two hundred pounds of equipment on their backs. The pilot would take the plane through a parabolic trajectory. There would be a period of twenty-two seconds at the top of the curve when a simulation of one-sixth gravity would be present, and the two hundred pounds of equipment would weigh no more than on the moon, no more than thirty-plus pounds, and one could take loping steps down the aisle of the plane, staggering through unforeseen wobbles or turbulence. Then the parabolic trajectory was done, the plane was diving, and it would have to pull out of the dive. That created the reverse of one-sixth gravity — it multiplied gravity by two and a half times. The two hundred pounds of equipment now weighed five hundred pounds and the astronauts had to be supported by other men straining to help them bear the weight. So simulations gave them time for hardly more than a clue before heavy punishment was upon them. But now he was out in the open endless lunar gravity, his body and the reflexes of his life obliged to adopt a new rhythm and schedule of effort, a new disclosure of grace.

12   Still, he seemed pleased after the first few steps. "There seems to be no difficulty in moving around as we suspected. It's even perhaps easier than the simulations . . ." He would run a few steps and stop, run a few steps and stop. Perhaps it was not unlike directing the Lem when it hovered over the ground. One moved faster than on earth and with less effort, but it was harder to stop — one had to pick the place to halt from several yards ahead. Yes, it was easier once moving, but awkward at the beginning and the end because of the obdurate plastic bendings of the suit. And once standing at rest, the sense of the vertical was sly. One could be leaning further forward than one knew. Or leaning backward. Like a needle on a dial one would have to oscillate from side to side of the vertical to find position. Conceivably the sensation was not unlike skiing with a child on one's back.

It was time for Aldrin to descend the ladder from the Lem to the   13
ground, and Armstrong's turn to give directions: "The shoes are about
to come over the sill. Okay, now drop your PLSS down. There you go.
You're clear. . . . About an inch clearance on top of your PLSS."

Aldrin spoke for future astronauts: "Okay, you need a little bit   14
of arching of the back to come down . . .''

When he reached the ground, Aldrin took a big and exuberant   15
leap up the ladder again, as if to taste the pleasures of one-sixth gravity
all at once. "Beautiful, beautiful," he exclaimed.

Armstrong: "Isn't that something. Magnificent sight out here."   16

Aldrin: "Magnificent desolation."   17

They were looking at a terrain which lived in a clarity of focus   18
unlike anything they had ever seen on earth. There was no air, of
course, and so no wind, nor clouds, nor dust, nor even the finest scat-
tering of light from the smallest dispersal of microscopic particles on
a clear day on earth, no, nothing visible or invisible moved in the
vacuum before them. All light was pure. No haze was present, not
even the invisible haze of the finest day — therefore objects did not go
out of focus as they receded into the distance. If one's eyes were good
enough, an object at a hundred yards was as distinct as a rock at a few
feet. And their eyes were good enough. Just as one could not determine
one's altitude above the moon, not from fifty miles up nor five, so now
along the ground before them no distance was real, for all distances
had the faculty to appear equally near if one peered at them through
blinders and could not see the intervening details. Again the sense of
being on a stage or on the lighted floor of a room so large one could
not see where the dark ceiling began must have come upon them, for
there were no hints of gathering evanescence in ridge beyond ridge;
rather each outline was as severe as the one in front of it, and since
the ground was filled with small craters of every size, from antholes
to potholes to empty pools, and the horizon was near, four times
nearer than on earth and sharp as the line drawn by a pencil, the moon
ground seemed to slope and drop in all directions "like swimming in
an ocean with six-foot or eight-foot swells and waves," Armstrong
said later. "In that condition, you never can see very far away from
where you are." But what they could see, they could see entirely — to
the depth of their field of view at any instant their focus was complete.
And as they swayed from side to side, so a sense of the vertical kept
eluding them, the slopes of the craters about them seeming to tilt a
few degrees to one side of the horizontal, then the other. On earth, one
had only to incline one's body an inch or two and a sense of the

vertical was gone, but on the moon they could lean over, then further over, lean considerably further over without beginning to fall. So verticals slid and oscillated. Rolling from side to side, they could as well have been on water, indeed their sense of the vertical was probably equal to the subtle uncertainty of the body when a ship is rolling on a quiet sea. "I say," said Aldrin, "the rocks are rather slippery."

19   They were discovering the powder of the moon soil was curious indeed, comparable in firmness and traction to some matter between sand and snow. While the Lem looked light as a kite, for its pads hardly rested on the ground and it appeared ready to lift off and blow away, yet their own feet sometimes sank for two or three inches into the soft powder on the slope of very small craters, and their soles would slip as the powder gave way under their boots. In other places the ground was firm and harder than sand, yet all of these variations were to be found in an area not a hundred feet out from the legs of the Lem. As he explored his footing, Aldrin sent back comments to Mission Control, reporting in the rapt professional tones of a coach instructing his team on the conditions of the turf in a new plastic football field.

20   Meanwhile Armstrong was transporting the television camera away from the Lem to a position where it could cover most of their activities. Once properly installed, he revolved it through a full panorama of their view in order that audiences on earth might have a clue to what he saw. But in fact the transmission was too rudimentary to give any sense of what was about them, that desert sea of rocks, rubble, small boulders, and crater lips.

21   Aldrin was now working to set up the solar wind experiment, a sheet of aluminum foil hung on a stand. For the next hour and a half, the foil would be exposed to the solar wind, an invisible, unfelt, but high-velocity flow of noble gases from the sun like argon, krypton, neon and helium. For the astronauts, it was the simplest of procedures, no more difficult than setting up a piece of sheet music on a music stand. At the end of the EVA, however, the aluminum foil would be rolled up, inserted in the rock box, and delivered eventually to a laboratory in Switzerland uniquely equipped for the purpose. There any noble gases which had been trapped in the atomic lattice of the aluminum would be baked out in virtuoso procedures of quantitative analysis, and a closer knowledge of the components of the solar wind would be gained. Since the solar wind, it may be recalled, was diverted by the magnetosphere away from the earth it had not hitherto been available for casual study.

That was the simplest experiment to set up; the other two would 22
be deployed about an hour later. One was a passive seismometer to
measure erratic disturbances and any periodic vibrations, as well as
moonquakes, and the impact of meteors in the weeks and months to
follow; it was equipped to radio this information to earth, the energy
for transmission derived from solar panels which extended out to
either side, and thereby gave it the look of one of those spaceships of
the future with thin extended paperlike wings which one sees in science fiction drawings. In any case it was so sensitive that the steps of
the astronauts were recorded as they walked by. Finally there was a
Laser Ranging Retro-Reflector, an LRRR (or LRQ, or L R-cubed), and
that was a mirror whose face was a hundred quartz crystals, black as
coal, cut to a precision never obtained before in glass — one-third of
an arc/sec. Since each quartz crystal was a corner of a rectangle, any
ray of light striking one of the three faces in each crystal would bounce
off the other two in such a way that the light would return in exactly
the same direction it had been received. A laser beam sent up from
earth would therefore reflect back to the place from which it was sent.
The time it required to travel this half-million miles from earth to
moon round trip, a journey of less than three seconds, could be measured so accurately that physicists might then discern whether the
moon was drifting away from the earth a few centimeters a year, or
(by using two lasers) whether Europe and America might be drifting
apart some comparable distance, or even if the Pacific Ocean were
contracting. These measurements could then be entered into the caverns of Einstein's General Theory of Relativity, and new proof or
disproof of the great thesis could be obtained.

We may be certain the equipment was remarkable. Still, its pack- 23
aging and its ease of deployment had probably done as much to
advance its presence on the ship as any clear priority over other scientific equipment; the beauty of these items from the point of view of
NASA was that the astronauts could set them up in a few minutes
while working in their space suits, even set them up with inflated
gloves so insensitive that special silicone pads had to be inserted at
the fingertips in order to leave the astronauts not altogether numb-
fingered in their manipulations. Yet these marvels of measurement
would soon be installed on the moon with less effort than it takes to
remove a vacuum cleaner from its carton and get it operating.

It was at this point that patriotism, the corporation, and the 24
national taste all came to occupy the same head of a pin, for the
astronauts next proceeded to set up the flag. But that operation, as

always, presented its exquisite problems. There was, we remind ourselves, no atmosphere for the flag to wave in. Any flag made of cloth
would droop, indeed it would dangle. Therefore, a species of starched
plastic flag had to be employed, a flag which would stand out, there,
out to the nonexistent breeze, flat as a slab of plywood. No, that would
not do either. The flag was better crinkled and curled. Waves and
billows were bent into it, and a full corkscrew of a curl at the end.
There it stands for posterity, photographed in the twists of a high gale
on the windless moon, curled up tin flag, numb as a pickled pepper.

25   Aldrin would hardly agree. "Being able to salute that flag was one
of the more humble yet proud experiences I've ever had. To be able to
look at the American flag and know how much so many people had
put of themselves and their work into getting it where it was. We
sensed — we really did — this almost mystical identification of all the
people in the world at that instant."

26   Two minutes after the flag was up, the President of the United
States put in his phone call. Let us listen one more time:

27   "Because of what you have done," said Nixon, "the heavens have
become a part of man's world. And as you talk to us from the Sea of
Tranquility, it inspires us to redouble our efforts to bring peace and
tranquility to earth . . ."

28   "Thank you, Mr. President. It's a great honor and privilege for us
to be here representing not only the United States, but men of peace
of all nations . . ."

29   In such piety is the schizophrenia of the ages.

30   Immediately afterward, Aldrin practiced kicking moon dust, but
he was somewhat broken up. Either reception was garbled, or Aldrin
was temporarily incoherent. "They seem to leave," he said to the
Capcom, referring to the particles, "and most of them have about the
same angle of departure and velocity. From where I stand, a large
portion of them will impact at a certain distance out. Several — the
percentage is, of course, that will impact . . ."

31   Capcom: "Buzz, this is Houston. You're cutting out on the end
of your transmissions. Can you speak a little more forward into your
microphone. Over."

32   Aldrin: "Roger, I'll try that."

33   Capcom: "Beautiful."

34   Aldrin: "Now I had that one inside my mouth that time."

35   Capcom: "It sounded a little wet."

36   And on earth, a handful of young scientists were screaming,
"Stop wasting time with flags and presidents — collect some rocks!"

_____ **CONSIDERATIONS** _____

1. Mailer's task — to narrate what the moon-walkers experienced — is complicated by the necessity to describe technical operations, equipment, and navigational procedures. Is Mailer successful in keeping human experience uppermost? Explain.

2. Look closely at Mailer's account of setting up the American flag on the moon and at the remarks immediately following by Aldrin, President Nixon, and Mailer himself. "In such piety is the schizophrenia of the ages," says Mailer. Is this straight reporting? Is it loaded? If so, can you justify it?

3. What are some differences between the astronauts' moon exploration and the travels of others in this book, such as Lillian Hellman (pages 199–205) and N. Scott Momaday (pages 259–265)?

4. "If it were spelled 'mune,'" wrote Jack Spicer, the American poet, "it would not cause madness." The moon has been surrounded by worlds of mythology, superstition, and fond fantasy. Will exact information about the moon affect our way of thinking of or responding to "moon"? Does knowledge affect belief?

5. A man in Houston tells a man on the moon when to put his left foot down. Discuss the remote control feature in moon explorations. Are there parallels in medicine, or oceanographic research, or electronic games?

Andrew Marvell (1621–1678) lived during a time of turmoil in England — during Cromwell's revolution, the beheading of a king, and the restoration of the monarchy. He was a political man, a member of Parliament, and at different times espoused different sides, without ever turning hypocrite. Some of his poems are political; the best are not, unless "To His Coy Mistress" is a manifesto of sexual politics. Many readers find it less concerned with sexuality than with mortality.

44

ANDREW MARVELL

To His Coy Mistress

Had we but world enough, and time,
This coyness, lady, were no crime.
We would sit down, and think which way
To walk, and pass our long love's day.
5 Thou by the Indian Ganges' side
Shouldst rubies find; I by the tide
Of Humber would complain. I would
Love you ten years before the flood,
And you should, if you please, refuse
10 Till the conversion of the Jews.
My vegetable love should grow
Vaster than empires and more slow;
An hundred years should go to praise
Thine eyes, and on thy forehead gaze;
15 Two hundred to adore each breast,
But thirty thousand to the rest;
An age at least to every part,
And the last age should show your heart.

For, lady, you deserve this state,
Nor would I love at lower rate   20
      But at my back I always hear
Time's wingéd chariot hurrying near;
And yonder all before us lie
Deserts of vast eternity.
Thy beauty shall no more be found;   25
Nor, in thy marble vault, shall sound
My echoing song; then worms shall try
That long-preserved virginity,
And your quaint honor turn to dust,
And into ashes all my lust: 30
The grave's a fine and private place,
But none, I think, do there embrace.
      Now therefore, while the youthful hue
Sits on thy skin like morning dew,
And while thy willing soul transpires   35
At every pore with instant fires,
Now let us sport us while we may,
And now, like amorous birds of prey,
Rather at once our time devour
Than languish in his slow-chapped° power.   40
Let us roll all our strength and all
Our sweetness up into one ball,
And tear our pleasures with rough strife
Thorough the iron gates of life:
Thus, though we cannot make our sun   45
Stand still, yet we will make him run.

° slow-jawed

H. L. Mencken (1880–1956), the dominant editor of his day, edited the magazines Smart Set *and* American Mercury, *and wrote funny, intelligent, cantankerous, irascible, mocking essays about American political, artistic, and social mores. He collected the best of his periodical writing in six books of* Prejudices *(1919, 1920, 1922, 1924, 1926, 1927) and in* A Book of Prefaces *(1917). (See Richard Wright's reminiscence of reading Mencken, on pages 480–488.) His* The American Language *(1919) and its two* Supplements *(1945, 1948) looked at the difference between American and English, and argued the vitality of the American language. Later in life he wrote an autobiography in three volumes,* Happy Days *(1940),* Newspaper Days *(1941) and* Heathen Days *(1943).*

"Gamalielese" shows Mencken's talents as a social critic, as a debunker of popular idiocy. It also demonstrates his tight observation of the American language, and his humor. Warren Gamaliel Harding was twenty-ninth president of the United States. On the question of President Harding's intellectual qualifications for office, history has been as unkind as Harding's contemporary.

45

H. L. MENCKEN
Gamalielese

1   On the question of the logical content of Dr. Harding's harangue of last Friday I do not presume to have views. The matter has been debated at great length by the editorial writers of the Republic, all of them experts in logic; moreover, I confess to being prejudiced. When a man arises publicly to argue that the United States entered the late

From the *Baltimore Sun*, March 7, 1921. Reprinted by permission of the *Baltimore Sun*.

war because of a "concern for preserved civilization," I can only snicker in a superior way and wonder why he isn't holding down the chair of history in some American university. When he says that the U.S. has "never sought territorial aggrandizement through force," the snicker rises to the virulence of a chuckle, and I turn to the first volume of General Grant's memoirs. And when, gaining momentum, he gravely informs the boobery that "ours is a constitutional freedom where the popular will is supreme, and minorities are sacredly protected," then I abandon myself to a mirth that transcends, perhaps, the seemly, and send picture postcards of A. Mitchell Palmer,[1] and the Atlanta Penitentiary to all of my enemies who happen to be Socialists.

But when it comes to the style of a great man's discourse, I can   2
speak with a great deal less prejudice, and maybe with somewhat more competence, for I have earned most of my livelihood for twenty years past by translating the bad English of a multitude of authors into measurably better English. Thus qualified professionally, I rise to pay my small tribute to Dr. Harding. Setting aside a college professor or two and half a dozen dipsomaniacal newspaper reporters, he takes the first place in my Valhall of literati. That is to say, he writes the worst English that I have ever encountered. It reminds me of a string of wet sponges; it reminds me of tattered washing on the line; it reminds me of a stale bean-soup, of college yells, of dogs barking idiotically through endless nights. It is so bad that a sort of grandeur creeps into it. It drags itself out of the dark abysm (I was about to write abscess!) of pish, and crawls insanely up the topmost pinnacle of posh. It is rumble and bumble. It is flap and doodle. It is balder and dash.

But I grow lyrical. More scientifically, what is the matter with   3
it? Why does it seem so flabby, so banal, so confused and childish, so stupidly at war with sense? If you first read the inaugural address and then hear it intoned, as I did (at least in part), then you will perhaps arrive at an answer. That answer is very simple. When Dr. Harding prepares a speech he does not think it out in terms of an educated reader locked up in jail, but in terms of a great horde of stoneheads gathered around a stand. That is to say, the thing is always a stump speech; it is conceived as a stump speech and written as a stump speech. More, it is a stump speech addressed primarily to the sort of audience that the speaker has been used to all his life, to wit, an audience of small town yokels, of low political serfs, of morons

---

[1] Seventh U.S. attorney general, who ordered arrests in the red scare of 1919 and 1920. — ED.

scarcely able to understand a word of more than two syllables, and wholly unable to pursue a logical idea for more than two centimeters.

4   Such imbeciles do not want ideas — that is, new ideas, ideas that are unfamiliar, ideas that challenge their attention. What they want is simply a gaudy series of platitudes, of threadbare phrases terrifically repeated, of sonorous nonsense driven home with gestures. As I say, they can't understand many words of more than two syllables, but that is not saying that they do not esteem such words. On the contrary, they like them and demand them. The roll of incomprehensible polysyllables enchants them. They like phrases which thunder like salvos of artillery. Let that thunder sound, and they take all the rest on trust. If a sentence begins furiously and then peters out into fatuity, they are still satisfied. If a phrase has a punch in it, they do not ask that it also have a meaning. If a word slides off the tongue like a ship going down the ways, they are content and applaud it and wait for the next.

5   Brought up amid such hinds, trained by long practice to engage and delight them, Dr. Harding carries over his stump manner into everything he writes. He is, perhaps, too old to learn a better way. He is, more likely, too discreet to experiment. The stump speech, put into cold type, maketh the judicious to grieve. But roared from an actual stump, with arms flying and eyes flashing and the old flag overhead, it is certainly and brilliantly effective. Read the inaugural address, and it will gag you. But hear it recited through a sound-magnifier, with grand gestures to ram home its periods, and you will begin to understand it.

6   Let us turn to a specific example. I exhume a sentence from the latter half of the eminent orator's discourse:

7   "I would like government to do all it can to mitigate; then, in understanding, in mutuality of interest, in concern for the common good, our tasks will be solved."

8   I assume that you have read it. I also assume that you set it down as idiotic — a series of words without sense. You are quite right; it is. But now imagine it intoned as it was designed to be intoned. Imagine the slow tempo of a public speech. Imagine the stately unrolling of the first clause, the delicate pause upon the word "then" — and then the loud discharge of the phrases "in understanding," "in mutuality of interest," "in concern for the common good," each with its attendant glare and roll of the eyes, each with its sublime heave, each with its gesture of a blacksmith bringing down his sledge upon an egg — imagine all this, and then ask yourself where you have got. You have got, in brief, to a point where you don't know what it is all about. You hear

and applaud the phrases, but their connection has already escaped you. And so, when in violation of all sequence and logic, the final phrase, "our tasks will be solved," assaults you, you do not notice its disharmony — all you notice is that, if this or that, already forgotten, is done, "our tasks will be solved." Whereupon, glad of the assurance and thrilled by the vast gestures that drive it home, you give a cheer.

That is, if you are the sort of man who goes to political meetings,   9 which is to say, if you are the sort of man that Dr. Harding is used to talking to, which is to say, if you are a jackass.

The whole inaugural address reeked with just such nonsense.   10 The thing started off with an error in English in its very first sentence — the confusion of pronouns in the *one-he* combination, so beloved of bad newspaper reporters. It bristled with words misused: *civic* for *civil, luring* for *alluring, womanhood* for *women, referendum* for *reference,* even *task* for *problem.* "The *task* is to be *solved"* — what could be worse? Yet I find it twice. "The expressed views of world opinion" — what irritating tautology! "The expressed conscience of progress" — what on earth does it mean? "This is not selfishness, it is sanctity" — what intelligible idea do you get out of that? "I know that Congress and the administration will favor every wise government policy to aid the resumption and encourage continued progress" — the resumption of what? "Service is the supreme *commitment* of life" — *ach, du heiliger!*

But is such bosh out of place in a stump speech? Obviously not.   11 It is precisely and thoroughly in place in a stump speech. A tight fabric of ideas would weary and exasperate the audience; what it wants is simply a loud burble of words, a procession of phrases that roar, a series of whoops. This is what it got in the inaugural address of the Hon. Warren Gamaliel Harding. And this is what it will get for four long years — unless God sends a miracle and the corruptible puts on incorruption . . . Almost I long for the sweeter song, the rubber-stamps of more familiar design, the gentler and more seemly bosh of the late Woodrow.

_____ **CONSIDERATIONS** _____

1. In his first sentence, Mencken denies having opinions about "the logical content" in Harding's address, promising instead to concentrate on Harding's style. How successful is he in avoiding comment on the content of the Harding speech? What is the relationship between content and style?

2. Can you find two or three phrases that suggest Mencken's irony? What do his ironic twists and turns contribute to his essay?

3. Mencken wrote his review of Harding's address at least twenty years before George Orwell published his "Politics and the English Language" (pages 310–322). Would Orwell applaud or criticize Mencken's treatment of the president?

4. Study the variety of Mencken's words, perhaps setting up two columns, one to list words like "pish" and "posh," and the other for words or phrases like "incomprehensible polysyllables." Do such extremes of diction confuse the reader, enliven the writer's argument, both, or neither?

5. Is Mencken himself guilty of any sins that he attributes to Harding? Explain, with examples.

6. How does Mencken's style support his opinionated view of politicians and political language?

N. Scott Momaday (b. 1934) was born in Oklahoma, and attended schools on Navaho, Apache, and Pueblo reservations. After graduating from the University of New Mexico, he took a Ph.D. at Stanford and now teaches there. He won the Pulitzer Prize in 1969 for his novel House Made of Dawn, *and in 1976 collected his poems in* The Gourd Dancer.

Momaday's father is a pure-blooded Kiowa, a teacher, and an artist. His mother, also a teacher, and author of books for older children, is part English, part French, and part Cherokee. Momaday spent summers as a child with his Kiowa grandmother, and has continually turned to his Indian ancestry as a source for writing. The essay below introduces The Way to Rainy Mountain *(1969), in which Momaday collected Kiowa legends.*

American writers continually dwell upon the return to origins — the farm in the country, the village in Sicily, the ghetto in Poland. Many of us can tell a story of going backward in time, on a journey to grandmother's house. Momaday's journey takes him further, and he takes us with him by the force of his language, to an America inside America, all but invisible to most Americans.

46

N. SCOTT MOMADAY
The Way to Rainy Mountain

A single knoll rises out of the plain in Oklahoma, north and west   1
of the Wichita Range. For my people, the Kiowas, it is an old land-
mark, and they gave it the name Rainy Mountain. The hardest
weather in the world is there. Winter brings blizzards, hot tornadic
winds arise in the spring, and in summer the prairie is an anvil's edge.

First published in *The Reporter*, January 26, 1967. Reprinted by permission from *The Way to Rainy Mountain*, copyright 1969, The University of New Mexico Press.

The grass turns brittle and brown, and it cracks beneath your feet. There are green belts along the rivers and creeks, linear groves of hickory and pecan, willow and witch hazel. At a distance in July or August the steaming foliage seems almost to writhe in fire. Great green and yellow grasshoppers are everywhere in the tall grass, popping up like corn to sting the flesh, and tortoises crawl about on the red earth, going nowhere in the plenty of time. Loneliness is an aspect of the land. All things in the plain are isolate; there is no confusion of objects in the eye, but *one* hill or *one* tree or *one* man. To look upon that landscape in the early morning, with the sun at your back, is to lose the sense of proportion. Your imagination comes to life, and this, you think, is where Creation was begun.

2   I returned to Rainy Mountain in July. My grandmother had died in the spring, and I wanted to be at her grave. She had lived to be very old and at last infirm. Her only living daughter was with her when she died, and I was told that in death her face was that of a child.

3   I like to think of her as a child. When she was born, the Kiowas were living the last great moment of their history. For more than a hundred years they had controlled the open range from the Smoky Hill River to the Red, from the headwaters of the Canadian to the fork of the Arkansas and Cimarron. In alliance with the Comanches, they had ruled the whole of the southern Plains. War was their sacred business, and they were among the finest horsemen the world has ever known. But warfare for the Kiowas was preeminently a matter of disposition rather than of survival, and they never understood the grim, unrelenting advance of the U.S. Cavalry. When at last, divided and ill-provisioned, they were driven onto the Stake Plains in the cold rains of autumn, they fell into panic. In Palo Duro Canyon they abandoned their crucial stores to pillage and had nothing then but their lives. In order to save themselves, they surrendered to the soldiers at Fort Sill and were imprisoned in the old stone corral that now stands as a military museum. My grandmother was spared the humiliation of those high gray walls by eight or ten years, but she must have known from birth the affliction of defeat, the dark brooding of old warriors.

4   Her name was Aho, and she belonged to the last culture to evolve in North America. Her forebears came down from the high country in western Montana nearly three centuries ago. They were a mountain people, a mysterious tribe of hunters whose language has never been positively classified in any major group. In the late seventeenth century they began a long migration to the south and east. It was a journey toward the dawn, and it led to a golden age. Along the way the Kiowas

were befriended by the Crows, who gave them the culture and religion of the Plains. They acquired horses, and their ancient nomadic spirit was suddenly free of the ground. They acquired Tai-me, the sacred Sun Dance doll, from that moment the object and symbol of their worship, and so shared in the divinity of the sun. Not least, they acquired the sense of destiny, therefore courage and pride. When they entered upon the southern Plains they had been transformed. No longer were they slaves to the simple necessity of survival; they were a lordly and dangerous society of fighters and thieves, hunters and priests of the sun. According to their origin myth, they entered the world through a hollow log. From one point of view, their migration was the fruit of an old prophecy, for indeed they emerged from a sunless world.

Although my grandmother lived out her long life in the shadow of Rainy Mountain, the immense landscape of the continental interior lay like memory in her blood. She could tell of the Crows, whom she had never seen, and of the Black Hills, where she had never been. I wanted to see in reality what she had seen more perfectly in the mind's eye, and traveled fifteen hundred miles to begin my pilgrimage. 5

Yellowstone, it seemed to me, was the top of the world, a region of deep lakes and dark timber, canyons and waterfalls. But, beautiful as it is, one might have the sense of confinement there. The skyline in all directions is close at hand, the high wall of the woods and deep cleavages of shade. There is a perfect freedom in the mountains, but it belongs to the eagle and the elk, the badger and the bear. The Kiowas reckoned their stature by the distance they could see, and they were bent and blind in the wilderness. 6

Descending eastward, the highland meadows are a stairway to the plain. In July the inland slope of the Rockies is luxuriant with flax and buckwheat, stonecrop and larkspur. The earth unfolds and the limit of the land recedes. Clusters of trees, and animals grazing far in the distance, cause the vision to reach away and wonder to build upon the mind. The sun follows a longer course in the day, and the sky is immense beyond all comparison. The great billowing clouds that sail upon it are shadows that move upon the grain like water, dividing light. Farther down, in the land of the Crows and Blackfeet, the plain is yellow. Sweet clover takes hold of the hills and bends upon itself to cover and seal the soil. There the Kiowas paused on their way; they had come to the place where they must change their lives. The sun is at home on the plains. Precisely there does it have the certain character of a god. When the Kiowas came to the land of the Crows, they 7 could see the dark lees of the hills at dawn across the Bighorn River, the profusion of light on the grain shelves, the oldest diety ranging after the solstices. Not yet would they veer southward to the caldron of the land that lay below; they must wean their blood from the northern winter and hold the mountains a while longer in their view. They bore Tai-me in procession to the east.

8 A dark mist lay over the Black Hills, and the land was like iron. At the top of a ridge I caught sight of Devil's Tower upthrust against the gray sky as if in the birth of time the core of the earth had broken through its crust and the motion of the world was begun. There are things in nature that engender an awful quiet in the heart of man; Devil's Tower is one of them. Two centuries ago, because they could not do otherwise, the Kiowas made a legend at the base of the rock. My grandmother said:

> Eight children were there at play, seven sisters and their brother. Suddenly the boy was struck dumb; he trembled and began to run upon his hands and feet. His fingers became claws, and his body was covered with fur. Directly there was a bear where the boy had been. The sisters were terrified; they ran, and the bear after them. They came to the stump of a great tree, and the tree spoke to them. It bade them climb upon it, and as they did so it began to rise into the air. The bear came to kill them, but they were just beyond its reach. It reared against the tree and scored the bark all around with its claws. The seven sisters were borne into the sky, and they became the stars of the Big Dipper.

From that moment, and so long as the legend lives, the Kiowas have kinsmen in the night sky. Whatever they were in the mountains, they could be no more. However tenuous their well-being, however much they had suffered and would suffer again, they had found a way out of the wilderness.

9 My grandmother had a reverence for the sun, a holy regard that now is all but gone out of mankind. There was a wariness in her, and an ancient awe. She was a Christian in her later years, but she had come a long way about, and she never forgot her birthright. As a child she had been to the Sun Dances; she had taken part in those annual rites, and by them she had learned the restoration of her people in the presence of Tai-me. She was about seven when the last Kiowa Sun Dance was held in 1887 on the Washita River above Rainy Mountain Creek. The buffalo were gone. In order to consummate the ancient sacrifice — to impale the head of a buffalo bull upon the medicine tree — a delegation of old men journeyed into Texas, there to beg and

barter for an animal from the Goodnight herd. She was ten when the Kiowas came together for the last time as a living Sun Dance culture. They could find no buffalo; they had to hang an old hide from the sacred tree. Before the dance could begin, a company of soldiers rode out from Fort Sill under orders to disperse the tribe. Forbidden without cause the essential act of their faith, having seen the wild herds slaughtered and left to rot upon the ground, the Kiowas backed away forever from the medicine tree. That was July 20, 1890, at the great bend of the Washita. My grandmother was there. Without bitterness, and for as long as she lived, she bore a vision of deicide.

Now that I can have her only in memory, I see my grandmother   10 in the several postures that were peculiar to her: standing at the wood stove on a winter morning and turning meat in a great iron skillet; sitting at the south window, bent above her beadwork, and afterwards, when her vision failed, looking down for a long time into the fold of her hands; going out upon a cane, very slowly as she did when the weight of age came upon her; praying. I remember her most often at prayer. She made long, rambling prayers out of suffering and hope, having seen many things. I was never sure that I had the right to hear, so exclusive were they of all mere custom and company. The last time I saw her she prayed standing by the side of her bed at night, naked to the waist, the light of a kerosene lamp moving upon her dark skin. Her long, black hair, always drawn and braided in the day, lay upon her shoulders and against her breasts like a shawl. I do not speak Kiowa, and I never understood her prayers, but there was something inherently sad in the sound, some merest hestitation upon the sylla-bles of sorrow. She began in a high and descending pitch, exhausting her breath to silence; then again and again — and always the same intensity of effort, of something that is, and is not, like urgency in the human voice. Transported so in the dancing light among the shadows of her room, she seemed beyond the reach of time. But that was illu-sion; I think I knew then that I should not see her again.

Houses are like sentinels in the plain, old keepers of the weather   11 watch. There, in a very little while, wood takes on the appearance of great age. All colors wear soon away in the wind and rain, and then the wood is burned gray and the grain appears and the nails turn red with rust. The windowpanes are black and opaque; you imagine there is nothing within, and indeed there are many ghosts, bones given up to the land. They stand here and there against the sky, and you approach them for a longer time than you expect. They belong in the distance; it is their domain.

12   Once there was a lot of sound in my grandmother's house, a lot of coming and going, feasting and talk. The summers there were full of excitement and reunion. The Kiowas are a summer people; they abide the cold and keep to themselves, but when the season turns and the land becomes warm and vital they cannot hold still; an old love of going returns upon them. The aged visitors who came to my grandmother's house when I was a child were made of lean and leather, and they bore themselves upright. They wore great black hats and bright ample shirts that shook in the wind. They rubbed fat upon their hair and wound their braids with strips of colored cloth. Some of them painted their faces and carried the scars of old and cherished enmities. They were an old council of warlords, come to remind and be reminded of who they were. Their wives and daughters served them well. The women might indulge themselves; gossip was at once the mark and compensation of their servitude. They made loud and elaborate talk among themselves, full of jest and gesture, fright and false alarm. They went abroad in fringed and flowered shawls, bright beadwork and German silver. They were at home in the kitchen, and they prepared meals that were banquets.

13   There were frequent prayer meetings, and great nocturnal feasts. When I was a child I played with my cousins outside, where the lamplight fell upon the ground and the singing of the old people rose up around us and carried away into the darkness. There were a lot of good things to eat, a lot of laughter and surprise. And afterwards, when the quiet returned, I lay down with my grandmother and could hear the frogs away by the river and feel the motion of the air.

14   Now there is a funeral silence in the rooms, the endless wake of some final word. The walls have closed in upon my grandmother's house. When I returned to it in mourning, I saw for the first time in my life how small it was. It was late at night, and there was a white moon, nearly full. I sat for a long time on the stone steps by the kitchen door. From there I could see out across the land; I could see the long row of trees by the creek, the low light upon the rolling plains, and the stars of the Big Dipper. Once I looked at the moon and caught sight of a strange thing. A cricket had perched upon the handrail, only a few inches away from me. My line of vision was such that the creature filled the moon like a fossil. It had gone there, I thought, to live and die, for there, of all places, was its small definition made whole and eternal. A warm wind rose up and purled like the longing within me.

15   The next morning I awoke at dawn and went out on the dirt road

to Rainy Mountain. It was already hot, and the grasshoppers began to fill the air. Still, it was early in the morning, and the birds sang out of the shadows. The long yellow grass on the mountain shone in the bright light, and a scissortail hied above the land. There, where it ought to be, at the end of a long and legendary way, was my grandmother's grave. Here and there on the dark stones were ancestral names. Looking back once, I saw the mountain and came away.

___ **CONSIDERATIONS** _____

1. Momaday attempts a large, general topic — the quest and migrations of a people, the Kiowas — yet he concentrates on one person, his grandmother. Why? A beginning writer may find an important guiding principle in this answer.

2. Momaday's essay is studded with names of native plants, such as hickory, pecan, willow, witch hazel, flax, buckwheat, stonecrop, larkspur. What do particulars do for an account like this?

3. Momaday writes that according to their origin myth, the Kiowas entered the world "through a hollow log." Why do people preserve such myths? Are you aware of any comparable myths in our culture of supermarkets, freeways, and television? Or do you believe, with some social historians, that twentieth-century Americans are a mythless people?

4. The sense of place seems to be important to human consciousness and identity. Compare Momaday's treatment of place with Annie Dillard's in "Strangers to Darkness."

5. After reading Momaday, read Flannery O'Connor's essay, "Total Effect and the Eighth Grade," paying particular attention to Paragraphs 7, 8, and 9. Can you connect Momaday's need to find his history with O'Connor's insistence that schoolchildren also need a historical base on which to develop?

6. Do you *see* the image that Momaday wants us to see, when he describes the cricket against the moon in his next to last paragraph? Why does the image belong in that paragraph? If you have read Norman Mailer's account of moon exploration (pages 244–250), invent a similar image — some little object held up by one of the astronauts against the pale earth a quarter million miles away.

Alice Morgan (b. 1940) took her Ph.D. in English at Harvard,
where she later taught expository writing. The notions expressed
in this brief article first occurred to her, as we might expect,
when she was an undergraduate facing final exams.

47

ALICE B. MORGAN
Exam-Week Unrealities

1   It has long been acceptable to criticize colleges as ivory towers, sheltered from life's harsher realities. To some this is the best thing about college, however, and it is never more evident than during the last days of a course. The very concept of a course enforces the idea: the student isolates one area of study, temporarily, from the rest, commences learning in that area, and finally concludes the process. Both he and the instructor know that subjects are immutably entangled with each other, and that learning does not start and stop on key dates in the academic calendar. Yet a course's conclusion has a gratifying unreality, offering us an option we so rarely have elsewhere — a clean break. If we choose, we can cease to think about this subject, cease to confront this teacher, cease to talk with or even to see the other students in the class. We can end the whole experience, leaving behind only the relatively trivial residue of the grade.

2   How exceptional this is! What a contrast to the usual messy durability of our ideas, our obsessions! As we grow older, we come to recognize that most experiences are hard to conclude, and that they leave behind untidy, unwieldy, and unwanted effects. People do not disappear comfortably; we must repel them, or they must abandon us.

No relationship has so natural an end as that between student and teacher, or between students in the same course. This is not to say that no such relationship can continue, or that knowledge should be forgotten or thinking suspended because a course is over. That, we must hope, rarely happens. The marvelous thing is that it can happen, if that is what we want. In this artificial world of thought and experience, we can close the books, without insult or offense, for good and all.

____ **CONSIDERATIONS** _____

1. Morgan says that both student and instructor "know that subjects are immutably entangled with each other." Is that your experience? Or are you surprised when you notice that separate courses are interconnected? Write a short essay on the relationship between two courses of interest to you — say, art history and gymnastics, or history and biology, or French and logic.

2. Much of the success of Morgan's mini-essay depends upon the ability of the student to infer much meaning from relatively spare statements — not unlike what has to happen when one reads a poem. Write out two or three inferences that you are able to draw from highly compressed lines in Morgan's essay, and use those examples in a discussion on the joys and/or frustrations of reading such material.

3. Is Morgan's description of college life, "this artificial world of thought and experience," at all related to the common remark that school is a preparation for life? What's wrong — or right — with such a conception of the college years?

4. In what sense is Morgan's essay an argument? An exposition? If it is an argument, does she anticipate the points of her opponents?

*Wright Morris (b. 1910) won the National Book Award in 1956
for his novel* The Field of Vision, *and in 1981 the American
Book Award for his novel* Plains Songs. *Altogether, he has published more than twenty volumes of prose, most of it fiction,
most of it set in the Nebraska where he grew up. His most recent
book is* Will's Boy *(1981).*

*In much of his writing, Morris specializes in viewing things
with the strange clarity of a Martian visitor. People have written
about sports from a variety of points of view; rarely, we believe,
have they kept their eye on the ball.*

48

WRIGHT MORRIS

Odd Balls

1   Most games that involve the use of a ball can be described, but
seldom explained. Consider the ball itself.

2   We begin with the golf ball, white until soiled, hard as a rock, the
surface uniformly pitted with mini-craters, in size about that of a
meatball. This ball is stroked with a slender, wandlike shaft, about
the length of a cane, the bottom end tipped with a blade, variously
tilted, or a fistlike wooden knob. A mystical belief that the club, not
the player, directs the ball, and the ball, not the player, determines its
direction, is common among most players. With their needs in mind,
a ball is promised that will correct the mistakes made by the club. A
ball could more easily be drawn to the hole by a magnet, but the
excitement generated among the spectators is based on the role in the
game that chance plays. No thrill equals the sight of a peerless player
missing a nine-inch putt. Golf balls not stroked are often given to

babies, found in car seats, stored in raincoat pockets, or left where
they can be stepped on.

Golf is played in the open, preferably on grass, over a course   3
cunningly strewn with obstructions. Bunkers, sand traps, trees,
streams, ponds, and spectators, along with rain, sleet, cold, and lightning, make the game of golf what it is. What it is was not known to
many golfers until they saw the game on TV. The mock-ups used by
the commentators made clear a fact that many golfers found puzzling.
What they were doing was walking up and down, back and forth. Most
ball games seem to have in common the going back and forth, rather
than going anyplace.

The very smallness of the ball may substantially contribute to   4
the high moral tone of the game. What is there to fight over? Each
player has several balls of his own. Although equipped with sticks that
would make good clubs, the golf player refrains from striking his opponents, making loud slurring remarks, or coughing or hissing when
another player is putting. It is not at all unusual to hear another player
described as a great gentleman.

In this game alone the opinion of an official is accepted in a   5
depressed, sportsmanlike manner. The player does not scream and
curse, as in baseball, or stage riots, as in football, but accepts without
comment or demonstration the fickle finger of fate. Law and order
prevail on the links, if viewed on prime time. The game was once
played for the health of it, by amateurs (a term currently applied to
unemployed track stars); now the lonely, single golfer is burdened
with the knowledge that he does for nothing what others are paid for.
This condition is technically described as a handicap.

Some players hit the ball and stand, dejected, waiting for it to   6
land; others turn away and leave it up to the caddy. Some enjoy the
pain they give to others, some like to torture themselves. Although
the physical challenge is substantial — miles and miles of walking,
hours of waiting, the possibility of heatstroke or of being stuck by
lightning — the crucial element is mental. If not in a seizure of tor-
ment and self-doubt, the player must pass hole after hole daydreaming,
or wondering why he has so many clubs to choose from. A loss of
concentration on the easy holes will invariably cost him the hard
ones. In summary we can say that the smallness of the ball is no
measure of the effort it takes to stroke it or of the reward it brings.

Between the small golf ball and the palm-sized baseball is the   7
billiard or pool ball. Even those ignorant of the game know what it is
to be behind the eight ball. The game is played on an oblong table in a

smoke-filled room, off bounds to growing boys and women. The ball is stroked with a long, tapering cue, first rolled on the table to see if the table is flat. If it is not flat, you use a warped cue. The way the chalk is applied to the cue's leather tip, and the green chalk dust is then blown from the fingers, distinguishes men from boys. Pocket billiards is best under lights hung low over the table, in such a manner that one sees only the hands of the players. If smoke conceals the balls, one can hear them rebound on the cushions, click when they collide, or drop into a pocket and rattle down the chute. Without billiards, small boys in YMCA lobbies would have had no cause to grow up and be men.

8   The game is rich in ceremony, symbolic objects, stroking, fondling, thrusting, chalking, cursing, shot-calling, with the dramatic dimness of light necessary to a monastic order. Once identified with masculine odors and pursuits, pool halls, YMCAs, vice dens, conclaves of sleeve-rolled toughs and ward politicians, brazenly sexist, the game will surely interest the new liberated woman. Billiard balls are also used to roll across tile floors, crush the skull of an opponent, or serve as a knob on the sportier type of gearshift. The meaning of being *in front* of the eight ball remains to be explored.

9   Once relatively rare, hidden away in drawers with flannel trousers, like a huge mothball, the snow-white, cotton-fuzzy tennis ball with the visible seams is now commonplace.

10   The aura of breeding and snobbery, so important to tennis, a game played and observed by royalty, is now on the wane as the masses have puzzled out the scoring system. If both players know how to keep score, it comes down to how to psych the opponent. This can be done by hissing at him openly, wearing unmatched socks, varying the bounce of the ball before serving, pretending to sulk, screaming at the linesmen, or delaying the game by blowing softly on the fingers of one hand. These strategies were poorly observed in the past but are now intimately revealed on the TV screen. Many players seem blinded by their own long hair, but this might well be tactical cunning.

11   Nor has tennis stood still, living in the shadow of bygone times and grass-stained balls; it has kept pace with the times with the introduction of the two-handed backhand. Theories vary, but anyone who has played the game badly has experienced the irresistible urge to club the ball with both hands. To everyone's surprise there was nothing in the rules to prevent it. Both ladies and gentlemen whack the ball in this manner, using racquets of wood and metal. Metal racquets are not new: they were used by players in the madcap twenties, one known to

me personally, the steel strings noted for their length of life and the fuzz they removed from the balls. In those days matches were observed by eight or ten girls, seated in Scripps-Booth roadsters, holding the players' sweaters and their racquet presses. Any player with a racquet *and* a press was sure to have a good girl.

In other ball games, the frenzy and enthusiasm of the spectators   12
stimulates the player to greater efforts, but in tennis absolute silence testifies to the moments of crisis. The bong of the ball, the twang of the net cord, the voice of the umpire are all that is heard, unless one of the maverick hot-blooded types is involved in a dispute. This is well known to be bad for tennis, but great for higher receipts.

Team tennis, which may puzzle some observers, is for those who   13
dislike tennis but like to bet on winners and identify with places.

The baseball is small enough to be thrown and caught by a boy   14
but large enough to be seen from the bleachers by a grownup. The use of a round bat to hit a round ball testifies to native inventive genius. Balls were once made of the materials found under beds, and became lopsided when batted, or split at the seams. Official balls were once made of miles and miles of string wound into a tight ball and covered with horsehide. God knows what they use now. Sensible players are afraid to look.

The big games are played in cities that have a ball park. The field   15
is shaped like a large wedge of pie, straight along the sides, curved at the back. There are official positions for nine players, but once the ball is batted they run about wildly. Collisions are common.

The rules of the game lull some into feeling that the object of the   16
game is the scoring of runs. *Quelle bêtise!*[1] Observe how one player, crouched as in prayer, holds the bat across his knee in a ceremonial manner. He is calm and assured. His appointed task, surely, is to crouch and wait. Another walks to the box reserved for the batter, his manner both insolent and indecisive. He steps in, then he steps back, he soils his hands with dirt, then he wipes them, he looks to see if the bat is his own, or another's, if it has the proper length, heft, and roundness; if he is assured of all these points, he re-enters the box. With his spikes he paws his own hole to stand in; straddle-legged he threatens the pitcher with his bat. No words are spoken. Both know this is the moment of truth. See how the pitcher rubs, turns, fondles, and conceals the ball; see how he stoops for the resin, note how he discards it, fingers the bill of his cap, strokes away perspiration,

[1] What stupidity! — ED.

glances slantwise down his cheeks at a potential runner; how he begins and stops, how he delays and stares, how he may rudely turn his back on the batter, actions designed to arouse, to incite, to distract the man at the plate from hitting the ball. In spite of these precautions it sometimes happens, to the relief and consternation of the players. Some may have dozed off, or have thoughts on their minds.

17   There are players, as well as the idly curious, who ask why the game is called "the national pastime." For one thing, if nothing else, time *passes:* sometimes the better part of an afternoon or evening, if you allow two hours or more for the game and at least an hour getting to and from the ball park. In the old days games were called off because of darkness, but in the new days they might go on forever, under the lights. Somebody has to win. That's what it says in the rules.

18   The football is oval in shape, usually thrown in a spiral, and when kicked end over end may prove difficult to catch. If not caught on the fly it bounces around erratically.

19   The apparent intent of the game is to deposit the ball across the opponent's goal line. Any child with a ball of its own might do it, six days a week and most of Sunday morning, but the rules of the game specify it must be done with members of both teams present and on the field. Owing to large-scale substitutions this is often difficult.

20   In the old days people went crazy trying to follow the ball. The players still do, but the viewing public, who are watching the game on TV, can relax and wait for the replay. If anything happens, that's where you'll see it. The disentanglement of bodies on the goal line is one of the finer visual moments available to sports fans. The tight knot bursts open, the arms and legs miraculously return to the point of rest, before the ball was snapped. Some find it unsettling. Is this what it means to be born again?

21   All ball games feature hitting and socking, chopping and slicing, smashing, slamming, stroking, and whacking, but only in football are these blows diverted from the ball to the opponent. And the more the players are helped or carried from the field, the more attendance soars. This truly male game is also enjoyed by women who find group therapy less rewarding. The sacking of the passer by the front four is especially gratifying. Charges that a criminal element threatens the game are a characteristic, but hopeful, exaggeration. What to do with big, mean, boyish-hearted men, long accustomed to horsing around in good clean dormitories, unaccustomed to the rigors of life in the Alaska oilfields, was, until football, a serious national dilemma.

All games are peculiar, one to the other, and defy the comprehension of nonplayers, but none is so bizarre as the game of dunking the ball through the basket. Until basketball, boys seven feet tall ran off and hid in the woods or joined a circus. Now the woods are combed in search of them. If they can dribble and dunk a ball, they've got it made. Rules are rules, and all the rules say is that the ball has to enter the basket at the top. The tall boys dunk it. There's nothing against it, according to the rules. 22

If may surprise people to learn that basketball was once played by normal, flat-chested boys who shot the ball with two hands. The show-off who shot the ball with one hand was hooted off the court. The first change in the game was the one-hand shooter, several known to me personally. The next change in the game was the dunk shot. The normal thing to do would be to raise the basket and let the seven-foot boys mull around beneath it, but what is normal about basketball? People who watch the game understand this problem, but people who play it think they're normal. They think of six-foot, long-winded, flat-chested boys as being handicapped. 23

The importance of drafting basketball players early is to keep them from playing anything but soccer. If they want to play soccer they have personal problems they need to work out. Most athletes have nothing to fear but fear itself, and that's how they feel. When they run off the field at the half, or between innings, some observers have the feeling that they won't come back. Why should they, if it's raining and they're losing? They come back, not because they are paid to, as you might think, but because of what it says in the rules. Hard and fast rules are hard to come by, as you may know. When a player runs off the field and tries to hide in the shower room, he's a free man, and that scares him. Whose side is he on? Where does he play? Without his Bank of America or American Express card, who is going to recognize him? Most of the games people play just go on and on without time-outs, vacations, or free ambulance service, but ball games have a beginning and an ending. It says so in the rules. In case you've often wondered, that may account for their strange appeal. 24

_____ **CONSIDERATIONS** _____

1. How far do you have to read before you suspect that Morris is not taking his sports very seriously? What are the surest clues to his attitude?

2. What does Morris imply with the final clause of the third sentence of Paragraph 5? Why? How important are the implications to Morris's essay?

3. To what extent are ritual and ceremony important in sports? Collect the several comments Morris makes on this question, add your own observations, and state your conclusion.

4. How does Morris's article differ from McPhee's account of Bradley on the basketball court (pages 239–242)? Consider the difference in voice and tone, using specific examples of each in the two essays.

5. Which of the sports does Morris see as the most bizarre? Does he like one sport more than the others? Using the *Reader's Guide to Periodical Literature*, locate magazine articles on Morris and read them to find out whether he himself is a sportsman of any kind.

6. In what way are the terms "sports," "recreation," and "play" synonymous? How are they different? If an amateur becomes a professional, must he then call his activity work? How do you distinguish between play and work? Or do you see them as part of the same thing?

Anaïs Nin (1903–1977) was born in Paris. When her father, a Spanish musician and composer, left her mother in 1914, the family sailed to New York. She adored her father and began a diary addressed to him, hoping that some day she would send it to him, and by its excellence win his approval. She continued writing the diary — more than sixty-five volumes — throughout her life. At the age of fifteen she began to support her mother and her brothers, first as a model, and later as a Spanish dancer. For decades her writings were unpublished but attained a reputation among other writers, who read portions privately. She was a friend and confidant of Henry Miller, author of Tropic of Cancer *and other novels. In 1939 she printed her novel* Winter of Artifice *herself, on a foot-powered printing press, and won more readers among a small but powerful elite. Later in the forties, a New York publisher attempted to distribute several of her novels, but without commercial success. In the 1960s, the Swallow Press reissued her novels, and her reputation widened. The publication of her diaries, in seven volumes, greatly increased her audience.*

Many of the entries in the diaries of Anaïs Nin mean little detached from the body of the text, so closely related are the references. Here we print a brief excerpt about her premature delivery of a dead child. It begins in the hospital delivery room after four difficult hours of labor. Images with the fantastic intensity of dream ("Will the ice come . . .? At the end of the dark tunnel, a knife gleams") are common in Anaïs Nin's writing.

49

ANAÏS NIN

Journal Entry

1   The nurses begin to talk again. I say, "Let me alone." I place my two hands on my stomach and very slowly, very softly, with the tips of my fingers I drum, drum, drum on my stomach, in circles. Round and round, softly, with eyes open in great serenity. The doctor comes near and looks with amazement. The nurses are silent. Drum drum drum drum drum in soft circles, in soft quiet circles. "Like a savage," they whisper. The mystery.

2   Eyes open, nerves quiet, I drum gently on my stomach for a long while. The nurses begin to quiver. A mysterious agitation runs through them. I hear the ticking of the clock. It ticks inexorably, separately. The little nerves awaken, stir. I say, "I can push now!" and I push violently. They are shouting, "A little more! Just a little more!"

3   Will the ice come, and the darkness, before I am through? At the end of the dark tunnel, a knife gleams. I hear the clock and my heart. I say, "Stop!" The doctor holds the instrument, and he is leaning over. I sit up and shout at him. He is afraid again. "Let me alone, all of you!"

4   I lie back so quietly. I hear the ticking. Softly I drum, drum, drum. I feel my womb stirring, dilating. My hands are so weary, they will fall off. They will fall off, and I will lie there in darkness. The womb is stirring and dilating. Drum drum drum drum drum. "I am ready!" The nurse puts her knee on my stomach. There is blood in my eyes. A tunnel. I push into this tunnel. I bite my lips and push. There is fire, flesh ripping and no air. Out of the tunnel! All my blood is spilling out. "Push! Push! It is coming! It is coming!" I feel the slipperiness, the sudden deliverance, the weight is gone. Darkness.

I hear voices. I open my eyes. I hear them saying, "It was a little   5
girl. Better not show it to her." All my strength is coming back. I sit
up. The doctor shouts, "For God's sake, don't sit up, don't move!"

"Show me the child," I say.   6

"Don't show it," says the nurse, "it will be bad for her."   7

The nurses try to make me lie down. My heart is beating so   8
loudly I can hardly hear myself repeating, "Show it to me!" The doctor
holds it up. It looks dark, and small, like a diminutive man. But it is a
little girl. It has long eyelashes on its closed eyes, it is perfectly made,
and all glistening with the waters of the womb. It was like a doll, or
like a miniature Indian, about one foot long, skin on bones, no flesh.
But completely formed. The doctor told me afterwards that it had
hands and feet exactly like mine. The head was bigger than average.
As I looked at the dead child, for a moment I hated it for all the pain it
had caused me, and it was only later that this flare of anger turned
into great sadness.

____ CONSIDERATIONS ____

1. A surprisingly little-used grammatical technique adds to the tension
of the narrative. The same characteristic was used by Kenneth Tynan in his
account of Johnny Carson (pages 427–430). What is it? How does it add to the
drama? Why is it so rarely used by writers?

2. "At the end of the dark tunnel, a knife gleams." What tunnel?

3. In the first paragraph, Nin describes herself as serene; in the third, "I
sit up and shout at him." How do you account for this apparent contradiction?

4. Notice how repetition raises suspense in this short narrative. How
does Nin adapt her style to make the most of the repetition in the fourth
paragraph? Do you hear that repetition echoed in Paragraph 5?

5. Take a dramatic moment from your own experience and write a short
account of it, imitating Nin's style.

6. How might those either for or against natural childbirth methods
make use of Nin's experience?

*Flannery O'Connor (1925–1964) was born in Savannah, and
moved with her family to her mother's birthplace, Milledgeville,
Georgia, when she was twelve years old. When she was fifteen
her father died of the inherited degenerative disease, lupus. She
took her B.A. at Milledgeville's Georgia State College for Women
(now Georgia College) and then studied the writing of fiction at
the University of Iowa. From 1947 until 1951 she moved among
New York, Connecticut, and Georgia. When she discovered that
she was ill, she returned to live with her mother on the Milledgeville farm called Andalusia, surrounded by pet peacocks and
peahens, writing her remarkable fiction and staying in touch
with friends by letter. She died of lupus when she was thirty-
eight.*

*Flannery O'Connor wrote essays also, collected after her death
in a volume called* Mystery and Manners *(1969). This essay
appeared in the* Georgia Bulletin *in 1963, addressed to local and
immediate problems; in the American eighties its insights
remain urgent, as our culture, in O'Connor's word, becomes
increasingly "fractured."*

50

FLANNERY O'CONNOR

The Total Effect
and the Eighth Grade

In two recent instances in Georgia, parents have objected to their 1
eighth- and ninth-grade children's reading assignments in modern fiction. This seems to happen with some regularity in cases throughout
the country. The unwitting parent picks up his child's book, glances
through it, comes upon passages of erotic detail or profanity, and takes
off at once to complain to the school board. Sometimes, as in one of
the Georgia cases, the teacher is dismissed and hackles rise in liberal
circles everywhere.

The two cases in Georgia, which involved Steinbeck's *East of* 2
Eden and John Hersey's *A Bell for Adano*, provoked considerable
newspaper comment. One columnist, in commending the enterprise
of the teachers, announced that students do not like to read the fusty
works of the nineteenth century, that their attention can best be held
by novels dealing with the realities of our own time, and that the
Bible, too, is full of racy stories.

Mr. Hersey himself addressed a letter to the State School Super- 3
intendent in behalf of the teacher who had been dismissed. He pointed
out that his book is not scandalous, that it attempts to convey an
earnest message about the nature of democracy, and that it falls well
within the limits of the principle of "total effect," that principle

followed in legal cases by which a book is judged not for isolated parts but by the final effect of the whole book upon the general reader.

4   I do not want to comment on the merits of these particular cases. What concerns me is what novels ought to be assigned in the eighth and ninth grades as a matter of course, for if these cases indicate anything, they indicate the haphazard way in which fiction is approached in our high schools. Presumably there is a state reading list which contains "safe" books for teachers to assign; after that it is up to the teacher.

5   English teachers come in Good, Bad, and Indifferent, but too frequently in high schools anyone who can speak English is allowed to teach it. Since several novels can't easily be gathered into one textbook, the fiction that students are assigned depends upon their teacher's knowledge, ability, and taste: variable factors at best. More often than not, the teacher assigns what he thinks will hold the attention and interest of the students. Modern fiction will certainly hold it.

6   Ours is the first age in history which has asked the child what he would tolerate learning, but that is a part of the problem with which I am not equipped to deal. The devil of Educationism that possesses us is the kind that can be "cast out only by prayer and fasting." No one has yet come along strong enough to do it. In other ages the attention of children was held by Homer and Virgil, among others, but, by the reverse evolutionary process, that is no longer possible; our children are too stupid now to enter the past imaginatively. No one asks the student if algebra pleases him or if he finds it satisfactory that some French verbs are irregular, but if he prefers Hersey to Hawthorne, his taste must prevail.

7   I would like to put forward the proposition, repugnant to most English teachers, that fiction, if it is going to be taught in the high schools, should be taught as a subject and as a subject with a history. The total effect of a novel depends not only on its innate impact, but upon the experience, literary and otherwise, with which it is approached. No child needs to be assigned Hersey or Steinbeck until he is familiar with a certain amount of the best work of Cooper, Hawthorne, Melville, the early James, and Crane, and he does not need to be assigned these until he has been introduced to some of the better English novelists of the eighteenth and nineteenth centuries.

8   The fact that these works do not present him with the realities of his own time is all to the good. He is surrounded by the realities of his own time, and he has no perspective whatever from which to view them. Like the college student who wrote in her paper on Lincoln that

he went to the movies and got shot, many students go to college unaware that the world was not made yesterday; their studies began with the present and dipped backward occasionally when it seemed necessary or unavoidable.

There is much to be enjoyed in the great British novels of the 9 nineteenth century, much that a good teacher can open up in them for the young student. There is no reason why these novels should be either too simple or too difficult for the eighth grade. For the simple, they offer simple pleasures; for the more precocious, they can be made to yield subtler ones if the teacher is up to it. Let the student discover, after reading the nineteenth-century British novel, that the nineteenth-century American novel is quite different as to its literary characteristics, and he will thereby learn something not only about these individual works but about the sea-change which a new historical situation can effect in a literary form. Let him come to modern fiction with this experience behind him, and he will be better able to see and to deal with the more complicated demands of the best twentieth-century fiction.

Modern fiction often looks simpler than the fiction that preceded 10 it, but in reality it is more complex. A natural evolution has taken place. The author has for the most part absented himself from direct participation in the work and has left the reader to make his own way amid experiences dramatically rendered and symbolically ordered. The modern novelist merges the reader in experience; he tends to raise the passions he touches upon. If he is a good novelist, he raises them to effect by their order and clarity a new experience — the total effect — which is not in itself sensuous or simply of the moment. Unless the child has had some literary experience before, he is not going to be able to resolve the immediate passions the book arouses into any true, total picture.

It is here the moral problem will arise. It is one thing for a child 11 to read about adultery in the Bible or in *Anna Karenina*, and quite another for him to read about it in most modern fiction. This is not only because in both the former instances adultery is considered a sin, and in the latter, at most, an inconvenience, but because modern writing involves the reader in the action with a new degree of intensity, and literary mores now permit him to be involved in any action a human being can perform.

In our fractured culture, we cannot agree on morals; we cannot 12 even agree that moral matters should come before literary ones when there is a conflict between them. All this is another reason why the high schools would do well to return to their proper business of preparing foundations. Whether in the senior year students should be assigned modern novelists should depend both on their parents' consent and on what they have already read and understood.

13   The high-school English teacher will be fulfilling his responsibility if he furnishes the student a guided opportunity, through the best writing of the past, to come, in time, to an understanding of the best writing of the present. He will teach literature, not social studies or little lessons in democracy or the customs of many lands.

14   And if the student finds that this is not to his taste? Well, that is regrettable. Most regrettable. His taste should not be consulted; it is being formed.

____ **CONSIDERATIONS** _____

1. How far must you read in O'Connor's essay before you know her chief concern? Does it occupy her attention in her first three paragraphs? If not, how can you defend the organization of this essay?

2. O'Connor argues in Paragraph 8 that "it is all to the good" that the so-called classics do not present the child with realities of his own time. Is her argument anything like that of Langston Hughes's character, Simple, who asserts that "Everything I do is connected up with my past life"? Or is it more like the complaint of the historian who describes us today as "prisoners of the present"?

3. To what extent does O'Connor's Paragraph 10 help explain the principle of "total effect" mentioned in Paragraph 3? Do you consider that principle a reasonable means of sorting out acceptable from unacceptable reading matter?

4. Would D. H. Lawrence (in "Pornography") agree or disagree with O'Connor's solution to the moral problem explained in her Paragraph 12? Explain.

5. Write a response to O'Connor's answer to her question at the beginning of Paragraph 14. Try to take into account the rest of her essay as well as your own feelings.

6. What nineteenth-century British and American novels do you remember well enough to compare with modern novels? If your answer is "none," are you in any position to argue with O'Connor?

Flannery O'Connor's first novel, Wise Blood, *appeared in 1952, her second and last,* The Violent Bear It Away, *in 1960. Most readers believe her short stories to be her best fiction; they are available in* The Collected Stories of Flannery O'Connor *(1972). During her lifetime she published one volume of stories, bearing the title of the story that follows. This was the story she usually read aloud when asked to read.*

51

FLANNERY O'CONNOR

A Good Man Is Hard to Find

The grandmother didn't want to go to Florida. She wanted to visit some of her connections in east Tennessee and she was seizing every chance to change Bailey's mind. Bailey was the son she lived with, her only boy. He was sitting on the edge of his chair at the table, bent over the orange sports section of the *Journal.* "Now look here, Bailey," she said, "see here, read this," and she stood with one hand on her thin hip and the other rattling the newspaper at his bald head. "Here this fellow that calls himself The Misfit is aloose from the Federal Pen and headed toward Florida and you read here what it says he did to these people. Just you read it. I wouldn't take my children in any direction with a criminal like that aloose in it. I couldn't answer to my conscience if I did." 1

Bailey didn't look up from his reading so she wheeled around then and faced the children's mother, a young woman in slacks, whose 2 face was as broad and innocent as a cabbage and was tied around with a green headkerchief that had two points on the top like rabbit's ears. She was sitting on the sofa, feeding the baby his apricots out of a jar. "The children have been to Florida before," the old lady said. "You all ought to take them somewhere else for a change so they would see different parts of the world and be broad. They never have been to east Tennessee."

3   The children's mother didn't seem to hear her, but the eight-year-old boy, John Wesley, a stocky child with glasses, said, "If you don't want to go to Florida, why dontcha stay at home?" He and the little girl, June Star, were reading the funny papers on the floor.

4   "She wouldn't stay at home to be queen for a day," June Star said without raising her yellow head.

5   "Yes, and what would you do if this fellow, The Misfit, caught you?" the grandmother asked.

6   "I'd smack his face," John Wesley said.

7   "She wouldn't stay at home for a million bucks," June Star said. "Afraid she'd miss something. She has to go everywhere we go."

8   "All right, Miss," the grandmother said. "Just remember that the next time you want me to curl your hair."

9   June Star said her hair was naturally curly.

10   The next morning the grandmother was the first one in the car, ready to go. She had her big black valise that looked like the head of a hippopotamus in one corner, and underneath it she was hiding a basket with Pitty Sing, the cat, in it. She didn't intend for the cat to be left alone in the house for three days because he would miss her too much and she was afraid he might brush against one of the gas burners and accidentally asphyxiate himself. Her son, Bailey, didn't like to arrive at a motel with a cat.

11   She sat in the middle of the back seat with John Wesley and June Star on either side of her. Bailey and the children's mother and the baby sat in the front and they left Atlanta at eight forty-five with the mileage on the car at 55890. The grandmother wrote this down because she thought it would be interesting to say how many miles they had been when they got back. It took them twenty minutes to reach the outskirts of the city.

12   The old lady settled herself comfortably, removing her white cotton gloves and putting them up with her purse on the shelf in front of the back window. The children's mother still had on slacks and still had her head tied up in a green kerchief, but the grandmother had on a navy blue straw sailor hat with a bunch of white violets on the brim

and a navy blue dress with a small white dot in the print. Her collar and cuffs were white organdy trimmed with lace and at her neckline she had pinned a purple spray of cloth violets containing a sachet. In case of an accident, anyone seeing her dead on the highway would know at once that she was a lady.

She said she thought it was going to be a good day for driving, 13 neither too hot nor too cold, and she cautioned Bailey that the speed limit was fifty-five miles an hour and that the patrolmen hid themselves behind bill-boards and small clumps of trees and sped out after you before you had a chance to slow down. She pointed out interesting details of the scenery: Stone Mountain; the blue granite that in some places came up to both sides of the highway; the brilliant red clay banks slightly streaked with purple; and the various crops that made rows of green lace-work on the ground. The trees were full of silver-white sunlights and the meanest of them sparkled. The children were reading comic magazines and their mother had gone back to sleep.

"Let's go through Georgia fast so we won't have to look at it 14 much," John Wesley said.

"If I were a little boy," said the grandmother, "I wouldn't talk 15 about my native state that way. Tennessee has the mountains and Georgia has the hills."

"Tennessee is just a hillbilly dumping ground," John Wesley said, 16 "and Georgia is a lousy state too."

"You said it," June Star said. 17

"In my time," said the grandmother, folding her thin veined fin- 18 gers, "children were more respectful of their native states and their parents and everything else. People did right then. Oh look at the cute little pickaninny!" she said and pointed to a Negro child standing in the door of a shack. "Wouldn't that make a picture, now?" she asked and they all turned and looked at the little Negro out of the back window. He waved.

"He didn't have any britches on," June Star said. 19

"He probably didn't have any," the grandmother explained. 20 "Little niggers in the country don't have things like we do. If I could paint, I'd paint that picture," she said.

The children exchanged comic books. 21

The grandmother offered to hold the baby and the children's 22 mother passed him over the front seat to her. She set him on her knee and bounced him and told him about the things they were passing. She rolled her eyes and screwed up her mouth and stuck her leathery thin face into his smooth bland one. Occasionally he gave her a far-away smile. They passed a large cotton field with five or six graves fenced in the middle of it, like a small island. "Look at the graveyard!" the grandmother said, pointing it out. "That was the old family burying ground. That belonged to the plantation."

23   "Where's the plantation?" John Wesley asked.

24   "Gone With the Wind," said the grandmother. "Ha. Ha."

25   When the children finished all the comic books they had brought, they opened the lunch and ate it. The grandmother ate a peanut butter sandwich and an olive and would not let the children throw the box and the paper napkins out the window. When there was nothing else to do they played a game by choosing a cloud and making the other two guess what shape it suggested. John Wesley took one the shape of a cow and June Star guessed a cow and John Wesley said, no, an automobile, and June Star said he didn't play fair, and they began to slap each other over the grandmother.

26   The grandmother said she would tell them a story if they would keep quiet. When she told a story, she rolled her eyes and waved her head and was very dramatic. She said once when she was a maiden lady she had been courted by a Mr. Edgar Atkins Teagarden from Jasper, Georgia. She said he was a very good-looking man and a gentleman and that he brought her a watermelon every Saturday afternoon with his initials cut in it, E.A.T. Well, one Saturday, she said, Mr. Teagarden brought the watermelon and there was nobody at home and he left it on the front porch and returned in his buggy to Jasper, but she never got the watermelon, she said, because a nigger boy ate it when he saw the initials, E.A.T.! This story tickled John Wesley's funny bone and he giggled and giggled but June Star didn't think it was any good. She said she wouldn't marry a man that just brought her a watermelon on Saturday. The grandmother said she would have done well to marry Mr. Teagarden because he was a gentleman and had bought Coca-Cola stock when it first came out and that he had died only a few years ago, a very wealthy man.

27   They stopped at The Tower for barbecued sandwiches. The Tower was a part-stucco and part-wood filling station and dance hall set in a clearing outside of Timothy. A fat man named Red Sammy Butts ran it and there were signs stuck here and there on the building and for miles up and down the highway saying, TRY RED SAMMY'S FAMOUS BARBECUE. NONE LIKE FAMOUS RED SAMMY'S! RED SAM! THE FAT BOY WITH THE HAPPY LAUGH. A VETERAN! RED SAMMY'S YOUR MAN!

28   Red Sammy was lying on the bare ground outside The Tower with his head under a truck while a gray monkey about a foot high,

chained to a small chinaberry tree, chattered nearby. The monkey sprang back into the tree and got on the highest limb as soon as he saw the children jump out of the car and run toward him.

Inside, The Tower was a long dark room with a counter at one 29 end and tables at the other and dancing space in the middle. They all sat down at a broad table next to the nickelodeon and Red Sam's wife, a tall burnt-brown woman with hair and eyes lighter than her skin, came and took their order. The children's mother put a dime in the machine and played "The Tennessee Waltz," and the grandmother said that tune always made her want to dance. She asked Bailey if he would like to dance but he only glared at her. He didn't have a naturally sunny disposition like she did and trips made him nervous. The grandmother's brown eyes were very bright. She swayed her head from side to side and pretended she was dancing in her chair. June Star said play something she could tap to so the children's mother put in another dime and played a fast number and June Star stepped out onto the dance floor and did her tap routine.

"Ain't she cute?" Red Sam's wife said, leaning over the counter. 30 "Would you like to come be my little girl?"

"No, I certainly wouldn't," June Star said. "I wouldn't live in a 31 broken-down place like this for a million bucks!" and she ran back to the table.

"Ain't she cute?" the woman repeated, stretching her mouth 32 politely.

"Aren't you ashamed?" hissed the grandmother. 33

Red Sam came in and told his wife to quit lounging on the 34 counter and hurry up with these people's order. His khaki trousers reached just to his hip bones and his stomach hung over them like a sack of meal swaying under his shirt. He came over and sat down at a table nearby and let out a combination sigh and yodel. "You can't win," he said. "You can't win," and he wiped his sweating red face off with a gray handkerchief. "These days you don't know who to trust," he said. "Ain't that the truth?"

"People are certainly not nice like they used to be," said the 35 grandmother.

"Two fellers come in here last week," Red Sammy said, "driving 36 a Chrysler. It was an old beat-up car but it was a good one and these boys looked all right to me. Said they worked at the mill and you know I let them fellers charge the gas they bought? Now why did I do that?"

"Because you're a good man!" the grandmother said at once. 37

38   "Yes'm, I suppose so," Red Sam said as if he were struck with this answer.

39   His wife brought the orders, carrying the five plates all at once without a tray, two in each hand and one balanced on her arm. "It isn't a soul in this green world of God's that you can trust," she said. "And I don't count nobody out of that, not nobody," she repeated, looking at Red Sammy.

40   "Did you read about that criminal, The Misfit, that's escaped?" asked the grandmother.

41   "I wouldn't be a bit surprised if he didn't attack this place right here," said the woman. "If he hears about it being here, I wouldn't be none surprised to see him. If he hears it's two cent in the cash register, I wouldn't be a tall surprised if he . . ."

42   "That'll do," Red Sam said. "Go bring these people their Co'-Colas," and the woman went off to get the rest of the order.

43   "A good man is hard to find," Red Sammy said. "Everything is getting terrible. I remember the day you could go off and leave your screen door unlatched. Not no more."

44   He and the grandmother discussed better times. The old lady said that in her opinion Europe was entirely to blame for the way things were now. She said the way Europe acted you would think we were made of money and Red Sam said it was no use talking about it, she was exactly right. The children ran outside into the white sunlight and looked at the monkey in the lacy chinaberry tree. He was busy catching fleas on himself and biting each one carefully between his teeth as if it were a delicacy.

45   They drove off again into the hot afternoon. The grandmother took cat naps and woke up every few minutes with her own snoring. Outside of Toombsboro she woke up and recalled an old plantation that she had visited in this neighborhood once when she was a young lady. She said the house had six white columns across the front and that there was an avenue of oaks leading up to it and two little wooden trellis arbors on either side in front where you sat down with your suitor after a stroll in the garden. She recalled exactly which road to turn off to get to it. She knew that Bailey would not be willing to lose any time looking at an old house, but the more she talked about it, the more she wanted to see it once again and find out if the little twin arbors were still standing. "There was a secret panel in this house," she said craftily, not telling the truth but wishing that she were, "and the story went that all the family silver was hidden in it when Sherman came through but it was never found. . . ."

"Hey!" John Wesley said. "Let's go see it! We'll find it! We'll 46
poke all the wood work and find it! Who lives there? Where do you
turn off at? Hey Pop, can't we turn off there?"

"We never have seen a house with a secret panel!" June Star 47
shrieked. "Let's go to the house with the secret panel! Hey, Pop, can't
we go see the house with the secret panel!"

"It's not far from here, I know," the grandmother said. "It 48
wouldn't take over twenty minutes."

Bailey was looking straight ahead. His jaw was as rigid as a horse- 49
shoe. "No," he said.

The children began to yell and scream that they wanted to see 50
the house with the secret panel. John Wesley kicked the back of the
front seat and June Star hung over her mother's shoulder and whined
desperately into her ear that they never had any fun even on their
vacation, that they could never do what THEY wanted to do. The baby
began to scream and John Wesley kicked the back of the seat so hard
that his father could feel the blows in his kidney.

"All right!" he shouted and drew the car to a stop at the side of 51
the road. "Will you all shut up? Will you all just shut up for one
second? If you don't shut up, we won't go anywhere."

"It would be very educational for them," the grandmother mur- 52
mured.

"All right," Bailey said, "but get this. This is the only time 53
we're going to stop for anything like this. This is the one and only
time."

"The dirt road that you have to turn down is about a mile back," 54
the grandmother directed. "I marked it when we passed."

"A dirt road," Bailey groaned. 55

After they had turned around and were headed toward the dirt 56
road, the grandmother recalled other points about the house, the beautiful glass over the front doorway and the candle lamp in the hall. John
Wesley said that the secret panel was probably in the fireplace.

"You can't go inside the house," Bailey said. "You don't know 57
who lives there."

"While you all talk to the people in front, I'll run around behind 58
and get in a window," John Wesley suggested.

"We'll all stay in the car," his mother said. 59

They turned onto the dirt road and the car raced roughly along in 60
a swirl of pink dust. The grandmother recalled the times when there
were no paved roads and thirty miles was a day's journey. The dirt
road was hilly and there were sudden washes in it and sharp curves on

dangerous embankments. All at once they would be on a hill, looking down over the blue tops of trees for miles around, then the next minute, they would be in a red depression with the dust-coated trees looking down on them.

61   "This place had better turn up in a minute," Bailey said, "or I'm going to turn around."

62   The road looked as if no one had traveled on it in months.

63   "It's not much farther," the grandmother said and just as she said it, a horrible thought came to her. The thought was so embarrassing that she turned red in the face and her eyes dilated and her feet jumped up, upsetting her valise in the corner. The instant the valise moved, the newspaper top she had over the basket under it rose with a snarl and Pitty Sing, the cat, sprang onto Bailey's shoulder.

64   The children were thrown to the floor and their mother, clutching the baby, was thrown out the door onto the ground; the old lady was thrown into the front seat. The car turned over once and landed right-side-up in a gulch on the side of the road. Bailey remained in the driver's seat with the cat—gray-striped with a broad white face and an orange nose—clinging to his neck like a caterpillar.

65   As soon as the children saw they could move their arms and legs, they scrambled out of the car, shouting, "We've had an ACCIDENT!" The grandmother was curled up under the dashboard, hoping she was injured so that Bailey's wrath would not come down on her all at once. The horrible thought she had had before the accident was that the house she had remembered so vividly was not in Georgia but in Tennessee.

66   Bailey removed the cat from his neck with both hands and flung it out the window against the side of a pine tree. Then he got out of the car and started looking for the children's mother. She was sitting against the side of the red gutted ditch, holding the screaming baby, but she only had a cut down her face and a broken shoulder. "We've had an ACCIDENT!" the children screamed in a frenzy of delight.

67   "But nobody's killed," June Star said with disappointment as the grandmother limped out of the car, her hat still pinned to her head but the broken front brim standing up at a jaunty angle and the violet spray hanging off the side. They all sat down in the ditch, except the children, to recover from the shock. They were all shaking.

68   "Maybe a car will come along," said the children's mother hoarsely.

69   "I believe I have injured an organ," said the grandmother, pressing her side, but no one answered her. Bailey's teeth were clattering.

He had on a yellow sport shirt with bright blue parrots designed in it and his face was as yellow as the shirt. The grandmother decided that she would not mention that the house was in Tennessee.

The road was about ten feet above and they could see only the 70 tops of the trees on the other side of it. Behind the ditch they were sitting in there were more woods, tall and dark and deep. In a few minutes they saw a car some distance away on top of a hill, coming slowly as if the occupants were watching them. The grandmother stood up and waved both arms dramatically to attract their attention. The car continued to come on slowly, disappeared around a bend and appeared again, moving even slower, on top of the hill they had gone over. It was a big black battered hearselike automobile. There were three men in it.

It came to a stop just over them and for some minutes, the driver 71 looked down with a steady expressionless gaze to where they were sitting, and didn't speak. Then he turned his head and muttered something to the other two and they got out. One was a fat boy in black trousers and a red sweat shirt with a silver stallion embossed on the front of it. He moved around on the right side of them and stood staring, his mouth partly open in a kind of loose grin. The other had on khaki pants and a blue striped coat and a gray hat pulled down very low, hiding most of his face. He came around slowly on the left side. Neither spoke.

The driver got out of the car and stood by the side of it, looking 72 down at them. He was an older man than the other two. His hair was just beginning to gray and he wore silver-rimmed spectacles that gave him a scholarly look. He had a long creased face and didn't have on any shirt or undershirt. He had on blue jeans that were too tight for him and was holding a black hat and a gun. The two boys also had guns.

"We've had an ACCIDENT!" the children screamed. 73

The grandmother had the peculiar feeling that the bespectacled 74 man was someone she knew. His face was as familiar to her as if she had known him all her life but she could not recall who he was. He moved away from the car and began to come down the embankment, placing his feet carefully so that he wouldn't slip. He had on tan and white shoes and no socks, and his ankles were red and thin. "Good afternoon," he said. "I see you all had you a little spill."

"We turned over twice!" said the grandmother. 75

"Oncet," he corrected. "We see it happen. Try their car and see 76 will it run, Hiram," he said quietly to the boy with the gray hat.

77   "What you got that gun for?" John Wesley asked. "Whatcha gonna do with that gun?"

78   "Lady," the man said to the children's mother, "would you mind calling them children to sit down by you? Children make me nervous. I want all you all to sit down right together there were you're at."

79   "What are you telling us what to do for?" June Star asked.

80   Behind them the line of woods gaped like a dark open mouth. "Come here," said their mother.

81   "Look here now," Bailey began suddenly, "we're in a predicament! We're in . . ."

82   The grandmother shrieked. She scrambled to her feet and stood staring.

83   "You're The Misfit!" she said. "I recognized you at once!"

84   "Yes'm," the man said, smiling slightly as if he were pleased in spite of himself to be known. "But it would have been better for all of you, lady, if you hadn't of reckernized me."

85   Bailey turned his head sharply and said something to his mother that shocked even the children. The old lady began to cry and The Misfit reddened.

86   "Lady," he said, "don't you get upset. Sometimes a man says things he don't mean. I don't reckon he meant to talk to you thataway."

87   "You wouldn't shoot a lady, would you?" the grandmother said and removed a clean handkerchief from her cuff and began to slap at her eyes with it.

88   The Misfit pointed the toe of his shoe into the ground and made a little hole and then covered it up again. "I would hate to have to," he said.

89   "Listen," the grandmother almost screamed, "I know you're a good man. You don't look a bit like you have common blood. I know you must come from nice people!"

90   "Yes mam," he said, "finest people in the world." When he smiled he showed a row of strong white teeth. "God never made a finer woman than my mother and my daddy's heart was pure gold," he said. The boy with the red sweat shirt had come around behind them and was standing with his gun at his hip. The Misfit squatted down on the ground. "Watch them children, Bobby Lee," he said. "You know they make me nervous." He looked at the six of them huddled together in front of him and he seemed to be embarrassed as if he couldn't think of anything to say. "Ain't a cloud in the sky," he

remarked, looking up at it. "Don't see no sun but don't see no cloud neither."

"Yes, it's a beautiful day," said the grandmother. "Listen," she said, "you shouldn't call yourself The Misfit because I know you're a good man at heart. I can just look at you and tell." 91

"Hush!" Bailey yelled. "Hush! Everybody shut up and let me handle this!" He was squatting in the position of a runner about to sprint forward but he didn't move. 92

"I pre-chate that, lady," The Misfit said and drew a little circle in the ground with the butt of his gun. 93

"It'll take a half a hour to fix this here car," Hiram called, looking over the raised hood of it. 94

"Well, first you and Bobby Lee get him and that little boy to step over yonder with you," The Misfit said, pointing to Bailey and John Wesley. "The boys want to ask you something," he said to Bailey. "Would you mind stepping back in them woods there with them?" 95

"Listen," Bailey began, "we're in a terrible predicament! Nobody realizes what this is," and his voice cracked. His eyes were as blue and intense as the parrots in his shirt and he remained perfectly still. 96

The grandmother reached up to adjust her hat brim as if she were going to the woods with him but it came off in her hand. She stood staring at it and after a second she let it fall on the ground. Hiram pulled Bailey up by the arm as if he were assisting an old man. John Wesley caught hold of his father's hand and Bobby Lee followed. They went off toward the woods and just as they reached the dark edge, Bailey turned and supporting himself against a gray naked pine trunk, he shouted, "I'll be back in a minute, Mamma, wait on me!" 97

"Come back this instant!" his mother shrilled but they all disappeared into the woods. 98

"Bailey Boy!" the grandmother called in tragic voice but she found she was looking at The Misfit squatting on the ground in front of her. "I just know you're a good man," she said desperately. "You're not a bit common!" 99

"Nome, I ain't a good man," The Misfit said after a second as if he had considered her statement carefully, "but I ain't the worst in the world neither. My daddy said I was a different breed of dog from my brothers and sisters. 'You know,' Daddy said, 'it's some that can live their whole life out without asking about it and it's others has to know why it is, and this boy is one of the latters. He's going to be into 100 everything!' " He put on his black hat and looked up suddenly and then away deep into the woods as if he were embarrassed again. "I'm sorry, I don't have on a shirt before you ladies," he said, hunching his shoulders slightly. "We buried our clothes that we had on when we escaped and we're just making do until we can get better. We borrowed these from some folks we met," he explained.

101   "That's perfectly all right," the grandmother said. "Maybe Bailey has an extra shirt in his suitcase."

102   "I'll look and see terrectly," The Misfit said.

103   "Where are they taking him?" the children's mother screamed.

104   "Daddy was a card himself," The Misfit said. "You couldn't put anything over on him. He never got in trouble with the Authorities though. Just had the knack of handling them."

105   "You could be honest too if you'd only try," said the grandmother. "Think how wonderful it would be to settle down and live a comfortable life and not have to think about somebody chasing you all the time."

106   The Misfit kept scratching in the ground with the butt of his gun as if he were thinking about it. "Yes'm, somebody is always after you," he murmured.

107   The grandmother noticed how thin his shoulder blades were just behind his hat because she was standing up looking down on him. "Do you ever pray?" she asked.

108   He shook his head. All she saw was the black hat wiggle between his shoulder blades. "Nome," he said.

109   There was a pistol shot from the woods, followed closely by another. Then silence. The old lady's head jerked around. She could hear the wind move through the tree tops like a long satisfied insuck of breath. "Bailey Boy!" she called.

110   "I was a gospel singer for a while," The Misfit said. "I been most everything. Been in the arm service, both land and sea, at home and abroad, been twict married, been an undertaker, been with the railroads, plowed Mother Earth, been in a tornado, seen a man burnt alive oncet," and he looked up at the children's mother and the little girl who were sitting close together, their faces white and their eyes glassy; "I even seen a woman flogged," he said.

111   "Pray, pray," the grandmother began, "pray, pray . . ."

112   "I never was a bad boy that I remember of," The Misfit said in an almost dreamy voice, "but somewheres along the line I done something wrong and got sent to the penitentiary. I was buried alive," and he looked up and held her attention to him by a steady stare.

"That's when you should have started to pray," she said. "What 113
did you do to get sent to the penitentiary that first time?"

"Turn to the right, it was a wall," The Misfit said, looking up 114
again at the cloudless sky. "Turn to the left, it was a wall. Look up it
was a ceiling, look down it was a floor. I forgot what I done, lady. I set
there and set there, trying to remember what it was I done and I ain't
recalled it to this day. Oncet in a while, I would think it was coming
to me, but it never come."

"Maybe they put you in by mistake," the old lady said vaguely. 115

"Nome," he said. "It wasn't no mistake. They had the papers on 116
me."

"You must have stolen something," she said. 117

The Misfit sneered slightly. "Nobody had nothing I wanted," he 118
said. "It was a head-doctor at the penitentiary said what I had done
was kill my daddy but I known that for a lie. My daddy died in nineteen ought nineteen of the epidemic flu and I never had a thing to do
with it. He was buried in the Mount Hopewell Baptist churchyard
and you can go there and see for yourself."

"If you would pray," the old lady said, "Jesus would help you." 119

"That's right," The Misfit said. 120

"Well then, why don't you pray?" she asked trembling with de- 121
light suddenly.

"I don't want no hep," he said, "I'm doing all right by myself." 122

Bobby Lee and Hiram came ambling back from the woods. Bobby 123
Lee was dragging a yellow shirt with bright blue parrots in it.

"Throw me that shirt, Bobby Lee," The Misfit said. The shirt 124
came flying at him and landed on his shoulder and he put it on. The
grandmother couldn't name what the shirt reminded her of. "No,
lady," The Misfit said while he was buttoning it up, "I found out the
crime don't matter. You can do one thing or you can do another, kill
a man or take a tire off his car, because sooner or later you're going to
forget what it was you done and just be punished for it."

The children's mother had begun to make heaving noises as if 125
she couldn't get her breath. "Lady," he asked, "would you and that
little girl like to step off yonder with Bobby Lee and Hiram and join
your husband?"

"Yes, thank you," the mother said faintly. Her left arm dangled 126
helplessly and she was holding the baby, who had gone to sleep, in the
other. "Hep that lady up, Hiram," The Misfit said as she struggled to
climb out of the ditch, "and Bobby Lee, you hold onto that little girl's
hand."

127 "I don't want to hold hands with him," June Star said. "He reminds me of a pig."

128 The fat boy blushed and laughed and caught her by the arm and pulled her off into the woods after Hiram and her mother.

129 Alone with The Misfit, the grandmother found that she had lost her voice. There was not a cloud in the sky nor any sun. There was nothing around her but woods. She wanted to tell him that he must pray. She opened and closed her mouth several times before anything came out. Finally she found herself saying, "Jesus. Jesus," meaning, Jesus will help you, but the way she was saying it, it sounded as if she might be cursing.

130 "Yes'm," The Misfit said as if he agreed. "Jesus thrown everything off balance. It was the same case with Him as with me except He hadn't committed any crime and they could prove I had committed one because they had the papers on me. Of course," he said, "they never shown me any papers. That's why I sign myself now. I said long ago, you get you a signature and sign everything you do and keep a copy of it. Then you'll know what you done and you can hold up the crime to the punishment and see do they match and in the end you'll have something to prove you ain't been treated right. I call myself The Misfit," he said, "because I can't make what all I done wrong fit what all I gone through in punishment."

131 There was a piercing scream from the woods, followed closely by a pistol report. "Does it seem right to you, lady, that one is punished a heap and another ain't punished at all?"

132 "Jesus!" the old lady cried. "You've got blood! I know you wouldn't shoot a lady! I know you come from nice people! Pray! Jesus, you ought not to shoot a lady. I'll give you all the money I've got!"

133 "Lady," The Misfit said, looking beyond her far into the woods, "there never was a body that give the undertaker a tip."

134 There were two more pistol reports and the grandmother raised her head like a parched old turkey hen crying for water and called, "Bailey Boy, Bailey Boy!" as if her heart would break.

135 "Jesus was the only One that ever raised the dead," The Misfit continued, "and He shouldn't have done it. He thrown everything off balance. If He did what He said, then it's nothing for you to do but throw away everything and follow Him, and if He didn't then it's nothing for you to do but enjoy the few minutes you got left the best way you can — by killing somebody or burning down his house or doing some other meanness to him. No pleasure but meanness," he said and his voice had become almost a snarl.

"Maybe He didn't raise the dead," the old lady mumbled, not   136
knowing what she was saying and feeling so dizzy that she sank down
in the ditch with her legs twisted under her.

"I wasn't there so I can't say He didn't," The Misfit said. "I wisht   137
I had of been there," he said, hitting the ground with his fist. "It ain't
right I wasn't there because if I had of been there I would of known.
Listen lady," he said in a high voice, "if I had of been there I would of
known and I wouldn't be like I am now." His voice seemed about to
crack and the grandmother's head cleared for an instant. She saw the
man's face twisted close to her own as if he were going to cry and she
murmured, "Why, you're one of my babies. You're one of my own
children!" She reached out and touched him on the shoulder. The
Misfit sprang back as if a snake had bitten him and shot her three
times through the chest. Then he put his gun down on the ground and
took off his glasses and began to clean them.

Hiram and Bobby Lee returned from the woods and stood over   138
the ditch, looking down at the grandmother who half sat and half lay
in a puddle of blood with her legs crossed under her like a child's and
her face smiling up at the cloudless sky.

Without his glasses, The Misfit's eyes were red-rimmed and pale   139
and defenseless-looking. "Take her off and throw her where you
thrown the others," he said, picking up the cat that was rubbing itself
against his leg.

"She was a talker, wasn't she?" Bobby Lee said, sliding down the   140
ditch with a yodel.

"She would of been a good woman," The Misfit said, "if it had   141
been somebody there to shoot her every minute of her life."

"Some fun!" Bobby Lee said.   142

"Shut up, Bobby Lee," The Misfit said. "It's no real pleasure in   143
life."

_____ **CONSIDERATIONS** _____

1. In order to keep the children quiet, the grandmother tells the ridiculous story of Mr. Edgar Atkins Teagarden, who cut his initials, E.A.T., in a watermelon. How do you account for O'Connor's including such an anecdote in a story about a psychopathic murderer?

2. One respected scholar and critic describes O'Connor's story as a "satire on the half-and-half Christian faced with nihilism and death." In what sense would the grandmother qualify as a "half-and-half Christian"? Is there

anything in O'Connor's letters to John Hawkes and Alfred Corn (see pages 300–306) that might help you understand what O'Connor thought a real Christian was?

3. Does this story contain characteristics of satire as seen in Jonathan Swift's "A Modest Proposal" or Mark Twain's "Was the World Made for Man"?

4. O'Connor borrows a line from her own story to serve as a title. Find the line, study the context and comment on it as a title.

5. When the Misfit tells the grandmother, "it would have been better for all of you, lady, if you hadn't of reckernized me," what purpose does his warning serve, in furthering the story?

6. Study three elderly women: the grandmother in this story, Faulkner's Emily, and Welty's Phoenix Jackson. Do you think it fair to say that all three are used to convey the point of their respective authors' stories? Explain.

*In 1979 a selection of Flannery O'Connor's letters, edited by
Sally Fitzgerald, appeared as* The Habit of Being. *The letters are
affectionate, often funny, rich with literary and religious
thought.*

*The following excerpts begin with passages from two letters
about "A Good Man Is Hard to Find." The letter* To a Professor
of English *is prefaced by Sally Fitzgerald's explanatory note. The
other passage comes from a letter addressed to the novelist John
Hawkes, a leading writer of O'Connor's generation, author of*
The Lime Twig, Blood Oranges, *and* The Passion Artist *among
other novels. Here O'Connor speaks of the theology of her story.
In the letter that follows, also to John Hawkes, O'Connor's
Catholicism is clear and certain; Hawkes is of another mind.
The last letter is addressed to Alfred Corn, who is now a well-
known poet. In 1962 he was an undergraduate at Emory University in Atlanta, Georgia; when he heard Flannery O'Connor
speak to an English class, he wrote her about a subject that troubled him.*

52

FLANNERY O'CONNOR

From Flannery O'Connor's Letters

TO JOHN HAWKES

14 April 60

1   Thanks for your letter of some time back. I have been busy keeping my blood pressure down while reading various reviews of my book. Some of the favorable ones are as bad as the unfavorable; most reviewers seem to have read the book in fifteen minutes and written the review in ten. . . . I hope that when yours comes out you'll fare better.

2   It's interesting to me that your students naturally work their way to the idea that the Grandmother in "A Good Man" is not pure evil and may be a medium for Grace. If they were Southern students I would say this was because they all had grandmothers like her at home. These old ladies exactly reflect the banalities of the society and the effect of the comical rather than the seriously evil. But Andrew [Lytle] insists that she is a witch, even down to the cat. These children, yr. students, know their grandmothers aren't witches.

3   Perhaps it is a difference in theology, or rather the difference that ingrained theology makes in the sensibility. Grace, to the Catholic way of thinking, can and does use as its medium the imperfect, purely human, and even hypocritical. Cutting yourself off from Grace is a very decided matter, requiring a real choice, act of will, and affecting the very ground of the soul. The Misfit is touched by the Grace that

comes through the old lady when she recognizes him as her child, as she has been touched by the Grace that comes through him in his particular suffering. His shooting her is a recoil, a horror at her humanness, but after he has done it and cleaned his glasses, the Grace has worked in him and he pronounces his judgment: she would have been a good woman if *he* had been there every moment of her life. True enough. In the Protestant view, I think Grace and nature don't have much to do with each other. The old lady, because of her hypocrisy and humanness and banality couldn't be a medium for Grace. In the sense that I see things the other way, I'm a Catholic writer.

TO A PROFESSOR OF ENGLISH

A professor of English had sent Flannery the following letter: "I am writing as spokesman for three members of our department and some ninety university students in three classes who for a week now have been discussing your story 'A Good Man Is Hard to Find.' We have debated at length several possible interpretations, none of which fully satisfies us. In general we believe that the appearance of the Misfit is not "real" in the same sense that the incidents of the first half of the story are real. Bailey, we believe, imagines the appearance of the Misfit, whose activities have been called to his attention on the night before the trip and again during the stopover at the roadside restaurant. Bailey, we further believe, identifies himself with the Misfit and so plays two roles in the imaginary last half of the story. But we cannot, after great effort, determine the point at which reality fades into illusion or reverie. Does the accident literally occur, or is it a part of Bailey's dream? Please believe me when I say we are not seeking an easy way out of our difficulty. We admire your story and have examined it with great care, but we are convinced that we are missing something important which you intended for us to grasp. We will all be very grateful if you comment on the interpretation which I have outlined above and if you will give us further comments about your intention in writing 'A Good Man Is Hard to Find.' "

She replied:

28 March 61

The interpretation of your ninety students and three teachers is fantastic and about as far from my intentions as it could get to be. If it were a legitimate interpretation, the story would be little more than a trick and its interest would be simply for abnormal psychology. I am not interested in abnormal psychology.

2   There is a change of tension from the first part of the story to the second where the Misfit enters, but this is no lessening of reality. This story is, of course, not meant to be realistic in the sense that it portrays the everyday doings of people in Georgia. It is stylized and its conventions are comic even though its meaning is serious.

3   Bailey's only importance is as the Grandmother's boy and the driver of the car. It is the Grandmother who first recognizes the Misfit and who is most concerned with him throughout. The story is a duel of sorts between the Grandmother and her superficial beliefs and the Misfit's more profoundly felt involvement with Christ's action which set the world off balance for him.

4   The meaning of a story should go on expanding for the reader the more he thinks about it, but meaning cannot be captured in an interpretation. If teachers are in the habit of approaching a story as if it were a research problem for which any answer is believable so long as it is not obvious, then I think students will never learn to enjoy fiction. Too much interpretation is certainly worse than too little, and where feeling for a story is absent, theory will not supply it.

5   My tone is not meant to be obnoxious. I am in a state of shock.

TO JOHN HAWKES

28 November 61

1   I have been fixing to write you ever since last summer when we saw the goat man.[1] We went up to north Georgia to buy a bull and when we were somewhere above Conyers we saw up ahead a pile of rubble some eight feet high on the side of the road. When we got about fifty feet from it, we could begin to make out that some of the rubble was distributed around something like a cart and that some of it was alive. Then we began to make out the goats. We stopped in front of it and looked back. About half the goats were asleep, venerable and exhausted, in a kind of heap. I didn't see Chess. Then my mother located an arm around the neck of one of the goats. We also saw a knee. The old man was lying on the road, asleep amongst them, but we never located his face.

---

[1] The founder of the Free Thinking Christian Mission, a wandering witness who traveled with a cart and a clutch of goats.

That is wonderful about the new baby. I can't equal that but I do 2
have some new additions to my ménage. For the last few years I have
been hunting a pair of swans that I could afford. Swans cost $250 a
pair and that was beyond me. My friend in Florida, the one I wrote you
about once, took upon herself to comb Florida for cheap swans. What
she sets out to do, she does. . . . So now I am the owner of a one-eyed
swan and her consort. They are Polish, or immutable, swans and very
tractable and I radiate satisfaction every time I look at them.

I had brief notes from Andrew [Lytle][2] a couple of times lately. In 3
fact he has a story of mine but I haven't heard from him whether he's
going to use it or not. He said he had asked you to write an article
about my fiction and that if he used my story I might want to send it
to you. If he does take it and you write an article and want to see the
story ["The Lame Shall Enter First"], I'll send it. It's about one of
Tarwater's terrible cousins, a lad named Rufus Johnson, and it will
add fuel to your theory though not legitimately I think.

You haven't convinced me that I write with the Devil's will or 4
belong in the romantic tradition and I'm prepared to argue some more
with you on this if I can remember where we left off at. I think the
reason we can't agree on this is because there is a difference in our
two devils. My Devil has a name, a history and a definite plan. His
name is Lucifer, he's a fallen angel, his sin is pride, and his aim is the
destruction of the Divine plan. Now I judge that your Devil is co-equal
to God, not his creature; that pride is his virtue, not his sin; and that
his aim is not to destroy the Divine plan because there isn't any
Divine plan to destroy. My Devil is objective and yours is subjective.
You say one becomes "evil" when one leaves the herd. I say that
depends entirely on what the herd is doing.

The herd has been known to be right, in which case the one who 5
leaves it is doing evil. When the herd is wrong, the one who leaves it
is not doing evil but the right thing. If I remember rightly, you put
that word, evil, in quotation marks which means the standards you
judge it by there are relative; in fact you would be looking at it there
with the eyes of the herd.

I think I would admit to writing what Hawthorne called 6
"romances," but I don't think that has anything to do with the romantic mentality. Hawthorne interests me considerably. I feel more of a
kinship with him than with any other American, though some of what
he wrote I can't make myself read through to the end.

---

[2] Novelist, editor at this time of the *Sewanee Review*.

7   I didn't write the note to *Wise Blood.* I just let it go as is. I thought here I am wasting my time saying what I've written when I've already written it and I could be writing something else. I couldn't hope to convince anybody anyway. A friend of mine wrote me that he had read a review in one of the university magazines of *The Violent Bear etc.* that said that since the seeds that had opened one at a time in Tarwater's blood were put there in the first place by the great uncle that the book was about homosexual incest. When you have a generation of students who are being taught to think like that, there's nothing to do but wait for another generation to come along and hope it won't be worse. . . .

8   I've introduced *The Lime Twig* to several people and they're all enthusiastic. Somebody has gone off with my copy now. I hope you are at another one.

TO ALFRED CORN

30 May 62

1   I think that this experience you are having of losing your faith, or as you think, of having lost it, is an experience that in the long run belongs to faith; or at least it can belong to faith if faith is still valuable to you, and it must be or you would not have written me about this.

2   I don't know how the kind of faith required of a Christian living in the 20th century can be at all if it is not grounded on this experience that you are having right now of unbelief. This may be the case always and not just in the 20th century. Peter said, "Lord, I believe. Help my unbelief." It is the most natural and most human and most agonizing prayer in the gospels, and I think it is the foundation prayer of faith.

3   As a freshman in college you are bombarded with new ideas, or rather pieces of ideas, new frames of reference, an activation of the intellectual life which is only beginning, but which is already running ahead of your lived experience. After a year of this, you think you cannot believe. You are just beginning to realize how difficult it is to have faith and the measure of a commitment to it, but you are too young to decide you don't have faith just because you feel you can't believe. About the only way we know whether we believe or not is by what we do, and I think from your letter that you will not take the path of least resistance in this matter and simply decide that you have lost your faith and that there is nothing you can do about it.

One result of the stimulation of your intellectual life that takes   4
place in college is usually a shrinking of the imaginative life. This
sounds like a paradox, but I have often found it to be true. Students
get so bound up with difficulties such as reconciling the clashing of so
many different faiths such as Buddhism, Mohammedanism, etc., that
they cease to look for God in other ways. Bridges once wrote Gerard
Manley Hopkins and asked him to tell him how he, Bridges, could
believe. He must have expected from Hopkins a long philosophical
answer. Hopkins wrote back, "Give alms." He was trying to say to
Bridges that God is to be experienced in Charity (in the sense of love
for the divine image in human beings). Don't get so entangled with
intellectual difficulties that you fail to look for God in this way.

The intellectual difficulties have to be met, however, and you   5
will be meeting them for the rest of your life. When you get a reasonable hold on one, another will come to take its place. At one time, the
clash of the different world religions was a difficulty for me. Where
you have absolute solutions, however, you have no need of faith. Faith
is what you have in the absence of knowledge. The reason this clash
doesn't bother me any longer is because I have got, over the years, a
sense of the immense sweep of creation, of the evolutionary process
in everything, of how incomprehensible God must necessarily be to be
the God of heaven and earth. You can't fit the Almighty into your
intellectual categories. I might suggest that you look into some of the
works of Pierre Teilhard de Chardin *(The Phenomenon of Man* et al.).
He was a paleontologist — helped to discover Peking man — and also
a man of God. I don't suggest you go to him for answers but for different questions, for that stretching of the imagination that you need to
make you a sceptic in the face of much that you are learning, much of
which is new and shocking but which when boiled down becomes less
so and takes its place in the general scheme of things. What kept me
a sceptic in college was precisely my Christian faith. It always said:
wait, don't bite on this, get a wider picture, continue to read.

If you want your faith, you have to work for it. It is a gift, but for   6
very few is it a gift given without any demand for equal time devoted
to its cultivation. For every book you read that is anti-Christian, make
it your business to read one that presents the other side of the picture;
if one isn't satisfactory read others. Don't think that you have to
abandon reason to be a Christian. A book that might help you is *The
Unity of Philosophical Experience* by Etienne Gilson. Another is
Newman's *The Grammar of Assent.* To find out about faith, you have
to go to the people who have it and you have to go to the most intel-

ligent ones if you are going to stand up intellectually to agnostics and the general run of pagans that you are going to find in the majority of people around you. Much of the criticism of belief that you find today comes from people who are judging it from the standpoint of another and narrower discipline. The Biblical criticism of the 19th century, for instance, was the product of historical disciplines. It has been entirely revamped in the 20th century by applying broader criteria to it, and those people who lost their faith in the 19th century because of it, could better have hung on in blind trust.

7   Even in the life of a Christian, faith rises and falls like the tides of an invisible sea. It's there, even when he can't see it or feel it, if he wants it to be there. You realize, I think, that it is more valuable, more mysterious, altogether more immense than anything you can learn or decide upon in college. Learn what you can, but cultivate Christian scepticism. It will keep you free — not free to do anything you please, but free to be formed by something larger than your own intellect or the intellects of those around you.

8   I don't know if this is the kind of answer that can help you, but any time you care to write me, I can try to do better.

_____ **CONSIDERATIONS** _____

Letter to John Hawkes: April 14, 1960

1. What does O'Connor mean when she says that some of the favorable reviews of her book "are as bad as the unfavorable"? How do you go about judging the quality of a book review? As a writer, how do you judge the comments on your own papers when they are returned by your instructors?

2. In Paragraph 2 O'Connor suggests that the grandmother in her story is like a lot of grandmothers in the South, but in her letter to the Professor of English (p. 301) she says her story is not realistic in the "everyday" sense. Can you reconcile this apparent contradiction?

3. O'Connor's comments on the term "grace" in Paragraph 3 might be more understandable if you pursued the word itself in a good dictionary where you will find at least a dozen different definitions of the word. Keep in mind that she is using the word according to her own view of Catholic theology.

4. O'Connor says at the end of Paragraph 3 that she is a Catholic writer. Does she mean that Protestant readers are not welcome or that Protestants could not understand her work? Is it possible to disagree with — or even disapprove of — a writer's ideas and still appreciate that writer's work? Explain.

5. While she does not always agree with John Hawkes's reading of her stories, O'Connor's letters to him (see also that of 11/28/61) express a good deal more respect for his ideas than can be found in her letter to a professor of English. Read a little of the work of John Hawkes to see if you can discover qualities he shares with O'Connor.

Letter to a Professor of English, March 28, 1961

1. O'Connor says her story is realistic, not in an "everyday" but "stylized" sense. Compare a paragraph or two of her story with a passage in Eudora Welty's "The Worn Path" to see if you can determine what O'Connor means by "stylized." You might also get some help on that word by consulting a history of art.

2. Find passages in "A Good Man Is Hard to Find" that will illustrate what O'Connor means by Grandmother's "superficial beliefs" and the Misfit's "more profoundly felt involvement." Does such a close examination of the story push you closer to or further away from O'Connor's belief that the heart of the story is a "duel of sorts" between the Grandmother and the Misfit?

3. In Paragraph 4 O'Connor makes an interesting distinction between "meaning" and "interpretation" as she deplores the "habit of approaching a story as if it were a research problem for which any answer is believable so long as it is not obvious." Discuss some experience of your own in which insistence upon a particular interpretation (yours or anyone else's) interfered with the expanded meaning O'Connor mentions.

4. O'Connor says in her last paragraph that her tone in the letter "is not meant to be obnoxious." If you were the professor to whom she had written, what particular lines or words in the letter might you think gave it an obnoxious tone. Can you find any other writers in your text whose tone is obnoxious? Explain.

5. In what sense, if any, do you think a short story (or poem or novel or play or essay for that matter) can be taught? What assistance do you expect or want from your own instructor and/or text in reading a story like O'Connor's?

Letter to John Hawkes, November 28, 1961

1. O'Connor's remarkable versatility in the use of the English language is demonstrated in her letters as well as in her stories. This letter to John Hawkes, for example, shows her ability to shift from one voice to another at will. Find examples.

2. At the end of Paragraph 4, O'Connor tells Hawkes, "You say one becomes 'evil' when one leaves the herd. I say that depends entirely on what the herd is doing." Write an essay on relative versus absolute morality.

3. O'Connor, speaking of her interest in Hawthorne, makes a distinction between writing "romances" and having a "romantic mentality." What

did Hawthorne mean by "romances," and why does O'Connor "feel more of a kinship with him than with any other American"?

4. O'Connor's letters are filled with brief reports on local events and people, like the one on the goat man in the letter to John Hawkes. Eudora Welty, in discussing one of her own stories — see her essay "The Point of the Story" — says that her story began when she observed an old woman in Mississippi. How might O'Connor's observations of her surroundings have contributed to "A Good Man Is Hard to Find"?

Letter to Alfred Corn, May 30, 1962

1. "You can't fit the Almighty into your intellectual categories," says O'Connor. Does she advise her correspondent to ignore the intellectual challenges of college? Study her discussion of the clash between intellectual inquiry and faith, especially in Paragraphs 5 and 6, and write an essay on her conclusions.

2. How, according to O'Connor, can we know whether we believe or not?

3. Look over Consideration 1 regarding O'Connor's 1961 letter to John Hawkes and think about voice. How would you describe the voice in this letter to Alfred Corn? Does O'Connor play with changes of voice in this letter? Why?

4. Compare O'Connor's advice to a troubled freshman with F. Scott Fitzgerald's letters to his daughter. Point out differences and similarities, particularly with regard to the two writers' attitudes toward the young. Remember that Fitzgerald was writing to his daughter and O'Connor to a young man she did not know.

5. Read Langston Hughes' essay "Salvation"; how might O'Connor have consoled the disillusioned boy?

George Orwell (1903–1950) was the pen name of Eric Blair, who was born in India of English parents, attended Eton on a scholarship, and returned to the East as a member of the Imperial Police. He quit his position after five years because he wanted to write, and because he came to feel that imperialism was "very largely a racket." For eight years he wrote with small success and in considerable poverty. His first book, Down and Out in Paris and London *(1933), described those years. Further memoirs and novels followed, including* Burmese Days *(1935) and* Keep the Aspidistra Flying *(1938). His last books were the political fable* Animal Farm *(1945) and his great anti-utopia* 1984, *which appeared in 1949, shortly before his death. He died of tuberculosis, his health first afflicted when he was a policeman in Burma, undermined by years of poverty, and further worsened by a wound he received during the civil war in Spain.*

*Best known for his fiction, Orwell was essentially an essayist; even his novels are essays. He made his living most of his adult life by writing reviews and articles for English weeklies. His collected essays, reviews, and letters form an impressive four volumes. Politics is at the center of his work — a personal politics. After his disaffection from imperialism, he became a leftist, and fought on the Loyalist side against Franco in Spain. (*Homage to Catalonia *comes out of this time.) But his experience of Communist duplicity there, and his early understanding of the paranoid totalitarianism of Stalin, turned him anti-Communist. He could swear allegiance to no party. His anti-Communism made him in no way conservative; he considered himself a socialist until his death, but other socialists would have nothing to do with him. He found politics shabby and politicians dishonest. With an empirical, English turn of mind, he looked skeptically at all saviors and panaceas. In this famous essay, he attacks the rhetoric of politics. He largely attacks the left — because his audience was an English intellectual class that was largely leftist.*

53

GEORGE ORWELL
Politics and
the English Language

1   Most people who bother with the matter at all would admit that
the English language is in a bad way, but it is generally assumed that
we cannot by conscious action do anything about it. Our civilization
is decadent and our language — so the argument runs — must inevitably share in the general collapse. It follows that any struggle against
the abuse of language is a sentimental archaism, like preferring can-
dles to electric light or hansom cabs to aeroplanes. Underneath this
lies the half-conscious belief that language is a natural growth and not
an instrument which we shape for our own purposes.

2   Now, it is clear that the decline of a language must ultimately
have political and economic causes: it is not due simply to the bad
influence of this or that individual writer. But an effect can become a
cause, reinforcing the original cause and producing the same effect in
an intensified form, and so on indefinitely. A man may take to drink
because he feels himself to be a failure, and then fail all the more
completely because he drinks. It is rather the same thing that is happening to the English language. It becomes ugly and inaccurate
because our thoughts are foolish, but the slovenliness of our language
makes it easier for us to have foolish thoughts. The point is that the
process is reversible. Modern English, especially written English, is
full of bad habits which spread by imitation and which can be avoided

if one is willing to take the necessary trouble. If one gets rid of these habits one can think more clearly, and to think clearly is a necessary first step towards political regeneration: so that the fight against bad English is not frivolous and is not the exclusive concern of professional writers. I will come back to this presently, and I hope that by that time the meaning of what I have said here will have become clearer. Meanwhile, here are five specimens of the English language as it is now habitually written.

These five passages have not been picked out because they are 3 especially bad — I could have quoted far worse if I had chosen — but because they illustrate various of the mental vices from which we now suffer. They are a little below the average, but are fairly representative samples. I number them so that I can refer back to them when necessary:

> (1) I am not, indeed, sure whether it is not true to say that the Milton who once seemed not unlike a seventeenth-century Shelley had not become, out of an experience ever more bitter in each year, more alien [*sic*] to the founder of that Jesuit sect which nothing could induce him to tolerate.
>
> <div align="right">Professor Harold Laski
[Essay in <i>Freedom of Expression</i>].</div>

> (2) Above all, we cannot play ducks and drakes with a native battery of idioms which prescribes such egregious collocations of vocables as the Basic *put up with* for *tolerate* or *put at a loss* for *bewilder.*
>
> <div align="right">Professor Lancelot Hogben [<i>Interglossa</i>].</div>

> (3) On the one side we have the free personality: by definition it is not neurotic, for it has neither conflict nor dream. Its desires, such as they are, are transparent, for they are just what institutional approval keeps in the forefront of consciousness; another institutional pattern would alter their number and intensity, there is little in them that is natural, irreducible, or culturally dangerous. But *on the other side,* the social bond itself is nothing but the mutual reflection of these self-secure integrities. Recall the definition of love. Is not this the very picture of a small academic? Where is there a place in this hall of mirrors for either personality or fraternity?
>
> <div align="right">Essay on psychology in <i>Politics</i> [New York].</div>

> (4) All the "best people" from the gentlemen's clubs, and all the frantic fascist captains, united in common hatred of Socialism and bestial horror of the rising tide of the mass revolutionary move-

ment, have turned to acts of provocation, to foul incendiarism, to medieval legends of poisoned wells, to legalize their own destruction of proletarian organizations, and rouse the agitated petty-bourgeoisie to chauvinistic fervor on behalf of the fight against the revolutionary way out of the crisis.

Communist pamphlet.

(5) If a new spirit is to be infused into this old country, there is one thorny and contentious reform which must be tackled, and that is the humanization and galvanization of the B.B.C. Timidity here will bespeak canker and atrophy of the soul. The heart of Britain may be sound and of strong beat, for instance, but the British lion's roar at present is like that of Bottom in Shakespeare's *Midsummer Night's Dream* — as gentle as any sucking dove. A virile new Britain cannot continue indefinitely to be traduced in the eyes, or rather ears, of the world by the effete languors of Langham Place, brazenly masquerading as "standard English." When the Voice of Britain is heard at nine o'clock, better far and infinitely less ludicrous to hear aitches honestly dropped than the present priggish, inflated, inhibited, school-ma'amish arch braying of blameless bashful mewing maidens!

Letter in *Tribune*.

4　　　Each of these passages has faults of its own, but, quite apart from avoidable ugliness, two qualities are common to all of them. The first is staleness of imagery; the other is lack of precision. The writer either has a meaning and cannot express it, or he inadvertently says something else, or he is almost indifferent as to whether his words mean anything or not. This mixture of vagueness and sheer incompetence is the most marked characteristic of modern English prose, and especially of any kind of political writing. As soon as certain topics are raised, the concrete melts into the abstract and no one seems able to think of turns of speech that are not hackneyed: prose consists less and less of *words* chosen for the sake of their meaning, and more and more of *phrases* tacked together like the sections of a prefabricated hen-house. I list below, with notes and examples, various of the tricks by means of which the work of prose-construction is habitually dodged:

DYING METAPHORS

5　　　A newly invented metaphor assists thought by evoking a visual image, while on the other hand a metaphor which is technically "dead" (e.g. *iron resolution*) has in effect reverted to being an ordinary word and can generally be used without loss of vividness. But in between these two classes there is a huge dump of worn-out metaphors which have lost all evocative power and are merely used because they save people the trouble of inventing phrases for themselves. Examples are: *Ring the changes on, take up the cudgels for, toe the line, ride roughshod over, stand shoulder to shoulder with, play into the hands of, no axe to grind, grist to the mill, fishing in troubled waters, on the order of the day, Achilles' heel, swan song, hotbed.* Many of these are used without knowledge of their meaning (what is a "rift," for instance?), and incompatible metaphors are frequently mixed, a sure sign that the writer is not interested in what he is saying. Some metaphors now current have been twisted out of their original meaning without those who use them even being aware of the fact. For example, *toe the line* is sometimes written *tow the line.* Another example is *the hammer and the anvil,* now always used with the implication that the anvil gets the worst of it. In real life it is always the anvil that breaks the hammer, never the other way about: a writer who stopped to think what he was saying would be aware of this, and would avoid perverting the original phrase.

OPERATORS OR VERBAL FALSE LIMBS

These save the trouble of picking out appropriate verbs and nouns, and at the same time pad each sentence with extra syllables which give it an appearance of symmetry. Characteristic phrases are *render inoperative, militate against, make contact with, be subjected to, give rise to, give grounds for, have the effect of, play a leading part (role) in, make itself felt, take effect, exhibit a tendency to, serve the purpose of,* etc., etc. The keynote is the elimination of simple verbs. Instead of being a single word, such as *break, stop, spoil, mend, kill* a verb becomes a *phrase,* made up of a noun or adjective tacked on to some general-purpose verb such as *prove, serve, form, play, render.* In addition, the passive voice is wherever possible used in preference to the active, and noun constructions are used instead of gerunds *(by examination of* instead of *by examining).* The range of verbs is further cut down by means of the *-ize* and *de-* formations, and the banal statements are given an appearance of profundity by means of the *not un-* formation. Simple conjunctions and prepositions are replaced by such phrases as *with respect to, having regard to, the fact that, by dint of, in view of, in the interests of, on the hypothesis that;* and the

6

ends of sentences are saved from anticlimax by such resounding commonplaces as *greatly to be desired, cannot be left out of account, a
development to be expected in the near future, deserving of serious
consideration, brought to a satisfactory conclusion* and so on and so
forth.

PRETENTIOUS DICTION

7   Words like *phenomenon, element, individual* (as noun), *objective, categorical, effective, virtual, basic, primary, promote, constitute, exhibit, exploit, utilize, eliminate, liquidate,* are used to dress
up simple statements and give an air of scientific impartiality to
biased judgments. Adjectives like *epoch-making, epic, historic, unfor-
gettable, triumphant, age-old, inevitable, inexorable, veritable,* are
used to dignify the sordid processes of international politics, while
writing that aims at glorifying war usually takes on an archaic color,
its characteristic words being: *realm, throne, chariot, mailed fist, tri-
dent, sword, shield, buckler, banner, jackboot, clarion.* Foreign words
and expressions such as *cul de sac, ancien régime, deus ex machina,
mutatis mutandis, status quo, gleichschaltung, weltanschauung,* are
used to give an air of culture and elegance. Except for the useful abbre-
viations *i.e., e.g.,* and *etc.,* there is no real need for any of the hundreds
of foreign phrases now current in English. Bad writers, and especially
scientific, political and sociological writers, are nearly always haunted
by the notion that Latin or Greek words are grander than Saxon ones,
and unnecessary words like *expedite, ameliorate, predict, extraneous,
deracinated, clandestine, subaqueous* and hundreds of others constantly gain ground from their Anglo-Saxon opposite numbers.[1] The
jargon peculiar to Marxist writing (*hyena, hangman, cannibal, petty
bourgeois, these gentry, lacquey, flunkey, mad dog, White Guard,*
etc.) consists largely of words and phrases translated from Russian,
German or French; but the normal way of coining a new word is to
use a Latin or Greek root with the appropriate affix and, where necessary, the *-ize* formation. It is often easier to make up words of this
kind (*deregionalize, impermissible, extramarital, non-fragmentary*

---

[1] An interesting illustration of this is the way in which the English flower names
which were in use till very recently are being ousted by Greek ones, *snapdragon* becoming *antirrhinum, forget-me-not* becoming *myosotis,* etc. It is hard to see any practical
reason for this change of fashion: it is probably due to an instinctive turning-away from
the more homely word and a vague feeling that the Greek is scientific.

and so forth) than to think up the English words that will cover one's meaning. The result, in general, is an increase in slovenliness and vagueness.

MEANINGLESS WORDS

In certain kinds of writing, particularly in art criticism and liter- 8 ary criticism, it is normal to come across long passages which are almost completely lacking in meaning.[2] Words like *romantic, plastic, values, human, dead, sentimental, natural, vitality,* as used in art criticism, are strictly meaningless, in the sense that they not only do not point to any discoverable object, but are hardly ever expected to do so by the reader. When one critic writes, "The outstanding feature of Mr. X's work is its living quality," while another writes, "The immediately striking thing about Mr. X's work is its peculiar dead-ness," the reader accepts this as a simple difference of opinion. If words like *black* and *white* were involved, instead of the jargon words *dead* and *living,* he would see at once that language was being used in an improper way. Many political words are similarly abused. The word *Fascism* has now no meaning in so far as it signifies "something not desirable." The words *democracy, socialism, freedom, patriotic, realistic, justice,* have each of them several different meanings which cannot be reconciled with one another. In the case of a word like *democracy,* not only is there no agreed definition, but the attempt to make one is resisted from all sides. It is almost universally felt that when we call a country democratic we are praising it: consequently the defenders of every kind of régime claim that it is a democracy, and fear that they might have to stop using the word if it were tied down to any one meaning. Words of this kind are often used in a consciously dishonest way. That is, the person who uses them has his own private definition, but allows his hearer to think he means something quite different. Statements like *Marshal Pétain was a true patriot, The Soviet Press is the freest in the world, The Catholic Church is opposed to persecution,* are almost always made with intent to deceive. Other

---

[2] Example: "Comfort's catholicity of perception and image, strangely Whitman-esque in range, almost the exact opposite in aesthetic compulsion, continues to evoke that trembling atmospheric accumulative hinting at a cruel, an inexorably serene time-lessness. . . . Wrey Gardiner scores by aiming at simple bull's-eyes with precision. Only they are not so simple, and through his contented sadness runs more than the surface bitter-sweet of resignation." (Poetry Quarterly.)

words used in variable meanings, in most cases more or less dishonestly, are: *class, totalitarian, science, progressive, reactionary, bourgeois, equality.*

9   Now that I have made this catalogue of swindles and perversions, let me give another example of the kind of writing that they lead to. This time it must of its nature be an imaginary one. I am going to translate a passage of good English into modern English of the worst sort. Here is a well-known verse from *Ecclesiastes:*

> I returned and saw under the sun, that the race is not to the swift, nor the battle to the strong, neither yet bread to the wise, nor yet riches to men of understanding, nor yet favour to men of skill, but time and chance happeneth to them all.

10   Here it is in modern English:

> Objective consideration of contemporary phenomena compels the conclusion that success or failure in competitive activities exhibits no tendency to be commensurate with innate capacity, but that a considerable element of the unpredictable must invariably be taken into account.

11   This is a parody, but not a very gross one. Exhibit (3), above, for instance, contains several patches of the same kind of English. It will be seen that I have not made a full translation. The beginning and ending of the sentence follow the original meaning fairly closely, but in the middle the concrete illustrations — race, battle, bread — dissolve into the vague phrase "success or failure in competitive activities." This had to be so, because no modern writer of the kind I am discussing — no one capable of using phrases like "objective consideration of contemporary phenomena" — would ever tabulate his thoughts in that precise and detailed way. The whole tendency of modern prose is away from concreteness. Now analyse these two sentences a little more closely. The first contains forty-nine words but only sixty syllables, and all its words are those of everyday life. The second contains thirty-eight words of ninety syllables: eighteen of its words are from Latin roots, and one from Greek. The first sentence contains six vivid images, and only one phrase ("time and chance") that could be called vague. The second contains not a single fresh, arresting phrase, and in spite of its ninety syllables it gives only a shortened version of the meaning contained in the first. Yet without a doubt it is the second kind of sentence that is gaining ground in modern English. I do not want to exaggerate. This kind of writing is

not yet universal, and outcrops of simplicity will occur here and there in the worst-written page. Still, if you or I were told to write a few lines on the uncertainty of human fortunes, we should probably come much nearer to my imaginary sentence than to the one from *Ecclesiastes*.

As I have tried to show, modern writing at its worst does not   12
consist in picking out words for the sake of their meaning and inventing images in order to make the meaning clearer. It consists in gumming together long strips of words which have already been set in order by someone else, and making the results presentable by sheer humbug. The attraction of this way of writing is that it is easy. It is easier — even quicker, once you have the habit — to say *In my opinion it is not an unjustifiable assumption that* than to say *I think*. If you use ready-made phrases, you not only don't have to hunt about for words; you also don't have to bother with the rhythms of your sentences, since these phrases are generally so arranged as to be more or less euphonious. When you are composing in a hurry — when you are dictating to a stenographer, for instance, or making a public speech — it is natural to fall into a pretentious, Latinized style. Tags like *a consideration which we should do well to bear in mind* or *a conclusion to which all of us would readily assent* will save many a sentence from coming down with a bump. By using stale metaphors, similes and idioms, you save much mental effort, at the cost of leaving your meaning vague, not only for your reader but for yourself. This is the significance of mixed metaphors. The sole aim of a metaphor is to call up a visual image. When these images clash — as in *The Fascist octopus has sung its swan song, the jackboot is thrown into the melting pot* — it can be taken as certain that the writer is not seeing a mental image of the objects he is naming; in other words he is not really thinking. Look again at the examples I gave at the beginning of this essay. Professor Laski (1) uses five negatives in fifty-three words. One of these is superfluous, making nonsense of the whole passage, and in addition there is the slip *alien* for *akin*, making further nonsense, and several avoidable pieces of clumsiness which increase the general vagueness. Professor Hogben (2) plays ducks and drakes with a battery which is able to write prescriptions, and, while disapproving of the everyday phrase *put up with*, is unwilling to look *egregious* up in the dictionary and see what it means; (3), if one takes an uncharitable attitude towards it, is simply meaningless: probably one could work out its intended meaning by reading the whole of the article in which it occurs. In (4), the writer knows more or less what he wants to say,

but an accumulation of stale phrases chokes him, like tea leaves blocking a sink. In (5), words and meaning have almost parted company. People who write in this manner usually have a general emotional meaning — they dislike one thing and want to express solidarity with another — but they are not interested in the detail of what they are saying. A scrupulous writer, in every sentence that he writes, will ask himself at least four questions, thus: What am I trying to say? What words will express it? What image or idiom will make it clearer? Is this image fresh enough to have an effect? And he will probably ask himself two more: Could I put it more shortly? Have I said anything that is avoidably ugly? But you are not obliged to go to all this trouble. You can shirk it by simply throwing your mind open and letting the ready-made phrases come crowding in. They will construct your sentences for you — even think your thoughts for you, to a certain extent — and at need they will perform the important service of partially concealing your meaning even from yourself. It is at this point that the special connection between politics and the debasement of language becomes clear.

13   In our time it is broadly true that political writing is bad writing. Where it is not true, it will generally be found that the writer is some kind of rebel, expressing his private opinions and not a "party line." Orthodoxy, of whatever color, seems to demand a lifeless, imitative style. The political dialects to be found in pamphlets, leading articles, manifestos, White Papers and the speeches of undersecretaries do, of course, vary from party to party, but they are all alike in that one almost never finds in them a fresh, vivid, home-made turn of speech. When one watches some tired hack on the platform mechanically repeating the familiar phrases — *bestial atrocities, iron heel, bloodstained tyranny, free people of the world, stand shoulder to shoulder* — one often has a curious feeling that one is not watching a live human being but some kind of dummy: a feeling which suddenly becomes stronger at moments when the light catches the speaker's spectacles and turns them into blank discs which seem to have no eyes behind them. And this is not altogether fanciful. A speaker who uses that kind of phraseology has gone some distance towards turning himself into a machine. The appropriate noises are coming out of his larynx, but his brain is not involved as it would be if he were choosing his words for himself. If the speech he is making is one that he is accustomed to make over and over again, he may be almost unconscious of what he is saying, as one is when one utters the responses in church. And this reduced state of consciousness, if not indispensable, is at any rate favorable to political conformity.

In our time, political speech and writing are largely the defence 14
of the indefensible. Things like the continuance of British rule in
India, the Russian purges and deportations, the dropping of the atom
bombs on Japan, can indeed be defended, but only by arguments which
are too brutal for most people to face, and which do not square with
the professed aims of political parties. Thus political language has to
consist largely of euphemism, question-begging and sheer cloudy
vagueness. Defenceless villages are bombarded from the air, the inhabitants driven out into the countryside, the cattle machine-gunned, the
huts set on fire with incendiary bullets: this is called *pacification*.
Millions of peasants are robbed of their farms and sent trudging along
the roads with no more than they can carry: this is called *transfer of
population* or *rectification of frontiers*. People are imprisoned for years
without trial, or shot in the back of the neck or sent to die of scurvy
in Arctic lumber camps: this is called *elimination of unreliable elements*. Such phraseology is needed if one wants to name things without calling up mental pictures of them. Consider for instance some
comfortable English professor defending Russian totalitarianism. He
cannot say outright, "I believe in killing off your opponents when you
can get good results by doing so." Probably, therefore, he will say
something like this:

"While freely conceding that the Soviet régime exhibits certain 15
features which the humanitarian may be inclined to deplore, we must,
I think, agree that a certain curtailment of the right to political opposition is an unavoidable concomitant of transitional periods, and that
the rigors which the Russian people have been called upon to undergo
have been amply justified in the sphere of concrete achievement."

The inflated style is itself a kind of euphemism. A mass of Latin 16
words falls upon the facts like soft snow, blurring the outlines and
covering up all the details. The great enemy of clear language is insin-
cerity. When there is a gap between one's real and one's declared aims,
one turns as it were instinctively to long words and exhausted idioms,
like a cuttlefish squirting out ink. In our age there is no such thing as
"keeping out of politics." All issues are political issues, and politics
itself is a mass of lies, evasions, folly, hatred and schizophrenia. When
the general atmosphere is bad, language must suffer. I should expect
to find — this is a guess which I have not sufficient knowledge to
verify — that the German, Russian and Italian languages have all de-
teriorated in the last ten or fifteen years, as a result of dictatorship.

But if thought corrupts language, language can also corrupt 17
thought. A bad usage can spread by tradition and imitation, even
among people who should and do know better. The debased language

that I have been discussing is in some ways very convenient. Phrases like *a not unjustifiable assumption, leaves much to be desired, would serve no good purpose, a consideration which we should do well to bear in mind,* are a continuous temptation, a packet of aspirins always at one's elbow. Look back through this essay, and for certain you will find that I have again and again committed the very faults I am protesting against. By this morning's post I have received a pamphlet dealing with conditions in Germany. The author tells me that he "felt impelled" to write it. I open it at random, and here is almost the first sentence that I see: "[The Allies] have an opportunity not only of achieving a radical transformation of Germany's social and political structure in such a way as to avoid a nationalistic reaction in Germany itself, but at the same time of laying the foundations of a co-operative and unified Europe." You see, he "feels impelled" to write — feels, presumably, that he has something new to say — and yet his words, like cavalry horses answering the bugle, group themselves automatically into the familiar dreary pattern. This invasion of one's mind by ready-made phrases (*lay the foundations, achieve a radical transformation*) can only be prevented if one is constantly on guard against them, and every such phrase anaesthetizes a portion of one's brain.

18   I said earlier that the decadence of our language is probably curable. Those who deny this would argue, if they produced an argument at all, that language merely reflects existing social conditions, and that we cannot influence its development by any direct tinkering with words and constructions. So far as the general tone or spirit of a language goes, this may be true, but it is not true in detail. Silly words and expressions have often disappeared, not through any evolutionary process but owing to the conscious action of a minority. Two recent examples were *explore every avenue* and *leave no stone unturned,* which were killed by the jeers of a few journalists. There is a long list of flyblown metaphors which could similarly be got rid of if enough people would interest themselves in the job; and it should also be possible to laugh the *not un-* formation out of existence,[3] to reduce the amount of Latin and Greek in the average sentence, to drive out foreign phrases and strayed scientific words, and, in general, to make pretentiousness unfashionable. But all these are minor points. The defence of the English language implies more than this, and perhaps it is best to start by saying what it does *not* imply.

---

[3] One can cure oneself of the *not un-* formation by memorizing this sentence: *A not unblack dog was chasing a not unsmall rabbit across a not ungreen field.*

To begin with it has nothing to do with archaism, with the sal- 19
vaging of obsolete words and turns of speech, or with the setting up of
a "standard English" which must never be departed from. On the
contrary, it is especially concerned with the scrapping of every word
or idiom which has outworn its usefulness. It has nothing to do with
correct grammar and syntax, which are of no importance so long as
one makes one's meaning clear, or with the avoidance of American-
isms, or with having what is called a "good prose style." On the other
hand it is not concerned with fake simplicity and the attempt to make
written English colloquial. Nor does it even imply in every case preferring the Saxon word to the Latin one, though it does imply using
the fewest and shortest words that will cover one's meaning. What is
above all needed is to let the meaning choose the word, and not the
other way about. In prose, the worst thing one can do with words is to
surrender to them. When you think of a concrete object, you think
wordlessly, and then, if you want to describe the thing you have been
visualizing you probably hunt about till you find the exact words that
seem to fit it. When you think of something abstract you are more
inclined to use words from the start, and unless you make a conscious
effort to prevent it, the existing dialect will come rushing in and do
the job for you, at the expense of blurring or even changing your meaning. Probably it is better to put off using words as long as possible and
get one's meaning as clear as one can through pictures or sensations.
Afterwards one can choose — not simply *accept* — the phrases that
will best cover the meaning, and then switch round and decide what
impression one's words are likely to make on another person. This
last effort of the mind cuts out all stale or mixed images, all prefabricated phrases, needless repetitions, and humbug and vagueness generally. But one can often be in doubt about the effect of a word or a
phrase, and one needs rules that one can rely on when instinct fails. I
think the following rules will cover most cases:

(i) Never use a metaphor, simile or other figure of speech which
you are used to seeing in print.
(ii) Never use a long word where a short one will do.
(iii) If it is possible to cut a word out, always cut it out.
(iv) Never use the passive where you can use the active.
(v) Never use a foreign phrase, a scientific word or a jargon word
if you can think of an everyday English equivalent.
(vi) Break any of these rules sooner than say anything outright
barbarous.

These rules sound elementary, and so they are, but they demand a deep change of attitude in anyone who has grown used to writing in the style now fashionable. One could keep all of them and still write bad English, but one could not write the kind of stuff that I quoted in those five specimens at the beginning of this article.

20   I have not here been considering the literary use of language, but merely language as an instrument for expressing and not for concealing or preventing thought. Stuart Chase and others have come near to claiming that all abstract words are meaningless, and have used this as a pretext for advocating a kind of political quietism. Since you don't know what Fascism is, how can you struggle against Fascism? One need not swallow such absurdities as this, but one ought to recognize that the present political chaos is connected with the decay of language, and that one can probably bring about some improvement by starting at the verbal end. If you simplify your English, you are freed from the worst follies of orthodoxy. You cannot speak any of the necessary dialects, and when you make a stupid remark its stupidity will be obvious, even to yourself. Political language — and with variations this is true of all political parties, from Conservatives to Anarchists — is designed to make lies sound truthful and murder respectable, and to give an appearance of solidity to pure wind. One cannot change this all in a moment, but one can at least change one's own habits, and from time to time one can even, if one jeers loudly enough, send some worn-out and useless phrase — some *jackboot, Achilles' heel, hotbed, melting pot, acid test, veritable inferno* or other lump of verbal refuse — into the dustbin where it belongs.

_____ **CONSIDERATIONS** _____

1. "Style is the man himself." How well, and in what ways, does Orwell's essay illustrate Buffon's aphorism? Select another author in the text, someone with a distinct style, and test it against Buffon's statement.

2. Assuming that Orwell's statement in Paragraph 2, "the fight against bad English is not frivolous and is not the exclusive concern of professional writers," is the conclusion of a syllogism, reconstruct the major and minor premises of that syllogism by studying the steps Orwell takes to reach his conclusion. See Robert Gorham Davis's "Logic and Logical Fallacies" for help in understanding a syllogism.

3. Orwell documents his argument by quoting five passages by writers who wrote in the forties. From comparable sources, assembly a gallery of

current specimens to help confirm or refute his contention that "the English language is in a bad way."

4. Orwell concludes with six rules. From the rest of his essay, how do you think he would define "anything outright barbarous" (in rule vi)?

5. Has Orwell broken some of his own rules? Point out and explain any examples you find. Look over his "Shooting an Elephant" and "A Hanging" as well as "Politics and the English Language."

6. In Paragraph 16, Orwell asserts that "The inflated style is itself a kind of euphemism." Look up the meaning of "euphemism" and compile examples from your local newspaper. Do you agree with Orwell that they are "swindles and perversions"? Note how Ambrose Bierce counts on our understanding of euphemisms in his Devil's Dictionary (pages 59–62).

Two of George Orwell's best essays derive from his experience as a colonial policeman, upholder of law and order for the British empire. Many political thinkers derive an ideology from thought and theory; Orwell's politics grew empirically from the life he lived. He provides us models for learning by living — and for learning by writing out of one's life.

54

GEORGE ORWELL

Shooting an Elephant

1   In Moulmein, in Lower Burma, I was hated by large numbers of people — the only time in my life that I have been important enough for this to happen to me. I was sub-divisional police officer of the town, and in an aimless, petty kind of way anti-European feeling was very bitter. No one had the guts to raise a riot, but if a European woman went through the bazaars alone somebody would probably spit betel juice over her dress. As a police officer I was an obvious target and was baited whenever it seemed safe to do so. When a nimble Burman tripped me up on the football field and the referee (another Burman) looked the other way, the crowd yelled with hideous laughter. This happened more than once. In the end the sneering yellow faces of young men that met me everywhere, the insults hooted after me when I was at a safe distance, got badly on my nerves. The young Buddhist priests were the worst of all. There were several thousands of them in the town and none of them seemed to have anything to do except stand on street corners and jeer at Europeans.

All this was perplexing and upsetting. For at that time I had 2 already made up my mind that imperialism was an evil thing and the sooner I chucked up my job and got out of it the better. Theoretically — and secretly, of course — I was all for the Burmese and all against their oppressors, the British. As for the job I was doing, I hated it more bitterly than I can perhaps make clear. In a job like that you see the dirty work of Empire at close quarters. The wretched prisoners huddling in the stinking cages of the lock-ups, the grey, cowed faces of the long-term convicts, the scarred buttocks of the men who had been flogged with bamboos — all these oppressed me with an intolerable sense of guilt. But I could get nothing into perspective. I was young and ill-educated and I had had to think out my problems in the utter silence that is imposed on every Englishman in the East. I did not even know that the British Empire is dying, still less did I know that it is a great deal better than the younger empires that are going to supplant it. All I knew was that I was stuck between my hatred of the empire I served and my rage against the evil-spirited little beasts who tried to make my job impossible. With one part of my mind I thought of the British Raj as an unbreakable tyranny, as something clamped down, in *saecula saeculorum*, upon the will of prostrate peoples; with another part I thought that the greatest joy in the world would be to drive a bayonet into a Buddhist priest's guts. Feelings like these are the normal by-products of imperialism; ask any Anglo-Indian official, if you can catch him off duty.

One day something happened which in a roundabout way was 3 enlightening. It was a tiny incident in itself, but it gave me a better glimpse than I had had before of the real nature of imperialism — the real motives for which despotic governments act. Early one morning the sub-inspector at a police station the other end of town rang me up on the phone and said that an elephant was ravaging the bazaar. Would I please come and do something about it? I did not know what I could do, but I wanted to see what was happening and I got on to a pony and started out. I took my rifle, an old .44 Winchester and much too small to kill an elephant, but I thought the noise might be useful *in terrorem*. Various Burmans stopped me on the way and told me about the elephant's doings. It was not, of course, a wild elephant, but a tame one which had gone "must." It had been chained up, as tame elephants always are when their attack of "must" is due, but on the previous night it had broken its chain and escaped. Its mahout, the only person who could manage it when it was in that state, had set out in pursuit, but had taken the wrong direction and was now twelve hours' journey away, and in the morning the elephant had suddenly reappeared in the town. The Burmese population had no weapons and were quite help-less against it. It had already destroyed somebody's bamboo hut, killed a cow and raided some fruit-stalls and devoured the stock; also it had met the municipal rubbish van and, when the driver jumped out and took to his heels, had turned the van over and inflicted violences upon it.

4   The Burmese sub-inspector and some Indian constables were waiting for me in the quarter where the elephant had been seen. It was a very poor quarter, a labyrinth of squalid bamboo huts, thatched with palmleaf, winding all over a steep hillside. I remember that it was a cloudy, stuffy morning at the beginning of the rains. We began ques-tioning the people as to where the elephant had gone and, as usual, failed to get any definite information. That is invariably the case in the East; a story always sounds clear enough at a distance, but the nearer you get to the scene of events the vaguer it becomes. Some of the people said that the elephant had gone in one direction, some said that he had gone in another, some professed not even to have heard of any elephant. I had almost made up my mind that the whole story was a pack of lies, when we heard yells a little distance away. There was a loud, scandalized cry of "Go away, child! Go away this instant!" and an old woman with a switch in her hand came round the corner of a hut, violently shooing away a crowd of naked children. Some more women followed, clicking their tongues and exclaiming; evidently there was something that the children ought not to have seen. I rounded the hut and saw a man's dead body sprawling in the mud. He was an Indian, a black Dravidian coolie, almost naked, and he could not have been dead many minutes. The people said that the elephant had come suddenly upon him round the corner of the hut, caught him with its trunk, put its foot on his back and ground him into the earth. This was the rainy season and the ground was soft, and his face had scored a trench a foot deep and a couple of yards long. He was lying on his belly with arms crucified and head sharply twisted to one side. His face was coated with mud, the eyes wide open, the teeth bared and grinning with an expression of unendurable agony. (Never tell me, by the way, that the dead look peaceful. Most of the corpses I have seen looked devilish.) The friction of the great beast's foot had stripped the skin from his back as neatly as one skins a rabbit. As soon as I saw the dead man I sent an orderly to a friend's house nearby to borrow an elephant rifle. I had already sent back the pony, not wanting it to go mad with fright and throw me if it smelt the elephant.

5   The orderly came back in a few minutes with a rifle and five

cartridges, and meanwhile some Burmans had arrived and told us that the elephant was in the paddy fields below, only a few hundred yards away. As I started forward practically the whole population of the quarter flocked out of the houses and followed me. They had seen the rifle and were all shouting excitedly that I was going to shoot the elephant. They had not shown much interest in the elephant when he was merely ravaging their homes, but it was different now that he was going to be shot. It was a bit of fun to them, as it would be to an English crowd; besides they wanted the meat. It made me vaguely uneasy. I had no intention of shooting the elephant — I had merely sent for the rifle to defend myself if necessary — and it is always unnerving to have a crowd following you. I marched down the hill, looking and feeling a fool, with the rifle over my shoulder and an ever-growing army of people jostling at my heels. At the bottom, when you got away from the huts, there was a metalled road and beyond that a miry waste of paddy fields a thousand yards across, not yet ploughed but soggy from the first rains and dotted with coarse grass. The elephant was standing eight yards from the road, his left side towards us. He took not the slightest notice of the crowd's approach. He was tearing up bunches of grass, beating them against his knees to clean them and stuffing them into his mouth.

I had halted on the road. As soon as I saw the elephant I knew   6 with perfect certainty that I ought not to shoot him. It is a serious matter to shoot a working elephant — it is comparable to destroying a huge and costly piece of machinery — and obviously one ought not to do it if it can possibly be avoided. And at that distance, peacefully eating, the elephant looked no more dangerous than a cow. I thought then and I think now that his attack of "must" was already passing off; in which case he would merely wander harmlessly about until the mahout came back and caught him. Moreover, I did not in the least want to shoot him. I decided that I would watch him for a little while to make sure that he did not turn savage again, and then go home.

But at that moment, I glanced round at the crowd that had fol-   7 lowed me. It was an immense crowd, two thousand at the least and growing every minute. It blocked the road for a long distance on either side. I looked at the sea of yellow faces above the garish clothes — faces all happy and excited over this bit of fun, all certain that the elephant was going to be shot. They were watching me as they would watch a conjuror about to perform a trick. They did not like me, but with the magical rifle in my hands I was momentarily worth watching. And suddenly I realized that I should have to shoot the elephant after all. The people expected it of me and I had got to do it; I could feel their two thousand wills pressing me forward, irresistibly. And it was at this moment, as I stood there with the rifle in my hands, that I first grasped the hollowness, the futility of the white man's dominion in the East. Here was I, the white man with his gun, standing in front of the unarmed native crowd — seemingly the leading actor of the piece; but in reality I was only an absurd puppet pushed to and fro by the will of those yellow faces behind. I perceived in this moment that when the white man turns tyrant it is his own freedom that he destroys. He becomes a sort of hollow, posing dummy, the conventionalized figure of a sahib. For it is the condition of his rule that he shall spend his life in trying to impress the "natives," and so in every crisis he has got to do what the "natives" expect of him. He wears a mask, and his face grows to fit it. I had got to shoot the elephant. I had committed myself to doing it when I sent for the rifle. A sahib has got to act like a sahib; he has got to appear resolute, to know his own mind and do definite things. To come all that way, rifle in hand, with two thousand people marching at my heels, and then to trail feebly away, having done nothing — no, that was impossible. The crowd would laugh at me. And my whole life, every white man's life in the East, was one long struggle not to be laughed at.

8   But I did not want to shoot the elephant. I watched him beating his bunch of grass against his knees, with that preoccupied grandmotherly air that elephants have. It seemed to me that it would be murder to shoot him. At that age I was not squeamish about killing animals, but I had never shot an elephant and never wanted to. (Somehow it always seems worse to kill a *large* animal.) Besides, there was the beast's owner to be considered. Alive, the elephant was worth at least a hundred pounds; dead, he would only be worth the value of his tusks, five pounds, possibly. But I had got to act quickly. I turned to some experienced-looking Burmans who had been there when we arrived, and asked them how the elephant had been behaving. They all said the same thing: he took no notice of you if you left him alone, but he might charge if you went too close to him.

9   It was perfectly clear to me what I ought to do. I ought to walk up to within, say, twenty-five yards of the elephant and test his behavior. If he charged, I could shoot; if he took no notice of me, it would be safe to leave him until the mahout came back. But also I knew that I was going to do no such thing. I was a poor shot with a rifle and the ground was soft mud into which one would sink at every step. If the elephant charged and I missed him, I should have about as much chance as a toad under a steam-roller. But even then I was not thinking particularly of my own skin, only of the watchful yellow faces behind.

For at that moment, with the crowd watching me, I was not afraid in the ordinary sense, as I would have been if I had been alone. A white man mustn't be frightened in front of "natives"; and so, in general, he isn't frightened. The sole thought in my mind was that if anything went wrong those two thousand Burmans would see me pursued, caught, trampled on and reduced to a grinning corpse like that Indian up the hill. And if that happened it was quite probable that some of them would laugh. That would never do. There was only one alternative. I shoved the cartridges into the magazine and lay down on the road to get a better aim.

The crowd grew very still, and a deep, low, happy sigh, as of 10 people who see the theatre curtain go up at last, breathed from innumerable throats. They were going to have their bit of fun after all. The rifle was a beautiful German thing with cross-hair sights. I did not then know that in shooting an elephant one would shoot to cut an imaginary bar running from ear-hole to ear-hole. I ought, therefore, as the elephant was sideways on, to have aimed straight at his ear-hole; actually I aimed several inches in front of this, thinking the brain would be further forward.

When I pulled the trigger I did not hear the bang or feel the kick 11 — one never does when a shot goes home — but I heard the devilish roar of glee that went up from the crowd. In that instant, in too short a time, one would have thought, even for the bullet to get there, a mysterious, terrible change had come over the elephant. He neither stirred nor fell, but every line of his body had altered. He looked suddenly stricken, shrunken, immensely old, as though the frightful impact of the bullet had paralysed him without knocking him down. At last, after what seemed a long time — it might have been five seconds, I dare say — he sagged flabbily to his knees. His mouth slobbered. An enormous senility seemed to have settled upon him. One could have imagined him thousands of years old. I fired again into the same spot. At the second shot he did not collapse but climbed with desperate slowness to his feet and stood weakly upright, with legs sagging and head drooping. I fired a third time. That was the shot that did for him. You could see the agony of it jolt his whole body and knock the last remnant of strength from his legs. But in falling he seemed for a moment to rise, for as his hind legs collapsed beneath him he seemed to tower upward like a huge rock toppling, his trunk reaching skywards like a tree. He trumpeted, for the first and only time. And then down he came, his belly towards me, with a crash that seemed to shake the ground even where I lay.

I got up. The Burmans were already racing past me across the 12 mud. It was obvious that the elephant would never rise again, but he was not dead. He was breathing very rhythmically with long rattling gasps, his great mound of a side painfully rising and falling. His mouth was wide open. I could see far down into caverns of pale pink throat. I waited a long time for him to die, but his breathing did not weaken. Finally I fired my two remaining shots into the spot where I thought his heart must be. The thick blood welled out of him like red velvet, but still he did not die. His body did not even jerk when the shots hit him, the tortured breathing continued without a pause. He was dying, very slowly and in great agony, but in some world remote from me where not even a bullet could damage him further. I felt I had got to put an end to that dreadful noise. It seemed dreadful to see the great beast lying there, powerless to move and yet powerless to die, and not even to be able to finish him. I sent back for my small rifle and poured shot after shot into his heart and down his throat. They seemed to make no impression. The tortured gasps continued as steadily as the ticking of a clock.

13   In the end I could not stand it any longer and went away. I heard later that it took him half an hour to die. Burmans were bringing dahs and baskets even before I left, and I was told they had stripped his body almost to the bones by the afternoon.

14   Afterwards, of course, there were endless discussions about the shooting of the elephant. The owner was furious, but he was only an Indian and could do nothing. Besides, legally I had done the right thing, for a mad elephant has to be killed, like a mad dog, if its owner fails to control it. Among the Europeans opinion was divided. The older men said I was right, the younger men said it was a damn shame to shoot an elephant for killing a coolie, because the elephant was worth more than any damn Coringhee coolie. And afterwards I was very glad that the coolie had been killed; it put me legally in the right and it gave me sufficient pretext for shooting the elephant. I often wondered whether any of the others grasped that I had done it solely to avoid looking a fool.

___ **CONSIDERATIONS** _____

1. Some of Orwell's remarks about the Burmese make him sound like a racist; collect a half dozen of them on a separate sheet of paper, then look for lines or phrases that counter the first samples. Discuss your findings, particularly in terms of Orwell's purposes in his essay.

2. "In a job like that you see the dirty work of Empire at close quarters." If you ponder Orwell's capitalizing "Empire" (Paragraph 2) and then substitute other abstract terms for "Empire" — say, Government, Poverty, War, Hatred — you may discover one of the most important principles of effective writing, a principle beautifully demonstrated by Orwell's whole account.

3. In Paragraph 4, Orwell says, "the nearer you get to the scene of events the vaguer it becomes." Have you had any experience that would help you understand his remark? Would it hold true for the soldier caught in battle, a couple suffering a divorce, a football player caught in a pile-up on the scrimmage line?

4. Some years after his experience in Burma, Orwell became a well-known opponent of fascism. Explain how shooting the elephant taught him to detest totalitarianism.

5. "Somehow it always seems worse to kill a *large* animal," Orwell writes in Paragraph 8. Why? Are some lives more equal than others?

6. In Paragraph 10, Orwell describes his rifle as a "beautiful German thing." Does he use the word "beautiful" in the same way Don Sharp uses it in the last paragraph of his essay "Under the Hood"? Neither of the writers means "pulchritude" when he uses "beautiful." What synonyms might fit their sense of the word?

7. After two substantial paragraphs of agonizing detail, Orwell's elephant is still dying. Why does the writer inflict this punishment on the reader?

55

GEORGE ORWELL

A Hanging

1   It was in Burma, a sodden morning of the rains. A sickly light, like yellow tinfoil, was slanting over the high walls into the jail yard. We were waiting outside the condemned cells, a row of sheds fronted with double bars, like small animal cages. Each cell measured about ten feet by ten and was quite bare within except for a plank bed and a pot for drinking water. In some of them brown, silent men were squatting at the inner bars, with their blankets draped round them. These were the condemned men, due to be hanged within the next week or two.

2   One prisoner had been brought out of his cell. He was a Hindu, a puny wisp of a man, with a shaven head and vague liquid eyes. He had a thick, sprouting mustache, absurdly too big for his body, rather like the moustache of a comic man on the films. Six tall Indian warders were guarding him and getting him ready for the gallows. Two of them stood by with rifles and fixed bayonets, while the others handcuffed him, passed a chain through his handcuffs and fixed it to their belts, and lashed his arms tight to his sides. They crowded very close about him, with their hands always on him in a careful, caressing grip, as though all the while feeling him to make sure he was there. It was like men handling a fish which is still alive and may jump back into the water. But he stood quite unresisting, yielding his arms limply to the ropes, as though he hardly noticed what was happening.

3   Eight o'clock struck and a bugle call, desolately thin in the wet

From *Shooting an Elephant and Other Essays* by George Orwell, copyright 1950 by Sonia Brownell Orwell, 1978 by Sonia Pitt-Rivers. Reprinted by permission of Harcourt Brace Jovanovich, Inc., the estate of the late George Orwell, and Martin Secker & Warburg.

air, floated from the distant barracks. The superintendent of the jail, who was standing apart from the rest of us, moodily prodding the gravel with his stick, raised his head at the sound. He was an army doctor, with a grey toothbrush moustache and a gruff voice. "For God's sake hurry up, Francis," he said irritably. "The man ought to have been dead by this time. Aren't you ready yet?"

Francis, the head jailer, a fat Dravidian in a white drill suit and 4 gold spectacles, waved his black hand. "Yes sir, yes sir," he bubbled. "All iss satisfactorily prepared. The hangman iss waiting. We shall proceed."

"Well, quick march, then. The prisoners can't get their breakfast 5 till this job's over."

We set out for the gallows. Two warders marched on either side 6 of the prisoner, with their rifles at the slope; two others marched close against him, gripping him by arm and shoulder, as though at once pushing and supporting him. The rest of us, magistrates and the like, followed behind. Suddenly, when we had gone ten yards, the procession stopped short without any order or warning. A dreadful thing had happened — a dog, come goodness knows whence, had appeared in the yard. It came bounding among us with a loud volley of barks and leapt round us wagging its whole body, wild with glee at finding so many human beings together. It was a large woolly dog, half Airedale, half pariah. For a moment it pranced round us, and then, before anyone could stop it, it had made a dash for the prisoner, and jumping up tried to lick his face. Everybody stood aghast, too taken aback even to grab the dog.

"Who let that bloody brute in here?" said the superintendent 7 angrily. "Catch it, someone!"

A warder detached from the escort, charged clumsily after the 8 dog, but it danced and gambolled just out of his reach, taking everything as part of the game. A young Eurasian jailer picked up a handful of gravel and tried to stone the dog away, but it dodged the stones and came after us again. Its yaps echoed from the jail walls. The prisoner, in the grasp of the two warders, looked on incuriously, as though this was another formality of the hanging. It was several minutes before someone managed to catch the dog. Then we put my handkerchief through its collar and moved off once more, with the dog still straining and whimpering.

It was about forty yards to the gallows. I watched the bare brown 9 back of the prisoner marching in front of me. He walked clumsily with his bound arms, but quite steadily, with that bobbing gait of the

Indian who never straightens his knees. At each step his muscles slid neatly into place, the lock of hair on his scalp danced up and down, his feet printed themselves on the wet gravel. And once, in spite of the men who gripped him by each shoulder, he stepped lightly aside to avoid a puddle on the path.

10   It is curious; but till that moment I had never realized what it means to destroy a healthy, conscious man. When I saw the prisoner step aside to avoid the puddle I saw the mystery, the unspeakable wrongness, of cutting a life short when it is in full tide. This man was not dying, he was alive just as we are alive. All the organs of his body were working — bowels digesting food, skin renewing itself, nails growing, tissues forming — all toiling away in solemn foolery. His nails would still be growing when he stood on the drop, when he was falling through the air with a tenth-of-a-second to live. His eyes saw the yellow gravel and the grey walls, and his brain still remembered, foresaw, reasoned — even about puddles. He and we were a party of men walking together, seeing, hearing, feeling, understanding the same world; and in two minutes, with a sudden snap, one of us would be gone — one mind less, one world less.

11   The gallows stood in a small yard, separate from the main grounds of the prison, and overgrown with tall prickly weeds. It was a brick erection like three sides of a shed, with planking on top, and above that two beams and a crossbar with the rope dangling. The hangman, a greyhaired convict in the white uniform of the prison, was waiting beside his machine. He greeted us with a servile crouch as we entered. At a word from Francis the two warders, gripping the prisoner more closely than ever, half led, half pushed him to the gallows and helped him clumsily up the ladder. Then the hangman climbed up and fixed the rope round the prisoner's neck.

12   We stood waiting, five yards away. The warders had formed in a rough circle round the gallows. And then, when the noose was fixed, the prisoner began crying out to his god. It was a high, reiterated cry of "Ram! Ram! Ram! Ram!" not urgent and fearful like a prayer or cry for help, but steady, rhythmical, almost like the tolling of a bell. The dog answered the sound with a whine. The hangman, still standing on the gallows, produced a small cotton bag like a flour bag and drew it down over the prisoner's face. But the sound, muffled by the cloth, still persisted, over and over again: "Ram! Ram! Ram! Ram! Ram!"

13   The hangman climbed down and stood ready, holding the lever. Minutes seemed to pass. The steady, muffled crying from the prisoner

went on and on, "Ram! Ram! Ram!" never faltering for an instant. The superintendent, his head on his chest, was slowly poking the ground with his stick; perhaps he was counting the cries, allowing the prisoner a fixed number — fifty, perhaps, or a hundred. Everyone had changed colour. The Indians had gone grey like bad coffee, and one or two of the bayonets were wavering. We looked at the lashed, hooded man on the drop, and listened to his cries — each cry another second of life; the same thought was in all our minds; oh, kill him quickly, get it over, stop that abominable noise!

Suddenly the superintendent made up his mind. Throwing up his head he made a swift motion with his stick. "Chalo!" he shouted almost fiercely. 14

There was a clanking noise, and then dead silence. The prisoner had vanished, and the rope was twisting on itself. I let go of the dog, and it galloped immediately to the back of the gallows; but when it got there it stopped short, barked, and then retreated into a corner of the yard, where it stood among the weeds, looking timorously out at us. We went round the gallows to inspect the prisoner's body. He was dangling with his toes pointed straight downwards, very slowly revolving, as dead as a stone. 15

The superintendent reached out with his stick and poked the bare brown body; it oscillated slightly. *"He's* all right," said the superintendent. He backed out from under the gallows, and blew out a deep breath. The moody look had gone out of his face quite suddenly. He glanced at his wrist-watch. "Eight minutes past eight. Well, that's all for this morning, thank God." 16

The warders unfixed bayonets and marched away. The dog, sobered and conscious of having misbehaved itself, slipped after them. We walked out of the gallows yard, past the condemned cells with their waiting prisoners, into the big central yard of the prison. The convicts, under the command of warders armed with lathis, were already receiving their breakfast. They squatted in long rows, each man holding a tin pannikin, while two warders with buckets marched round ladling out rice; it seemed quite a homely, jolly scene, after the hanging. An enormous relief had come upon us now that the job was done. One felt an impulse to sing, to break into a run, to snigger. All at once everyone began chatting gaily. 17

The Eurasian boy walking beside me nodded towards the way we had come, with a knowing smile: "Do you know, sir, our friend (he meant the dead man) when he heard his appeal had been dismissed, 18 he pissed on the floor of his cell. From fright. Kindly take one of my cigarettes, sir. Do you not admire my new silver case, sir? From the boxwallah, two rupees eight annas. Classy European style."

19   Several people laughed — at what, nobody seemed certain.

20   Francis was walking by the superintendent, talking garrulously: "Well, sir, all has passed off with the utmost satisfactoriness. It was all finished — flick! Like that. It iss not always so — oah, no! I have known cases where the doctor wass obliged to go beneath the gallows and pull the prissoner's legs to ensure decease. Most disagreeable!"

21   "Wriggling about, eh? That's bad," said the superintendent.

22   "Ach, sir, it iss worse when they become refractory! One man, I recall, clung to the bars of hiss cage when we went to take him out. You will scarcely credit, sir, that it took six warders to dislodge him, three pulling at each leg. We reasoned with him, 'My dear fellow,' we said, 'think of all the pain and trouble you are causing to us!' But no, he would not listen! Ach, he wass very troublesome!"

23   I found that I was laughing quite loudly. Everyone was laughing. Even the superintendent grinned in a tolerant way. "You'd better all come out and have a drink," he said quite genially. "I've got a bottle of whiskey in the car. We could do with it."

24   We went through the big double gates of the prison into the road. "Pulling at his legs!" exclaimed a Burmese magistrate suddenly, and burst into a loud chuckling. We all began laughing again. At that moment Francis' anecdote seemed extraordinarily funny. We all had a drink together, native and European alike, quite amicably. The dead man was a hundred yards away.

____ CONSIDERATIONS _____

1. Many readers have described Orwell's "A Hanging" as a powerful condemnation of capital punishment. Study Orwell's technique in drawing from his readers the desired inference. It might be helpful to read another master of implication — Ernest Hemingway in his short story "Hills Like White Elephants."

2. Point out examples of Orwell's skillful use of detail to establish the place and the mood of "A Hanging." Adapt his technique to your purpose in your next essay.

3. What minor incident caused Orwell suddenly to see "the unspeakable wrongness . . . of cutting a life short"? Why?

4. What effect, in Paragraph 6, does the boisterous dog have on the players of this scene? On you, the reader? Explain in terms of the whole essay.

5. "One mind, one world less" is the way Orwell sums up the demise of the Hindu prisoner. Obviously, Orwell's statement is highly compressed, jamming into its short length many ideas, hopes, and fears. Write a short essay, opening up his aphorism so that your readers get some idea of what can be packed into five short words. For additional examples of compressed expression, see Ambrose Bierce, Benjamin Franklin, and some of the poems in this book (by Arnold, Dickinson, Hughes, Marvell, Plath, Stafford).

6. The warden and others present were increasingly disconcerted by the prisoner's continued cry, "Ram! Ram! Ram! Ram!" But note Orwell's description of that cry in Paragraphs 12 and 13. Does that description give you a clue as to the nature of the man's cry? Why doesn't Orwell explain it?

John A. Parrish (b. 1939) came from Kentucky, received a B.A. at Duke and an M.D. at Yale, and became a resident at the University of Michigan Hospital. He now teaches at Harvard Medical School and is a dermatologist on the staff of Massachusetts General Hospital. Between Michigan and Harvard, he served in Vietnam, and later wrote 12, 20 & 5: A Doctor's Year in Vietnam *(1972). In 1973 he tried out briefly — and comically — for the Pittsburgh Pirates, and wrote about his experiences in* Playing Around *(1974).*

56

JOHN A. PARRISH
Welcome to Vietnam

1   We introduced ourselves and stated our home states and places of training. Any special training beyond internship was listed beneath our names on the blackboard. There were four doctors straight from internship, one anesthesiologist, one general surgeon, and two partially trained internists. The four without specialty training were immediately assigned to infantry battalions, three of which were out in the field on maneuvers. The remaining four of us were assigned to the hospital company in Phu Bai.

2   Captain Street walked with us to the hospital compound to show us our new place of work. He was in no hurry. He had spent his entire tour of duty in Phu Bai except when in Da Nang on business. He was going home in eighty more days, and anything that would take up a few hours, or even minutes, was welcome. We were his most recent time passers.

3   The hospital company was on the edge of the compound situated

next to the airstrip. The location not only made it easy to receive casualties, but also placed the hospital directly adjacent to the prime target for enemy mortars or rockets. The airstrip was always an early target during any kind of enemy attack.

The building farthest from the airstrip was a single, wooden   4
"hooch" with a large mobile refrigeration unit attached to the rear of the building. Three layers of sandbags protected each side. The sign on the front read, "Graves Registration."

Street did not even slow down as we passed. "This is Graves," he   5
said, as we walked by the front of the building. "This is the only part of the hospital company completely staffed by marines. From the field, the dead come directly here where they are washed down, identified, and put in the freezer until the next flight south. They are embalmed in Da Nang or Saigon before shipment back to the States. The marines who staff this place are 'grunts' (foot soldiers) who volunteer for this duty, usually because they are cowards. Some are being punished. Others may be mentally ill or may want to be embalmers someday. On a hot, busy day this place smells terrible." Street seemed disgusted not only with the marines who worked in Graves, but also with any-body who would be stupid or inconsiderate enough to get killed on a hot and busy day.

We passed two large portable units that looked like large inflated   6
tubes. "These are the MUST (Medical Unit Self-Contained Transport-able) units; one is used as a medical ward, and the other as a surgery ward. The smaller units are attached to the main building. They house our operating rooms. We have six O.R.'s and an X-ray unit. Helicopters land here on the edge of the airstrip, and the casualties go directly to the main casualty sorting area called triage."

As Captain Street was talking, a helicopter settled down beyond   7
us. Several marines ran out from the main building to meet the craft. They were handed a stretcher with a wounded marine, and the heli-copter was gone. The stretcher bearers ran past us carrying a big Negro kid. He was completely nude. His M16 hung over the stretcher handle, and his boots rode between his legs. He was so black that the mud on his skin was light by comparison. He was long and muscular, and his spidery fingers curled tightly around the sides of the bouncing litter. His whole body was glistening with sweat that reflected highlights of the bright morning sun. The sweat on his forehead did not drip. It remained like tiny drops of oil and glue fastened tightly to his skin.

His eyelids were forced widely apart, and his stare was straight   8
ahead into nowhere, seeing nothing, having seen too much. He threw back his head, and his white teeth parted as if he were trying to speak,

to curse, to cry. A spasm of intolerable pain wrenched the muscles of his face into a mask that hid a grinning skeleton beneath. His chest heaved rapidly. The muscles of his steel arms bulged as he grasped the muddy stretcher. A small hole in his rigid abdomen permitted a steady snake of red and brown to spill onto the litter. The fluids created red blacks and brown purples on the green canvas. His left knee was flexed, and his long, uncircumsized penis lay over on his right upper thigh. His left foot arched as his toes grasped for the litter.

9   As he passed by, he raised his head almost involuntarily. It seemed as if the contracting straps of his neck muscles would tear off his jaw should his head not rise. His neck veins swelled in protest. His mouth began to open, at first for air, but then as a silent plea for help. He extended his dirty hand directly toward me, and I turned to follow him into triage.

10   Captain Street had not noticed him go by. He was still talking about the compound — something about the marines putting the retaining wall in the wrong place. He was ready to show us triage.

11   It was a large, open room measuring fifteen by twenty meters. Reinforced on the outside with sandbags, the walls protected floor-to-ceiling shelves filled with bandages, first-aid gear, and bottles of intra-venous fluids. An unprotected tin roof was supported by four-by-fours. At the time, there were six men lined up on stretchers supported at either end by two lightweight metal sawhorses. Several doctors and corpsmen were quickly, but unexcitedly, working over the wounded. Captain Street was still talking, but I couldn't listen any longer.

12   On the first stretcher lay a boy whom, earlier in the day, any coach would have wanted as a tackle or a defensive end. But now, as he lay on his back, his left thigh pointed skyward and ended in a red brown, meaty mass of twisted ligaments, jellylike muscle, blood clots, and long bony splinters. There was no knee, and parts of the lower leg hung loosely by skin strips and fascial strings. A tourniquet had been placed around his thigh, and a corpsman was cutting through the strips of tissue with shears to remove the unviable dangling calf. Lying separately on the stretcher was a boot from which the lower leg still protruded.

13   In the second position a sweating doctor was administering closed cardiac massage on a flaccid, pale, thin boy with multiple wounds. A second doctor was bag-breathing the boy. The vigorous chest compression seemed to be producing only the audible cracking of ribs.

14   In position three was the boy who minutes earlier had been car-

ried past us. He already had intravenous fluids running into his arm, and a bandage was in place over his abdomen. He was vigorously protesting efforts to turn him over in order to examine his back. Positions four and five were occupied by two nude bodies quietly awaiting treatment. Their wounds were not serious. The next few positions for litters were empty. Off in the corner (position ten) lay a young man with his head wrapped tightly in blood-soaked, white bandages. No part of his body moved except for the slow, unsteady respiratory efforts of his chest. He had an endotracheal tube emerging from his nose, and each respiration made a grunting snort. No one was paying any attention to this man — a hopelessly damaged brain was awaiting death.

Captain Street never looked directly at any of the casualties. He   15
showed us the rest of the hospital compound and left us with the hospital commander, a general surgeon who proved to be an intolerable, immature, egotistical, Napoleonic SOB, and an excellent surgeon. I liked him from the very first.

"Welcome to Vietnam," he said.   16

_____ **CONSIDERATIONS** _____

1. Narrative essays most often proceed chronologically, as Parrish's does. But another organizing principle is here. It is most apparent in the first two pages. Identify it and discuss how naturally it works with the chronological sequence.

2. Study the three paragraphs on the wounded black marine carried on a stretcher. Identify the separate sentences as description or narration. By what criteria do you make this distinction?

3. List the technical jargon in Parrish's account — MUST, O.R., and the rest. Why is such terminology so common in military and governmental language? What are the uses of such words? The abuses?

4. Parrish's account of his stint in Vietnam seems straightforward and objective, but we can sense his attitudes toward people and events. How? Point out several examples. Is he consistent in these attitudes?

5. At the end of Paragraph 6, Captain Street uses the word "triage." You might have to consult more than one dictionary to find the word, but the hunt is worth the effort. The meaning of the word opens up moral questions. Discuss.

Octavio Paz (b. 1914) is a Mexican poet and essayist who has lived in the United States. He served Mexico as diplomat in France, India, Japan, Switzerland, and other countries. Volumes of his poems in English translation, some with facing Spanish texts, include Configurations *(1971),* Early Poems 1935–1955 *(1973),* Eagle or Sun? *(1976), and* A Draft of Shadows and Other Poems *(1979).*

__57__

OCTAVIO PAZ

Mexican-American Differences

1   The history of Mexico is the history of a man seeking his parentage, his origins. He has been influenced at one time or another by France, Spain, the United States and the militant indigenists of his own country, and he crosses history like a jade comet, now and then giving off flashes of lightning. What is he pursuing in his eccentric course? He wants to go back beyond the catastrophe he suffered: he wants to be a sun again, to return to the center of that life from which he was separated one day. (Was that day the Conquest? Independence?) Our solitude has the same roots as religious feelings. It is a form of orphanhood, an obscure awareness that we have been torn from the All, and an ardent search: a flight and a return, an effort to re-establish the bonds that unite us with the universe.

2   Nothing could be further from this feeling than the solitude of the North American. In the United States man does not feel that he

has been torn from the center of creation and suspended between hostile forces. He has built his own world and it is built in his own image: it is his mirror. But now he cannot recognize himself in his inhuman objects, nor in his fellows. His creations, like those of an inept sorcerer, no longer obey him. He is alone among his works, lost — to use the phrase by José Gorostiza — in a "wilderness of mirrors."

Some people claim that the only differences between the North American and ourselves are economic. That is, they are rich and we are poor, and while their legacy is Democracy, Capitalism and the Industrial Revolution, ours is the Counterreformation, Monopoly and Feudalism. But however influential the systems of production may be in the shaping of a culture, I refuse to believe that as soon as we have heavy industry and are free of all economic imperialism, the differences will vanish. (In fact, I look for the opposite to happen, and I consider this possibility one of the greatest virtues of the Revolution of 1910.) But why search history for an answer that only we ourselves can give? If it is we who feel ourselves to be different, what makes us so, and in what do the differences consist? 3

I am going to suggest an answer that will perhaps not be wholly satisfactory. I am only trying to clarify the meaning of certain experiences for my own self, and I admit that what I say may be worth no more than a personal answer to a personal question. 4

When I arrived in the United States I was surprised above all by the self-assurance and confidence of the people, by their apparent happiness and apparent adjustment to the world around them. This satisfaction does not stifle criticism, however, and the criticism is valuable and forthright, of a sort not often heard in the countries of the south, where long periods of dictatorship have made us more cautious about expressing our points of view. But it is a criticism that respects the existing systems and never touches the roots. I thought of Ortega y Gasset's distinction between uses and abuses, in his definition of the "revolutionary spirit." The revolutionary is always a radical, that is, he is trying to correct the uses themselves rather than the mere abuses of them. Almost all the criticisms I heard from the lips of North Americans were of the reformist variety: they left the social or cultural structures intact and were only intended to limit or improve this or that procedure. It seemed to me then, and it still does, that the United States is a society that wants to realize its ideals, has no wish to exchange them for others, and is confident of surviving, no matter how dark the future may appear. I am not interested in discussing whether this attitude is justified by reason and reality; I simply want 5 to point out that it exists. It is true that this faith in the natural goodness of life, or in its infinite wealth of possibilities, cannot be found in recent North American literature, which prefers to depict a much more somber world; but I found it in the actions, the words and even the faces of almost everyone I met.[1]

6   On the other hand, I heard a good deal of talk about American realism and also about American ingenuousness, qualities that would seem to be mutually exclusive. To us a realist is always a pessimist. And an ingenuous person would not remain so for very long if he truly contemplated life realistically. Would it not be more accurate to say that the North American wants to use reality rather than to know it? In some matters — death, for example — he not only has no desire to understand it, he obviously avoids the very idea. I met some elderly ladies who still had illusions and were making plans for the future as if it were inexhaustible. Thus they refused Nietzsche's statement condemning women to an early onset of skepticism because "men have ideals but women only have illusions." American realism, then, is of a very special kind, and American ingenuousness does not exclude dissimulation and even hypocrisy. When hypocrisy is a character trait it also affects one's thinking, because it consists in the negation of all the aspects of reality that one finds disagreeable, irrational or repugnant.

7   In contrast, one of the most notable traits of the Mexican's character is his willingness to contemplate horror: he is even familiar and complacent in his dealings with it. The bloody Christs in our village churches, the macabre humor in some of our newspaper headlines, our wakes, the custom of eating skull-shaped cakes and candies on the Day of the Dead, are habits inherited from the Indians and the Spaniards and are now an inseparable part of our being. Our cult of death is also a cult of life, in the same way that love is a hunger for life and a longing for death. Our fondness for self-destruction derives not only from our masochistic tendencies but also from a certain variety of religious emotion.

8   And our differences do not end there. The North Americans are credulous and we are believers; they love fairy tales and detective stories and we love myths and legends. The Mexican tells lies because

---

[1] These lines were written before the public was clearly cognizant of the danger of universal annihilation made possible by nuclear weapons. Since then the North Americans have lost their optimism but not their confidence, a confidence based on resignation and obstinacy. The truth is that although many people talk about the danger, secretly no one believes — no one wants to believe — that it is real and immediate.

he delights in fantasy, or because he is desperate, or because he wants to rise above the sordid facts of his life; the North American does not tell lies, but he substitutes social truth for the real truth, which is always disagreeable. We get drunk in order to confess; they get drunk in order to forget. They are optimists and we are nihilists — except that our nihilism is not intellectual but instinctive, and therefore irrefutable. We are suspicious and they are trusting. We are sorrowful and sarcastic and they are happy and full of jokes. North Americans want to understand and we want to contemplate. They are activists and we are quietists; we enjoy our wounds and they enjoy their inventions. They believe in hygiene, health, work and contentment, but perhaps they have never experienced true joy, which is an intoxication, a whirlwind. In the hubbub of a fiesta night our voices explode into brilliant lights, and life and death mingle together, while their vitality becomes a fixed smile that denies old age and death but that changes life to motionless stone.

_____ CONSIDERATIONS _____

1. Study the differences and similarities between Paz's comparison of American and Mexican attitudes and any one of the following: Adams's "Winter and Summer," Bergmann's "Two Sides of Freedom," and Catton's "Grant and Lee." Then try your hand at a comparison/contrast essay.

2. In Paragraph 2, speaking of the technology of North America, Paz says, "His creations, like those of an inept sorcerer, no longer obey him." The full force of his statement can only be felt if one understands his allusion to a very famous piece of music by a little-known French composer, Paul Dukas's *The Sorcerer's Apprentice*. Read the story related by that music, and write a short essay on the nature, function, and value of allusions.

3. Referring to the statement by Paz in Consideration 2 above, write an answer in response to the generalization, building your essay on concrete examples.

4. How does Paz attempt to anticipate the criticism that his short essay is made up largely of generalizations?

5. In thinking about the last sentence in Paz's Paragraph 6, refer to the essay by Ronald Blythe for an example of attitudes toward the elderly that many Anglo-Americans apparently find "disagreeable, irrational or repugnant." Does such an example justify Paz's identification of American ingenuousness with hypocrisy?

6. Do you find any evidence that Americans are acquiring what he calls one of the most notable traits of the Mexican's character: "his willingness to contemplate horror"?

Robert M. Pirsig (b. 1928), in his book Zen and the Art of Motorcycle Maintenance *(1974), describes a motorcycle journey he takes with his young son, and among passages of narrative and description, explains and argues ideas about education, technology, and thought. Pirsig also reminisces about the past. Especially he remembers the thoughts of one "Phaedrus" — the "he" of this essay — who is Pirsig's earlier self, before a mental breakdown and shock treatments altered his personality. Here, he remembers Phaedrus's Church of Reason lecture to his composition course students in a western university. The lecture argues the distinction between the university as we know it and the ideal university, starting with analogy and moving on to contrast. See how Pirsig uses analogy to analyze, to suggest the separation of material and ideal.*

58

ROBERT M. PIRSIG

The Church of Reason

1   That night, for the next day's lecture, he wrote out his defense of what he was doing. This was the Church of Reason lecture, which in contrast to his usual sketchy lecture notes, was very long and very carefully elaborated.

2   It begins with reference to a newspaper article about a country church building with an electric beer sign hanging right over the front entrance. The building had been sold and was being used as a bar. One can guess that some classroom laughter started at this point. The college was well-known for drunken partying and the image vaguely

fit. The article said a number of people had complained to the church officials about it. It had been a Catholic church, and the priest who had been delegated to respond to the criticism had sounded quite irritated about the whole thing. To him it had revealed an incredible ignorance of what a church really was. Did they think that bricks and boards and glass constituted a church? Or the shape of the roof? Here, posing as piety, was an example of the very materialism the church opposed. The building in question was not holy ground. It had been desanctified. That was the end of it. The beer sign resided over a bar, not a church, and those who couldn't tell the difference were simply revealing something about themselves.

Phaedrus said the same confusion existed about the University 3 and that was why loss of accreditation was hard to understand. The real University is not a material object. It is not a group of buildings that can be defended by police. He explained that when a college lost its accreditation, nobody came and shut down the school. There were no legal penalties, no fines, no jail sentences. Classes did not stop. Everything went on just as before. Students got the same education they would if the school didn't lose its accreditation. All that would happen, Phaedrus said, would simply be an official recognition of a condition that already existed. It would be similar to excommunication. What would happen is that the *real* University, which no legislature can dictate to and which can never be identified by any location of bricks or boards or glass, would simply declare that this place was no longer "holy ground." The real University would vanish from it, and all that would be left was the bricks and the books and the material manifestation.

It must have been a strange concept to all of the students, and I 4 can imagine him waiting for a long time for it to sink in, and perhaps then waiting for the question, What do you think the real University is?

His notes, in response to his question, state the following: 5

The real University, he said, has no specific location. It owns no 6 property, pays no salaries and receives no material dues. The real University is a state of mind. It is that great heritage of rational thought that has been brought down to us through the centuries and which does not exist at any specific location. It's a state of mind which is regenerated throughout the centuries by a body of people who traditionally carry the title of professor, but even that title is not part of the real University. The real University is nothing less than the continuing body of reason itself.

7   In addition to this state of mind, "reason," there's a legal entity which is unfortunately called by the same name but which is quite another thing. This is a nonprofit corporation, a branch of the state with a specific address. It owns property, is capable of paying salaries, of receiving money and of responding to legislative pressures in the process.

8   But this second university, the legal corporation, cannot teach, does not generate new knowledge or evaluate ideas. It is not the real University at all. It is just a church building, the setting, the location at which conditions have been made favorable for the real church to exist.

9   Confusion continually occurs in people who fail to see this difference, he said, and think that control of the church buildings implies control of the church. They see professors as employees of the second university who should abandon reason when told to and take orders with no backtalk, the same way employees do in other corporations.

10   They see the second university, but fail to see the first.

_____ **CONSIDERATIONS** _____

1. What are the telltale signs that the "real University" is present or absent on your campus?

2. What happens when a school loses its accreditation? How is accreditation maintained? Why?

3. Pirsig's definition of the "real University" puts a great deal of weight on rational thought. Do you agree with that emphasis?

4. Can you think of institutions other than the church and the university whose essence might be explained as in Pirsig's essay?

5. What techniques does Pirsig use that differ from those employed in other argumentative essays?

*Sylvia Plath (1932–1963) grew up in Massachusetts and gradu-
ated from Smith College. She was a precocious writer, publishing
professionally even as an undergraduate. Her first devotion was
to poetry but she also worked in fiction and the essay. On a Ful-
bright Fellowship to England she met and married the English
poet Ted Hughes; they had two children. Her first book of poetry,*
The Colossus, *was published in 1960, her novel* The Bell Jar *in
1963. The poems of* Ariel *(1965) are her best work — poems of
intense suffering and power, including "The Bee Meeting." In
February of 1963 she killed herself.*

The journal entry that follows is from Johnny Panic and the
Bible of Dreams *(1978), a posthumous collection of short stories
and miscellaneous prose. Here we watch a young writer at work
— first on her journal — observant, careful, distinctive; then we
watch her refine her prose into the lines of the finished poem.*

59

SYLVIA PLATH

Journal Entries: Charlie Pollard and the Beekeepers

JUNE 7 [1962]

The midwife stopped up to see Ted at noon to remind him that   1
the Devon beekeepers were having a meeting at six at Charlie Pollard's. We were interested in starting a hive, so dumped the babies in

bed and jumped in the car and dashed down the hill past the old factory to Mill Lane, a row of pale orange stucco cottages on the Taw, which gets flooded whenever the river rises. We drove into the dusty, ugly paved parking lot under the gray peaks of the factory buildings, unused since 1928 and now only used for wool storage. We felt very new & shy, I hugging my bare arms in the cool of the evening, for I had not thought to bring a sweater. We crossed a little bridge to the yard where a group of miscellaneous Devonians were standing — an assortment of shapeless men in brown-speckled, bulgy tweeds, Mr. Pollard in white shirtsleeves, with his dark, nice brown eyes and oddly Jewy head, tan, balding, dark-haired. I saw two women, one very large, tall, stout, in a glistening aqua-blue raincoat, the other cadaverous as a librarian in a dun raincoat. Mr. Pollard glided toward us & stood for a moment on the bridge end, talking. He indicated a pile of hives, like white and green blocks of wood with little gables, & said we could have one, if we would like to fix it up. A small pale blue car pulled into the yard: the midwife. Her moony beam came at us through the windshield. Then the rector came pontificating across the bridge, & there was a silence that grew round him. He carried a curious contraption — a dark felt hat with a screen box built on under it, and cloth for a neckpiece under that. I thought the hat a clerical beekeeping hat, and that he must have made it for himself. Then I saw, on the grass, and in hands, everybody was holding a bee hat, some with netting of nylon, most with box screening, some with khaki round hats. I felt barer and barer. People became concerned. Have you no hat? Have you no coat? Then a dry little woman came up, Mrs. P, the secretary of the society, with tired, short blond hair. "I have a boiler suit." She went to her car and came back with a small white silk button-down smock, the sort pharmacist's assistants use. I put it on and buttoned it & felt more protected. Last year, said the midwife, Charlie Pollard's bees were bad-tempered and made everybody run. Everyone seemed to be waiting for someone. But then we all slowly filed after Charlie Pollard to his beehives. We threaded our way through neatly weeded allotment gardens, one with bits of tinfoil and a fan of black and white feathers on a string, very decorative, to scare the birds, and twiggy lean-tos over the plants. Black-eyed sweetpea-like blooms: broad beans, somebody said. The gray ugly backs of the factory. Then we came to a clearing, roughly scythed, with one hive, a double-brood hive, two layers. From this hive Charlie Pollard wanted to make three hives. I understood very little. The men gathered round the hive. Charlie Pollard started squirting smoke from a little funnel with a hand bellows attached to it round the entry at the bottom of the hive. "Too much smoke," hissed the large, blue-raincoated woman next to me. "What do you do if they sting?" I whispered, as the bees, now Charlie had lifted the top off the hive, were zinging out and dancing round as at the end of long elastics. (Charlie had produced a fashionable white straw Italian hat for me with a black nylon veil that collapsed perilously into my face in the least wind. The rector had tucked it into my collar, much to my surprise. "Bees always crawl up, never down," he said. I had drawn it down loose over my shoulders.) The woman said, "Stand behind me, I'll protect you." I did. (I had spoken to her husband earlier, a handsome, rather sarcastic man standing apart, silver hair, a military blue eye. Plaid tie, checked shirt, plaid vest, all different. Tweedy suit, navy blue beret. His wife, he had said, kept twelve hives & was the expert. The bees always stung him. His nose & lips, his wife later said.)

The men were lifting out rectangular yellow slides, crusted with bees, crawling, swarming. I felt prickles all over me, & itches. I had one pocket & was advised to keep my hands in this and not move. "See all the bees round the rector's dark trousers!" whispered the woman. "They don't seem to like white." I was grateful for my white smock. The rector was somehow an odd man out, referred to now and then by Charlie jestingly: "Eh, rector?" "Maybe they want to join his church," one man, emboldened by the anonymity of the hats, suggested.

The donning of the hats had been an odd ceremony. Their ugliness & anonymity very compelling, as if we were all party to a rite. They were brown or gray or faded green felt, mostly, but there was one white straw boater with a ribbon. All faces, shaded, became alike. Commerce became possible with complete strangers.

The men were lifting slides, Charlie Pollard squirting smoke, into another box. They were looking for queen cells — long, pendulous, honey-colored cells from which the new queens would come. The blue-coated woman pointed them out. She was from British Guiana, had lived alone in the jungle for eighteen years, lost £25 on her first bees there — there had been no honey for them to eat. I was aware of bees buzzing and stalling before my face. The veil seemed hallucinatory. I could not see it for moments at a time. Then I became aware I was in a bone-stiff trance, intolerably tense, and shifted round to where I could see better. "Spirit of my dead father, protect me!" I arrogantly prayed. A dark, rather nice, "unruly"-looking man came up through the cut grasses. Everyone turned, murmured, "O Mr. Jenner, we didn't think you were coming."

5   This, then, the awaited expert, the "government man" from Exeter. An hour late. He donned a white boiler suit and a very expert bee hat — a vivid green dome, square black screen box for head, joined with yellow cloth at the corners, and a white neckpiece. The men muttered, told what had been done. They began looking for the old queen. Slide after slide was lifted, examined on both sides. To no avail. Myriads of crawling, creeping bees. As I understood it from my blue bee-lady, the first new queen out would kill the old ones, so the new queen cells were moved to different hives. The old queen would be left in hers. But they couldn't find her. Usually the old queen swarmed before the new queen hatched. This was to prevent swarming. I heard words like "supersede," "queen excluder" (a slatted screen of metal only workers could crawl through). The rector slipped away unnoticed, then the midwife. "He used too much smoke" was the general criticism of Charlie Pollard. The queen hates smoke. She might have swarmed earlier. She might be hiding. She was not marked. It grew later. Eight. Eight-thirty. The hives were parceled up, queen excluders put on. An old beamy brown man wisely jutted a forefinger as we left. "She's in that one." The beekeepers clustered around Mr. Jenner with questions. The secretary sold chances for a bee festival.

FRIDAY, JUNE 8

6   Ted & I drove down to Charlie Pollard's about nine tonight to collect our hive. He was standing at the door of his cottage in Mill Lane, the corner one, in white shirtsleeves, collar open, showing dark chest hairs & a white mail-knit undershirt. His pretty blond wife smiled & waved. We went over the bridge to the shed, with its roto-vator, orange, resting at the end. Talked of floods, fish, Ash Ridge: the Taw flooded his place over & over. He was wanting to move up, had an eye on the lodge at Ash Ridge, had hives up there. His father-in-law had been head gardener when they had six gardeners. Told of great heaters to dry hay artificially & turn it to meal: two thousand, four thousand, the machines cost, were lying up there now, hardly used. He hadn't been able to get any more flood insurance once he had claimed. Had his rugs cleaned, but they were flat: you can live with them, I can't, he told the inspector. Had to have the upholstered sofa

& chairs all redone at the bottom. Walked down the first step from the second floor one night & put his foot in water. A big salmon inhabited his reach of the Taw. "To be honest with you," he said, over & over. "To be honest with you." Showed us his big barny black offices. A honey ripener with a beautiful sweet-smelling, slow gold slosh of honey at the bottom. Loaned us a bee book. We loaded with our creaky old wood hive. He said if we cleaned it and painted it over Whitsun, he'd order a swarm of docile bees. Had showed us his beautiful red-gold Italian queen the day before, with her glossy green mark on the thorax, I think. He had made it. To see her the better. The bees were bad-tempered, though. She would lay a lot of docile bees. We said: Docile, be sure now, & drove home.

These few lines were typed at the top margin of the original MS:

Noticed: a surround of tall white cow parsley, pursy yellow gorse bloom, an old Christmas tree, white hawthorn, strong-smelling.

60

SYLVIA PLATH

The Bee Meeting

Who are these people at the bridge to meet me? They are the villagers ——
The rector, the midwife, the sexton, the agent for bees.
In my sleeveless summery dress I have no protection,
And they are all gloved and covered, why did nobody tell me?
5 They are smiling and taking out veils tacked to ancient hats.

I am nude as a chicken neck, does nobody love me?
Yes, here is the secretary of bees with her white shop smock,
Buttoning the cuffs at my wrists and the slit from my neck to my knees.
Now I am milkweed silk, the bees will not notice.
10 They will not smell my fear, my fear, my fear.

Which is the rector now, is it that man in black?
Which is the midwife, is that her blue coat?
Everybody is nodding a square black head, they are knights in visors,
Breastplates of cheesecloth knotted under the armpits.
15 Their smiles and their voices are changing. I am led through a beanfield.

Strips of tinfoil winking like people,
Feather dusters fanning their hands in a sea of bean flowers,

Creamy bean flowers with black eyes and leaves like bored hearts.
Is it blood clots the tendrils are dragging up that string?
No, no, it is scarlet flowers that will one day be edible.   20

Now they are giving me a fashionable white straw Italian hat
And a black veil that moulds to my face, they are making me one of
    them.
They are leading me to the shorn grove, the circle of hives.
Is it the hawthorn that smells so sick?
The barren body of hawthorn, etherizing its children.   25

Is it some operation that is taking place?
It is the surgeon my neighbours are waiting for,
This apparition in a green helmet,
Shining gloves and white suit.
Is it the butcher, the grocer, the postman, someone I know?   30

I cannot run, I am rooted, and the gorse hurts me
With its yellow purses, its spiky armoury.
I could not run without having to run forever.
The white hive is snug as a virgin,
Sealing off her brood cells, her honey, and quietly humming.   35

Smoke rolls and scarves in the grove.
The mind of the hive thinks this is the end of everything.
Here they come, the outriders, on their hysterical elastics.
If I stand very still, they will think I am cow parsley,
A gullible head untouched by their animosity,   40

Not even nodding, a personage in a hedgerow.
The villagers open the chambers, they are hunting the queen.
Is she hiding, is she eating honey? She is very clever.
She is old, old, old, she must live another year, and she knows it.
While in their fingerjoint cells the new virgins   45

Dream of a duel they will win inevitably,
A curtain of wax dividing them from the bride flight,
The upflight of the murderess into a heaven that loves her.
The villagers are moving the virgins, there will be no killing.
The old queen does not show herself, is she so ungrateful?   50

I am exhausted, I am exhausted ——
Pillar of white in a blackout of knives.
I am the magician's girl who does not flinch.
The villagers are untying their disguises, they are shaking hands.
55 Whose is that long white box in the grove, what have they accomplished, why am I cold?

—— CONSIDERATIONS ——————————————————————

1. To what extent did Sylvia Plath draw upon her notebook for material in writing her poem, "The Bee Meeting"? Read both pieces carefully and list any phrases, characters, events, and ideas that notebook and poem share. Note changes in the material as it moved from notebook to poem.

2. Compare Plath's notebook entries with passages from other notebooks appearing in this book — those of F. Scott Fitzgerald, Anaïs Nin, and Thomas Wolfe. Discuss differences and similarities. Compare your own daily writing or journal.

3. Study the brief but graphic descriptions of each of the people Plath meets at the gathering of beekeepers. How do they differ? What do her observations reveal, other than the physical appearance of the subjects?

4. Study the details Plath notes of the places themselves — the parking lot, the gardens. Do these details reveal Plath's feelings, or are they incidental?

5. "Commerce became possible with complete strangers," writes Plath at the end of Paragraph 3. Consider this curious phenomenon: that strangers will often speak more freely than will acquaintances. Can you explain this behavior?

6. Reread Plath's notebook account, looking especially for points that would allow you to explain either that Plath felt very much a part of the beekeeping crowd or that she remained aloof, an interested but uninvolved observer. It might be helpful to read Carol Bly's account of driving a tractor in Minnesota; see her "Getting Tired."

Plato (427?–347 B.C.) was the pupil of Socrates, whom he quotes or paraphrases, and the teacher of Aristotle. In this passage from Plato, Socrates has been unjustly condemned to death for misleading the young, and explains why he chooses execution as more dignified than the alternative of flight and exile. Shortly after delivering these words, Socrates swallowed the poisonous hemlock.

61

PLATO

Socrates to His Accusers

Not much time will be gained, O Athenians, in return for the evil name which you will get from the detractors of the city, who will say that you killed Socrates, a wise man; for they will call me wise even though I am not wise when they want to reproach you. If you had waited a little while, your desire would have been fulfilled in the course of nature. For I am far advanced in years, as you may perceive, and not far from death. I am speaking now only to those of you who have condemned me to death. And I have another thing to say to them: You think that I was convicted through deficiency of words — I mean, that if I had thought fit to leave nothing undone, nothing unsaid, I might have gained an acquittal. Not so; the deficiency which led to my conviction was not of words — certainly not. But I had not the boldness or impudence of inclination to address you as you would have liked me to address you, weeping and wailing and lamenting, and saying and doing many things which you have been accustomed to hear from others, and which, as I say, are unworthy of me. But I thought that I ought not to do anything common or mean in the hour of danger: nor do I now repent of the manner of my defence, and I would rather die having spoken after my manner, than speak in your manner and live. For neither in war nor yet at law ought any man to use every way of escaping death. For often in battle there is no doubt that if a man will throw away his arms, and fall on his knees before his pursuers, he may escape death; and in other dangers there are other ways of escaping death, if a man is willing to say and do anything. The difficulty, my friends, is not in avoiding death, but in avoiding unrighteousness; for that runs faster than death. I am old and move slowly, and the slower runner has overtaken me, and my accusers are keen and quick, and the faster runner, who is unrighteousness, has overtaken them. And now I depart hence condemned by you to suffer the penalty of death, and they, too, go their ways condemned by the truth to suffer the penalty of villainy and wrong; and I must abide by my award — let them abide by theirs. I suppose that these things may be regarded as fated — and I think that they are well.

2   And now, O men who have condemned me, I would fain prophesy to you; for I am about to die, and that is the hour in which men are gifted with prophetic power. And I prophesy to you who are my murderers, that immediately after my death punishment far heavier than you have inflicted on me will surely await you. Me you have killed because you wanted to escape the accuser, and not to give an account of your lives. But that will not be as you suppose: far otherwise. For I say that there will be more accusers of you than there are now; accusers whom hitherto I have restrained: and as they are younger they will be more severe with you, and you will be more offended at them. For if you think that by killing men you can avoid the accuser censuring your lives, you are mistaken; that is not a way of escape which is either possible or honorable; the easiest and noblest way is not to be crushing others, but to be improving yourselves. This is the prophecy which I utter before my departure, to the judges who have condemned me.

3   Friends, who would have acquitted me, I would like also to talk with you about this thing which has happened, while the magistrates are busy, and before I go to the place at which I must die. Stay then awhile, for we may as well talk with one another while there is time. You are my friends, and I should like to show you the meaning of this event which has happened to me. O my judges — for you I may truly call judges — I should like to tell you of a wonderful circumstance. Hitherto the familiar oracle within me has constantly been in the habit of opposing me even about trifles, if I was going to make a slip or error about anything; and now as you see there has come upon me that which may be thought, and is generally believed to be, the last and worst evil. But the oracle made no sign of opposition, either as I

was leaving my house and going out in the morning, or when I was going up into this court, or while I was speaking, at anything which I was going to say; and yet I have often been stopped in the middle of a speech; but now in nothing I either said or did touching this matter has the oracle opposed me. What do I take to be the explanation of this? I will tell you. I regard this as a proof that what has happened to me is a good, and that those of us who think that death is an evil are in error. This is a great proof to me of what I am saying, for the customary sign would surely have opposed me had I been going to evil and not to good.

Let us reflect in another way, and we shall see that there is great reason to hope that death is a good, for one of two things: either death is a state of nothingness and utter unconsciousness, or, as men say, there is a change and migration of the soul from this world to another. Now if you suppose that there is no consciousness, but a sleep like the sleep of him who is undisturbed even by the sight of dreams, death will be an unspeakable gain. For if a person were to select the night in which his sleep was undisturbed even by dreams, and were to compare with this the other days and nights of his life, and then were to tell us how many days and nights he had passed in the course of his life better and more pleasantly than this one, I think that any man, I will not say a private man, but even the great king, will not find many such days or nights, when compared with the others. Now if death is like this, I say that to die, is gain; for eternity is then only a single night. But if death is the journey to another place, and there, as men say, all the dead are, what good, O my friends and judges, can be greater than this? If indeed when the pilgrim arrives in the world below, he is delivered from the professors of justice in this world, and finds the true judges who are said to give judgment there, Minos and Rhadamanthus and Æacus and Triptolemus, and other sons of God who were righteous in their own life, that pilgrimage will be worth making. What would not a man give if he might converse with Orpheus and Musæus and Hesiod and Homer? Nay, if this be true, let me die again and again. I, too, shall have a wonderful interest in a place where I can converse with Palamedes, and Ajax the son of Telamon, and other heroes of old, who have suffered death through an unjust judgment; and there will be no small pleasure, as I think, in comparing my own sufferings with theirs. Above all, I shall be able to continue my search into true and false knowledge; as in this world, so also in that; I shall find out who is wise, and who pretends to be wise, and is not. What would not a man give, O judges, to be able to examine the leader of the great Trojan expedition; or Odysseus or Sisyphus, or numberless others, men and women too! What infinite delight would there be in conversing with them and asking them questions! For in that world they do not put a man to death for this; certainly not. For besides being happier in that world than in this, they will be immortal, if what is said is true.

5   Wherefore, O judges, be of good cheer about death, and know this of a truth — that no evil can happen to a good man, either in life or after death. He and his are not neglected by the gods; nor has my own approaching end happened by mere chance. But I see clearly that to die and be released was better for me; and therefore the oracle gave no sign. For which reason also, I am not angry with my accusers, or my condemners; they have done me no harm, although neither of them meant to do me any good; and for this I may gently blame them.

6   Still I have a favor to ask of them. When my sons are grown up, I would ask you, O my friends, to punish them; and I would have you trouble them, as I have troubled you, if they seem to care about riches, or anything, more than about virtue; or if they pretend to be something when they are really nothing — then reprove them, as I have reproved you, for not caring about that for which they ought to care, and thinking that they are something when they are really nothing. And if you do this, I and my sons will have received justice at your hands.

7   The hour of departure has arrived, and we go our ways — I to die, and you to live. Which is better, God only knows.

___ **CONSIDERATIONS** _____

1. Judging by his opening paragraph, how would you predict Socrates' response to the notion that "The end justifies the means"?

2. Socrates devotes Paragraph 4 to this proposition: death is good. Examine his argument with care, paying particular attention to his logic. You might find it instructive to compare William Cullen Bryant's treatment of the same argument in his famous poem "Thanatopsis."

3. Socrates asks as a favor from his friends that a certain punishment be inflicted. On whom? Why?

4. In Paragraph 2 what political advice does Socrates offer to those in power, advice frequently ignored by the powerful?

5. We are led to believe that Socrates's remarks are *spoken* language — a speech as opposed to a written essay. What are the characteristics of speech? Do you think of the difference between spoken and written language when you are writing? Does the work of other writers in this collection have the qualities of speech?

James Rettie (b. 1922) wrote this essay in 1948 when he worked for the National Forest Service; it was collected in For-ever the Land *(1950). A member of the Society of the Friends of the Land, Rettie raised bees on his farm outside Savannah, Georgia, until he retired in 1980 to devote full time to his collection of seed catalogues.*

62

JAMES C. RETTIE

"But a Watch in the Night": A Scientific Fable[1]

Out beyond our solar system there is a planet called Copernicus. 1
It came into existence some four or five billion years before the birth

[1] From the Bible, Psalm 90, apparently either slightly altered or using a translation other than the King James version, which reads:

Lord, thou has been our dwelling place
In all generations.
Before the mountains were brought forth,
Or ever thou hadst formed the earth and the world,
Even from everlasting to everlasting, thou art God.
Thou turnest man to destruction;
And sayest, "Return, ye children of men."
For a thousand years in thy sight
Are but as yesterday when it is past,
And as a watch in the night. . . .   — ED.

of our Earth. In due course of time it became inhabited by a race of intelligent men.

2   About 750 million years ago the Copernicans had developed the motion picture machine to a point well in advance of the stage that we have reached. Most of the cameras that we now use in motion picture work are geared to take twenty-four pictures per second on a continuous strip of film. When such film is run through a projector, it throws a series of images on the screen and these change with a rapidity that gives the visual impression of normal movement. If a motion is too swift for the human eye to see it in detail, it can be captured and artificially slowed down by means of the slow-motion camera. This one is geared to take many more shots per second — ninety-six or even more than that. When the slow-motion film is projected at the normal speed of twenty-four pictures per second, we can see just how the jumping horse goes over a hurdle.

3   What about motion that is too slow to be seen by the human eye? That problem has been solved by the use of the time-lapse camera. In this one, the shutter is geared to take only one shot per second, or one per minute, or even one per hour — depending upon the kind of movement that is being photographed. When the time-lapse film is projected at the normal speed of twenty-four pictures per second, it is possible to see a bean sprout growing up out of the ground. Time-lapse films are useful in the study of many types of motion too slow to be observed by the unaided human eye.

4   The Copernicans, it seems, had time-lapse cameras some 757 million years ago and they also had superpowered telescopes that gave them a clear view of what was happening upon this Earth. They decided to make a film record of the life history of Earth and to make it on the scale of one picture per year. The photography has been in progress during the last 757 million years.

5   In the near future, a Copernican interstellar expedition will arrive upon our Earth and bring with it a copy of the time-lapse film. Arrangements will be made for showing the entire film in one continuous run. This will begin at midnight of New Year's eve and continue day and night without a single stop until midnight of December 31. The rate of projection will be twenty-four pictures per second. Time on the screen will thus seem to move at the rate of twenty-four years per second; 1,440 years per minute; 86,400 years per hour; approximately two million years per day; and 62 million years per month. The normal life-span of individual man will occupy about three seconds. The full period of Earth history that will be unfolded on the

screen (some 757 million years) will extend from what the geologists call Pre-Cambrian times up to the present. This will, by no means, cover the full time-span of the Earth's geological history but it will embrace the period since the advent of living organisms.

During the months of January, February and March the picture   6
will be desolate and dreary. The shape of the land masses and the oceans will bear little or no resemblance to those that we know. The violence of geological erosion will be much in evidence. Rains will pour down on the land and promptly go booming down to the seas. There will be no clear streams anywhere except where the rains fall upon hard rock. Everywhere on the steeper ground the stream channels will be filled with boulders hurled down by rushing waters. Raging torrents and dry stream beds will keep alternating in quick succession. High mountains will seem to melt like so much butter in the sun. The shifting of land into the seas, later to be thrust up as new mountains, will be going on at a grand scale.

Early in April there will be some indication of the presence of   7
single-celled living organisms in some of the warmer and sheltered coastal waters. By the end of the month it will be noticed that some of these organisms have become multicellular. A few of them, including the Trilobites, will be encased in hard shells.

Toward the end of May, the first vertebrates will appear, but they   8
will still be aquatic creatures. In June about 60 percent of the land area that we know as North America will be under water. One broad channel will occupy the space where the Rocky Mountains now stand. Great deposits of limestone will be forming under some of the shallower seas. Oil and gas deposits will be in process of formation — also under shallow seas. On land there will still be no sign of vegetation. Erosion will be rampant, tearing loose particles and chunks of rock and grinding them into sand and silt to be spewed out by the streams into bays and estuaries.

About the middle of July the first land plants will appear and   9
take up the tremendous job of soil building. Slowly, very slowly, the mat of vegetation will spread, always battling for its life against the power of erosion. Almost foot by foot, the plant life will advance, lacing down with its root structures whatever pulverized rock material it can find. Leaves and stems will be giving added protection against the loss of the soil foothold. The increasing vegetation will pave the way for the land animals that will live upon it.

Early in August the seas will be teeming with fish. This will be   10
what geologists call the Devonian period. Some of the races of these

fish will be breathing by means of lung tissue instead of through gill tissues. Before the month is over, some of the lung fish will go ashore and take on a crude lizard-like appearance. Here are the first amphibians.

11   In early September the insects will put in their appearance. Some will look like huge dragon flies and will have a wingspread of 24 inches. Large portions of the land masses will now be covered with heavy vegetation that will include the primitive spore-propagating trees. Layer upon layer of this plant growth will build up, later to appear as the coal deposits. About the middle of this month, there will be evidence of the first seed-bearing plants and the first reptiles. Heretofore, the land animals will have been amphibians that could reproduce their kind only by depositing a soft egg mass in quiet waters. The reptiles will be shown to be freed from the aquatic bond because they can reproduce by means of a shelled egg in which the embryo and its nurturing liquids are sealed in and thus protected from destructive evaporation. Before September is over, the first dinosaurs will be seen — creatures destined to dominate the animal realm for about 140 million years and then to disappear.

12   In October there will be a series of mountain uplifts along what is now the eastern coast of the United States. A creature with feathered limbs — half bird and half reptile in appearance — will take itself into the air. Some small and rather unpretentious animals will be seen to bring forth their young in a form that is a miniature replica of the parents and to feed these young on milk secreted by mammary glands in the female parent. The emergence of this mammalian form of animal life will be recognized as one of the great events in geologic time. October will also witness the high water mark of the dinosaurs — creatures ranging in size from that of the modern goat to monsters like Brontosaurus that weighed some 40 tons. Most of them will be placid vegetarians, but a few will be hideous-looking carnivores, like Allosaurus and Tyrannosaurus. Some of the herbivorous dinosaurs will be clad in body armor for protection against their flesh-eating comrades.

13   November will bring pictures of a sea extending from the Gulf of Mexico to the Arctic in space now occupied by the Rocky Mountains. A few of the reptiles will take to the air on bat-like wings. One of these, called Pteranodon, will have a wingspread of 15 feet. There will be a rapid development of the modern flowering plants, modern trees, and modern insects. The dinosaurs will disappear. Toward the end of

the month there will be a tremendous land disturbance in which the Rocky Mountains will rise out of the sea to assume a dominating place in the North American landscape.

As the picture runs on into December it will show the mammals in command of the animal life. Seed-bearing trees and grasses will have covered most of the land with a heavy mantle of vegetation. Only the areas newly thrust up from the sea will be barren. Most of the streams will be crystal clear. The turmoil of geologic erosion will be confined to localized areas. About December 25 will begin the cutting of the Grand Canyon of the Colorado River. Grinding down through layer after layer of sedimentary strata, this stream will finally expose deposits laid down in Pre-Cambrian times. Thus in the walls of that canyon will appear geological formations dating from recent times to the period when the earth had no living organisms upon it.

The picture will run on through the latter days of December and even up to its final day with still no sign of mankind. The spectators will become alarmed in the fear that man has somehow been left out. But not so; sometime about noon on December 31 (one million years ago) will appear a stooped, massive creature of man-like proportions. This will be Pithecanthropus, the Java ape man. For tools and weapons he will have nothing but crude stone and wooden clubs. His children will live a precarious existence threatened on the one side by hostile animals and on the other by tremendous climatic changes. Ice sheets — in places 4000 feet deep — will form in the northern parts of North America and Eurasia. Four times this glacial ice will push southward to cover half the continents. With each advance the plant and animal life will be swept under or pushed southward. With each recession of the ice, life will struggle to reestablish itself in the wake of the retreating glaciers. The wooly mammoth, the musk ox, and the caribou all will fight to maintain themselves near the ice line. Sometimes they will be caught and put into cold storage — skin, flesh, blood, bones and all.

The picture will run on through supper time with still very little evidence of man's presence on the Earth. It will be about 11 o'clock when Neanderthal man appears. Another half hour will go by before the appearance of Cro-Magnon man living in caves and painting crude animal pictures on the walls of his dwelling. Fifteen minutes more will bring Neolithic man, knowing how to chip stone and thus produce sharp cutting edges for spears and tools. In a few minutes more it will appear that man has domesticated the dog, the sheep and, possibly, other animals. He will then begin the use of milk. He will also learn the arts of basket weaving and the making of pottery and dugout canoes.

17   The dawn of civilization will not come until about five or six minutes before the end of the picture. The story of the Egyptians, the Babylonians, the Greeks, and the Romans will unroll during the fourth, the third and the second minute before the end. At 58 minutes and 43 seconds past 11:00 P.M. (just 1 minute and 17 seconds before the end) will come the beginning of the Christian era. Columbus will discover the new world 20 seconds before the end. The Declaration of Independence will be signed just 17 seconds before the final curtain comes down.

18   In those few moments of geologic time will be the story of all that has happened since we became a nation. And what a story it will be! A human swarm will sweep across the face of the continent and take it away from the . . . red men. They will change it far more radically than it has ever been changed before in a comparable time. The great virgin forests will be seen going down before ax and fire. The soil, covered for aeons by its protective mantle of trees and grasses, will be laid bare to the ravages of water and wind erosion. Streams that had been flowing clear will, once again, take up a load of silt and push it toward the seas. Humus and mineral salts, both vital elements of productive soil, will be seen to vanish at a terrifying rate. The railroads and highways and cities that will spring up may divert attention, but they cannot cover up the blight of man's recent activities. In great sections of Asia, it will be seen that man must utilize cow dung and every scrap of available straw or grass for fuel to cook his food. The forests that once provided wood for this purpose will be gone without a trace. The use of these agricultural wastes for fuel, in place of returning them to the land, will be leading to increasing soil impoverishment. Here and there will be seen a dust storm darkening the landscape over an area a thousand miles across. Man-creatures will be shown counting their wealth in terms of bits of printed paper representing other bits of a scarce but comparatively useless yellow metal that is kept buried in strong vaults. Meanwhile, the soil, the only real wealth that can keep mankind alive on the face of this Earth is savagely being cut loose from its ancient moorings and washed into the seven seas.

19   We have just arrived upon this Earth. How long will we stay?

_____ **CONSIDERATIONS** _____

1. Rettie's essay, opening somewhat like a science-fiction story, is an ingenious example of the extended analogy. What are the advantages and disadvantages of such a device?

2. Rettie's Copernican film spins out a large segment of evolutionary history. Compare that with similar efforts by Loren Eiseley in "How Flowers Changed the World" and by Mark Twain in "Was the World Made for Man?" How do different styles and purposes affect the presentation of similar material?

3. An unusual feature of Rettie's style is that he writes almost entirely in the future tense. Why? What tense do most writers use? Why?

4. In Paragraph 12, Rettie mentions the emergence of mammals as an event that "will be recognized as one of the great events in geologic time." Recognized by whom? Might the answer to that question go a long way toward understanding why Rettie describes the event as "great"? Would the Copernican audiences of Rettie's imaginary film necessarily use the same adjective?

5. Do our feelings and ideas have "ancestral forms" and evolutionary histories, as our bodies seem to have? What device might an inventive writer employ to discuss such a topic?

6. "How long will we stay?" asks Rettie at the close of his hypothetical movie depicting 757 million years of earth history. The question is a rhetorical one because it is asked not so much to elicit an answer as to force a moment of reflection against the backdrop of his 750-million-year movie. What kinds of reflection would be appropriate?

Carl Sagan (b. 1934) is an astronomer and writer, whose thirteen-part Cosmos *series appeared on public television in 1980. His books include* Intelligent Life in the Universe *(1966),* Other Worlds *(1975),* The Dragons of Eden *(1977), for which he received a Pulitzer Prize,* Broca's Brain *(1979), and* Cosmos *(1980). He is director of the Laboratory for Planetary Studies and David Duncan Professor of Astronomy and Space Sciences at Cornell University.*

63

CARL SAGAN

The Measure of Eratosthenes

1   The earth is a place. It is by no means the only place. It is not even a typical place. No planet or star or galaxy can be typical, because the cosmos is mostly empty. The only typical place is within the vast, cold, universal vacuum, the everlasting night of intergalactic space, a place so strange and desolate that, by comparison, planets and stars and galaxies seem achingly rare and lovely.

2   If we were randomly inserted into the cosmos, the chance that we would find ourselves on or near a planet would be less than one in a billion trillion trillion (10^{33}, a one followed by 33 zeros). In everyday life, such odds are called compelling. Worlds are precious.

3   The discovery that the earth is a *little* world was made, as so many important human discoveries were, in the ancient Near East, in a time some humans call the third century B.C., in the greatest metropolis of the age, the Egyptian city of Alexandria.

4   Here there lived a man named Eratosthenes. One of his envious contemporaries called him "Beta," the second letter of the Greek

From *Harvard* Magazine, September-October 1980. Copyright © 1980 Harvard Magazine. Reprinted by permission.

alphabet, because, he said, Eratosthenes was the world's second best in everything. But it seems clear that, in almost everything, Eratosthenes was "alpha."

He was an astronomer, historian, geographer, philosopher, poet, theater critic, and mathematician. His writings ranged from "Astronomy" to "On Freedom from Pain." He was also the director of the great library of Alexandria, where one day he read, in a papyrus book, that in the southern frontier outpost of Syene (now Aswan), near the first cataract of the Nile, at noon on June 21 vertical sticks cast no shadows. On the summer solstice, the longest day of the year, as the hours crept toward midday, the shadows of the temple columns grew shorter. At noon, they were gone. A reflection of the sun could then be seen in the water at the bottom of a deep well. The sun was directly overhead.

It was an observation that someone else might easily have ignored. Sticks, shadows, reflections in wells, the position of the sun — of what possible importance could such simple, everyday matters be? But Eratosthenes was a scientist, and his musings on these commonplaces changed the world: in a way, they made the world.

Eratosthenes had the presence of mind to do an experiment — actually to observe whether *in Alexandria* vertical sticks cast shadows near noon on June 21. And, he discovered, sticks do.

Eratosthenes asked himself how, at the same moment, a stick in Syene could cast no shadow and a stick in Alexandria, far to the north, could cast a pronounced shadow.

Consider a map of ancient Egypt with two vertical sticks of equal length, one stuck in Alexandria, the other in Syene. Suppose that, at a certain moment, neither stick casts any shadow at all. This is perfectly easy to understand — provided the earth is flat. The sun would then be directly overhead. If the two sticks cast shadows of equal length, that also would make sense on a flat earth: the sun's rays would then be inclined at the same angle to the two sticks. But how could it be that at the same instant there was no shadow at Syene and a substantial shadow at Alexandria?

The only possible answer, he saw, was that the surface of the earth is curved. Not only that: the greater the curvature, the greater the difference in the shadow lengths. The sun is so far away that its rays are parallel when they reach the earth. Sticks placed at different angles to the sun's rays cast shadows of different lengths. For the observed difference in the shadow lengths, the distance between Alexandria and Syene had to be about seven degrees along the surface of the earth; that is, if you imagine the sticks extending down to the center of the earth, they would intersect there at an angle of seven degrees.

11   Seven degrees is something like one-fiftieth of 360 degrees, the full circumference of the earth. Eratosthenes knew that the distance between Alexandria and Syene was approximately 800 kilometers, because he had hired a man to pace it out.

12   Eight hundred kilometers times 50 is 40,000 kilometers; so that must be the circumference of the earth. (Or, if you like to measure things in miles, the distance between Alexandria and Syene is about 500 miles, and 500 miles times 50 is 25,000 miles.)

13   This is the right answer.

14   Eratosthenes' only tools were sticks, eyes, feet, and brains, plus a taste for experiment. With them he deduced the circumference of the earth with an error of only a few percent, a remarkable achievement for 2,200 years ago. He was the first person accurately to measure the size of a planet.

_____ **CONSIDERATIONS** _____

1. Sagan's short essay is a tribute to the power of deduction, the thought process that made Sherlock Holmes famous. How does deduction differ from induction?

2. The great Alexandrian library has long been described as one of the truly great human accomplishments. But what happened to it? Is there any truth to the story that Arabian conquerors shoveled it into furnaces to heat the public baths for six months?

3. Sagan's explanation of Eratosthenes's deductions is a good example of process analysis, which attempts to show how something works. Select some process that you know well — how to change a tire, how to derive the square root of a number, how to make a sunsuit, how to talk to a computer, how to tune a violin — and write a process essay. Study Sagan's techniques for making the process lively.

4. Eratosthenes was, according to Sagan, a "scientist" (Paragraph 6), but nearly 2,000 years would have to pass before the word "scientist" would be invented. (See the Oxford English Dictonary for the comparatively recent history of that word.) What did Sagan have in mind when he applied the term to Eratosthenes?

5. Sagan's essay begins with a series of short, simple sentences, and Paragraph 12 contains only one sentence five words long. College writers are usually urged to avoid such brevity. Does Sagan use those constructions successfully?

William Shakespeare (1564–1616) wrote three long poems and a sequence of sonnets, as well as the plays for which we know him best. He was born in Stratford-on-Avon to a middle-class family, came to London in his twenties, and began his theatrical career as an actor. His writing for the theater started with plays based on English history: the three parts of Henry VI *and* Richard III. The Tempest *was his last play, and by 1611 he had retired to Stratford with the money he had made upon the stage.*

This sonnet develops a common poetic theme with metaphors at once profuse and precise.

64

WILLIAM SHAKESPEARE

That time of year thou mayst in me behold

That time of year thou mayst in me behold
When yellow leaves, or none, or few, do hang
Upon those boughs which shake against the cold,
Bare ruined choirs, where late the sweet birds sang.
In me thou see'st the twilight of such day   5
As after sunset fadeth in the west;
Which by and by black night doth take away,
Death's second self, that seals up all in rest.
In me thou see'st the glowing of such fire,
That on the ashes of his youth doth lie,   10
As the deathbed whereon it must expire,
Consumed with that which it was nourished by.
This thou perceiv'st, which makes thy love more strong,
To love that well which thou must leave ere long.

Don Sharp (b. 1938) has taught in Alaska, Hawaii, and Australia, and once owned and operated a garage in Pennsylvania called Discriminating Services. He now lives in Massachusetts, where he writes for magazines and works on old cars. This essay won the Ken Purdy Award for Excellence in Automobile Journalism in 1981.

65

DON SHARP
Under the Hood

1   The owner of this 1966 Plymouth Valiant has made the rounds of car dealers. They will gladly sell him a new car — the latest model of government regulation and industrial enterprise — for $8,000, but they don't want his clattering, emphysemic old vehicle in trade. It isn't worth enough to justify the paperwork, a classified ad, and space on the used-car lot. "Sell it for junk," they tell him. "Scrap iron is high now, and they'll give you $25 for it."

2   The owner is hurt. He likes this car. It has served him well for 90,000-odd miles. It has a functional shape and he can get in and out of it easily. He can roll down his window in a light rain and not get his shoulder wet. The rear windows roll down, and he doesn't need an air conditioner. He can see out of it fore, aft, and abeam. He can hazard it on urban parking lots without fear of drastic, insurance-deductible casualty loss. His teenage children reject it as passé, so it is always available to him. It has no buzzers, and the only flashing lights are those he controls himself when signaling a turn. The owner, clearly

one of a vanishing tribe, brings the car to a kindred spirit and asks me to rebuild it.

We do not discuss the cost. I do not advertise my services and my   3
sign is discreet. My shop is known by word of mouth, and those who spread the word emphasize my house rule: "A blank check and a free hand." That is, I do to your car what I think it needs and you pay for it; you trust me not to take advantage, I guarantee you good brakes, sound steering, and prompt starting, and you pay without quarrel. This kind of arrangement saves a lot of time spent in making estimates and a lot of time haggling over the bill. It also imposes a tremendous burden of responsibility on me and on those who spread the word, and it puts a burden of trust on those who deliver their cars into my custody.

A relationship of that sort is about as profound as any that two   4
people can enjoy, even if it lasts no longer than the time required to reline a set of brakes. I think of hometown farmers who made sharecropping deals for the season on a handshake; then I go into a large garage and see the white-coated service writer noting the customer's every specification, calling attention to the fine print at the bottom of the work order, and requiring a contractual signature before even a brake-light bulb is replaced. I perceive in their transaction that ignorance of cause and effect breeds suspicion, and I wonder who is the smaller, the customer or the service writer, and how they came to be so small of spirit.

Under the hood of this ailing Valiant, I note a glistening line of   5
seeping oil where the oil pan meets the engine block. For thousands of miles, a piece of cork — a strip of bark from a Spanish tree — has stood firm between the pan and the block against churning oil heated to nearly 200 degrees, oil that sought vainly to escape its duty and was forced back to work by a stalwart gasket. But now, after years of perseverance, the gasket has lost its resilience and the craven oil escapes. Ecclesiastes allows a time for all things, and the time for this gasket has passed.

Higher up, between the block casting that forms the foundation   6
of the engine and the cylinder-head casting that admits fresh air and exhausts oxidized air and fuel, is the head gasket, a piece of sheet metal as thin as a matchbook cover that has confined the multiple fires built within the engine to their proper domains. Now, a whitish-gray deposit betrays an eroded area from which blue flame spits every time the cylinder fires. The gasket is "blown."

7   Let us stop and think of large numbers. In the four-cycle engines that power all modern cars, a spark jumps a spark-plug gap and sets off a fire in a cylinder every time the crankshaft goes around twice. The crankshaft turns the transmission shaft, which turns the driveshaft, which turns the differential gears, which turn the rear axles, which turn the wheels (what could Aquinas have done with something like that, had he addressed himself to the source of the spark or to the final destination of the wheels?). In 100,000 miles — a common life for modern engines — the engine will make some 260 million turns, and in half of those turns, 130 million of them, a gasoline-fueled fire with a maximum temperature of 2,000 degrees (quickly falling to about 1,200 degrees) is built in each cylinder. The heat generated by the fire raises the pressure in the cylinder to about 700 pounds per square inch, if only for a brief instant before the piston moves and the pressure falls. A head gasket has to contend with heat and pressure like this all the time the engine is running, and, barring mishap, it will put up with it indefinitely.

8   This Plymouth has suffered mishap. I know it as soon as I raise the hood and see the telltale line of rust running across the underside of the hood: the mark of overheating. A water pump bearing or seal gave way, water leaked out, and was flung off the fan blades with enough force to embed particles of rust in the undercoating. Without cooling water, the engine grew too hot, and that's why the head gasket blew. In an engine, no cause exists without an effect. Unlike a court of law, wherein criminals are frequently absolved of wrongdoing, no engine component is without duty and responsibility, and failure cannot be mitigated by dubious explanations such as parental neglect or a crummy neighborhood.

9   Just as Sherlock Holmes would not be satisfied with one clue if he could find others, I study the oil filter. The block and oil pan are caked with seepings and drippings, but below the filter the caking is visibly less thick and somewhat soft. So: once upon a time, a careless service-station attendant must have ruined the gasket while installing a new oil filter. Oil en route to the bearings escaped and washed away the grime that had accumulated. Odds are that the oil level fell too low and the crankshaft bearings were starved for oil.

10   Bearings are flat strips of metal, formed into half-circles about as thick as a matchbook match and about an inch wide. The bearing surface itself — the surface that *bears* the crankshaft and that *bears* the load imposed by the fire-induced pressure above the piston — is

half as thick. Bearing metal is a drab, gray alloy, the principal component of which is *babbitt,* a low-friction metal porous enough to absorb oil but so soft that it must be allowed to withstand high pressures. (I like to think that Sinclair Lewis had metallurgy in mind when he named his protagonist George Babbitt.) When the fire goes off above the piston and the pressure is transmitted to the crankshaft via the connecting rod, the babbitt-alloyed bearing pushes downward with a force of about 3,500 pounds per square inch. And it must not give way, must not be peened into foil and driven from its place in fragments.

11   Regard the fleshy end joint of your thumb and invite a 100-pound woman (or a pre-teen child, if no such woman be near to hand) to stand on it. Multiply the sensation by thirty-five and you get an idea of what the bearing is up against. Of course, the bearing enjoys a favorable handicap in the comparison because it works in a metal-to-metal environment heated to 180 degrees or so. The bearing is equal to its task so long as it is protected from direct metal-to-metal contact by a layer of lubricating oil, oil that must be forced into the space between the bearing and the crankshaft against that 3,500 pounds of force. True, the oil gets a lot of help from hydrodynamic action as the spinning crankshaft drags oil along with it, but lubrication depends primarily on a pump that forces oil through the engine at around 40 pounds of pressure.

12   If the oil level falls too low, the oil pump sucks in air. The oil gets as frothy as whipped cream and doesn't flow. In time, oil pressure will fall so low that the "idiot" light on the dashboard will flash, but long before then the bearing may have run "dry" and suffered considerable amounts of its metal to be peened away by those 3,500-pound hammer blows. "Considerable" may mean only .005 inches, or about the thickness of one sheet of 75-percent-cotton, 25-pound-per-ream dissertation bond — not much metal, but enough to allow oil to escape from the bearing even after the defective filter gasket is replaced and the oil supply replenished. From the time of oil starvation onward, the beaten bearing is a little disaster waiting to spoil a vacation or a commute to an important meeting.

13   Curious, that an unseen .005 inches of drab, gray metal worthy only to inspire the name of a poltroonish bourgeois should enjoy more consequence for human life than almost any equal thickness of a randomly chosen doctoral dissertation. Life is full of ironies.

14   The car I confront does not have an "idiot" light. It has an old-fashioned oil-pressure gauge. As the driver made his rounds from condominium to committee room, he could — if he cared or was ever so

alert — monitor the health of his engine bearings by noting the oil pressure. Virtually all cars had these gauges in the old days, but they began to disappear in the mid-'50s, and nowadays hardly any cars have them. In eliminating oil-pressure gauges, the car makers pleaded that, in their dismal experience, people didn't pay much attention to gauges. Accordingly, Detroit switched to the warning light, which was cheaper to manufacture anyway (and having saved a few bucks on the mechanicals, the manufacturer could afford to etch a design in the opera windows; this is called "progress"). Curious, in the midst of all this, that Chrysler Corporation, the maker of Plymouths and the victim of so much bad management over the past fifteen years, should have been the one car manufacturer to constantly assert, via a standard-equipment oil-pressure gauge, a faith in the awareness, judgment, and responsibility of drivers. That Chrysler did so may have something to do with its current problems.

15   The other car makers were probably right. Time was when most men knew how to replace their own distributor points, repair a flat tire, and install a battery. Women weren't assumed to know as much, but they were expected to know how to put a gear lever in neutral, set a choke and throttle, and crank a car by hand if the battery was dead. Now, odds are that 75 percent of men and a higher percentage of women don't even know how to work the jacks that come with their cars. To be sure, a bumper jack is an abominable contraption — the triumph of production economies over good sense — but it will do what it is supposed to do, and the fact that most drivers cannot make one work says much about the way motorists have changed over the past forty years.

16   About all that people will watch on the downslide of this century is the fuel gauge, for they don't like to be balked in their purpose. A lack of fuel will stop a car dead in its tracks and categorically prevent the driver from arriving at the meeting to consider tenure for a male associate professor with a black grandfather and a Chinese mother. Lack of fuel will stall a car in mid-intersection and leave dignity and image prey to the honks and curses of riffraff driving taxicabs and beer trucks, so people watch the fuel gauge as closely as they watch a pubescent daughter or a bearish stock.

17   But for the most part, once the key goes into the ignition, people assign responsibility for the car's smooth running to someone else — to anybody but themselves. If the engine doesn't start, that's not because the driver has abused it, but because the manufacturer was

remiss or the mechanic incompetent. (Both suspicions are reasonable, but they do not justify the driver's spineless passivity.) The driver considers himself merely a client of the vehicle. He proudly disclaims, at club and luncheon, any understanding of the dysfunctions of the machine. He must so disclaim, for to admit knowledge or to seek it actively would require an admission of responsibility and fault. To be wrong about inflation or the political aspirations of the Albanians doesn't cost anybody anything, but to claim to know why the car won't start and then to be proved wrong is both embarrassing and costly.

Few people would remove $500 from someone's pocket without   18 a qualm and put it in their own. Yet, the job-lot run of mechanics do it all the time. Mechanics and drivers are alike: they gave up worrying long ago about the intricacies and demands of cause and effect. The mechanics do not attend closely to the behavior of the vehicle. Rather, they consult a book with flow-charts that says, "Try this, and if it doesn't work, try that." Or they hook the engine up to another machine and read gauges or cathode-ray-tube squiggles, but without realizing that gauges and squiggles are not reality but only tools used to aid perception of reality. A microscope is also a wonderful tool, but you still have to comprehend what you're looking for; else, like James Thurber, you get back the reflection of your own eye.

Mechanics, like academics and bureaucrats, have retreated too   19 far from the realities of their tasks. An engine runs badly. They consult the book. The book says to replace part A. They replace A. The engine still runs badly, but the mechanic can deny the fact as handily as a socialist can deny that minimum-wage laws eventually lead to unemployment. Just as the driver doesn't care to know why his oil pressure drops from 40 to 30 to 20 pounds and then to zero, so the mechanic cares little for the casuistic distinctions that suggest that part A is in good order but that some subtle conjunction of wholesome part B with defective part C may be causing the trouble. (I don't know about atheists in foxholes, but I doubt that many Jesuits are found among incompetent mechanics.)

And why should the mechanic care? He gets paid in any event.   20 From the mechanic's point of view, he should get paid, for he sees a federal judge hire academic consultants to advise about busing, and after the whites have fled before the imperious column of yellow buses and left the schools blacker than ever, the judge hires the consultants again to find out why the whites moved out. The consultant gets paid in public money, whatever effects his actions have, even when he causes things he said would never happen.

21   Consider the garden-variety Herr Doktor who has spent a pleasant series of warm fall weekends driving to a retreat in the Catskills; his car has started with alacrity and run well despite a stuck choke. Then, when the first blue norther of the season sends temperatures toward zero, the faithful machine must be haggled into action and proceeds haltingly down the road, gasping and backfiring. "Needs a new carburetor," the mechanic says, and, to be sure, once a new carburetor is installed, the car runs well again. Our Herr Doktor is happy. His car did not run well; it got a new carburetor and ran well again; ergo, the carburetor was at fault. Q.E.D.'

22   Curious that in personal matters the classic *post hoc* fallacy should be so readily accepted when it would be mocked in academic debate. Our Herr Doktor should know, or at least suspect, that the carburetor that functioned so well for the past several months could hardly have changed its nature overnight, and we might expect of him a more diligent inquiry into its problems. But "I'm no mechanic," he chuckles to his colleagues, and they nod agreeably. Such skinned-knuckle expertise would be unfitting in a man whose self-esteem is equivalent to his uselessness with a wrench. Lilies of the postindustrial field must concern themselves with weighty matters beyond the ken of greasy laborers who drink beer at the end of a workday.

23   Another example will illustrate the point. A battery cable has an end that is designed to connect to a terminal on the battery. Both cable-end and battery-terminal surfaces look smooth, but aren't. Those smooth surfaces are pitted and peaked, and only the peaks touch each other. The pits collect water from the air, and the chemistry of electricity-carrying metals causes lead oxides to form in the pits. The oxides progressively insulate the cable end and battery terminal from each other until the day that turning the key produces only a single, resounding *clunk* and no more. The road service mechanic installs a new $75 battery and collects $25 for his trouble. Removing the cables from the old battery cleans their ends somewhat, so things work for a few days, and then the car again fails to start. The mechanic installs a $110 alternator, applies a $5 charge to the battery, and collects another $25; several days later he gives the battery another $5 charge, installs a $75 starter, and collects $25 more. In these instances, to charge the battery — to send current backwards from cable end to battery terminal — disturbs the oxides and temporarily improves their

conductivity. Wriggling the charger clamps on the cable ends probably helps too. On the driver's last $25 visit, the mechanic sells another $5 battery charge and a pair of $25 battery cables. Total bill: $400, and all the car needed was to have its cable ends and battery terminals cleaned. The mechanic wasn't necessarily a thief. Perhaps, like academic education consultants, he just wasn't very smart — and his ilk abound; they are as plentiful as the drivers who will pay generously for the privilege of an aristocratic disdain of elementary cause and effect in a vehicular electrical system.

After a tolerably long practice as a mechanic, I firmly believe 24 that at least two-thirds of the batteries, starters, alternators, ignition coils, carburetors, and water pumps that are sold are not needed. Batteries, alternators, and starters are sold because battery-cable ends are dirty. A maladjusted or stuck automatic choke is cured by a new carburetor. Water pumps and alternators are sold to correct problems from loose fan belts. In the course of the replacement, the fan belt gets properly tightened, so the original problem disappears in the misguided cure, with mechanic and owner never the wiser.

I understand the venality (and laziness and ignorance) of mechanics, 25 and I understand the shop owner's need to pay a salary to someone to keep up with the IRS and OSHA forms. The shop marks up parts by 50 to 100 percent. When the car with the faulty choke comes in the door, the mechanic must make a choice: he can spend fifteen minutes fixing it and charge a half-hour's labor, or he can spend a half-hour replacing the carburetor (and charge for one hour) with one he buys for $80 and sells for $135. If the shop is a profit-making enterprise, the mechanic can hardly be blamed for selling the unneeded new carburetor, especially if the customer will stand still to be fleeced. Whether the mechanic acts from ignorance or larceny (the odds are about equal), the result is still a waste, one that arises from the driver's refusal to study the cause and effect of events that occur under the hood of his car.

The willingness of a people to accept responsibility for the 26 machines they depend on is a fair barometer of their sense of individual worth and of the moral strength of a culture. According to popular reports, the Russian working folk are a sorrowfully vodka-besotted lot; likewise, reports are that Russian drivers abuse their vehicles atrociously. In our unhappy country, as gauges for battery-charging (ammeters), cooling-water temperature, and oil pressure disappeared from the dashboards, they were replaced by a big-brotherly series of cacophonous buzzers and flashing lights, buzzers and lights mandated by regulatory edict for the sole purpose of reminding the driver that the government considers him a hopeless fool. Concurrent with these developments has come social agitation and law known as "consumer protection," which is, in fact, an extension of the philosophy that people are morons for whom the government must provide outpatient care. People pay handsome taxes to be taught that they are not responsible and do not need to be. This is a long way from what the Puritans paid their tithes for, and, Salem witch trials aside, the Puritans got a better product for their money.

27   What is astounding and dismaying is how quickly people came to believe in their own incompetence. In 1951, Eric Hoffer noted in *The True Believer* that a leader so disposed could make free people into slaves easier than he could turn slaves into free people (cf. Moses). Hoffer must be pained by the accuracy of his perception.

28   I do not claim that Everyman can be his own expert mechanic, for I know that precious few can. I do claim that disdain for the beautiful series of cause-and-effect relationships ("beautiful" in the way that provoked Archimedes to proclaim "Eureka!") that move machines, and particularly the automobile, measures not only a man's wit but also a society's morals.

_____ **CONSIDERATIONS** _____

1. At the end of Paragraph 4, Sharp poses a question. What sentence toward the end of his essay answers this question? Is that sentence the thesis of his essay? What do you think of his choice of a moral barometer? Would Carol Bly approve? See her essay "Getting Tired," especially the final paragraph.

2. What would James Thurber think of Sharp's use of "which" in Paragraph 7? (See Thurber's short essay "Which.")

3. In Paragraphs 10, 11, and 12, Sharp offers an exposition of a process. Study his success in explaining technical matters without lapsing into terminology too specialized for the general reader.

4. Sharp calls a particular device on the dashboard an "idiot light." Why? Does this epithet connect with other parts of his essay?

5. Sharp refers (in Paragraph 9) to Sherlock Holmes's renowned skill in deduction, and (in Paragraph 22) to a common logical fallacy called *post hoc ergo propter hoc*, both of which are explained by Robert Gorham Davis in his essay, "Logic and Logical Fallacies." With Davis's help, reread Sharp's essay with an eye to any problems of logic.

William Stafford (b. 1914) is a poet who grew up in Kansas and taught for many years at Lewis and Clark College in Oregon. Traveling through the Dark *won the National Book Award in 1963, and was followed by* The Rescued Year *(1966),* Allegiances *(1970), and* Some Day, Maybe *(1973). In 1977, Stafford collected his poems into one volume called* Stories That Could Be True. *His essays appear in* Writing the Australian Crawl *(1978).*

Stafford's poetry and his account of writing his poetry look simple. In a way, they are simple, but their simplicity deepens as you look at it. His poetry is simple and deep, rather than complex and superficial. Reading about his way of writing, you feel the style of the man as intensely in his prose as in his poems.

66

WILLIAM STAFFORD

A Way of Writing

A writer is not so much someone who has something to say as he is someone who has found a process that will bring about new things he would not have thought of if he had not started to say them. That is, he does not draw on a reservoir; instead, he engages in an activity that brings to him a whole succession of unforeseen stories, poems, essays, plays, laws, philosophies, religions, or — but wait! 1

Back in school, from the first when I began to try to write things, I felt this richness. One thing would lead to another; the world would give and give. Now, after twenty years or so of trying, I live by that certain richness, an idea hard to pin, difficult to say, and perhaps offensive to some. For there are strange implications in it. 2

From *Field: Contemporary Poetry and Poetics,* #2. Spring 1970. Reprinted by permission of *Field,* Oberlin College, Oberlin, Ohio.

3   One implication is the importance of just plain receptivity. When I write, I like to have an interval before me when I am not likely to be interrupted. For me, this means usually the early morning, before others are awake. I get pen and paper, take a glance out the window (often it is dark out there), and wait. It is like fishing. But I do not wait very long, for there is always a nibble — and this is where receptivity comes in. To get started I will accept anything that occurs to me. Something always occurs, of course, to any of us. We can't keep from thinking. Maybe I have to settle for an immediate impression: it's cold, or hot, or dark, or bright, or in between! Or — well, the possibilities are endless. If I put down something, that thing will help the next thing come, and I'm off. If I let the process go on, things will occur to me that were not at all in my mind when I started. These things, odd or trivial as they may be, are somehow connected. And if I let them string out, surprising things will happen.

4   If I let them string out. . . . Along with initial receptivity, then, there is another readiness: I must be willing to fail. If I am to keep on writing, I cannot bother to insist on high standards. I must get into action and not let anything stop me, or even slow me much. By "standards" I do not mean "correctness" — spelling, punctuation, and so on. These details become mechanical for anyone who writes for a while. I am thinking about what many people would consider "important" standards, such matters as social significance, positive values, consistency, etc. I resolutely disregard these. Something better, greater, is happening! I am following a process that leads so wildly and originally into new territory that no judgment can at the moment be made about values, significance, and so on. I am making something new, something that has not been judged before. Later others — and maybe I myself — will make judgments. Now, I am headlong to discover. Any distraction may harm the creating.

5   So, receptive, careless of failure, I spin out things on the page. And a wonderful freedom comes. If something occurs to me, it is all right to accept it. It has one justification: it occurs to me. No one else can guide me. I must follow my own weak, wandering, diffident impulses.

6   A strange bonus happens. At times, without my insisting on it, my writings become coherent; the successive elements that occur to me are clearly related. They lead by themselves to new connections. Sometimes the language, even the syllables that happen along, may start a trend. Sometimes the materials alert me to something waiting in my mind, ready for sustained attention. At such times, I allow myself to be eloquent, or intentional, or for great swoops (treacherous!

not to be trusted!) reasonable. But I do not insist on any of that; for I know that back of my activity there will be the coherence of my self, and that indulgence of my impulses will bring recurrent patterns and meanings again.

This attitude toward the process of writing creatively suggests a 7 problem for me, in terms of what others say. They talk about "skills" in writing. Without denying that I do have experience, wide reading, automatic orthodoxies and maneuvers of various kinds, I still must insist that I am often baffled about what "skill" has to do with the precious little area of confusion when I do not know what I am going to say and then I find out what I am going to say. That precious interval I am unable to bridge by skill. What can I witness about it? It remains mysterious, just as all of us must feel puzzled about how we are so inventive as to be able to talk along through complexities with our friends, not needing to plan what we are going to say, but never stalled for long in our confident forward progress. Skill? If so, it is the skill we all have, something we must have learned before the age of three or four.

A writer is one who has become accustomed to trusting that 8 grace, or luck, or — skill.

Yet another attitude I find necessary: most of what I write, like 9 most of what I say in casual conversation, will not amount to much. Even I will realize, and even at the time, that it is not negotiable. It will be like practice. In conversation I allow myself random remarks — in fact, as I recall, that is the way I learned to talk — , so in writing I launch many expendable efforts. A result of this free way of writing is that I am not writing for others, mostly; they will not see the product at all unless the activity eventuates in something that later appears to be worthy. My guide is the self, and its adventuring in the language brings about communication.

This process-rather-than-substance view of writing invites a 10 final, dual reflection:

1. Writers may not be special — sensitive or talented in any usual sense. They are simply engaged in sustained use of a language skill we all have. Their "creations" come about through confident reliance on stray impulses that will, with trust, find occasional patterns that are satisfying.

2. But writing itself is one of the great, free human activities. There is scope for individuality, and elation, and discovery, in writing. For the person who follows with trust and forgiveness what occurs to him, the world remains always ready and deep, an inexhaustible environment, with the combined vividness of an actuality and flexibility

of a dream. Working back and forth between experience and thought, writers have more than space and time can offer. They have the whole unexplored realm of human vision.

A sample daily-writing sheet and the poem as revised.

Shadows

I

Out in places like Wyoming some of the shadows

are cut out and pasted on fossils.

There are mountains that erode when
clouds drag across them. You can hear ~~the tick~~ the tick

~~the tick~~ of the light breaking edges off white stones.

At ~~the~~ a fountain on Main Street I saw

our shadow. It did not drink but

waited on cement and water while I drank.

There were two people and but one shadow.

I looked up so hard outward that a bird

flying past made a shadow on the sky.

There is a place in the air where our house
used to be.

Once I crawled through grassblades to hear

the sounds of their shadows. One of the shadows

moved, and it was the earth where a mole

was passing. I could hear little

paws in the dirt, and fur brush along

the tunnel, and even, somehow, the mole shadow.

In churches ~~these~~ when hearts pump sermons

from wells full of shadows.

In my prayers I let yesterday begin

and then go behind this hour now.

SHADOWS

Out in places like Wyoming some of the shadows
are cut out and pasted on fossils.
There are mountains that erode when
clouds drag across them. You hear the tick
of sunlight breaking edges off white stones.

At a fountain on Main Street I saw
our shadow. It did not drink but
waited on cement and water while I drank.
There were two people and but one shadow.
I looked up so hard outward that a bird
flying past made a shadow on the sky.
There is a place in the air where
our old house used to be.

Once I crawled through grassblades to hear
the sounds of their shadows. One shadow
moved, and it was the earth where a mole
was passing. I could hear little
paws in the dirt, and fur brush along
the tunnel, and even, somehow, the mole shadow.

In my prayers I let yesterday begin
and then go behind this hour now,
in churches where hearts pump sermons
from wells full of shadows.

——— CONSIDERATIONS ————————————————

1. Stafford is clearly and openly talking about himself — how *he* writes, what writing means to *him* — and yet most readers agree that he successfully avoids the egotism or self-consciousness that sours many first-person essays. Compare his style with three or four other first-person pieces in this book to see how he does it.

2. In his first paragraph, Stafford tells of an idea that might be called writing as discovery. Thinking back through your own writing, can you recall this experience — when, after struggling to write an essay or letter that you *had* to write, you discovered something you *wanted* to write? What did you do about it? More important, what might you do next time it happens?

3. What, according to Stafford, is more important to a writer than "social significance, or positive values, or consistency"?

4. Stafford is talking about writing a poem. How do his discoveries and conclusions bear on *your* problems in writing an essay? Be specific.

5. Do the opening and closing paragraphs differ in style? If so, what is the difference, and why does Stafford allow it?

6. Study the three versions of Stafford's poem "Shadows." Do you find anything that belies the easygoing impression his essay gives of Stafford at work? Explain.

Jonathan Swift (1667–1745), the author of Gulliver's Travels, was a priest, a poet, and a master of English prose. Some of his strongest satire took the form of reasonable defense of the unthinkable, like his argument in favor of abolishing Christianity in the British Isles. Born in Dublin, he was angry all his life at England's misuse and mistreatment of the subject Irish people. In 1729, he made this modest proposal for solving the Irish problem.

67

JONATHAN SWIFT
A Modest Proposal

FOR PREVENTING THE CHILDREN OF POOR PEOPLE IN IRELAND FROM BEING A BURDEN TO THEIR PARENTS OR COUNTRY, AND FOR MAKING THEM BENEFICIAL TO THE PUBLIC

1   It is a melancholy object to those who walk through this great town or travel in the country, when they see the streets, the roads, and cabin doors, crowded with beggars of the female sex, followed by three, four, or six children, all in rags and importuning every passenger for an alms. These mothers, instead of being able to work for their honest livelihood, are forced to employ all their time in strolling to beg sustenance for their helpless infants, who, as they grow up, either turn thieves for want of work, or leave their dear native country to fight for the Pretender in Spain, or sell themselves to the Barbadoes.

2   I think it is agreed by all parties that this prodigious number of children in the arms, or on the backs, or at the heels of their mothers, and frequently of their fathers, is in the present deplorable state of the kingdom a very great additional grievance; and therefore whoever could find out a fair, cheap, and easy method of making these children

sound, useful members of the commonwealth would deserve so well of the public as to have his statue set up for a preserver of the nation.

But my intention is very far from being confined to provide only 3 for the children of professed beggars; it is of a much greater extent, and shall take in the whole number of infants at a certain age who are born of parents in effect as little able to support them as those who demand our charity in the streets.

As to my own part, having turned my thoughts for many years 4 upon this important subject, and maturely weighed the several schemes of other projectors, I have always found them grossly mistaken in their computation. It is true, a child just dropped from its dam may be supported by her milk for a solar year, with little other nourishment; at most not above the value of two shillings, which the mother may certainly get, or the value in scraps, by her lawful occupation of begging; and it is exactly at one year old that I propose to provide for them in such a manner as instead of being a charge upon their parents or the parish, or wanting food and raiment for the rest of their lives, they shall on the contrary contribute to the feeding, and partly to the clothing, of many thousands.

There is likewise another great advantage in my scheme, that it 5 will prevent those voluntary abortions, and that horrid practice of women murdering their bastard children, alas, too frequent among us, sacrificing the poor innocent babes, I doubt, more to avoid the expense than the shame, which would move tears and pity in the most savage and inhuman breast.

The number of souls in this kingdom being usually reckoned one 6 million and a half, of these I calculate there may be about two hundred thousand couples whose wives are breeders; from which number I subtract thirty thousand couples who are able to maintain their own children, although I apprehend there cannot be so many under the present distress of the kingdom; but this being granted, there will remain an hundred and seventy thousand breeders. I again subtract fifty thousand for those women who miscarry, or whose children die by accident or disease within the year. There only remain an hundred and twenty thousand children of poor parents annually born. The question therefore is, how this number shall be reared and provided for, which, as I have already said, under the present situation of affairs, is utterly impossible by all the methods hitherto proposed. For we can neither employ them in handicraft or agriculture; we neither build houses (I mean in the country) nor cultivate land. They can very seldom pick up a livelihood by stealing till they arrive at six years old, except where they are of towardly parts; although I confess they learn the rudiments much earlier, during which time they can however be looked upon only as probationers, as I have been informed by a principal gentleman in the country of Cavan, who protested to me that he never knew above one or two instances under the age of six, even in a part of the kingdom so renowned for the quickest proficiency in that art.

7   I am assured by our merchants that a boy or a girl before twelve years old is no salable commodity; and even when they come to this age they will not yield above three pounds, or three pounds and half a crown at most on the Exchange; which cannot turn to account either to the parents or the kingdom, the charge of nutriment and rags having been at least four times that value.

8   I shall now therefore humbly propose my own thoughts, which I hope will not be liable to the least objection.

9   I have been assured by a very knowing American of my acquaintance in London, that a young healthy child well nursed is at a year old a most delicious, nourishing, and wholesome food, whether stewed, roasted, baked, or boiled; and I make no doubt that it will equally serve in a fricassee or a ragout.

10   I do therefore humbly offer it to public consideration that of the hundred and twenty thousand children, already computed, twenty thousand may be reserved for breed, whereof only one fourth part to be males, which is more than we allow to sheep, black cattle, or swine; and my reason is that these children are seldom the fruits of marriage, a circumstance not much regarded by our savages, therefore one male will be sufficient to serve four females. That the remaining hundred thousand may at a year old be offered in sale to the persons of quality and fortune through the kingdom, always advising the mother to let them suck plentifully in the last month, so as to render them plump and fat for a good table. A child will make two dishes at an entertainment for friends; and when the family dines alone, the fore or hind quarter will make a reasonable dish, and seasoned with a little pepper or salt will be very good boiled on the fourth day, especially in winter.

11   I have reckoned upon a medium that a child just born will weigh twelve pounds, and in a solar year if tolerably nursed increaseth to twenty-eight pounds.

12   I grant this food will be somewhat dear, and therefore very proper for landlords, who, as they have already devoured most of the parents, seem to have the best title to the children.

Infant's flesh will be in season throughout the year, but more 13
plentiful in March, and a little before and after. For we are told by a
grave author, an eminent French physician, that fish being a prolific
diet, there are more children born in Roman Catholic countries about
nine months after Lent than at any other season; therefore, reckoning
a year after Lent, the markets will be more glutted than usual, because
the number of popish infants is at least three to one in this kingdom;
and therefore it will have one other collateral advantage, by lessening
the number of Papists among us.

I have already computed the charge of nursing a beggar's child (in 14
which list I reckon all cottagers, laborers, and four fifths of the farmers) to be about two shillings per annum, rags included; and I believe
no gentleman would repine to give ten shillings for the carcass of a
good fat child, which, as I have said, will make four dishes of excellent
nutritive meat, when he hath only some particular friend or his own
family to dine with him. Thus the squire will learn to be a good
landlord, and grow popular among the tenants; the mother will have
eight shillings net profit, and be fit for work till she produces another
child.

Those who are more thrifty (as I must confess the times require) 15
may flay the carcass; the skin of which artificially dressed will make
admirable gloves for ladies, and summer boots for fine gentlemen.

As to our city of Dublin, shambles may be appointed for this 16
purpose in the most convenient parts of it, and butchers we may be
assured will not be wanting; although I rather recommend buying the
children alive, and dressing them hot from the knife as we do roasting
pigs.

A very worthy person, a true lover of his country, and whose 17
virtues I highly esteem, was lately pleased in discoursing on this matter to offer a refinement upon my scheme. He said that many gentlemen of his kingdom, having of late destroyed their deer, he conceived
that the want of venison might be well supplied by the bodies of young
lads and maidens, not exceeding fourteen years of age nor under
twelve, so great a number of both sexes in every county being now
ready to starve for want of work and service; and these to be disposed
of by their parents, if alive, or otherwise by their nearest relations. But
with due deference to so excellent a friend and so deserving a patriot,
I cannot be altogether in his sentiments; for as to the males, my American acquaintance assured me from frequent experience that their
flesh was generally tough and lean, like that of our schoolboys, by
continual exercise, and their taste disagreeable; and to fatten them

would not answer the charge. Then as to the females, it would, I think with humble submission, be a loss to the public, because they soon would become breeders themselves: and besides, it is not improbable that some scrupulous people might be apt to censure such a practice (although indeed very unjustly) as a little bordering upon cruelty; which, I confess, hath always been with me the strongest objection against any project, how well soever intended.

18 But in order to justify my friend, he confessed that this expedient was put into his head by the famous Psalmanazar, a native of the island Formosa, who came from thence to London above twenty years ago, and in conversation told my friend that in his country when any young person happened to be put to death, the executioner sold the carcass to persons of quality as a prime dainty; and that in his time the body of a plump girl of fifteen, who was crucified for an attempt to poison the emperor, was sold to his Imperial Majesty's prime minister of state, and other great mandarins of the court, in joints from the gibbet, at four hundred crowns. Neither indeed can I deny that if the same use were made of several plump young girls in this town, who without one single groat to their fortunes cannot stir abroad without a chair, and appear at the playhouse and assemblies in foreign fineries which they never will pay for, the kingdom would not be the worse.

19 Some persons of a desponding spirit are in great concern about that vast number of poor people who are aged, diseased, or maimed, and I have been desired to employ my thoughts what course may be taken to ease the nation of so grievous an encumbrance. But I am not in the least pain upon that matter, because it is very well known that they are every day dying and rotting by cold and famine, and filth and vermin, as fast as can be reasonably expected. And as to the younger laborers, they are now in almost as hopeful a condition. They cannot get work, and consequently pine away for want of nourishment to a degree that if at any time they are accidentally hired to common labor, they have not strength to perform it; and thus the country and themselves are happily delivered from the evils to come.

20 I have too long digressed, and therefore shall return to my subject. I think the advantages by the proposal which I have made are obvious and many, as well as of the highest importance.

21 For first, as I have already observed, it would greatly lessen the number of Papists, with whom we are yearly overrun, being the principal breeders of the nation as well as our most dangerous enemies; and who stay at home on purpose to deliver the kingdom to the Pretender, hoping to take their advantage by the absence of so many good

Protestants, who have chosen rather to leave their country than to stay at home and pay tithes against their conscience to an Episcopal curate.

Secondly, the poorer tenants will have something valuable of 22 their own, which by law may be made liable to distress, and help to pay their landlord's rent, their corn and cattle being already seized and money a thing unknown.

Thirdly, whereas the maintenance of an hundred thousand chil- 23 dren, from two years old and upwards, cannot be computed at less than ten shillings a piece per annum, the nation's stock will be thereby increased fifty thousand pounds per annum, besides the profit of a new dish introduced to the tables of all gentlemen of fortune in the kingdom who have any refinement in taste. And the money will circulate among ourselves, the goods being entirely of our own growth and manufacture.

Fourthly, the constant breeders, besides the gain of eight shillings 24 sterling per annum by the sale of their children, will be rid of the charge of maintaining them after the first year.

Fifthly, this food would likewise bring great custom to taverns, 25 where the vintners will certainly be so prudent as to procure the best receipts for dressing it to perfection, and consequently have their houses frequented by all the fine gentlemen, who justly value themselves upon their knowledge in good eating; and a skillful cook, who understands how to oblige his guests, will contrive to make it as expensive as they please.

Sixthly, this would be a great inducement to marriage, which all 26 wise nations have either encouraged by rewards of enforced by laws and penalties. It would increase the care and tenderness of mothers toward their children, when they were sure of a settlement for life to the poor babes, provided in some sort by the public, to their annual profit instead of expense. We should see an honest emulation among the married women, which of them could bring the fattest child to the market. Men would become as fond of their wives during the time of their pregnancy as they are now of their mares in foal, their cows in calf, or sows when they are ready to farrow; nor offer to beat or kick them (as is too frequent a practice) for fear of a miscarriage.

Many other advantages might be enumerated. For instance, the 27 addition of some thousand carcasses in our exportation of barreled beef, the propagation of swine's flesh, and improvements in the art of making good bacon, so much wanted among us by the great destruction of pigs, too frequent at our tables, which are no way comparable in taste or magnificence to a well-grown, fat, yearling child, which roasted whole will make a considerable figure at a lord mayor's feast or any other public entertainment. But this and many others I omit, being studious of brevity.

28   Supposing that one thousand families in this city would be constant customers for infants' flesh, besides others who might have it at merry meetings, particularly weddings and christenings, I compute that Dublin would take off annually about twenty thousand carcasses, and the rest of the kingdom (where probably they will be sold somewhat cheaper) the remaining eighty thousand.

29   I can think of no one objection that will possibly be raised against this proposal, unless it should be urged that the number of people will be thereby much lessened in the kingdom. This I freely own, and it was indeed one principal design in offering it to the world. I desire the reader will observe, that I calculate my remedy for this one individual kingdom of Ireland and for no other that ever was, is, or I think ever can be upon earth. Therefore let no man talk to me of other expedients: of taxing our absentees at five shillings a pound: of using neither clothes nor household furniture except what is of our own growth and manufacture; of utterly rejecting the materials and instruments that promote foreign luxury: of curing the expensiveness of pride, vanity, idleness, and gaming in our women: of introducing a vein of parsimony, prudence, and temperance: of learning to love our country, in the want of which we differ even from Laplanders and the inhabitants of Topinamboo: of quitting our animosities and factions, nor acting any longer like the Jews, who were murdering one another at the very moment their city was taken: of being a little cautious not to sell our country and conscience for nothing: of teaching landlords to have at least one degree of mercy toward their tenants: lastly, of putting a spirit of honesty, industry, and skill into our shopkeepers; who, if a resolution could now be taken to buy only our native goods, would immediately unite to cheat and exact upon us in the price, the measure, and the goodness, nor could ever yet be brought to make one fair proposal of just dealing, though often and earnestly invited to it.

30   Therefore I repeat, let no man talk to me of these and the like expedients, till he hath at least some glimpse of hope that there will ever be some hearty and sincere attempt to put them in practice.

31   But as to myself, having been wearied out for many years with offering vain, idle, visionary thoughts, and at length utterly despairing of success, I fortunately fell upon this proposal, which, as it is wholly new, so it hath something solid and real, of no expense and little

trouble, full in our own power, and whereby we can incur no danger in disobliging England. For this kind of commodity will not bear exportation, the flesh being of too tender a consistence to admit a long continuance in salt, although perhaps I could name a country which would be glad to eat up our whole nation without it.

After all, I am not so violently bent upon my own opinion as to   32
reject any offer proposed by wise men, which shall be found equally innocent, cheap, easy, and effectual. But before something of that kind shall be advanced in contradiction to my scheme, and offering a better, I desire the author or authors will be pleased maturely to consider two points. First, as things now stand, how they will be able to find food and raiment for an hundred thousand useless mouths and backs. And secondly, there being a round million of creatures in human figure throughout this kingdom, whose sole subsistence put into a common stock would leave them in debt two millions of pounds sterling, adding those who are beggars by profession to the bulk of farmers, cottagers, and laborers, with their wives and children who are beggars in effect; I desire those politicians who dislike my overture, and may perhaps be so bold to attempt an answer, that they will first ask the parents of these mortals whether they would not at this day think it a great happiness to have been sold for food at a year old in this manner I prescribe, and thereby have avoided such a perpetual scene of misfortunes as they have since gone through by the oppression of landlords, the impossibility of paying rent without money or trade, the want of common sustenance, with neither house nor clothes to cover them from the inclemencies of the weather, and the most inevitable prospect of entailing the like or greater miseries upon their breed forever.

I profess, in the sincerity of my heart, that I have not the least   33
personal interest in endeavoring to promote this necessary work, having no other motive than the public good of my country, by advancing our trade, providing for infants, relieving the poor, and giving some pleasure to the rich. I have no children by which I can propose to get a single penny; the youngest being nine years old, and my wife past childbearing.

___ **CONSIDERATIONS** _____

1. The biggest risk a satirist runs is that his reader will not understand that he is reading satire; that he will be too literal-minded. Can you imagine a reader missing the satiric nature of Swift's "A Modest Proposal"? It has

happened many times. What might such a reader think of the author? Consider the same problem with regard to Ambrose Bierce (pages 59–62), Mark Twain (pages 421–425), or Flannery O'Connor in her short story "A Good Man Is Hard to Find" (pages 283–297).

2. One clue to the satire is Swift's choice of diction in certain passages. In Paragraph 4, for example, note the phrase, "just dropped from its dam," in reference to a newborn child. How do these words make a sign to the reader? Look for other such words.

3. What words and phrases does Swift use to give the impression of straightforward seriousness?

4. How does Swift turn his satirical talent against religious intolerance?

5. What is the chief target of his satire toward the end of the essay?

6. If you have read Swift's *Gulliver's Travels* only in the version usually offered to children, you are in for a surprise when you read the complete, unexpurgated *Gulliver's Travels*, a devastating satire of British political, moral, and religious values.

*Studs Terkel (b. 1912) has been an actor on stage and televi-
sion, and has conducted a successful radio interview show in
Chicago. His best known books, collections of interviews, are*
Division Street America *(1966),* Hard Times *(1970), and* Working
*(1974) — from which we take this example of American speech.
In 1977, he published* Talking to Myself, *his autobiography.*

68

STUDS TERKEL

Phil Stallings, Spot Welder

He is a spot-welder at the Ford assembly plant on the far South 1
*Side of Chicago. He is twenty-seven years old; recently married. He
works the third shift: 3:30 P.M. to midnight.*

"I start the automobile, the first welds. From there it goes to 2
*another line, where the floor's put on, the roof, the trunk hood, the
doors. Then it's put on a frame. There is hundreds of lines.*

"The welding gun's got a square handle, with a button on the 3
*top for high voltage and a button on the bottom for low. The first is to
clamp the metal together. The second is to fuse it.*

"The gun hangs from a ceiling, over tables that ride on a track. 4
*It travels in a circle, oblong, like an egg. You stand on a cement
platform, maybe six inches from the ground."*

I stand in one spot, about two- or three-feet area, all night. The 5
only time a person stops is when the line stops. We do about thirty-
two jobs per car, per unit. Forty-eight units an hour, eight hours a day.

From *Working: People Talk about What They Do All Day and How They Feel
about What They Do,* by Studs Terkel. Copyright © 1972, 1974 by Studs Terkel.
Reprinted by permission of Pantheon Books, a Division of Random House, Inc.

Thirty-two times forty-eight times eight. Figure it out. That's how many times I push that button.

6   The noise, oh it's tremendous. You open your mouth and you're liable to get a mouthful of sparks. (Shows his arms.) That's a burn, these are burns. You don't compete against the noise. You go to yell and at the same time you're straining to maneuver the gun to where you have to weld.

7   You got some guys that are uptight, and they're not sociable. It's too rough. You pretty much stay to yourself. You get involved with yourself. You dream, you think of things you've done. I drift back continuously to when I was a kid and what me and my brothers did. The things you love most are the things you drift back into.

8   Lots of times I worked from the time I started to the time of the break and I never realized I had even worked. When you dream, you reduce the chances of friction with the foreman or with the next guy.

9   It don't stop. It just goes and goes and goes. I bet there's men who have lived and died out there, never seen the end of that line. And they never will — because it's endless. It's like a serpent. It's just all body, no tail. It can do things to you . . . (Laughs.)

10   Repetition is such that if you were to think about the job itself, you'd slowly go out of your mind. You'd let your problems build up, you'd get to a point where you'd be at the fellow next to you — his throat. Every time the foreman came by and looked at you, you'd have something to say. You just strike out at anything you can. So if you involve yourself by yourself, you overcome this.

11   I don't like the pressure, the intimidation. How would you like to go up to someone and say, "I would like to go to the bathroom?" If the foreman doesn't like you, he'll make you hold it, just ignore you. Should I leave this job to go to the bathroom I risk being fired. The line moves all the time.

12   I work next to Jim Grayson and he's preoccupied. The guy on my left, he's a Mexican, speaking Spanish, so it's pretty hard to understand him. You just avoid him. Brophy, he's a young fella, he's going to college. He works catty-corner from me. Him and I talk from time to time. If he ain't in the mood, I don't talk. If I ain't in the mood, he knows it.

13   Oh sure, there's tension here. It's not always obvious, but the whites stay with the whites and the coloreds stay with the coloreds. When you go into Ford, Ford says, "Can you work with other men?" This stops a lot of trouble, 'cause when you're working side by side with a guy, they can't afford to have guys fighting. When two men

don't socialize, that means two guys are gonna do more work, know what I mean?

I don't understand how come more guys don't flip. Because 14 you're nothing more than a machine when you hit this type of thing. They give better care to that machine than they will to you. They'll have more respect, give more attention to that machine. And you *know* this. Somehow you get the feeling that the machine is better than you are. (Laughs.)

You really begin to wonder. What price do they put on me? Look 15 at the price they put on the machine. If that machine breaks down, there's somebody out there to fix it right away. If I break down, I'm just pushed over to the other side till another man takes my place. The only thing they have on their mind is to keep that line running.

I'll do the best I can. I believe in an eight-hour pay for an eight- 16 hour day. But I will not try to outreach my limits. If I can't cut it, I just don't do it. I've been there three years and I keep my nose pretty clean. I never cussed anybody or anything like that. But I've had some real brushes with foremen.

What happened was my job was overloaded. I got cut and it got 17 infected. I got blood poisoning. The drill broke. I took it to the foreman's desk. I says, "Change this as soon as you can." We were running specials for XL hoods. I told him I wasn't a repair man. That's how the conflict began. I says, "If you want, take me to the Green House." Which is a superintendent's office — disciplinary station. This is when he says, "Guys like you I'd like to see in the parking lot."

One foreman I know, he's about the youngest out here, he has 18 this idea: I'm it and if you don't like it, you know what you can do. Anything this other foreman says, he usually overrides. Even in some cases, the foremen don't get along. They're pretty hard to live with, even with each other.

Oh yeah, the foreman's got somebody knuckling down on him, 19 putting the screws to him. But a foreman is still free to go to the bathroom, go get a cup of coffee. He doesn't face the penalties. When I first went in there, I kind of envied foremen. Now, I wouldn't have a foreman's job. I wouldn't give 'em the time of the day.

When a man becomes a foreman, he has to forget about even 20 being human, as far as feelings are concerned. You see a guy there bleeding to death. So what, buddy? That line's gotta keep goin'. I can't live like that. To me, if a man gets hurt, first thing you do is get him some attention.

About the blood poisoning. It came from the inside of a hood 21 rubbin' against me. It caused quite a bit of pain. I went down to the medics. They said it was a boil. Got to my doctor that night. He said blood poisoning. Running fever and all this. Now I've smartened up.

22   They have a department of medics. It's basically first aid. There's no doctor on our shift, just two or three nurses, that's it. They've got a door with a sign on it that says Lab. Another door with a sign on it: Major Surgery. But my own personal opinion, I'm afraid of 'em. I'm afraid if I were to get hurt, I'd get nothin' but back talk. I got hit square in the chest one day with a bar from a rack and it cut me down this side. They didn't take x-rays or nothing. Sent me back on the job. I missed three and a half days two weeks ago. I had bronchitis. They told me I was all right. I didn't have a fever. I went home and my doctor told me I couldn't go back to work for two weeks. I really needed the money, so I had to go back the next day. I woke up still sick, so I took off the rest of the week.

23   I pulled a muscle on my neck, straining. This gun, when you grab this thing from the ceiling, cable, weight, I mean you're pulling every- thing. Your neck, your shoulders, and your back. I'm very surprised more accidents don't happen. You have to lean over, at the same time holding down the gun. This whole edge here is sharp. I go through a shirt every two weeks, it just goes right through. My coveralls catch on fire. I've had gloves catch on fire. (Indicates arms.) See them little holes? That's what sparks do. I've got burns across here from last night.

24   I know I could find better places to work. But where could I get the money I'm making? Let's face it, $4.32 an hour. That's real good money now. Funny thing is, I don't mind working at body construc- tion. To a great degree, I enjoy it. I love using my hands — more than I do my mind. I love to be able to put things together and see some- thing in the long run. I'll be the first to admit I've got the easiest job on the line. But I'm against this thing where I'm being held back. I'll work like a dog until I get what I want. The job I really want is utility.

25   It's where I can stand and say I can do any job in this department, and nobody has to worry about me. As it is now, out of say, sixty jobs, I can do almost half of 'em. I want to get away from standing in one spot. Utility can do a different job every day. Instead of working right there for eight hours I could work over there for eight, I could work the other place for eight. Every day it would change. I would be around more people. I go out on my lunch break and work on the fork truck for a half-hour — to get the experience. As soon as I got it down pretty good, the foreman in charge says he'll take me. I don't want the other

guys to see me. When I hit that fork lift, you just stop your thinking and you concentrate. Something right there in front of you, not in the past, not in the future. This is real healthy.

I don't eat lunch at work. I may grab a candy bar, that's enough. I wouldn't be able to hold it down. The tension your body is put under by the speed of the line . . . When you hit them brakes, you just can't stop. There's a certain momentum that carries you forward. I could hold the food, but it wouldn't set right.

Proud of my work? How can I feel pride in a job where I call a foreman's attention to a mistake, a bad piece of equipment, and he'll ignore it. Pretty soon you get the idea they don't care. You keep doing this and finally you're titled a troublemaker. So you just go about your work. You *have* to have pride. So you throw it off to something else. And that's my stamp collection.

I'd break both my legs to get into social work. I see all over so many kids really gettin' a raw deal. I think I'd go into juvenile. I tell kids on the line, "Man, go out there and get that college." Because it's too late for me now.

When you go into Ford, first thing they try to do is break your spirit. I seen them bring a tall guy where they needed a short guy. I seen them bring a short guy where you have to stand on two guys' backs to do something. Last night, they brought a fifty-eight-year-old man to do the job I was on. That man's my father's age. I know damn well my father couldn't do it. To me, this is humanely wrong. A job should be a job, not a death sentence.

The younger worker, when he gets uptight, he talks back. But you take an old fellow, he's got a year, two years, maybe three years to go. If it was me, I wouldn't say a word, I wouldn't care what they did. 'Cause, baby, for another two years I can stick it out. I can't blame this man. I respect him because he had enough will power to stick it out for thirty years.

It's gonna change. There's a trend. We're getting younger and younger men. We got this new Thirty and Out. Thirty years seniority and out. The whole idea is to give a man more time, more time to slow down and live. While he's still in his fifties, he can settle down in a camper and go out and fish. I've sat down and thought about it. I've got twenty-seven years to go. (Laughs.) That's why I don't go around causin' trouble or lookin' for a cause.

The only time I get involved is when it affects me or it affects a man on the line in a condition that could be me. I don't believe in lost causes, but when it all happened . . . (He pauses, appears bewildered.)

33   The foreman was riding the guy. The guy either told him to go away or pushed him, grabbed him . . . You can't blame the guy — Jim Grayson. I don't want nobody stickin' their finger in my face. I'd've probably hit him beside the head. The whole thing was: Damn it, it's about time we took a stand. Let's stick up for the guy. We stopped the line. (He pauses, grins.) Ford lost about twenty units. I'd figure about five grand a unit — whattaya got? (Laughs.)

34   I said, "Let's all go home." When the line's down like that, you can go up to one man and say, "You gonna work?" If he says no, they can fire him. See what I mean? But if nobody was there, who the hell were they gonna walk up to and say, "Are you gonna work?" Man, there woulda been nobody there! If it were up to me, we'd gone home.

35   Jim Grayson, the guy I work next to, he's colored. Absolutely. That's the first time I've seen unity on that line. Now it's happened once, it'll happen again. Because everybody just sat down. Believe you me. (Laughs.) It stopped at eight and it didn't start till twenty after eight. Everybody and his brother were down there. It was really nice to see, it really was.

____ **CONSIDERATIONS** _____

1. Terkel is famous for his ability to catch the voice of the people he interviews. Study the language of Phil Stallings and list some of the features of his voice.

2. In addition to diction, what about this selection takes it out of the category of "essay"?

3. How does Stallings show that the company puts a higher value on its machines than on its men?

4. Does Stallings agree with what Caroline Bird says in her essay on the value of college (pages 64–73)?

5. What occurrence on the line, described toward the end of the interview, reveals Stallings's social consciousness?

6. Interview someone you find interesting, or, if you're too shy, some imaginary character.

Lewis Thomas (b. 1913) received his M.D. from Harvard Medical School in 1937, and since 1973 has headed the Memorial Sloan-Kettering Cancer Center in New York City. In 1971 he began to contribute meticulous essays to the New England Journal of Medicine, *since collected in* The Lives of a Cell *(1974) and* The Medusa and the Snail *(1979), from which we take this physician's elegant observations on punctuation.*

69

LEWIS THOMAS
Notes on Punctuation

There are no precise rules about punctuation (Fowler lays out some general advice (as best he can under the complex circumstances of English prose (he points out, for example, that we possess only four stops (the comma, the semicolon, the colon and the period (the question mark and exclamation point are not, strictly speaking, stops; they are indicators of tone (oddly enough, the Greeks employed the semicolon for their question mark (it produces a strange sensation to read a Greek sentence which is a straightforward question: Why weepest thou; (instead of Why weepest thou? (and, of course, there are parentheses (which are surely a kind of punctuation making this whole matter much more complicated by having to count up the left-handed parentheses in order to be sure of closing with the right number (but if the parentheses were left out, with nothing to work with but the stops, we would have considerably more flexibility in the deploying of layers of meaning than if we tried to separate all the clauses by physical barriers (and in the latter case, while we might have more precision

1

and exactitude for our meaning, we would lose the essential flavor of language, which is its wonderful ambiguity))))))))))))).

2   The commas are the most useful and usable of all the stops. It is highly important to put them in place as you go along. If you try to come back after doing a paragraph and stick them in the various spots that tempt you you will discover that they tend to swarm like minnows into all sorts of crevices whose existence you hadn't realized and before you know it the whole long sentence becomes immobilized and lashed up squirming in commas. Better to use them sparingly, and with affection, precisely when the need for each one arises, nicely, by itself.

3   I have grown fond of semicolons in recent years. The semicolon tells you that there is still some question about the preceding full sentence; something needs to be added; it reminds you sometimes of the Greek usage. It is almost always a greater pleasure to come across a semicolon than a period. The period tells you that that is that; if you didn't get all the meaning you wanted or expected, anyway you got all the writer intended to parcel out and now you have to move along. But with a semicolon there you get a pleasant little feeling of expectancy; there is more to come; read on; it will get clearer.

4   Colons are a lot less attractive, for several reasons: firstly, they give you the feeling of being rather ordered around, or at least having your nose pointed in a direction you might not be inclined to take if left to yourself, and, secondly, you suspect you're in for one of those sentences that will be labeling the points to be made: firstly, secondly and so forth, with the implication that you haven't sense enough to keep track of a sequence of notions without having them numbered. Also, many writers use this system loosely and incompletely, starting out with number one and number two as though counting off on their fingers but then going on and on without the succession of labels you've been led to expect, leaving you floundering about searching for the ninthly or seventeenthly that ought to be there but isn't.

5   Exclamation points are the most irritating of all. Look! they say, look at what I just said! How amazing is my thought! It is like being forced to watch someone else's small child jumping up and down crazily in the center of the living room shouting to attract attention. If a sentence really has something of importance to say, something quite remarkable, it doesn't need a mark to point it out. And if it is really, after all, a banal sentence needing more zing, the exclamation point simply emphasizes its banality!

6   Quotation marks should be used honestly and sparingly, when

there is a genuine quotation at hand, and it is necessary to be very rigorous about the words enclosed by the marks. If something is to be quoted, the *exact* words must be used. If part of it must be left out because of space limitations, it is good manners to insert three dots to indicate the omission, but it is unethical to do this if it means connecting two thoughts which the original author did not intend to have tied together. Above all, quotation marks should not be used for ideas that you'd like to disown, things in the air so to speak. Nor should they be put in place around clichés; if you want to use a cliché you must take full responsibility for it yourself and not try to job it off on anon., or on society. The most objectionable misuse of quotation marks, but one which illustrates the dangers of misuse in ordinary prose, is seen in advertising, especially in advertisements for small restaurants, for example "just around the corner," or "a good place to eat." No single, identifiable, citable person every really said, for the record, "just around the corner," much less "a good place to eat," least likely of all for restaurants of the type that use this type of prose.

The dash is a handy device, informal and essentially playful, 7 telling you that you're about to take off on a different tack but still in some way connected with the present course — only you have to remember that the dash is there, and either put a second dash at the end of the notion to let the reader know that he's back on course, or else end the sentence, as here, with a period.

The greatest danger in punctuation is for poetry. Here it is nec- 8 essary to be as economical and parsimonious with commas and periods as with the words themselves, and any marks that seem to carry their own subtle meanings, like dashes and little rows of periods, even semicolons and question marks, should be left out altogether rather than inserted to clog up the thing with ambiguity. A single exclamation point in a poem, no matter what else the poem has to say, is enough to destroy the whole work.

The things I like best in T. S. Eliot's poetry, especially in the 9 *Four Quartets*, are the semicolons. You cannot hear them, but they are there, laying out the connections between the images and the ideas. Sometimes you get a glimpse of a semicolon coming, a few lines farther on, and it is like climbing a steep path through woods and seeing a wooden bench just at a bend in the road ahead, a place where you can expect to sit for a moment, catching your breath.

Commas can't do this sort of thing; they can only tell you how 10 the different parts of a complicated thought are to be fitted together, but you can't sit, not even take a breath, just because of a comma,

—— CONSIDERATIONS ——————————————

1. Why so many parentheses at the end of Thomas's first paragraph? How many are there? Why that number, precisely? What is this author up to?

2. Read Thomas's little lesson in punctuation in conjunction with James Thurber's "Which." Compare.

3. One of the blemishes in the works of beginning writers is often the faulty use of quotation marks. See Thomas's advice in Paragraph 6. Then look in newspapers, magazines, and your own papers for examples.

4. Both Thomas and Thurber allude to the best known of several available handbooks of usage: *A Dictionary of Modern English Usage,* by H. W. Fowler. It has been a trusted standby for writers through its many editions. It is also opinionated, sophisticated, and tartly amusing. Discover its worth for yourself by consulting a copy in your college library.

5. Thomas is obviously very conscious of the punctuation in this essay. It might be interesting to look at his punctuation in some of the other essays collected in *The Lives of a Cell* and *The Medusa and the Snail,* to see whether he follows his own advice.

6. Many students have commented that a humorous approach to grammar has not only proved more interesting but a surer way of learning the concept or convention involved than the customary humorless presentation. After reading Thomas and Thurber, try your hand at explaining, in a jocular way, a point of grammar that you have had some trouble with, such as pronoun reference, subject and verb agreement, dangling participles, or the like.

Henry David Thoreau (1817–1862) is one of the greatest American writers, and Walden one of the great American books. Thoreau attended Concord Academy, in the Massachusetts town where he was born and lived. Then he went to Harvard and completed his formal education, which was extensive in mathematics, literature, Greek, Latin, and French — and included smatterings of Spanish and Italian and some of the literature of India and China. He and his brother founded a school that lasted four years, and then he was a private tutor to a family. He also worked for his father, manufacturing pencils. But mostly Thoreau walked, meditated, observed nature, and wrote.

A friend of Ralph Waldo Emerson's, Thoreau was influenced by the older man, and by Transcendentalism — a doctrine that recognized the unity of man and nature. For Thoreau, an idea required testing by life itself; it never remained merely mental. In his daily work on his journals, and in the books he carved from them — A Week on the Concord and Merrimack Rivers (1849) as well as Walden (1854) — he observed the detail of daily life, human and natural, and he speculated on the universal laws he could derive from this observation.

The paragraphs below come from Walden, the book Thoreau wrote about his experience of living by himself, alone in the natural world, on the shores of Walden Pond in Concord. He had resolved — this civilized man of the nineteenth century, learned and cultured and educated — "to drive life into a corner, and reduce it to its lowest terms, and, if it be proven to be mean, why then to get the whole and genuine meanness of it, and publish its meanness to the world; and if it were sublime, to know it by experience, and be able to give a true account of it."

"To know it by experience, and be able to give a true account of it" — these words could be carved on Thoreau's gravestone. "To give a true account" he became a great writer, a master in particular of the long, inclusive sentence, which, built of many descriptive phrases and subordinate clauses, controls the position of observed detail, and sets the parts of a world in clear relation to each other.

70

HENRY DAVID THOREAU
To Build My House

1   Near the end of March, 1845, I borrowed an axe and went down to the woods by Walden Pond, nearest to where I intended to build my house, and began to cut down some tall arrowy white pines, still in their youth, for timber. It is difficult to begin without borrowing, but perhaps it is the most generous course thus to permit your fellow-men to have an interest in your enterprise. The owner of the axe, as he released his hold on it, said that it was the apple of his eye; but I returned it sharper than I received it. It was a pleasant hillside where I worked, covered with pine woods, through which I looked out on the pond, and a small open field in the woods where pines and hickories were springing up. The ice in the pond was all dark colored and saturated with water. There were some slight flurries of snow during the days that I worked there; but for the most part when I came out on to the railroad, on my way home, its yellow sand heap stretched away gleaming in the hazy atmosphere, and the rails shone in the spring sun, and I heard the lark and pewee and other birds already come to commence another year with us. They were pleasant spring days, in which the winter of man's discontent was thawing as well as the earth, and the life that had lain torpid began to stretch itself. One day, when my axe had come off and I had cut a green hickory for a wedge, driving it with a stone, and had placed the whole to soak in a pond hole in order to swell the wood, I saw a striped snake run into the water, and he lay on the bottom, apparently without inconvenience, as long as I staid there, or more than a quarter of an hour, perhaps because he had not yet fairly come out of the torpid state. It appeared to me that for a like reason men remain in their present low and primitive condition; but if they should feel the influence of the spring of springs arousing them, they would of necessity rise to a higher and

408

more ethereal life. I had previously seen the snakes in frosty mornings in my path with portions of their bodies still numb and inflexible, waiting for the sun to thaw them. On the 1st of April it rained and melted the ice, and in the early part of the day, which was very foggy, I heard a stray goose groping about over the pond and cackling as if lost, or like the spirit of the fog.

So I went on for some days cutting and hewing timber, and also 2 studs and rafters, all with my narrow axe, not having many communicable or scholar-like thoughts, singing to myself —

> Men say they know many things;
> But lo! they have taken wings, —
> The arts and sciences,
> And a thousand appliances;
> The wind that blows
> Is all that any body knows.

I hewed the main timbers six inches square, most of the studs on two sides only, and the rafters and floor timbers on one side, leaving the rest of the bark on, so that they were just as straight and much stronger than sawed ones. Each stick was carefully mortised or tenoned by its stump, for I had borrowed other tools by this time. My days in the woods were not very long ones; yet I usually carried my dinner of bread and butter, and read the newspaper in which it was wrapped, at noon, sitting amid the green pine boughs which I had cut off, and to my bread was imparted some of their fragrance, for my hands were covered with a thick coat of pitch. Before I had done I was more the friend than the foe of the pine tree, though I had cut down some of them, having become better acquainted with it. Sometimes a rambler in the wood was attracted by the sound of my axe, and we chatted pleasantly over the chips which I had made.

By the middle of April, for I made no haste in my work, but rather 3 made the most of it, my house was framed and ready for the raising. I had already bought the shanty of James Collins, an Irishman who worked on the Fitchburg Railroad, for boards. James Collins' shanty was considered an uncommonly fine one. When I called to see it he was not at home. I walked about the outside, at first unobserved from within, the window was so deep and high. It was of small dimensions, with a peaked cottage roof, and not much else to be seen, the dirt being raised five feet all around as if it were a compost heap. The roof was the soundest part, though a good deal warped and made brittle by the sun. Doorsill there was none, but a perennial passage for the hens

under the door board. Mrs. C. came to the door and asked me to view
it from the inside. The hens were driven in by my approach. It was
dark, and had a dirt floor for the most part, dank, clammy, and aguish,
only here a board and there a board which would not bear removal.
She lighted a lamp to show me the inside of the roof and the walls,
and also that the board floor extended under the bed, warning me not
to step into the cellar, a sort of dust hole two feet deep. In her own
words, they were "good boards overhead, good boards all around and a
good window," — of two whole squares originally, only the cat had
passed out that way lately. There was a stove, a bed, and a place to sit,
an infant in the house where it was born, a silk parasol, gilt-framed
looking-glass, and patent new coffee mill nailed to an oak sapling, all
told. The bargain was soon concluded, for James had in the meanwhile
returned. I to pay four dollars and twenty-five cents tonight, he to
vacate at five tomorrow morning, selling to nobody else meanwhile: I
to take possession at six. It were well, he said, to be there early, and
anticipate certain indistinct but wholly unjust claims on the score of
ground rent and fuel. This he assured me was the only encumbrance.
At six I passed him and his family on the road. One large bundle held
their all, — bed, coffee-mill, looking glass, hens, — all but the cat, she
took to the woods and became a wild cat, and, as I learned afterward,
trod in a trap set for woodchucks, and so became a dead cat at last.

4   I took down this dwelling the same morning, drawing the nails,
and removed it to the pond side by small cart-loads, spreading the
boards on the grass there to bleach and warp back again in the sun.
One early thrush gave me a note or two as I drove along the woodland
path. I was informed treacherously by a young Patrick that neighbor
Seeley, an Irishman, in the intervals of the carting, transferred the still
tolerable, straight, and drivable nails, staples, and spikes to his pocket
and then stood when I came back to pass the time of day, and look
freshly up, unconcerned, with spring thoughts, at the devastation;
there being a dearth of work, as he said. He was there to represent
spectatordom, and help make this seemingly insignificant event one
with the removal of the gods of Troy.

5   I dug my cellar in the side of a hill sloping to the south, where a
woodchuck had formerly dug his burrow, down through sumach and
blackberry roots, and the lowest stain of vegetation, six feet square by
seven deep, to a fine sand where potatoes would not freeze in any
winter. The sides were left shelving, and not stoned; but the sun having never shone on them, the sand still keeps its place. It was but two
hours' work. I took particular pleasure in this breaking of ground, for

in almost all latitudes men dig into the earth for an equable temperature. Under the most splendid house in the city is still to be found the
cellar where they store their roots as of old, and long after the superstructure has disappeared posterity remark its dent in the earth. The
house is still but a sort of porch at the entrance of a burrow.

At length, in the beginning of May, with the help of some of my   6
acquaintances, rather to improve so good an occasion for neighborli-
ness than from any necessity, I set up the frame of my house. No man
was ever more honored in the character of his raisers than I. They are
destined, I trust, to assist at the raising of loftier structures one day. I
began to occupy my house on the 4th of July, as soon as it was boarded
and roofed, for the boards were carefully feather-edged and lapped, so
that it was perfectly impervious to rain; but before boarding I laid the
foundation of a chimney at one end, bringing two cartloads of stones
up the hill from the pond in my arms. I built the chimney after my
hoeing in the fall, before a fire became necessary for warmth, doing
my cooking in the mean while out of doors on the ground, early in the
morning: which mode I still think is in some respects more convenient and agreeable than the usual one. When it stormed before my
bread was baked, I fixed a few boards over the fire, and sat under them
to watch my loaf, and passed some pleasant hours in that way. In
those days, when my hands were much employed, I read but little, but
the least scraps of paper which lay on the ground, my holder, or table-
cloth, afforded me as much entertainment, in fact answered the same
purpose as the Iliad.

It would be worth the while to build still more deliberately than   7
I did, considering, for instance, what foundation a door, a window, a
cellar, a garret, have in the nature of man, and perchance never raising
any superstructure until we found a better reason for it than our tem-
poral necessities even. There is some of the same fitness in a man's
building his own house that there is in a bird's building its own nest.
Who knows but if men constructed their dwellings with their own
hands, and provided food for themselves and families simply and honestly enough, the poetic faculty would be universally developed, as
birds universally sing when they are so engaged? But alas! we do like
cowbirds and cuckoos, which lay their eggs in nests which other birds
have built, and cheer no traveller with their chattering and unmusical
notes. Shall we forever resign the pleasure of construction to the carpenter? What does architecture amount to in the experience of the
mass of men? I never in all my walks came across a man engaged in so

simple and natural an occupation as building his house. We belong to the community. It is not the tailor alone who is the ninth part of a man, it is as much the preacher, and the merchant, and the farmer. Where is this division of labor to end? and what object does it finally serve? No doubt another *may* also think for me; but it is not therefore desirable that he should do so to the exclusion of my thinking for myself.

8   True, there are architects so called in this country, and I have heard of one at least possessed with the idea of making architectural ornaments have a core of truth, a necessity, and hence a beauty, as if it were a revelation to him. All very well perhaps from his point of view, but only a little better than the common dilettantism. A sentimental reformer in architecture, he began at the cornice, not at the foundation. It was only how to put a core of truth within the ornaments, that every sugar plum in fact might have an almond or caraway seed in it, — though I hold that almonds are most wholesome without the sugar — and not how the inhabitant, the indweller, might build truly within and without, and let the ornaments take care of themselves. What reasonable man ever supposed that ornaments were something outward and in the skin merely, — that the tortoise got his spotted shell, or the shellfish its mother-o'-pearl tints by such a contract as the inhabitants of Broadway their Trinity Church? But a man has no more to do with the style of architecture of his house than a tortoise with that of its shell: nor need the soldier be so idle as to try to paint the precise *color* of his virtue on his standard. The enemy will find it out. He may turn pale when the trial comes. This man seemed to me to lean over the cornice, and timidly whisper his half truth to the rude occupants who really knew it better than he. What of architectural beauty I now see, I know has gradually grown from within outward, out of the necessities and character of the indweller, who is the only builder — out of some unconscious truthfulness, and nobleness, without ever a thought for the appearance; and whatever additional beauty of this kind is destined to be produced will be preceded by a like unconscious beauty of life. The most interesting dwellings in this country, as the painter knows, are the most unpretending, humble log huts and cottages of the poor commonly; it is the life of the inhabitants whose shells they are, and not any peculiarity in their surfaces, merely, which makes them *picturesque*; and equally interesting will be the citizen's suburban box, when his life shall be as simple and as agreeable to the imagination, and there is as little straining after effect in the style of his dwelling. A great proportion of archi-

tectural ornaments are literally hollow, and a September gale would strip them off, like borrowed plumes, without injury to the substantials. They can do without *architecture* who have no olives nor wines in the cellar. What if an equal ado were made about the ornaments of style in literature, and the architects of our bibles spent as much time about their cornices as the architects of our churches do? So are made the *belles-lettres* and the *beaux-arts* and their professors. Much it concerns a man, forsooth, how a few sticks are slanted over him or under him and what colors are daubed upon his box. It would signify somewhat, if, in any earnest sense, *he* slanted them and daubed it; but the spirit having departed out of the tenant, it is of a piece with constructing his own coffin, — the architecture of the grave, and "carpenter," is but another name for "coffin-maker." One man says, in his despair or indifference to life, take up handful of the earth at your feet, and paint your house that color. Is he thinking of his last and narrow house? Toss up a copper for it as well. What an abundance of leisure he must have! Why do you take up a handful of dirt? Better paint your house your own complexion; let it turn pale or blush for you. An enterprise to improve the style of cottage architecture! When you have got my ornaments ready I will wear them.

Before winter I built a chimney, and shingled the sides of my 9 house, which were already impervious to rain, with imperfect and sappy shingles made of the first slice of the log, whose edges I was obliged to straighten with a plane.

I have thus a tight shingled and plastered house, ten feet wide by 10 fifteen long, and eight-feet posts, with a garret and a closet, a large window on each side, two trap doors, one door at the end, and a brick fireplace opposite. The exact cost of my house, paying the usual price for such materials as I used, but not counting the work, all of which was done by myself, was as follows; and I give the details because very few are able to tell exactly what their houses cost, and fewer still, if any, the separate cost of the various materials which compose them: —

Boards	$8 03½, mostly shanty boards.
Refuse shingles for roof and sides,	4 00
Laths,	1 25
Two second-hand windows with glass,	2 43

One thousand old brick,	4 00	
Two casks of lime,	2 40	That was high.
Hair,	0 31	More than I needed.
Mantle-tree iron,	0 15	
Nails,	3 90	
Hinges and screws,	0 14	
Latch,	0 10	
Chalk,	0 01	
Transportation,	1 40	I carried a good part on my back.
In all,	$28 12½	

11   These are all the materials excepting the timber, stones and sand, which I claimed by squatter's right. I have also a small wood-shed adjoining made chiefly of the stuff which was left after building the house.

12   I intend to build me a house which will surpass any on the main street in Concord in grandeur and luxury, as soon as it pleases me as much and will cost me no more than my present one.

13   I thus found that the student who wishes for a shelter can obtain one for a lifetime at an expense not greater than the rent which he now pays annually. If I seem to boast more than is becoming, my excuse is that I brag for humanity rather than for myself; and my shortcomings and inconsistencies do not affect the truth of my statement. Notwithstanding much cant and hypocrisy, — chaff which I find it difficult to separate from my wheat, but for which I am sorry as any man, — I will breathe freely and stretch myself in this respect, it is such a relief to both the moral and physical system; and I am resolved that I will not through humility become the devil's attorney. I will endeavor to speak a good word for the truth. At Cambridge College the mere rent of a student's room, which is only a little larger than my own, is thirty dollars each year, though the corporation had the advantage of building thirty-two side by side and under one roof, and the occupant suffers the inconvenience of many and noisy neighbors, and perhaps a residence in the fourth story. I cannot but think that if we had more true wisdom in these respects, not only less education would be needed, because, forsooth, more would already have been acquired, but the pecuniary expense of getting an education would in a great measure vanish. Those conveniences which the stu-

dent requires at Cambridge or elsewhere cost him or somebody else ten times as great a sacrifice of life as they would with proper management on both sides. Those things for which the most money is demanded are never the things which the student most wants. Tuition, for instance, is an important item in the term bill, while for the far more valuable education which he gets by associating with the most cultivated of his contemporaries no charge is made. The mode of founding a college is, commonly, to get up a subscription of dollars, and cents, and then following blindly the principles of a division of labor to its extreme, a principle which should never be followed but with circumspection, — to call in a contractor who makes this a subject of speculation, and he employs Irishmen or other operatives actually to lay the foundation, while the students that are to be are said to be fitting themselves for it; and for these oversights successive generations have to pay. I think that it would be *better than this*, for the students, or those who desire to be benefited by it, even to lay the foundation themselves. The student who secures his coveted leisure and retirement by systematically shirking any labor necessary to man obtains but an ignoble and unprofitable leisure, defrauding himself of the experience which alone can make leisure fruitful. "But," says one, "you do not mean that the students should go to work with their hands instead of their heads?" I do not mean that exactly, but I mean something which he might think a good deal like that; I mean that they should not *play* life, or *study* it merely, while the community supports them at this expensive game, but earnestly *live* it from beginning to end. How could youths better learn to live than by at once trying the experiment of living? Methinks this would exercise their minds as much as mathematics. If I wished a boy to know something about the arts and sciences, for instance, I would not pursue the common course, which is merely to send him into the neighborhood of some professor, where any thing is professed and practised but the art of life; — to survey the world through a telescope or a microscope, and never with his natural eye; to study chemistry, and not learn how his bread is made, or mechanics, and not learn how it is earned; to discover new satellites to Neptune, and not detect the motes in his eyes, or to what vagabond he is a satellite himself; or to be devoured by the monsters that swarm all around him, while contemplating the monsters in a drop of vinegar. Which would have advanced the most at the end of a month, — the boy who had made his own jackknife from the ore which he had dug and smelted, reading as much as would be necessary for this, — or the boy who had attended the lectures on metallurgy at the Institute in the mean while, and had received a Rogers' penknife from his father? Which would be most likely to cut his fingers? . . . To my astonishment I was informed on leaving college that I had studied navigation! — why, if I had taken one turn down the harbor I should have known more about it. Even the *poor* student studies and is taught only *political* economy, while that economy of living which is synonymous with philosophy is not even sincerely professed in our colleges. The consequence is, that while he is reading Adam Smith, Ricardo, and Say, he runs his father in debt irretrievably.

14   As with our colleges, so with a hundred "modern improvements"; there is an illusion about them; there is not always a positive advance. The devil goes on exacting compound interest to the last for his early share and numerous succeeding investments in them. Our inventions are wont to be pretty toys, which distract our attention from serious things. They are but too improved means to an improved end, an end which was already but too easy to arrive at; as railroads lead to Boston or New York. We are in great haste to construct a magnetic telegraph from Maine to Texas; but Maine and Texas, it may be, have nothing important to communicate. Either is in such a predicament as the man who was earnest to be introduced to a distinguished deaf woman, but when he was presented, and one end of her ear trumpet was put into his hand, had nothing to say. As if the main object were to talk fast and not to talk sensibly. We are eager to tunnel under the Atlantic and bring the old world some weeks nearer to the new; but perchance the first news that will leak through into the broad flapping American ear will be that the Princess Adelaide has the whooping cough. After all, the man whose horse trots a mile in a minute does not carry the most important messages; he is not an evangelist, nor does he come round eating locusts and wild honey. I doubt if Flying Childers[1] ever carried a peck of corn to mill.

_____ CONSIDERATIONS _____

1. Like many of his contemporaries, Thoreau kept extensive journals and from these culled prized sentences upon which he built many paragraphs, essays, and portions of books, including *Walden*. In this selection from *Wal-*

---

[1] According to Walter Harding, secretary of the Thoreau Society, Flying Childers was a famous race horse in eighteenth-century England, owned by a Mr. Childers of Carr House, and reputed to have been able to run a mile in one minute. — ED.

den, pick three or four sentences you think especially memorable. Explain why they seem exceptional.

2. Thoreau's sentences are rarely short and simple, and yet they are renowned for clarity. Study an especially complex sentence and observe how he manages its several parts. Rewrite it by breaking it down into three or four short sentences. Compare and contrast the two versions.

3. Thoreau is describing a specific project — how he built his house — yet he does not hesitate to include reflections on such large subjects as human nature. Finding an example, comment on his success in combining the particular and the general. Compare with the similar effort by Don Sharp in "Under the Hood."

4. When did Thoreau move into his house? Is anything symbolic about that date and that circumstance? What do you understand by "symbolic"?

5. What did Thoreau read during the early days of his occupancy? What is his curious remark about that reading material (remember that Thoreau was a student of classical literature)?

6. Why does Thoreau give us the cost of the materials for his house? In what way does that list expose an important thematic thread that is woven through the selection?

James Thurber (1894–1961) was born in Columbus, Ohio, the scene of many of his funniest stories. He graduated from Ohio State University, and after a period as a newspaper man in Paris, began to work for The New Yorker. *For years his comic writing and his cartoons — drawings of sausage-shaped dogs and of men and women forever at battle — were fixtures of that magazine. His collections of essays, short stories, and cartoons include* The Owl in the Attic and Other Perplexities *(1931),* The Seal in the Bedroom and Other Predicaments *(1932),* My Life and Hard Times *(1933),* Men, Women, and Dogs *(1943), and* Alarms and Diversions *(1957). He also wrote an account of life on* The New Yorker *staff,* The Years with Ross *(1959).*

An elegant stylist, Thurber was always fussy about language. "Which" is an example not only of his fascination with language — which became obsessive at times — but also of his humor.

71

JAMES THURBER
Which

1   The relative pronoun "which" can cause more trouble than any other word, if recklessly used. Foolhardy persons sometimes get lost in which-clauses and are never heard of again. My distinguished contemporary, Fowler, cites several tragic cases, of which the following is one: "It was rumoured that Beaconsfield intended opening the Conference with a speech in French, his pronounciation of which language leaving everything to be desired . . ." That's as much as Mr. Fowler quotes because, at his age, he was afraid to go any farther. The young man who originally got into that sentence was never found. His fate,

however, was not as terrible as that of another adventurer who became involved in a remarkable which-mire. Fowler has followed his devious course as far as he safely could on foot: "Surely what applies to games should also apply to racing, the leaders of which being the very people from whom an example might well be looked for . . ." Not even Henry James could have successfully emerged from a sentence with "which," "whom," and "being" in it. The safest way to avoid such things is to follow in the path of the American author, Ernest Hemingway. In his youth he was trapped in a which-clause one time and barely escaped with his mind. He was going along on solid ground until he got into this: "It was the one thing of which, being very much afraid — for whom has not been warned to fear such things — he . . ." Being a young and powerfully built man, Hemingway was able to fight his way back to where he had started, and begin again. This time he skirted the treacherous morass in this way: "He was afraid of one thing. This was the one thing. He had been warned to fear such things. Everybody has been warned to fear such things." Today Hemingway is alive and well, and many happy writers are following along the trail he blazed.

What most people don't realize is that one "which" leads to another. Trying to cross a paragraph by leaping from "which" to "which" is like Eliza crossing the ice. The danger is in missing a "which" and falling in. A case in point is this: "He went up to a pew which was in the gallery, which brought him under a colored window which he loved and always quieted his spirit." The writer, worn out, missed the last "which" — the one that should come just before "always" in that sentence. But supposing he had got it in! We would have: "He went up to a pew which was in the gallery, which brought him under a colored window which he loved and which always quieted his spirit." Your inveterate whicher in this way gives the effect of tweeting like a bird or walking with a crutch, and is not welcome in the best company.

It is well to remember that one "which" leads to two and that two "whiches" multiply like rabbits. You should never start out with the idea that you can get by with one "which." Suddenly they are all around you. Take a sentence like this: "It imposes a problem which we either solve, or perish." On a hot night, or after a hard day's work, a man often lets himself get by with a monstrosity like that, but suppose he dictates that sentence bright and early in the morning. It comes to him typed out by his stenographer and he instantly senses that something is the matter with it. He tries to reconstruct the sentence, still clinging to the "which," and gets something like this: "It imposes a problem which we either solve, or which, failing to solve, we must perish on account of." He goes to the water-cooler, gets a drink, sharpens his pencil, and grimly tries again. "It imposes a problem which we either solve or which we don't solve and . . ." He begins once more: "It imposes a problem which we either solve, or which we do not solve, and from which . . ." The more times he does it the more "whiches" he gets. The way out is simple: "We must either solve this problem, or perish." Never monkey with "which." Nothing except getting tangled up in a typewriter ribbon is worse.

—— **CONSIDERATIONS** ————————————

1. James Thurber concentrates on one word from an important class of function words. These relative pronouns often complicate life for the writer wishing to write clear sentences more complex than "I see Spot. Spot is a dog. Spot sees me." What other words belong to this class? Do you find any of them tripping you up in your sentences?

2. A grammar lesson may seem a peculiar place to find humor, but humor is Thurber's habit, whatever his subject. How does he make his treatment of the relative pronoun "which" entertaining?

3. Compare Fowler's book with an American version such as Wilson Follett's *Modern American Usage.* This could lead you into a study of the concept of usage as the ultimate authority in establishing conventions of grammar, spelling, definition, and punctuation.

4. "One 'which' leads to another" is a play on the old saying, "One drink leads to another." Consider how changing one word can revive a thought that George Orwell would call a hackneyed phrase. See how it is done by substituting a key word in several familiar sayings.

5. The two writers Thurber mentions, Henry James and Ernest Hemingway, are not idly chosen. Why not?

Mark Twain is the pseudonym of Samuel Clemens (1835–1910), who wrote Tom Sawyer *(1876),* Huckleberry Finn *(1884), and other novels, as well as short stories, essays, and an autobiography. Born in Missouri, he settled with his wife in Hartford, Connecticut; at his best he wrote out of his midwestern past. Twain's humor disguised his gloom and the misanthrophy that grew in his later years. The lightness of this essay's tone only thinly covers Twain's rage and contempt. His sense of man's littleness puts Twain's vision in the modern tradition.*

72

MARK TWAIN

Was the World Made for Man?

*Alfred Russel Wallace's revival of the theory that this earth is at the centre of the stellar universe, and is the only habitable globe, has aroused great interest in the world./*LITERARY DIGEST

*For ourselves we do thoroughly believe that man, as he lives just here on this tiny earth, is in essence and possibilities the most sublime existence in all the range of non-divine being — the chief love and delight of God./Chicago "*INTERIOR*" (Presb.)*

I seem to be the only scientist and theologian still remaining to   1
be heard from on this important matter of whether the world was
made for man or not. I feel that it is time for me to speak.

I stand almost with the others. They believe the world was made   2
for man, I believe it likely that it was made for man; they think there
is proof, astronomical mainly, that it was made for man, I think there

is evidence only, not proof, that it was made for him. It is too early, yet, to arrange the verdict, the returns are not all in. When they are all in, I think they will show that the world was made for man; but we must not hurry, we must patiently wait till they are all in.

3   Now as far as we have got, astronomy is on our side. Mr. Wallace has clearly shown this. He has clearly shown two things: that the world was made for man, and that the universe was made for the world — to stiddy it, you know. The astronomy part is settled, and cannot be challenged.

4   We come now to the geological part. This is the one where the evidence is not all in, yet. It is coming in, hourly, daily, coming in all the time, but naturally it comes with geological carefulness and deliberation, and we must not be impatient, we must not get excited, we must be calm, and wait. To lose our tranquillity will not hurry geology; nothing hurries geology.

5   It takes a long time to prepare a world for man; such a thing is not done in a day. Some of the great scientists, carefully ciphering the evidences furnished by geology, have arrived at the conviction that our world is prodigiously old, and they may be right, but Lord Kelvin is not of their opinion. He takes a cautious, conservative view, in order to be on the safe side, and feels sure it is not so old as they think. As Lord Kelvin is the highest authority in science now living, I think we must yield to him and accept his view. He does not concede that the world is more than a hundred million years old. He believes it is that old, but not older. Lyell believed that our race was introduced into the world 31,000 years ago, Herbert Spencer makes it 32,000. Lord Kelvin agrees with Spencer.

6   Very well. According to these figures it took 99,968,000 years to prepare the world for man, impatient as the Creator doubtless was to see him and admire him. But a large enterprise like this has to be conducted warily, painstakingly, logically. It was foreseen that man would have to have the oyster. Therefore the first preparation was made for the oyster. Very well, you cannot make an oyster out of whole cloth, you must make the oyster's ancestor first. This is not done in a day. You must make a vast variety of invertebrates, to start with — belemnites, trilobites, Jebusites, Amalekites, and that sort of fry; and put them to soak in a primary sea, and wait and see what will happen. Some will be a disappointment — the belemnites, the Ammonites and such; they will be failures, they will die out and become extinct, in the course of the nineteen million years covered by the experiment, but all is not lost, for the Amalekites will fetch the

homestake; they will develop gradually into encrinites, and stalactites, and blatherskites, and one thing and another as the mighty ages creep on and the Archaean and the Cambrian Periods pile their lofty crags in the primordial seas, and at last the first grand stage in the preparation of the world for man stands completed, the oyster is done. An oyster has hardly any more reasoning power than a scientist has; and so it is reasonably certain that this one jumped to the conclusion that the nineteen million years was a preparation for *him;* but that would be just like an oyster, which is the most conceited animal there is, except man. And anyway, this one could not know, at that early date, that he was only an incident in a scheme, and that there was some more to the scheme, yet.

The oyster being achieved, the next thing to be arranged for in the preparation of the world for man was fish. Fish and coal — to fry it with. So the Old Silurian seas were opened up to breed the fish in, and at the same time the great work of building Old Red Sandstone mountains eighty thousand feet high to cold-storage their fossils in was begun. This latter was quite indispensable, for there would be no end of failures again, no end of extinctions — millions of them — and it would be cheaper and less trouble to can them in the rocks than keep tally of them in a book. One does not build the coal beds and eighty thousand feet of perpendicular Old Red Sandstone in a brief time — no, it took twenty million years. In the first place, a coal bed is a slow and troublesome and tiresome thing to construct. You have to grow prodigious forests of tree-ferns and reeds and calamites and such things in a marshy region; then you have to sink them under out of sight and let them rot; then you have to turn the streams on them, so as to bury them under several feet of sediment, and the sediment must have time to harden and turn to rock; next you must grow another forest on top, then sink it and put on another layer of sediment and harden it; then more forest and more rock, layer upon layer, three miles deep — ah, indeed it is a sickening slow job to build a coal-measure and do it right! 7

So the millions of years drag on; and meantime the fish culture is lazying along and frazzling out in a way to make a person tired. You have developed ten thousand kinds of fishes from the oyster; and come to look, you have raised nothing but fossils, nothing but extinctions. There is nothing left alive and progressive but a ganoid or two and perhaps half a dozen asteroids. Even the cat wouldn't eat such. 8

Still, it is no great matter; there is plenty of time, yet, and they will develop into something tasty before man is ready for them. Even 9 a ganoid can be depended on for that, when he is not going to be called on for sixty million years.

10   The Paleozoic time limit having now been reached, it was necessary to begin the next stage in the preparation of the world for man, by opening up the Mesozoic Age and instituting some reptiles. For man would need reptiles. Not to eat, but to develop himself from. This being the most important detail of the scheme, a spacious liberality of time was set apart for it — thirty million years. What wonders followed! From the remaining ganoids and asteroids and alkaloids were developed by slow and steady and painstaking culture those stupendous saurians that used to prowl about the steamy world in those remote ages, with their snaky heads reared forty feet in the air and sixty feet of body and tail racing and thrashing after. All gone, now, alas — all extinct, except the little handful of Arkansawrians left stranded and lonely with us here upon this far-flung verge and fringe of time.

11   Yes, it took thirty million years and twenty million reptiles to get one that would stick long enough to develop into something else and let the scheme proceed to the next step.

12   Then the pterodactyl burst upon the world in all his impressive solemnity and grandeur, and all Nature recognized that the Cenozoic threshold was crossed and a new Period open for business, a new stage begun in the preparation of the globe for man. It may be that the pterodactyl thought the thirty million years had been intended as a preparation for himself, for there was nothing too foolish for a pterodactyl to imagine, but he was in error, the preparation was for man. Without doubt the pterodactyl attracted great attention, for even the least observant could see that there was the making of a bird in him. And so it turned out. Also the makings of a mammal, in time. One thing we have to say to his credit, that in the matter of picturesqueness he was the triumph of his Period; he wore wings and had teeth, and was a starchy and wonderful mixture altogether, a kind of long-distance premonitory symptom of Kipling's marine:

> 'E isn't one o' the reg'lar Line, nor 'e isn't one of the crew,
> 'E's a kind of giddy harumfrodite — soldier an' sailor too!

13   From this time onward for nearly another thirty million years the preparation moved briskly. From the pterodactyl was developed the bird; from the bird the kangaroo, from the kangaroo the other marsupials; from these the mastodon, the megatherium, the giant sloth, the Irish elk, and all that crowd that you make useful and

instructive fossils out of— then came the first great Ice Sheet, and they all retreated before it and crossed over the bridge at Bering Strait and wandered around over Europe and Asia and died. All except a few, to carry on the preparation with. Six Glacial Periods with two million years between Periods chased these poor orphans up and down and about the earth, from weather to weather — from tropic swelter at the poles to Arctic frost at the equator and back again and to and fro, they never knowing what kind of weather was going to turn up next; and if ever they settled down anywhere the whole continent suddenly sank under them without the least notice and they had to trade places with the fishes and scramble off to where the seas had been, and scarcely a dry rag on them; and when there was nothing else doing a volcano would let go and fire them out from wherever they had located. They led this unsettled and irritating life for twenty-five million years, half the time afloat, half the time aground, and always wondering what it was all for, they never suspecting, of course, that it was a preparation for man and had to be done just so or it wouldn't be any proper and harmonious place for him when he arrived.

And at last came the monkey, and anybody could see that man 14 wasn't far off, now. And in truth that was so. The monkey went on developing for close upon five million years, and then turned into a man — to all appearances.

Such is the history of it. Man has been here 32,000 years. That it 15 took a hundred million years to prepare the world for him is proof that that is what it was done for. I suppose it is. I dunno. If the Eiffel Tower were now representing the world's age, the skin of paint on the pinnacle-knob at its summit would represent man's share of that age; and anybody would perceive that that skin was what the tower was built for. I reckon they would, I dunno.

____ CONSIDERATIONS _____

1. How and when does Twain let us know what he is up to in this essay?

2. Twain urges us, as we study the history of man and the world, to be patient, to be calm, to jump to no conclusions. Note how he uses the oyster (Paragraph 6) and the pterodactyl (Paragraph 12) to strengthen his point.

3. "Was the World Made for Man?" begins with two epigraphs: quotations selected by the author and used to state or hint at the central theme or image of the piece. To learn the uses and limitations of this literary device, select epigraphs for one or two essays in this book. Consult Bartlett's *Familiar Quotations* for a little assistance.

73

KENNETH TYNAN

Here's Johnny! . . .

. . . Apart from two months in the late nineteen-fifties (when he 1 replaced Tom Ewell in a Broadway comedy called *The Tunnel of Love*), Johnny Carson has never been seen on the legitimate stage; and, despite a multitude of offers, he has yet to appear in his first film. He does not, in fact, much like appearing *anywhere* except (a) in the audience at the Wimbledon tennis championships, which he and his wife recently attended, (b) at his home in Bel Air, and (c) before the NBC cameras in Burbank, which act on him like an addictive and galvanic drug. Just how the drug works is not known to science, but its effect is witnessed — ninety minutes per night, four nights per week, thirty-seven weeks per year — by upward of fourteen million viewers; and it provoked the actor Robert Blake, while he was being interviewed by Carson on the "Tonight Show" in 1976, to describe him with honest adulation as "the ace comedian top-dog talk artist of the universe." I once asked a bright young Manhattan journalist whether he could define in a single word what makes television different from theatre or cinema. "For good or ill," he said, "Carson."

2   This pure and archetypal product of the box shuns large parties. Invitations from the Lazars are among the few he accepts. Tonight, he arrives alone (his wife, Joanna, has stopped off in New York for a few days' shopping), greets his host with the familiar smile, cordially wry, and scans the assembly, his eyes twinkling like icicles. Hard to believe, despite the pewter-colored hair, that he is fifty-one: he holds himself like the midshipman he once was, chin well tucked in, back as straight as a poker. (Carson claims to be five feet ten and a half inches in height. His pedantic insistence on that extra half inch betokens a man who suspects he looks small.) In repose, he resembles a king-sized ventriloquist's dummy. After winking impassively at de Cordova, he threads his way across the crowded living room and out through the ceiling-high sliding windows to the deserted swimming pool. Heads discreetly turn. Even in this posh peer group, Carson has cynosure status. Arms folded, he surveys Los Angeles by night — "glittering jewel of the Southland, gossamer web of loveliness," as Abe Burrows ironically called it. A waiter brings him a soft drink. "He looks like Gatsby," a young actress whispers to me. On the face of it, this is nonsense. Fitzgerald's hero suffers from star-crossed love, his wealth has criminal origins, and he loves to give flamboyant parties. But the simile is not without elements of truth. Gatsby, like Carson, is a midwesterner, a self-made millionaire, and a habitual loner, armored against all attempts to invade his emotional privacy. "He had come a long way to this blue lawn," Fitzgerald wrote of Gatsby — as far as Carson has come to these blue pools, from which steam rises on even the warmest nights.

3   "He doesn't drink now." I turn to find Lazar beside me, also peeking at the man outside. He continues, "But I remember Johnny when he was a *blackout* drunk." That was before the "Tonight Show" moved from New York to Los Angeles, in 1972. "A couple of drinks was all it took. He could get very hostile."

4   I point out to Lazar that Carson's family tree has deep Irish roots on the maternal side. Was there something atavistic in his drinking? Or am I glibly casting him as an ethnic ("black Irish") stereotype? At all events, I now begin to see in him — still immobile by the pool — the lineaments of a magnified leprechaun.

5   "Like a lot of people in our business," Lazar goes on, "he's a mixture of extreme ego and extreme cowardice." In Lazar's lexicon, a

coward is one who turns down starring roles suggested to him by Lazar.

Since Carson already does what nobody has ever done better, I 6 reply, why should he risk his reputation by plunging into movies or TV specials?

Lazar concedes that I may be right. "But I'll tell you something 7 else about him," he says, with italicized wonder. *"He's celibate."* He means "chaste." "In his position, he could have all the girls he wants. It wouldn't be difficult. But he never cheats."

It is thirty minutes later. Carson is sitting at a table by the pool, 8 where four or five people have joined him. He chats with impersonal affability, making no effort to dominate, charm, or amuse. I recall something that George Axelrod, the dramatist and screenwriter, once said to me about him: "Socially, he doesn't exist. The reason is that there are no television cameras in living rooms. If human beings had little red lights in the middle of their foreheads, Carson would be the greatest conversationalist on earth."

One of the guests is a girl whose hobby is numerology. Taking 9 Carson as her subject, she works out a series of arcane sums and then offers her interpretation of his character. "You are an enormously mercurial person," she says, "who swings between very high highs and very low lows."

His eyebrows rise, the corners of his lips turn down: this is the 10 mock-affronted expression he presents to the camera when a baby armadillo from some local zoo declines to respond to his caresses. "This girl is great," he says to de Cordova. "She makes me sound like a cross between Spring Byington and Adolf Hitler."

"Johnny Carson on TV," one of his colleagues confided to me, 11 "is the visible eighth of an iceberg called Johnny Carson." The remark took me back to something that Carson said of himself ten years ago, when, in the course of a question-and-answer session with viewers, he was asked, "What made you a star?" He replied, "I started out in a gaseous state, and then I cooled." Meeting him tête-à-tête is, as we shall see later, a curious experience. In 1966, writing for *Look*, Betty Rollin described Carson off camera as "testy, defensive, preoccupied, withdrawn, and wondrously inept and uncomfortable with people." Nowadays, his off-camera manner is friendly and impeccably diplomatic. Even so, you get the impression that you are addressing an elaborately wired security system. If the conversation edges toward areas in which he feels ill at ease or unwilling to commit himself, burglar alarms are triggered off, defensive reflexes rise around him like an invisible stockade, and you hear the distant baying of guard dogs. In addition to his childhood, his private life, and his income, these no-trespassing zones include all subjects of political controversy, any form of sexual behavior uncountenanced by the law, and such matters of social concern as abortion and the legalization of marijuana. His smile as he steers you away from forbidden territory is genial and unfading. It is only fair to remember that he does not pretend to be a pundit, employed to express his own opinions; rather, he is a professional explorer of other people's egos. In a magazine article that was published with annotations by Carson, Fred de Cordova wrote, "He's reluctant to talk much about himself because he is essentially a private person." To this Carson added a marginal gloss, intended as a gag, that had an eerie ring of truth: "I will not even talk to myself without an appointment." He has asked all the questions and knows all the evasive, equivocal answers. When he first signed to appear on the "Tonight Show," he was quizzed by the press so relentlessly that he refused after a while to submit to further interrogation. Instead, he issued a list of replies that journalists could append to any questions of their choice:

1. Yes, I did.
2. Not a bit of truth in that rumor.
3. Only twice in my life, both times on Saturday.
4. I can do either, but I prefer the first.
5. No. Kumquats.
6. I can't answer that question.
7. Toads and tarantulas.
8. Turkestan, Denmark, Chile, and the Komandorskie Islands.
9. As often as possible, but I'm not very good at it yet. I need much more practice.
10. It happened to some old friends of mine, and it's a story I'll never forget.

_____ **CONSIDERATIONS** _____

1. A sophisticated writer describing a sophisticated subject, Kenneth Tynan employs a wide-ranging vocabulary. List on a separate sheet the words from his essay you don't know, in the phrases in which they occur: for example, "addictive and *galvanic* drug," "cordially *wry* smile," "*archetypal* product of the box," "the *lineaments* of a magnified *leprechaun*." Then consult your

dictionary. See if the combination of dictionary and context, better than either alone, helps you understand the way Tynan uses these words.

2. Do short people, as Tynan suggests in Paragraph 2, try to look tall? What about tall people? Rely on your own observations to answer the questions.

3. What does Tynan hope to gain by comparing Carson with Fitzgerald's fictitious character, Gatsby? See also Bergmann's use of Dostoevski's work of fiction, *The Brothers Karamazov.* What character from a short story or a novel do you know well enough to use in an essay?

4. Tynan seems to take Carson seriously. Does he take him as seriously as McPhee takes Bradley, or Catton takes Grant and Lee? Discuss the making of a public figure. What qualities in a person prompt biographers to select him or her as a subject? Whom might you be tempted to write about? Why?

John Updike (b. 1932) grew up in Pennsylvania and went to Harvard, where he edited the humor magazine, the Lampoon. *On a fellowship year at Oxford, Updike sold a poem to* The New Yorker *and began his long relationship with that magazine. First he worked on the staff of* The New Yorker, *contributing to "The Talk of the Town." When he quit to free-lance, he continued to write stories, poems, reviews, and articles for the magazine. The* Poorhouse Fair *(1959), his first novel, appeared in the same year as his first collection of stories,* The Same Door, *from which we take "Ace in the Hole." This story appears to be the seed of his second novel,* Rabbit, Run *(1960) — also about an ex-basketball star with a deteriorating marriage.*

Updike has published stories, novels, poems, and two miscellaneous collections, Assorted Prose *(1965) and* Picked-up Pieces *(1975). Among his best-known novels are* The Centaur *(1963) and* The Coup *(1978). In "Ace in the Hole," Updike writes with his usual precision and finish, and with a final image that illuminates everything that has gone before it, gilding the dross of the present with a recollected gold.*

_74

JOHN UPDIKE
Ace in the Hole

1   No sooner did his car touch the boulevard heading home than Ace flicked on the radio. He needed the radio, especially today. In the seconds before the tubes warmed up, he said aloud, doing it just to hear a human voice, "Jesus. She'll pop her lid." His voice, though familiar, irked him; it sounded thin and scratchy, as if the bones in his

head were picking up static. In a deeper register Ace added, "She'll
murder me." Then the radio came on, warm and strong, so he stopped
worrying. The Five Kings were doing "Blueberry Hill"; to hear them
made Ace feel so sure inside that from the pack pinched between the
car roof and the sun shield he plucked a cigarette, hung it on his lower
lip, snapped a match across the rusty place on the dash, held the flame
in the instinctive spot near the tip of his nose, dragged, and blew out
the match, all in time to the music. He rolled down the window and
snapped the match so it spun end-over-end into the gutter. "Two
points," he said, and cocked the cigarette toward the roof of the car,
sucked powerfully, and exhaled two plumes through his nostrils. He
was beginning to feel like himself, Ace Anderson, for the first time
that whole day, a bad day. He beat time on the accelerator. The car
jerked crazily. "On Blueberry Hill," he sang, "my heart stood still.
The wind in the wil-low tree" — he braked for a red light — "played
love's suh-*weet* melodee —"

"Go, Dad, bust your lungs!" a kid's voice blared. The kid was   2
riding in a '52 Pontiac that had pulled up beside Ace at the light. The
profile of the driver, another kid, was dark over his shoulder.

Ace looked over at him and smiled slowly, just letting one side   3
of his mouth lift a little. "Shove it," he said, good-naturedly, across
the little gap of years that separated them. He knew how they felt,
young and mean and shy.

But the kid, who looked Greek, lifted his thick upper lip and   4
spat out the window. The spit gleamed on the asphalt like a half-
dollar.

"Now isn't that pretty?" Ace said, keeping one eye on the light.   5
"You miserable wop. You are *mis*erable." While the kid was trying to
think of some smart comeback, the light changed. Ace dug out so hard
he smelled burned rubber. In his rear-view mirror he saw the Pontiac
lurch forward a few yards, then stop dead, right in the middle of the
intersection.

The idea of them stalling their fat tin Pontiac kept him in a good   6
humor all the way home. He decided to stop at his mother's place and
pick up the baby, instead of waiting for Evey to do it. His mother must
have seen him drive up. She came out on the porch holding a plastic
spoon and smelling of cake.

"You're out early," she told him.   7

"Friedman fired me," Ace told her.   8

"Good for you," his mother said. "I always said he never treated   9
you right." She brought a cigarette out of her apron pocket and tucked

it deep into one corner of her mouth, the way she did when something pleased her.

10   Ace lighted it for her. "Friedman was O.K. personally," he said. "He just wanted too much for his money. I didn't mind working Saturdays, but until eleven, twelve Friday nights was too much. Everybody has a right to some leisure."

11   "Well, I don't dare think what Evey will say, but I, for one, thank dear God you had the brains to get out of it. I always said that job had no future to it — no future of any kind, Freddy."

12   "I guess," Ace admitted. "But I wanted to keep at it, for the family's sake."

13   "Now, I know I shouldn't be saying this, but any time Evey — this is just between us — any time Evey thinks she can do better, there's room for you *and* Bonnie right in your father's house." She pinched her lips together. He could almost hear the old lady think, *There, I've said it.*

14   "Look, Mom, Evey tries awfully hard, and anyway you know she can't work that way. Not that *that* — I mean, she's a realist, too . . ." He let the rest of the thought fade as he watched a kid across the street dribbling a basketball around a telephone pole that had a backboard and net nailed on it.

15   "Evey's a wonderful girl of her own kind. But I've always said, and your father agrees, Roman Catholics ought to marry among themselves. Now I know I've said it before, but when they get out in the greater world —"

16   "*No*, Mom."

17   She frowned, smoothed herself, and said, "Your name was in the paper today."

18   Ace chose to let that go by. He kept watching the kid with the basketball. It was funny how, though the whole point was to get the ball up into the air, kids grabbed it by the sides and squeezed. Kids just didn't think.

19   "Did you hear?" his mother asked.

20   "Sure, but so what?" Ace said. His mother's lower lip was coming at him, so he changed the subject. "I guess I'll take Bonnie."

21   His mother went into the house and brought back his daughter, wrapped in a blue blanket. The baby looked dopey. "She fussed all day," his mother complained. "I said to your father, 'Bonnie is a dear little girl, but without a doubt she's her mother's daughter.' You were the best-natured boy."

22   "Well I *had* everything," Ace said with an impatience that made

his mother blink. He nicely dropped his cigarette into a brown flow-erpot on the edge of the porch and took his daughter into his arms. She was getting heavier, solid. When he reached the end of the cement walk, his mother was still on the porch, waving to him. He was so close he could see the fat around her elbow jiggle, and he only lived a half block up the street, yet here she was, waving to him as if he was going to Japan.

At the door of his car, it seemed stupid to him to drive the measly half block home. His old coach, Bob Behn, used to say never to ride where you could walk. Cars were the death of legs. Ace left the igni-tion keys in his pocket and ran along the pavement with Bonnie laugh-ing and bouncing at his chest. He slammed the door of his landlady's house open and shut, pounded up the two flights of stairs, and was panting so hard when he reached the door of his apartment that it took him a couple of seconds to fit the key into the lock.

The run must have tuned Bonnie up. As soon as he lowered her into the crib, she began to shout and wave her arms. He didn't want to play with her. He tossed some blocks and a rattle into the crib and walked into the bathroom, where he turned on the hot water and began to comb his hair. Holding the comb under the faucet before every stroke, he combed his hair forward. It was so long, one strand curled under his nose and touched his lips. He whipped the whole mass back with a single pull. He tucked in the tufts around his ears, and ran the comb straight back on both sides of his head. With his fingers he felt for the little ridge at the back where the two sides met. It was there, as it should have been. Finally, he mussed the hair in front enough for one little lock to droop over his forehead, like Alan Ladd. It made the temple seem lower than it was. Every day, his hair-line looked higher. He had observed all around him how blond men went bald first. He remembered reading somewhere, though, that baldness shows virility.

On his way to the kitchen he flipped the left-hand knob of the television. Bonnie was always quieter with the set on. Ace didn't see how she could understand much of it, but it seemed to mean some-thing to her. He found a can of beer in the refrigerator behind some brownish lettuce and those hot dogs Evey never got around to cooking. She'd be home any time. The clock said 5:12. She'd pop her lid.

Ace didn't see what he could do but try and reason with her. "Evey," he'd say, "you ought to thank God I got out of it. It had no future to it at all." He hoped she wouldn't get too mad, because when she was mad he wondered if he should have married her, and doubting that made him feel crowded. It was bad enough, his mother always crowding him. He punched the two triangles in the top of the beer can, the little triangle first, and then the big one, the one he drank from. He hoped Evey wouldn't say anything that couldn't be forgotten. What women didn't seem to realize was that there were things you knew but shouldn't say.

27   He felt sorry he had called the kid in the car a wop.

28   Ace balanced the beer on a corner where two rails of the crib met and looked under the chairs for the morning paper. He had trouble finding his name, because it was at the bottom of a column on an inside sports page, in a small article about the county basketball statistics:

> "Dusty" Tremwick, Grosvenor Park's sure-fingered center, copped the individual scoring honors with a season's grand (and we do mean grand) total of 376 points. This is within eighteen points of the all-time record of 394 racked up in the 1949–1950 season by Olinger High's Fred Anderson.

29   Ace angrily sailed the paper into an armchair. Now it was Fred Anderson; it used to be Ace. He hated being called Fred, especially in print, but then the sportswriters were all office boys anyway, Behn used to say.

30   "Do not just ask for shoe polish," a man on television said, "but ask for *Emu Shoe Gloss,* the *only* polish that absolutely *guarantees* to make your shoes look shinier than new." Ace turned the sound off, so that the man moved his mouth like a fish blowing bubbles. Right away, Bonnie howled, so Ace turned it up loud enough to drown her out and went into the kitchen, without knowing what he wanted there. He wasn't hungry; his stomach was tight. It used to be like that when he walked to the gymnasium alone in the dark before a game and could see the people from town, kids and parents, crowding in at the lighted doors. But once he was inside, the locker room would be bright and hot, and the other guys would be there, laughing it up and towel-slapping, and the tight feeling would leave. Now there were whole days when it didn't leave.

31   A key scratched at the door lock. Ace decided to stay in the kitchen. Let *her* find *him.* Her heels clicked on the floor for a step or two; then the television set went off. Bonnie began to cry. "Shut up, honey," Evey said. There was a silence.

"I'm home," Ace called.   32

"No kidding. I thought Bonnie got the beer by herself."   33

Ace laughed. She was in a sarcastic mood, thinking she was Lau-   34
ren Bacall. That was all right, just so she kept funny. Still smiling, Ace
eased into the living room and got hit with, "What are *you* smirking
about? Another question: What's the idea running up the street with
Bonnie like she was a football?"

"You saw that?"   35

"Your mother told me."   36

"You saw her?"   37

"Of course I saw her. I dropped by to pick up Bonnie. What the   38
hell do you think? — I read her tiny mind?"

"Take it easy," Ace said, wondering if Mom had told her about   39
Friedman.

"Take it easy? Don't coach *me*. Another question: Why's the car   40
out in front of her place? You give the car to her?"

"Look, I parked it there to pick up Bonnie, and I thought I'd leave   41
it there."

"Why?"   42

"Whaddeya mean, why? I just did. I just thought I'd walk. It's not   43
that far, you know."

"No, I don't know. If you'd been on your feet all day a block   44
would look like one hell of a long way."

"Okay. I'm sorry."   45

She hung up her coat and stepped out of her shoes and walked   46
around the room picking up things. She stuck the newspaper in the
wastebasket.

Ace said, "My name was in the paper today."   47

"They spell it right?" She shoved the paper deep into the basket   48
with her foot. There was no doubt; she knew about Friedman.

"They called me Fred."   49

"Isn't that your name? What *is* your name anyway? Hero J.   50
Great?"

There wasn't any answer, so Ace didn't try any. He sat down on   51
the sofa, lighted a cigarette, and waited.

Evey picked up Bonnie. "Poor thing stinks. What does your   52
mother do, scrub out the toilet with her?"

"Can't you take it easy? I know you're tired."   53

"You should. I'm always tired."   54

Evey and Bonnie went into the bathroom; when they came out,   55

Bonnie was clean and Evey was calm. Evey sat down in an easy chair beside Ace and rested her stocking feet on his knees. "Hit me," she said, twiddling her fingers for the cigarette.

56   The baby crawled up to her chair and tried to stand, to see what he gave her. Leaning over close to Bonnie's nose, Evey grinned, smoke leaking through her teeth, and said, "Only for grownups, honey."

57   "Eve," Ace began, "there was no future in that job. Working all Saturday, and then Friday nights on top of it."

58   "I know. Your mother told *me* all that, too. All I want from you is what happened."

59   She was going to take it like a sport, then. He tried to remember how it *did* happen. "It wasn't my fault," he said. "Friedman told me to back this '51 Chevvy into the line that faces Church Street. He just bought it from an old guy this morning who said it only had thirteen thousand on it. So in I jump and start her up. There was a knock in the engine like a machine gun. I almost told Friedman he'd bought a squirrel, but you know I cut that smart stuff out ever since Palotta laid me off."

60   "You told me that story. What happens in this one?"

61   "Look, Eve. I *am* telling ya. Do you want me to go out to a movie or something?"

62   "Suit yourself."

63   "So I jump in the Chevvy and snap it back in line, and there was a kind of scrape and thump. I get out and look and Friedman's running over, his arms going like *this*" — Ace whirled his own arms and laughed — "and here was the whole back fender of a '49 Merc mashed in. Just looked like somebody took a planer and shaved off the bulge, you know, there at the back." He tried to show her with his hands. "The Chevvy, though, didn't have a dent. It even gained some paint. But *Friedman*, to *hear* him — Boy, they can rave when their pocket-book's hit. He said" — Ace laughed again — "never mind."

64   Evey said, "You're proud of yourself."

65   "No, listen. I'm not happy about it. But there wasn't a thing I could *do*. It wasn't my driving at all. I looked over on the other side, and there was just two or three inches between the Chevvy and a Buick. *Nobody* could have gotten into that hole. Even if it had hair on it." He thought this was pretty good.

66   She didn't. "You could have looked."

67   "There just wasn't the *space*. Friedman said stick it in; I stuck it in."

"But you could have looked and moved the others cars to make 68
more room."

"I guess that would have been the smart thing." 69

"I guess, too. Now what?" 70

"What do you mean?" 71

"I mean now what? Are you going to give up? Go back to the 72
Army? Your mother? Be a basketball pro? What?"

"You know I'm not tall enough. Anybody under six-six they 73
don't want."

"Is that so? Six-six? Well, please listen to this, Mr. Six-Foot-Five- 74
and-a-Half: I'm fed up. I'm ready as Christ to let you run." She stabbed
her cigarette into an ashtray on the arm of the chair so hard the ashtray
jumped to the floor. Evey flushed and shut up.

What Ace hated most in their arguments was these silences after 75
Evey had said something so ugly she wanted to take it back. "Better
ask the priest first," he murmured.

She sat right up. "If there's one thing I don't want to hear about 76
from you it's priests. You let the priests to me. You don't know a
damn thing about it. Not a damn thing."

"Hey, look at Bonnie," he said, trying to make a fresh start with 77
his tone.

Evey didn't hear him. "If you think," she went on, "if for one 78
rotten moment you think, Mr. Fred, that the be-all and end-all of my
life is you and your hot-shot stunts — "

"Look, Mother," Ace pleaded, pointing at Bonnie. The baby had 79
picked up the ashtray and put it on her head for a hat and was waiting
for praise.

Evey glanced down sharply at the child. "Cute," she said. "Cute 80
as her daddy."

The ashtray slid from Bonnie's head and she patted where it had 81
been and looked around puzzled.

"Yeah, but watch," Ace said. "Watch her hands. They're really 82
terrific hands."

"You're nuts," Evey said. 83

"No, honest. Bonnie's great. She's a natural. Get the rattle for 84
her. Never mind, I'll get it." In two steps, Ace was at Bonnie's crib,
picking the rattle out of the mess of blocks and plastic rings and
beanbags. He extended the rattle toward his daughter, shaking it deli-
cately. Made wary by this burst of attention, Bonnie reached with both
hands; like two separate animals they approached from opposite sides

and touched the smooth rattle simultaneously. A smile bubbled up on her face. Ace tugged weakly. She held on, and then tugged back. "She's a natural," Ace said, "and it won't do her any good because she's a girl. Baby, we got to have a boy."

85 "I'm not your baby," Evey said, closing her eyes.

86 Saying "Baby" over and over again, Ace backed up to the radio and, without turning around, switched on the volume knob. In the moment before the tubes warmed up, Evey had time to say, "Wise up, Freddy. What shall we do?"

87 The radio came in on something slow: dinner music. Ace picked Bonnie up and set her in the crib. "Shall we dance?" he asked his wife, bowing.

88 "I want to talk."

89 "Baby. It's the cocktail hour."

90 "This is getting us no place," she said, rising from her chair, though.

91 "Fred Junior. I can see him now," he said, seeing nothing.

92 "We will have no Juniors."

93 In her crib, Bonnie whimpered at the sight of her mother being seized. Ace fitted his hand into the natural place on Evey's back and she shuffled stiffly into his lead. When, with a sudden injection of saxophones, the tempo quickened, he spun her out carefully, keeping the beat with his shoulders. Her hair brushed his lips as she minced in, then swung away, to the end of his arm; he could feel her toes dig into the carpet. He flipped his own hair back from his eyes. The music ate through his skin and mixed with the nerves and small veins; he seemed to be great again, and all the other kids were around them, in a ring, clapping time.

—— **CONSIDERATIONS** ————————————————

1. Updike often uses minute physical observations. Do you find any of these in "Ace in the Hole"? How do they contribute to the story's effect?

2. How old is Ace? What information in the story prompts you to make a guess? What kind of age do you mean — chronological, mental, emotional? How important is his age to the story?

3. What are Ace's *real* interests: wife? child? job? future career? How does Updike help you discriminate between Ace's casual and lasting interests?

4. Which is most important to Ace — the past, the present, or the future? Cite evidence. Of what thematic significance is this question?

5. If you were a marriage counselor, would you have any advice for this young couple? Would you say that their marriage is in trouble? What are the chances that they would even consider consulting a marriage counselor? For your answers use the story itself.

6. What importance has play had in Ace's life? What particulars in the story reveal his attitude toward play, sport, games, fun, diversions, recreation?

7. Compare the reactions of Ace's mother and his wife to losing the job. How do their different attitudes toward this event reveal important things about Ace's life at this time?

Gore Vidal (b. 1925) entered the army after graduating from Phillips Exeter Academy and never attended college. He published his first novel the year he turned twenty-one. He has run for Congress, lived in Europe, and has written plays and essays but chiefly novels, including Julian *(1964),* Myra Breckinridge *(1968),* Burr *(1973), and* Kalki *(1979).*

_75

GORE VIDAL
Drugs

1   It is possible to stop most drug addiction in the United States within a very short time. Simply make all drugs available and sell them at cost. Label each drug with a precise description of what effect — good and bad — the drug will have on the taker. This will require heroic honesty. Don't say that marijuana is addictive or dangerous when it is neither, as millions of people know — unlike "speed," which kills most unpleasantly, or heroin, which is addictive and difficult to kick.

2   For the record, I have tried — once — almost every drug and liked none, disproving the popular Fu Manchu theory that a single whiff of opium will enslave the mind. Nevertheless many drugs are bad for certain people to take and they should be told why in a sensible way.

3   Along with exhortation and warning, it might be good for our citizens to recall (or learn for the first time) that the United States was the creation of men who believed that each man has the right to do what he wants with his own life as long as he does not interfere with

his neighbor's pursuit of happiness (that his neighbor's idea of happiness is persecuting others does confuse matters a bit).

This is a startling notion to the current generation of Americans. 4
They reflect a system of public education which has made the Bill of Rights, literally, unacceptable to a majority of high school graduates (see the annual Purdue reports) who now form the "silent majority" — a phrase which that underestimated wit Richard Nixon took from Homer who used it to describe the dead.

Now one can hear the warning rumble begin: if everyone is 5
allowed to take drugs everyone will and the GNP will decrease, the Commies will stop us from making everyone free, and we shall end up a race of Zombies, passively murmuring "groovie" to one another. Alarming thought. Yet it seems most unlikely that any reasonably sane person will become a drug addict if he knows in advance what addiction is going to be like.

Is everyone reasonably sane? No. Some people will always 6
become drug addicts just as some people will always become alcoholics, and it is just too bad. Every man, however, has the power (and should have the legal right) to kill himself if he chooses. But since most men don't, they won't be mainliners either. Nevertheless, forbidding people things they like or think they might enjoy only makes them want those things all the more. This psychological insight is, for some mysterious reason, perennially denied our governors.

It is a lucky thing for the American moralist that our country has 7
always existed in a kind of time-vacuum: we have no public memory of anything that happened before last Tuesday. No one in Washington today recalls what happened during the years alcohol was forbidden to the people by a Congress that thought it had a divine mission to stamp out Demon Rum — launching, in the process, the greatest crime wave in the country's history, causing thousands of deaths from bad alcohol, and creating a general (and persisting) contempt among the citizenry for the laws of the United States.

The same thing is happening today. But the government has 8
learned nothing from past attempts at prohibition, not to mention repression.

Last year when the supply of Mexican marijuana was slightly 9
curtailed by the Feds, the pushers got the kids hooked on heroin and deaths increased dramatically, particularly in New York. Whose fault? Evil men like the Mafiosi? Permissive Dr. Spock? Wild-eyed Dr. Leary? No.

The Government of the United States was responsible for those 10 deaths. The bureaucratic machine has a vested interest in playing cops and robbers. Both the Bureau of Narcotics and the Mafia want strong laws against the sale and use of drugs because if drugs are sold at cost there would be no money in it for anyone.

11   If there was no money in it for the Mafia, there would be no friendly playground pushers, and addicts would not commit crimes to pay for the next fix. Finally, if there was no money in it, the Bureau of Narcotics would wither away, something they are not about to do without a struggle.

12   Will anything sensible be done? Of course not. The American people are as devoted to the idea of sin and its punishment as they are to making money — and fighting drugs is nearly as big a business as pushing them. Since the combination of sin and money is irresistible (particularly to the professional politician), the situation will only grow worse.

____ CONSIDERATIONS _____

1. One mark of the experienced arguer is his ability to anticipate and thus neutralize his opponent's rebuttal. Where does Vidal do this? How effective is his attempt?

2. Vidal's argument (Paragraphs 10, 11, and 12) that "the bureaucratic machine has a vested interest in playing cops and robbers" rests on his implication that lawmen are at least as interested in preserving their jobs as they are in preserving law and order. Does he present any evidence to support this argument? What kind of evidence could he offer? How could you support a counterargument?

3. Vidal contends that every man "should have the legal right to kill himself." How far would he (or you) extend that "right"? To all varieties of suicide, for instance?

4. In Paragraph 3, Vidal introduces lightly a serious dilemma that often emerges in any discussion of individual liberty. See Boulding's essay "Nature and Artifice" for an example of that same dilemma. Then write your own solution.

5. Is the slang term "groovie" — usually spelled "groovy" — still current? Linguists often study slang because it changes faster than standard language. For the same reason, geneticists study fruit flies because the quick turnover of generations allows them to investigate principles of genetics within a brief period of time. In what way(s) do changes in slang parallel changes in English in general?

6. Given Vidal's belief in freedom of the individual, how do you think he would approach the question of gun control?

Eudora Welty (b. 1909) lives in her native Jackson, Mississippi, where she continues to write, deliberately and slowly, her perfect stories and novels. A Curtain of Green *(1941) was her first volume of collected stories. Her novels include* Losing Battles *(1970) and* The Optimist's Daughter *(1972), which won her a Pulitzer Prize. In 1980* The Collected Stories of Eudora Welty *was published.*

Here is one of her stories, followed by a useful essay she wrote about it years later, which appears in her book The Eye of the Story *(1978).*

76

EUDORA WELTY
A Worn Path

It was December — a bright frozen day in the early morning. Far 1
out in the country there was an old Negro woman with her head tied
in a red rag, coming along a path through the pinewoods. Her name
was Phoenix Jackson. She was very old and small and she walked
slowly in the dark pine shadows, moving a little from side to side in
her steps, with the balanced heaviness and lightness of a pendulum in
a grandfather clock. She carried a thin, small cane made from an
umbrella, and with this she kept tapping the frozen earth in front of
her. This made a grave and persistent noise in the still air, that seemed
meditative, like the chirping of a solitary little bird.

She wore a dark striped dress reaching down to her shoetops, and 2
an equally long apron of bleached sugar sacks, with a full pocket; all
neat and tidy, but every time she took a step she might have fallen

over her shoelaces, which dragged from her unlaced shoes. She looked straight ahead. Her eyes were blue with age. Her skin had a pattern all its own of numberless branching wrinkles and as though a whole little tree stood in the middle of her forehead, but a golden color ran underneath, and the two knobs of her cheeks were illuminated by a yellow burning under the dark. Under the red rag her hair came down on her neck in the frailest of ringlets, still black, and with an odor like copper.

3   Now and then there was a quivering in the thicket. Old Phoenix said, "Out of my way, all you foxes, owls, beetles, jack rabbits, coons, and wild animals! . . . Keep out from under these feet, little bob-whites. . . . Keep the big wild hogs out of my path. Don't let none of those come running my direction. I got a long way." Under her small black-freckled hand her cane, limber as a buggy whip, would switch at the brush as if to rouse up any hiding things.

4   On she went. The woods were deep and still. The sun made the pine needles almost too bright to look at, up where the wind rocked. The cones dropped as light as feathers. Down in the hollow was the mourning dove — it was not too late for him.

5   The path ran up a hill. "Seem like there is chains about my feet, time I get this far," she said, in the voice of argument old people keep to use with themselves. "Something always take a hold on this hill — pleads I should stay."

6   After she got to the top she turned and gave a full, severe look behind her where she had come. "Up through pines," she said at length. "Now down through oaks."

7   Her eyes opened their widest and she started down gently. But before she got to the bottom of the hill a bush caught her dress.

8   Her fingers were busy and intent, but her skirts were full and long, so that before she could pull them free in one place they were caught in another. It was not possible to allow the dress to tear. "I in the thorny bush," she said. "Thorns, you doing your appointed work. Never want to let folks past — no sir. Old eyes thought you was a pretty little *green* bush."

9   Finally, trembling all over, she stood free, and after a moment dared to stoop for her cane.

10   "Sun so high!" she cried, leaning back and looking, while the thick tears went over her eyes. "The time getting all gone here."

11   At the foot of this hill was a place where a log was laid across the creek.

12   "Now comes the trial," said Phoenix.

13   Putting her right foot out, she mounted the log and shut her eyes.

Lifting her skirt, leveling her cane fiercely before her, like a festival figure in some parade, she began to march across. Then she opened her eyes and she was safe on the other side.

"I wasn't as old as I thought," she said.   14

But she sat down to rest. She spread her skirts on the bank around   15
her and folded her hands over her knees. Up above her was a tree in a pearly cloud of mistletoe. She did not dare to close her eyes, and when a little boy brought her a little plate with a slice of marble-cake on it she spoke to him. "That would be acceptable," she said. But when she went to take it there was just her own hand in the air.

So she left that tree, and had to go through a barbed-wire fence.   16
There she had to creep and crawl, spreading her knees and stretching her fingers like a baby trying to climb the steps. But she talked loudly to herself: she could not let her dress be torn now, so late in the day, and she could not pay for having her arm or leg sawed off if she got caught fast where she was.

At last she was safe through the fence and risen up out in the   17
clearing. Big dead trees, like black men with one arm, were standing in the purple stalks of the withered cotton field. There sat a buzzard.

"Who you watching?"   18

In the furrow she made her way along.   19

"Glad this not the season for bulls," she said, looking sideways,   20
"and the good Lord made his snakes to curl up and sleep in the winter. A pleasure I don't see no two-headed snake coming around that tree, where it come once. It took a while to get by him, back in the summer."

She passed through the old cotton and went into a field of dead   21
corn. It whispered and shook, and was taller than her head. "Through the maze now," she said, for there was no path.

Then there was something tall, black, and skinny there, moving   22
before her.

At first she took it for a man. It could have been a man dancing   23
in the field. But she stood still and listened, and it did not make a sound. It was as silent as a ghost.

"Ghost," she said sharply, "who be you the ghost of? For I have   24
heard of nary death close by."

But there was no answer, only the ragged dancing in the wind.   25

She shut her eyes, reached out her hand, and touched a sleeve.   26
She found a coat and inside that an emptiness, cold as ice.

"You scarecrow," she said. Her face lighted. "I ought to be shut   27
up for good," she said with laughter. "My senses is gone. I too old. I

the oldest people I ever know. Dance, old scarecrow," she said, "while I dancing with you."

28   She kicked her foot over the furrow, and with mouth drawn down shook her head once or twice in a little strutting way. Some husks blew down and whirled in streamers about her skirts.

29   Then she went on, parting her way from side to side with the cane, through the whispering field. At last she came to the end, to a wagon track, where the silver grass blew between the red ruts. The quail were walking around like pullets, seeming all dainty and unseen.

30   "Walk pretty," she said. "This the easy place. This the easy going."

31   She followed the track, swaying through the quiet bare fields, through the little strings of trees silver in their dead leaves, past cabins silver from weather, with the doors and windows boarded shut, all like old women under a spell sitting there. "I walking in their sleep," she said, nodding her head vigorously.

32   In a ravine she went where a spring was silently flowing through a hollow log. Old Phoenix bent and drank. "Sweetgum makes the water sweet," she said, and drank more. "Nobody knows who made this well, for it was here when I was born."

33   The track crossed a swampy part where the moss hung as white as lace from every limb. "Sleep on, alligators, and blow your bubbles." Then the track went into the road.

34   Deep, deep the road went down between the high green-colored banks. Overhead the live-oaks met, and it was as dark as a cave.

35   A black dog with a lolling tongue came up out of the weeds by the ditch. She was meditating, and not ready, and when he came at her she only hit him a little with her cane. Over she went in the ditch, like a little puff of milk-weed.

36   Down there, her senses drifted away. A dream visited her, and she reached her hand up, but nothing reached down and gave her a pull. So she lay there and presently went to talking. "Old woman," she said to herself, "that black dog come up out of the weeds to stall you off, and now there he sitting on his fine tail, smiling at you."

37   A white man finally came along and found her — a hunter, a young man, with his dog on a chain.

38   "Well, Granny!" he laughed. "What are you doing there?"

39   "Lying on my back like a June-bug waiting to be turned over, mister," she said, reaching up her hand.

40   He lifted her up, gave her a swing in the air, and set her down, "Anything broken, Granny?"

"No sir, them old dead weeds is springy enough," said Phoenix,   41
when she had got her breath. "I thank you for your trouble."

"Where do you live, Granny?" he asked, while the two dogs were   42
growling at each other.

"Away back yonder, sir, behind the ridge. You can't even see it   43
from here."

"On your way home?" ·   44

"No, sir, I going to town."   45

"Why that's too far! That's as far as I walk when I come out   46
myself, and I get something for my trouble." He patted the stuffed bag
he carried, and there hung down a little closed claw. It was one of the
bobwhites, with its beak hooked bitterly to show it was dead. "Now
you go on home, Granny!"

"I bound to go to town, mister," said Phoenix. "The time come   47
around."

He gave another laugh, filling the whole landscape. "I know you   48
colored people! Wouldn't miss going to town to see Santa Claus!"

But something held Old Phoenix very still. The deep lines in her   49
face went into a fierce and different radiation. Without warning she
had seen with her own eyes a flashing nickel fall out of the man's
pocket on to the ground.

"How old are you, Granny?" he was saying.   50

"There is no telling, mister," she said, "no telling."   51

Then she gave a little cry and clapped her hands, and said, "Git   52
on away from here, dog! Look! Look at that dog!" She laughed as if in
admiration. "He ain't scared of nobody. He a big black dog." She whispered, "Sick him!"

"Watch me get rid of that cur," said the man. "Sick him, Pete!   53
Sick him!"

Phoenix heard the dogs fighting and heard the man running and   54
throwing sticks. She even heard a gunshot. But she was slowly bend-
ing forward by that time, further and further forward, the lids
stretched down over her eyes, as if she were doing this in her sleep.
Her chin was lowered almost to her knees. The yellow palm of her
hand came out from the fold of her apron. Her fingers slid down and
along the ground under the piece of money with the grace and care
they would have in lifting an egg from under a sitting hen. Then she
slowly straightened up, she stood erect, and the nickel was in her
apron pocket. A bird flew by. Her lips moved. "God watching me the
whole time. I come to stealing."

The man came back, and his own dog panted about them. "Well,   55

I scared him off that time," he said, and then he laughed and lifted his gun and pointed it at Phoenix.

56   She stood straight and faced him.

57   "Doesn't the gun scare you?" he said, still pointing it.

58   "No, sir, I seen plenty go off closer by, in my day, and for less what I done," she said, holding utterly still.

59   He smiled, and shouldered the gun. "Well, Granny," he said, "you must be a hundred years old, and scared of nothing. I'd give you a dime if I had any money with me. But you take my advice and stay home, and nothing will happen to you."

60   "I bound to go on my way, mister," said Phoenix. She inclined her head in the red rag. Then they went in different directions, but she could hear the gun shooting again and again over the hill.

61   She walked on. The shadows hung from the oak trees to the road like curtains. Then she smelled wood-smoke, and smelled the river, and she saw a steeple and the cabins on their steep steps. Dozens of little black children whirled around her. There ahead was Natchez shining. Bells were ringing. She walked on.

62   In the paved city it was Christmas time. There were red and green electric lights strung and crisscrossed everywhere, and all turned on in the daytime. Old Phoenix would have been lost if she had not distrusted her eyesight and depended on her feet to know where to take her.

63   She paused quietly on the sidewalk, where people were passing by. A lady came along in the crowd, carrying an armful of red-, green-, and silver-wrapped presents; she gave off perfume like the red roses in hot summer, and Phoenix stopped her.

64   "Please, missy, will you lace up my shoe?" She held up her foot.

65   "What do you want, Grandma?"

66   "See my shoe," said Phoenix. "Do all right for out in the country, but wouldn't look right to go in a big building."

67   "Stand still then, Grandma," said the lady. She put her packages down carefully on the sidewalk beside her and laced and tied both shoes tightly.

68   "Can't lace 'em with a cane," said Phoenix. "Thank you, missy. I doesn't mind asking a nice lady to tie up my shoe when I gets out on the street."

69   Moving slowly and from side to side, she went into the stone building and into a tower of steps, where she walked up and around and around until her feet knew to stop.

70   She entered a door, and there she saw nailed up on the wall the

document that had been stamped with the gold seal and framed in the gold frame which matched the dream that was hung up in her head.

"Here I be," she said. There was a fixed and ceremonial stiffness over her body.   71

"A charity case, I suppose," said an attendant who sat at the desk before her.   72

But Phoenix only looked above her head. There was sweat on her face; the wrinkles shone like a bright net.   73

"Speak up, Grandma," the woman said. "What's your name? We must have your history, you know. Have you been here before? What seems to be the trouble with you?"   74

Old Phoenix only gave a twitch to her face as if a fly were bothering her.   75

"Are you deaf?" cried the attendant.   76

But then the nurse came in.   77

"Oh, that's just old Aunt Phoenix," she said. "She doesn't come for herself — she has a little grandson. She makes these trips just as regular as clockwork. She lives away back off the Old Natchez Trace." She bent down. "Well, Aunt Phoenix, why don't you just take a seat? We won't keep you standing after your long trip." She pointed.   78

The old woman sat down, bolt upright in the chair.   79

"Now, how is the boy?" asked the nurse.   80

Old Phoenix did not speak.   81

"I said, how is the boy?"   82

But Phoenix only waited and stared straight ahead, her face very solemn and withdrawn into rigidity.   83

"Is his throat any better?" asked the nurse. "Aunt Phoenix, don't you hear me? Is your grandson's throat any better since the last time you came for the medicine?"   84

With her hand on her knees, the old woman waited, silent, erect and motionless, just as if she were in armor.   85

"You mustn't take up our time this way, Aunt Phoenix," the nurse said. "Tell us quickly about your grandson, and get it over. He isn't dead, is he?"   86

At last there came a flicker and then a flame of comprehension across her face, and she spoke.   87

"My grandson. It was my memory had left me. There I sat and forgot why I made my long trip."   88

"Forgot?" The nurse frowned. "After you came so far?"   89

Then Phoenix was like an old woman begging a dignified forgiveness for waking up frightened in the night. "I never did go to school   90

— I was too old at the Surrender," she said in a soft voice. "I'm an old woman without an education. It was my memory fail me. My little grandson, he is just the same, and I forgot it in the coming."

91   "Throat never heals, does it?" said the nurse, speaking in a loud, sure voice to Old Phoenix. By now she had a card with something written on it, a little list. "Yes. Swallowed lye. When was it — January — two — three years ago — "

92   Phoenix spoke unasked now. "No, missy, he not dead, he just the same. Every little while his throat begin to close up again, and he not able to swallow. He not get his breath. He not able to help himself. So the time come around, and I go on another trip for soothing medicine."

93   "All right. The doctor said as long as you came to get it you could have it," said the nurse. "But it's an obstinate case."

94   "My little grandson, he sit up there in the house all wrapped up, waiting by himself," Phoenix went on. "We is the only two left in the world. He suffer and it don't seem to put him back at all. He got a sweet look. He going to last. He wear a little patch quilt and peep out, holding his mouth open like a little bird. I remembers so plain now. I not going to forget him again, no, the whole enduring time. I could tell him from all the others in creation."

95   "All right." The nurse was trying to hush her now. She brought her a bottle of medicine. "Charity," she said, making a check mark in a book.

96   Old Phoenix held the bottle close to her eyes and then carefully put it into her pocket.

97   "I thank you," she said.

98   "It's Christmas time, Grandma," said the attendant. "Could I give you a few pennies out of my purse?"

99   "Five pennies is a nickel," said Phoenix stiffly.

100   "Here's a nickel," said the attendant.

101   Phoenix rose carefully and held out her hand. She received the nickel and then fished the other nickel out of her pocket and laid it beside the new one. She stared at her palm closely, with her head on one side.

102   Then she gave a tap with her cane on the floor.

103   "This is what come to me to do," she said. "I going to the store and buy my child a little windmill they sells, made out of paper. He going to find it hard to believe there such a thing in the world. I'll march myself back where he waiting, holding it straight up in this hand."

She lifted her free hand, gave a little nod, turned round, and 104
walked out of the doctor's office. Then her slow step began on the
stairs, going down.

_____ **CONSIDERATIONS** _____

1. Some features of Old Phoenix's long journey might bring to mind
Everyman's difficult travel through life. Do specific passages suggest that Old
Phoenix's journey is symbolic or archetypal?

2. Would you say that Old Phoenix is senile? Is she in excellent control
of her thoughts? What evidence can you find for your answer?

3. Is the grandson alive or dead? After you answer this question, read
Welty's own comments on the story in the next selection.

4. Who was the little boy with the slice of marble-cake? Why does he
appear and disappear so abruptly?

5. Eudora Welty makes no comment in the story on Old Phoenix's
encounter with the white man. Do the details of that encounter reveal anything about relations between whites and blacks?

6. What do you learn of Old Phoenix's sense of morality, and sense of
humor, and feeling of personal worth?

77

EUDORA WELTY
The Point of the Story

1   A story writer is more than happy to be read by students; the fact
that these serious readers think and feel something in response to his
work he finds life-giving. At the same time he may not always be able
to reply to their specific questions in kind. I wondered if it might
clarify something, for both the questioners and myself, if I set down a
general reply to the question that comes to me most often in the mail,
from both students and their teachers, after some classroom discussion. The unrivaled favorite is this: "Is Phoenix Jackson's grandson
really *dead?*" It refers to a short story I wrote years ago called "A Worn
Path," which tells of a day's journey an old woman makes on foot
from deep in the country into town and into a doctor's office on behalf
of her little grandson; he is at home, periodically ill, and periodically
she comes for his medicine; they give it to her as usual, she receives it
and starts the journey back.

2   I had not meant to mystify readers by withholding any fact; it is
not a writer's business to tease. The story is told through Phoenix's
mind as she undertakes her errand. As the author at one with the
character as I tell it, I must assume that the boy is alive. As the reader,
you are free to think as you like, of course: the story invites you to
believe that no matter what happens, Phoenix for as long as she is able
to walk and can hold to her purpose will make her journey. The *possibility* that she would keep on even if he were dead is there in her
devotion and its single-minded, single-track errand. Certainly the *artistic* truth, which should be good enough for the fact, lies in Phoenix's

From *The New York Times Book Review,* March 5, 1978. © 1978 by The New
York Times Company. Reprinted by permission.

own answer to that question. When the nurse asks, "He isn't dead, is he?" she speaks for herself: "He still the same. He going to last."

The grandchild is the incentive. But it is the journey, the going 3 of the errand, that is the story, and the question is not whether the grandchild is in reality alive or dead. It doesn't affect the outcome of the story or its meaning from start to finish. But it is not the question itself that has struck me as much as the idea, almost without exception implied in the asking, that for Phoenix's grandson to be dead would somehow make the story "better."

It's *all right*, I want to say to the students who write to me, for 4 things to be what they appear to be, and for words to mean what they say. It's all right, too, for words and appearances to mean more than one thing — ambiguity is a fact of life. A fiction writer's responsibility covers not only what he presents as the facts of a given story but what he chooses to stir up as their implications; in the end, these implications, too, become facts, in the larger, fictional sense. But it is not all right, not in good faith, for things not to mean what they say.

The grandson's plight was real and it made the truth of the story, 5 which is the story of an errand of love carried out. If the child no longer lived, the truth would persist in the "wornness" of the path. But his being dead can't increase the truth of the story, can't affect it one way or the other. I think I signal this, because the end of the story has been reached before old Phoenix gets home again: she simply starts back. To the question "Is the grandson really dead?" I could reply that it doesn't make any difference. I could also say that I did not make him up in order to let him play a trick on Phoenix. But my best answer would be: "Phoenix is alive."

The origin of a story is sometimes a trustworthy clue to the 6 author — or can provide him with the clue — to its key image; maybe in this case it will do the same for the reader. One day I saw a solitary old woman like Phoenix. She was walking; I saw her, at middle distance, in a winter country landscape, and watched her slowly make her way across my line of vision. That sight of her made me write the story. I invented an errand for her, but that only seemed a living part of the figure she was herself; what errand other than for someone else could be making her go? And her going was the first thing, her persisting in her landscape was the real thing, and the first and the real were what I wanted and worked to keep. I brought her up close enough, by imagination, to describe her face, make her present to the eyes, but the full-length figure moving across the winter fields was the indelible one and the image to keep, and the perspective extending into the vanishing distance the true one to hold in mind.

7   I invented for my character as I wrote, some passing adventures — some dreams and harassments and a small triumph or two, some jolts to her pride, some flights of fancy to console her, one or two encounters to scare her, a moment that gave her cause to feel ashamed, a moment to dance and preen—for it had to be a journey, and all these things belonged to that, parts of life's uncertainty.

8   A narrative line is in its deeper sense, of course, the tracing out of a meaning, and the real continuity of a story lies in this probing forward. The real dramatic force of a story depends on the strength of the emotion that has set it going. The emotional value is the measure of the reach of the story. What gives any such content to "A Worn Path" is not its circumstances but its subject: the deep-grained habit of love.

9   What I hoped would come clear was that in the whole surround of this story, the world it threads through, the only certain thing at all is the worn path. The habit of love cuts through confusion and stumbles or contrives its way out of difficulty, it remembers the way even when it forgets, for a dumbfounded moment, its reason for being. The path is the thing that matters.

10   Her victory — old Phoenix's — is when she sees the diploma in the doctor's office, when she finds "nailed up on the wall the document that had been stamped with the gold seal and framed in the gold frame, which matched the dream that was hung up in her head." The return with the medicine is just a matter of retracing her own footsteps. It is the part of the journey, and of the story, that can now go without saying.

11   In the matter of function, old Phoenix's way might even do as a sort of parallel to your way of work if you are a writer of stories. The way to get there is the all-important, all-absorbing problem, and this problem is your reason for undertaking the story. Your only guide, too, is your sureness about your subject, about what this subject is. Like Phoenix, you work all your life to find your way, through all the obstructions and the false appearances and the upsets you may have brought on yourself, to reach a meaning — using inventions of your imagination, perhaps helped out by your dreams and bits of good luck. And finally too, like Phoenix, you have to assume that what you are working in aid of is life, not death.

12   But you would make the trip anyway — wouldn't you? — just on hope.

_____ **CONSIDERATIONS** _____

1. Welty says that Old Phoenix's return trip is "the part of the journey, and of the story, that can now go without saying." If you were writing this story would you choose a different place to end it? Would you follow Old Phoenix all the way back into the hills? Would you show us the grandson? Why?

2. How does Welty feel about writers who intentionally mystify their readers?

3. Does "A Worn Path" illustrate what Welty means when she says, "A narrative line is in its deeper sense . . . the tracing out of a meaning"?

4. In Paragraph 4, Welty touches on the "factuality" of a work of fiction. This introduces a fascinating (if maddening) question: what is the difference between fiction and nonfiction?

5. Another southern writer, William Faulkner, wrote a short novel, *As I Lay Dying*, that can be read as a fuller version of "A Worn Path." It too is based on "an errand of love," as Welty puts it. Read the novel and discuss its parallels with Welty's story.

6. What do you think of Welty's response to the question about her story? Do her comments constitute the kind of critical analysis that Robert Gorham Davis mentions in Paragraph 8, page 116?

E. B. White (b. 1899) was born in Mount Vernon, New York, graduated from Cornell in 1921, and joined the staff of The New Yorker *in 1926. For many years, he wrote the brief essay which led off that magazine's "The Talk of the Town" and edited other "Talk" segments. In 1929, White collaborated with James Thurber on a book called* Is Sex Necessary? *and from time to time he has published collections of essays and poems, most of them taken from* The New Yorker *and* Harper's. *Some of his best-known collections are* One Man's Meat *(1942),* The Second Tree from the Corner *(1953), and* The Points of My Compass *(1962). He is also the author of children's books, most notably* Stuart Little *(1945) and* Charlotte's Web *(1952), and the celebrated book on prose,* The Elements of Style *(with William Strunk, Jr., 1959).*

In 1937, White retired from The New Yorker *and moved to a farm in Maine, where he continued to write those minimal, devastating comments attached to the proofhacks and other errors printed at the ends of* The New Yorker's *columns. And he continues his slow, consistent writing of superb prose. In recent years, the collected* Letters of E. B. White *(1976) and* Essays of E. B. White *(1977) have reconfirmed this country's infatuation with the versatile author. A special citation from the Pulitzer Prize Committee in 1978 celebrated the publication of White's letters.*

78

E. B. WHITE
Once More to the Lake

One summer, along about 1904, my father rented a camp on a lake in Maine and took us all there for the month of August. We all got ringworm from some kittens and had to rub Pond's Extract on our arms and legs night and morning, and my father rolled over in a canoe with all his clothes on; but outside of that the vacation was a success and from then on none of us ever thought there was any place in the world like that lake in Maine. We returned summer after summer — always on August 1st for one month. I have since become a salt-water man, but sometimes in summer there are days when the restlessness of the tides and the fearful cold of the sea water and the incessant wind that blows across the afternoon and into the evening make me wish for the placidity of a lake in the woods. A few weeks ago this feeling got so strong I bought myself a couple of bass hooks and a spinner and returned to the lake where we used to go, for a week's fishing and to revisit old haunts. 1

I took along my son, who had never had any fresh water up his nose and who had seen lily pads only from train windows. On the journey over to the lake I began to wonder what it would be like. I wondered how time would have marred this unique, this holy spot — the coves and streams, the hills that the sun set behind, the camps and the paths behind the camps. I was sure that the tarred road would have found it out and I wondered in what other ways it would be desolated. It is strange how much you can remember about places like that once you allow your mind to return into the grooves that lead 2 back. You remember one thing, and that suddenly reminds you of another thing. I guess I remembered clearest of all the early mornings, when the lake was cool and motionless, remembered how the bedroom smelled of the lumber it was made of and of the wet woods whose scent entered through the screen. The partitions in the camp were thin and did not extend clear to the top of the rooms, and as I was always the first up I would dress softly so as not to wake the others, and sneak out into the sweet outdoors and start out in the canoe, keeping close along the shore in the long shadows of the pines. I remembered being very careful never to rub my paddle against the gunwale for fear of disturbing the stillness of the cathedral.

3   The lake had never been what you would call a wild lake. There were cottages sprinkled around the shores, and it was in farming country although the shores of the lake were quite heavily wooded. Some of the cottages were owned by nearby farmers, and you would live at the shore and eat your meals at the farmhouse. That's what our family did. But although it wasn't wild, it was a fairly large and undisturbed lake and there were places in it which, to a child at least, seemed infinitely remote and primeval.

4   I was right about the tar: it led to within half a mile of the shore. But when I got back there, with my boy, and we settled into a camp near a farmhouse and into the kind of summertime I had known, I could tell that it was going to be pretty much the same as it had been before — I knew it, lying in bed the first morning, smelling the bedroom, and hearing the boy sneak quietly out and go off along the shore in a boat. I began to sustain the illusion that he was I, and therefore, by simple transposition, that I was my father. This sensation persisted, kept cropping up all the time we were there. It was not an entirely new feeling, but in this setting it grew much stronger. I seemed to be living a dual existence. I would be in the middle of some simple act, I would be picking up a bait box or laying down a table fork, or I would be saying something, and suddenly it would be not I but my father who was saying the words or making the gesture. It gave me a creepy sensation.

5   We went fishing the first morning. I felt the same damp moss covering the worms in the bait can, and saw the dragonfly alight on the tip of my rod as it hovered a few inches from the surface of the water. It was the arrival of this fly that convinced me beyond any doubt that everything was as it always had been, that the years were a mirage and there had been no years. The small waves were the same, chucking the rowboat under the chin as we fished at anchor, and the

boat was the same boat, the same color green and the ribs broken in the same places, and under the floor-boards the same fresh-water leavings and débris — the dead hellgrammite, the wisps of moss, the rusty discarded fishhook, the dried blood from yesterday's catch. We stared silently at the tips of our rods, at the dragonflies that came and went. I lowered the tip of mine into the water, tentatively, pensively dislodging the fly, which darted two feet away, poised, darted two feet back, and came to rest again a little farther up the rod. There had been no years between the ducking of this dragonfly and the other one — the one that was part of memory. I looked at the boy, who was silently watching his fly, and it was my hands that held his rod, my eyes watching. I felt dizzy and didn't know which rod I was at the end of.

We caught two bass, hauling them in briskly as though they were   6
mackerel, pulling them over the side of the boat in a businesslike manner without any landing net, and stunning them with a blow on the back of the head. When we got back for a swim before lunch, the lake was exactly where we had left it, the same number of inches from the dock, and there was only the merest suggestion of a breeze. This seemed an utterly enchanted sea, this lake you could leave to its own devices for a few hours and come back to, and find that it had not stirred, this constant and trustworthy body of water. In the shallows, the dark, water-soaked sticks and twigs, smooth and old, were undulating in clusters on the bottom against the clean ribbed sand, and the track of the mussel was plain. A school of minnows swam by, each minnow with its small individual shadow, doubling the attendance, so clear and sharp in the sunlight. Some of the other campers were in swimming, along the shore, one of them with a cake of soap, and the water felt thin and clear and unsubstantial. Over the years there had been this person with the cake of soap, this cultist, and here he was. There had been no years.

Up to the farmhouse to dinner through the teeming, dusty field,   7
the road under our sneakers was only a two-track road. The middle track was missing, the one with the marks of the hooves and splotches of dried, flaky manure. There had always been three tracks to choose from in choosing which track to walk in; now the choice was narrowed down to two. For a moment I missed terribly the middle alternative. But the way led past the tennis court, and something about the way it lay there in the sun reassured me; the tape had loosened along the backline, the alleys were green with plantains and other weeds, and the net (installed in June and removed in September) sagged in the dry noon, and the whole place steamed with midday heat and hunger

and emptiness. There was a choice of pie for dessert, and one was blueberry and one was apple, and the waitresses were the same country girls, there having been no passage of time, only the illusion of it as in a dropped curtain — the waitresses were still fifteen; their hair had been washed, that was the only difference — they had been to the movies and seen the pretty girls with the clean hair.

8   Summertime, oh summertime, pattern of life indelible, the fade-proof lake, the woods unshatterable, the pasture with the sweetfern and the juniper forever and ever, summer without end; this was the background, and the life along the shore was the design, the cottages with their innocent and tranquil design, their tiny docks with the flagpole and the American flag floating against the white clouds in the blue sky, the little paths over the roots of the trees leading from camp to camp and the paths leading back to the outhouses and the can of lime for sprinkling, and at the souvenir counters at the store the miniature birch-bark canoes and the post cards that showed things looking a little better than they looked. This was the American family at play, escaping the city heat, wondering whether the newcomers in the camp at the head of the cove were "common" or "nice," wondering whether it was true that the people who drove up for Sunday dinner at the farmhouse were turned away because there wasn't enough chicken.

9   It seemed to me, as I kept remembering all this, that those times and those summers had been infinitely precious and worth saving. There had been jollity and peace and goodness. The arriving (at the beginning of August) had been so big a business in itself, at the railway station the farm wagon drawn up, the first smell of the pine-laden air, the first glimpse of the smiling farmer, and the great importance of the trunks and your father's enormous authority in such matters, and the feel of the wagon under you for the long ten-mile haul, and at the top of the last long hill catching the first view of the lake after eleven months of not seeing this cherished body of water. The shouts and cries of the other campers when they saw you, and the trunks to be unpacked, to give up their rich burden. (Arriving was less exciting nowadays, when you sneaked up in your car and parked it under a tree near the camp and took out the bags and in five minutes it was all over, no fuss, no loud wonderful fuss about trunks.)

10   Peace and goodness and jollity. The only thing that was wrong now, really, was the sound of the place, an unfamiliar nervous sound of the outboard motors. This was the note that jarred, the one thing that would sometimes break the illusion and set the years moving. In those other summertimes all motors were inboard; and when they

were at a little distance, the noise they made was a sedative, an ingre-
dient of summer sleep. They were one-cylinder and two-cylinder
engines, and some were make-and-break and some were jump-spark,
but they all made a sleepy sound across the lake. The one-lungers
throbbed and fluttered, and the twin-cylinder ones purred and purred
and that was a quiet sound too. But now the campers all had out-
boards. In the daytime, in the hot mornings, these motors made a
petulant, irritable sound; at night, in the still evening when the after-
glow lit the water, they whined about one's ears like mosquitoes. My
boy loved our rented outboard, and his great desire was to achieve
singlehanded mastery over it, and authority, and he soon learned the
trick of choking it a little (but not too much), and the adjustment of
the needle valve. Watching him I would remember the things you
could do with the old one-cylinder engine with the heavy flywheel,
how you could have it eating out of your hand if you got really close
to it spiritually. Motor boats in those days didn't have clutches, and
you would make a landing by shutting off the motor at the proper
time and coasting in with a dead rudder. But there was a way of
reversing them, if you learned the trick, by cutting the switch and
putting it on again exactly on the final dying revolution of the flywheel, so that it would kick back against compression and begin
reversing. Approaching a dock in a strong following breeze, it was
difficult to slow up sufficiently by the ordinary coasting method, and
if a boy felt he had complete mastery over his motor, he was tempted
to keep it running beyond its time and then reverse it a few feet from
the dock. It took a cool nerve, because if you threw the switch a
twentieth of a second too soon you could catch the flywheel when it
still had speed enough to go up past center, and the boat would leap
ahead, charging bull-fashion at the dock.

We had a good week at the camp. The bass were biting well and   11
the sun shone endlessly, day after day. We would be tired at night and
lie down in the accumulated heat of the little bedrooms after the long
hot day and the breeze would stir almost imperceptibly outside and
the smell of the swamp drift in through the rusty screens. Sleep would
come easily and in the morning the red squirrel would be on the roof,
tapping out his gay routine. I kept remembering everything, lying in
bed in the mornings — the small steamboat that had a long rounded
stern like the lip of a Ubangi, and how quietly she ran on the moon-
light sails, when the older boys played their mandolins and the girls
sang and we ate doughnuts dipped in sugar, and how sweet the music
was on the water in the shining night, and what it had felt like to

think about girls then. After breakfast we would go up to the store and the things were in the same place — the minnows in a bottle, the plugs and spinners disarranged and pawed over by the youngsters from the boys' camp, the fig newtons and the Beeman's gum. Outside, the road was tarred and cars stood in front of the store. Inside, all was just as it had always been, except there was more Coca-Cola and not so much Moxie and root beer and birch beer and sarsaparilla. We would walk out with a bottle of pop apiece and sometimes the pop would backfire up our noses and hurt. We explored the streams, quietly, where the turtles slid off the sunny logs and dug their way into the soft bottom; and we lay on the town wharf and fed worms to the tame bass. Everywhere we went I had trouble making out which was I, the one walking at my side, the one walking in my pants.

12   One afternoon while we were there at that lake a thunderstorm came up. It was like the revival of an old melodrama that I had seen long ago with childish awe. The second-act climax of the drama of the electrical disturbance over a lake in America had not changed in any important respect. This was the big scene, still the big scene. The whole thing was so familiar, the first feeling of oppression and heat and a general air around camp of not wanting to go very far away. In midafternoon (it was all the same) a curious darkening of the sky, and a lull in everything that had made life tick; and then the way the boats suddenly swung the other way at their moorings with the coming of a breeze out of the new quarter, and the premonitory rumble. Then the kettle drum, then the snare, then the bass drum and cymbals, then crackling light against the dark, and the gods grinning and licking their chops in the hills. Afterward the calm, the rain steadily rustling in the calm lake, the return of light and hope and spirits, and the campers running out in joy and relief to go swimming in the rain, their bright cries perpetuating the deathless joke about how they were getting simply drenched, and the children screaming with delight at the new sensation of bathing in the rain, and the joke about getting drenched linking the generations in a strong indestructible chain. And the comedian who waded in carrying an umbrella.

13   When the others went swimming my son said he was going in too. He pulled his dripping trunks from the line where they had hung all through the shower, and wrung them out. Languidly, and with no thought of going in, I watched him, his hard little body, skinny and bare, saw him wince slightly as he pulled up around his vitals the small, soggy, icy garment. As he buckled the swollen belt suddenly my groin felt the chill of death.

_____ **CONSIDERATIONS** _____

1. A master of the personal essay, E. B. White transforms an exercise in memory into something universal, timeless, and profound. Study Paragraph 4 to see how.

2. White rejuvenates bits and pieces of language that have become worn and lackluster through repetition. Can you find an example of this technique in Paragraph 2?

3. White notes many changes at the old summer place, but he is more moved by the sameness. Locate examples of his feeling of sameness and consider how these examples contribute to his themes.

4. The author expresses a predictable dislike of outboard motors on the otherwise quiet lake. Does he avoid stereotype when he writes about motors elsewhere in this essay?

5. What is the chief device White uses in his description of the thunderstorm in Paragraph 12?

6. How is the last sentence of the essay a surprise? How has White prepared us for it?

Thomas Wolfe (1900–1938) wrote enormous autobiographical novels, most notably Look Homeward, Angel (1929) and Of Time and the River (1935), and two published posthumously, The Web and the Rock (1939) and You Can't Go Home Again (1940). He was born and grew up in Asheville, North Carolina, entered the University of North Carolina at fifteen, attended Harvard, and taught at New York University. Wolfe was a huge man, and he wrote hugely. His novels were unending journals of total recall. He sometimes wrote twenty thousand words — the equivalent of about sixty pages in A Writer's Reader — at one sitting. Patient editors, especially Maxwell Perkins at Scribner's, spent months carving each of his novels from packing cases full of disorganized manuscript. The finished novels were highly emotional, lyrical accounts of childhood, youth, and early manhood. Wolfe wrote one book about his unique method of writing, The Story of a Novel (1936). He died of complications following an attack of pneumonia, two weeks before he would have turned thirty-eight.

The journal from which these selections come was written shortly before his final illness and death. He had given a talk at Purdue University in Indiana, and then had traveled to the Pacific Northwest looking for some relatives on his mother's side. He took a notebook with him, thinking that later he might work his notes up into a book. Only these notes survive, presented here line by line, transcribed from the novelist's nearly illegible handwriting.

Brilliant descriptions, intense evocation — and no discipline or structure. Of course one would not expect discipline or structure from any writer in an unedited, posthumously published journal. This journal may serve as a model for students who wish to learn to write rapidly — in order to loosen up, and to accumulate detail and color, idea and recollection — before applying to their writing the formal disciplines of sentence, paragraph, and essay.

79

THOMAS WOLFE
Journal Entries

MONDAY JUNE 20 (CRATER LAKE)

Left Portland, University Club, 8:15 sharp —
Fair day, bright sunlight, no cloud in sky —
Went South by East through farmlands of upper
Willamette and around base of Mount Hood
which was glowing in brilliant sun — Then
climbed and crossed Cascades, and came down
with suddenness of knife into the dry lands of the
Eastern slope — Then over high plateau and
through bare hills and canyons and irrigated
farmlands here and there, low valley, etc., and
into Bend at 12:45 — 200 miles in 4½
hours —

1

Then lunch at hotel and view of the 3 Sisters and
the Cascade range — then up to the Pilot Butte
above the town — the great plain stretching
infinite away — and unapproachable the great line
of the Cascades with their snowspired sentinels
Hood, Adams, Jefferson, 3 sisters, etc, and out of
Bend at 3 and then through the vast and level
pinelands — somewhat reminiscent of the South

2

for 100 miles then down through the noble pines
to the vast plainlike valley of the Klamath? — the
virgin land of Canaan all again — the far-off
ranges — infinite — Oregon and the Promised
Land — then through the valley floor — past Indian
reservation — Capt Jack — the Modocs — the great
trees open approaching vicinity of the Park —
the entrance and the reservation — the forester —
the houses — the great snow patches underneath
the trees — then the great climb upwards — the
foresting, administration — up and up again —
through the passes the great plain behind and at
length the incredible crater of the lake — the hotel
and a certain cheerlessness in spite of cordialness
— dry tongues vain-licking for a feast — the return,
the cottages, the college boys and girls who serve
and wait — the cafeteria and the souvenirs —
the great crater fading coldly in incredible
cold light — at

3   length departure — and the forest rangers down
below — long, long talks — too long with them
about "our wonders," etc — then by darkness the
sixty or seventy miles down the great dim
expanse of Klamath Lake, the decision to stay
here for the night — 3 beers, a shower, and this,
reveille at 5:30 in the morning — and so to bed!
        First day: 404 miles

4   The gigantic unconscious humor of the situation
— C "making every national park" without
seeing any of them — the main thing is to "make
them" — and so on and on tomorrow

TUESDAY JUNE 21, 1938 (YOSEMITE)

5   Dies Irae: Wakened at 5:30 — dragged weary
bones erect, dressed, closed baggage, was ready
shortly before six, and we were off again "on

the dot" — at six oclock. So out of Klamath,
the lakes red, and a thread of silver river in
the desert, and immediately

    the desert, sage brush, and bare, naked, hills,   6
giant-molded, craterous, cupreous, glaciated
blasted — a demonic heath with reaches of great
pine, and volcanic glaciation, cupreous, fiendish,
desert, blasted — the ruins of old settlers home-
steads, ghost towns and the bleak little facades
of long forgotten postoffices lit bawdily by blazing
rising sun and the winding mainstreet, the
deserted station of the incessant railway — all
dominated now by the glittering snow — pale
masses of

    Mount Shasta — pine lands, canyons, sweeps and   7
rises, the naked crateric hills and the volcanic
lava masses and then Mount Shasta omnipresent
— Mount Shasta all the time — always Mt. Shasta
— and at last the town named Weed (with a
divine felicity) — and breakfast at Weed at 7:45 —
and the morning bus from Portland and the
tired people tumbling out and *in* for breakfast

    and away from Weed and towering Shasta at   8
8:15 — and up and climbing and at length into
the passes of the lovely timbered Siskiyous
and now down into canyon of the Sacramento
in among the lovely timbered Siskiyous and all
through the morning down and down and down
the canyon, and the road snaking, snaking
always with a thousand little punctual gashes,
and the freight trains and the engines turned
backward with the cabs in *front*

    down below along the lovely Sacramento snaking   9
snaking snaking — and at last into the town of
Redding and the timber fading, hills fading,
cupreous lavic masses fading — and almost at

once the mighty valley of the Sacramento — as
broad as a continent — and all through the morning through the great floor of that great plain
like valley — the vast fields thick with straw
grass lighter

10   than Swedes hair — and infinitely far and
unapproachable the towns down the mountain
on both sides — and great herds of fat brown
steers in straw light fields — a dry land, with
a strange hot heady fragrance and fertility —
and at last no mountains at all but the great
sun-bright, heat-hazed, straw-light plain and
the straight marvel of the road on which the
car rushes

11   on like magic and no sense of speed at 60 miles
an hour — At 11:30 a brief halt at — to look at
the hotel — and great palms now, and spanish
tiles and arches and pilasters and a patio in
the hotel and swimming pool — and on again and
on again across the great, hot, straw light plain,
and great fields mown new and scattered with
infinite bundles of baled hay and

12   occasional clumps of greenery and pastures and
houses and barns where water is and as Sacramento
nears a somewhat greener land, more unguent,
and better houses now, and great fat herds of
steers innumerable and lighter and more sun —
ovenhot towns and at length through the heat-
haze the slopes of Sacramento and over an
enormous viaduct across a flat

13   and marshy land and planes flying, and then
the far flung filling stations, hot dog stores,
3 Little Pigs, and Bar B-Q's of a California
town and then across the Sacramento into town —
the turn immediate and houses new and mighty
palms and trees and people walking. and the

State house with its gold leaf dome
and spaghetti at the first Greeks that we find,
and on out again immediate —

      pressing on — past state house — and past street   14
by street of leafy trees and palms and pleasant houses and out from
town now — but traffic
flashing past now — and loaded trucks and
whizzing cars — no more the lovely 50 mile
stretches and 60 miles an hour — but down across
the backbone of the state — and the whole backbone
of the state — cars and towns and farms
and people
flashing by — and still that same vast
billowy plain — no light *brown* now — the
San Joaquin Valley now — and bursting with
Gods plenty — orchards — peaches — apricots —
and vineyards — orange groves — Gods plenty of
the best — and glaring litle towns sown thick
with fruit packing houses — ovenhot, glittering
in the hot and shining air — town

      after town — each in the middle of Gods plenty —   15
and at length the turn at — toward Yosemite —
90 miles away — the barren, crateric, lavic, volcanic
blasted hills — but signs now telling us we can't
get in now across the washed out road save
behind the conductor — and now too late — already
5 of six and the last conductor leaves

      at six and we still 50 miles away — and telephone   16
calls now to rangers, superintendents and so
forth, a filling station and hot cabins, and the
end of a day of blazing heat and the wind
stirring in the sycamores about the cabins, and
on again now, and almost immediately the broken
ground, the straw light mouldings, the rises to
the crater hills and soon

      among them — climbing, climbing into timber —   17
and down down down into pleasant timbered

mountain folds — get no sensation yet and winding
in and out — and little hill towns here and there
and climbing, climbing, climbing, mountain
lodges, cabins, houses, and so on, and now in
terrific mountain folds, close packed, precipitous,
lapped together and down and over, down again

18   along breath taking curves and steepnesses and
sheer drops down below into a canyon cut a
mile below by great knifes blade — and at the
bottom the closed gate — the little store — calls upon
the phone again, and darkness and the sending
notes, and at last success — upon our own heads
be the risk but we may enter — and we do —
and so slowly up

19   we go along the washed out road — finding it
not near so dangerous as we feared — and at
length past the bad end and the closed gate and
release — and up now climbing and the sound of
mighty waters in the gorge and the sheer black-
nesses of beetling masses and the stars — and
presently the entrance and the rangers house —
a free pass now — and up and up — and boles of
trees terrific, cloven rock above the road

20   and over us and dizzy masses night black as a
cloud, a sense of the imminent terrific and at
length the valley of the Yosemite; roads forking
darkly, but the perfect sign — and now a smell
of smokes and of gigantic tentings and enormous
trees and gigantic cliff walls night black all
around and above the sky-bowl of starred night —
and Currys Lodge and

21   smoky gaiety and wonder — hundreds of young
faces and voices — the offices, buildings stores,
the dance floor crowded with its weary hundreds
and the hundreds of tents and cabins and the
absurdity of the life and the immensity of all —

and 1200 little shop girls and stenogs and new-
weds and schoolteachers and boys — all, God
bless their

little lives, necking, dancing, kissing, feeling,   22
and embracing in the great darkness of the giant
redwood trees — and the sound of the dark gigantic fall
of water — and so to bed!
  And 535 miles today!

_____ CONSIDERATIONS _____

1. Judging from the kinds of things he recorded in his journal, what were
Wolfe's chief interests during the journey? What was he searching for? Why
did he bother to keep a journal?

2. How many periods can you find in this selection? How does that
number help account for the sense of speed and constant motion we get from
the journal? What other characteristics of Wolfe's prose here contribute to that
sense?

3. Does Wolfe depend much in his journal on figurative language, or is
this selection chiefly literal and matter-of-fact?

4. How much of a typical American tourist was Wolfe? How often does
he break out of such a stereotype? As you consider these questions, think of
the phrases "see America first," "the American dream," and "middle-class
values."

5. Write journal entries of your own about a trip you've made, imitating
Wolfe's style. How do an imitation and a parody differ?

6. It would seem only fair to look at a sample of Wolfe's finished, published work. Try the opening pages of *Look Homeward, Angel,* or *You Can't
Go Home Again,* or *Of Time and the River.* Do you find any similarities
between his finished work and his rough notebook? Does anything suggest
that he might have used a good deal of journal material in his novels?

Virginia Woolf (1882–1941) is best known as a novelist. The Voyage Out *appeared in 1915, followed by* Night and Day *(1919),* Jacob's Room *(1922),* Mrs. Dalloway *(1925),* To The Lighthouse *(1927),* Orlando *(1928),* The Waves *(1931),* The Years *(1937), and* Between the Acts, *published shortly after her death. Daughter of Sir Leslie Stephen, Victorian critic and essayist who edited the* Dictionary of National Biography, *she was educated at home, and began her literary career as a critic for the* Times Literary Supplement. *She wrote essays regularly until her death; four volumes of her* Collected Essays *appeared in the United States in 1967. More recently, her publishers have issued six volumes of her collected letters, and her diary is being published.*

With her sister Vanessa, a painter, her husband Leonard Woolf, an editor and writer, and Vanessa's husband Clive Bell, an art critic, Virginia lived at the center of the Bloomsbury group — artists and intellectuals who gathered informally to talk and to amuse each other, and whose unconventional ideas and habits, when they were known, shocked the stolid British public. John Maynard Keynes, the economist, was a member of the varied group, which also included the biographer Lytton Strachey, the novelist E. M. Forster, and eventually the American poet living in England, T. S. Eliot. With her husband, Virginia Woolf founded The Hogarth Press, *a small firm dedicated to publishing superior works. Among its authors were T. S. Eliot and Virginia herself.*

A recent biography — Virginia Woolf *— by her nephew Quentin Bell gives an intimate picture of the whole group. Of all the Bloomsbury people, Virginia was perhaps the most talented. Through most of her life, she struggled against recurring mental illness, which brought intense depression and suicidal impulses. When she was fifty-nine she drowned herself in the River Ouse. The following famous passage from* A Room of One's Own *(1929) presents a feminist argument by means of a memorable supposition.*

written the plays of Shakespeare, I concluded, and I thought of that old gentleman, who is dead now, but was a bishop, I think, who declared that it was impossible for any woman, past, present, or to come, to have the genius of Shakespeare. He wrote to the papers about it. He also told a lady who applied to him for information that cats do not as a matter of fact go to heaven, though they have, he added, souls of a sort. How much thinking those old gentlemen used to save one! How the borders of ignorance shrank back at their approach! Cats do not go to heaven. Women cannot write the plays of Shakespeare.

3   Be that as it may, I could not help thinking, as I looked at the works of Shakespeare on the shelf, that the bishop was right at least in this; it would have been impossible, completely and entirely, for any woman to have written the plays of Shakespeare in the age of Shakespeare. Let me imagine, since facts are so hard to come by, what would have happened had Shakespeare had a wonderfully gifted sister, called Judith, let us say. Shakespeare himself went, very probably — his mother was an heiress — to the grammar school, where he may have learnt Latin — Ovid, Virgil and Horace — and the elements of grammar and logic. He was, it is well known, a wild boy who poached rabbits, perhaps shot a deer, and had, rather sooner than he should have done, to marry a woman in the neighbourhood, who bore him a child rather quicker than was right. That escapade sent him to seek his fortune in London. He had, it seemed, a taste for the theatre; he began by holding horses at the stage door. Very soon he got work in the theatre, became a successful actor, and lived at the hub of the universe, meeting everybody, knowing everybody, practising his art on the boards, exercising his wits in the streets, and even getting access to the palace of the queen. Meanwhile his extraordinarily gifted sister, let us suppose, remained at home. She was as adventurous, as imaginative, as agog to see the world as he was. But she was not sent to school. She had no chance of learning grammar and logic, let alone of reading Horace and Virgil. She picked up a book now and then, one of her brother's perhaps, and read a few pages. But then her parents came in and told her to mend the stockings or mind the stew and not moon about with books and papers. They would have spoken sharply but kindly, for they were substantial people who knew the conditions of life for a woman and loved their daughter — indeed, more likely than not she was the apple of her father's eye. Perhaps she scribbled some pages up in an apple loft on the sly, but was careful to hide them or set fire to them. Soon, however, before she was out of her teens, she was to be betrothed to the son of a neighbouring wool-stapler. She cried out that marriage was hateful to her, and for that she was

severely beaten by her father. Then he ceased to scold her. He begged her instead not to hurt him, not to shame him in this matter of her marriage. He would give her a chain of beads or a fine petticoat, he said; and there were tears in his eyes. How could she disobey him? How could she break his heart? The force of her own gift alone drove her to it. She made up a small parcel of her belongings, let herself down by a rope one summer's night and took the road to London. She was not seventeen. The birds that sang in the hedge were not more musical than she was. She had the quickest fancy, a gift like her brother's, for the tune of words. Like him, she had a taste for the theatre. She stood at the stage door; she wanted to act, she said. Men laughed in her face. The manager — a fat, loose-lipped man — guffawed. He bellowed something about poodles dancing and women acting — no woman, he said, could possibly be an actress. He hinted — you can imagine what. She could get no training in her craft. Could she even seek her dinner in a tavern or roam the streets at midnight? Yet her genius was for fiction and lusted to feed abundantly upon the lives of men and women and the study of their ways. At last — for she was very young, oddly like Shakespeare the poet in her face, with the same grey eyes and rounded brows — at last Nick Greene the actor-manager took pity on her; she found herself with child by that gentleman and so — who shall measure the heat and violence of the poet's heart when caught and tangled in a woman's body? — killed herself one winter's night and lies buried at some cross-roads where the omnibuses now stop outside the Elephant and Castle.

That, more or less, is how the story would run, I think, if a 4
woman in Shakespeare's day had had Shakespeare's genius. But for my part, I agree with the deceased bishop, if such he was — it is unthinkable that any woman in Shakespeare's day should have had Shakespeare's genius. For genius like Shakespeare's is not born among labouring, uneducated, servile people. It was not born in England among the Saxons and the Britons. It is not born today among the working classes. How, then, could it have been born among women whose work began, according to Professor Trevelyan, almost before they were out of the nursery, who were forced to it by their parents and held to it by all the power of law and custom?

——— CONSIDERATIONS ———————————————

1. In Paragraph 3, Woolf develops at length an imaginary sister of Shakespeare. Why does the writer call that sister Judith rather than Priscilla or

Richard Wright (1908–1960) was born on a plantation in Natchez, Mississippi. A restless and unruly child, at fifteen he left home and supported himself doing unskilled work, gradually improving his employment until he became a clerk in a post office. In this essay from his autobiography Black Boy *(1944) he writes about an occasion that transformed his life. By chance he became obsessed with the notion of reading H. L. Mencken, the iconoclastic editor and essayist. (See Mencken's "Gamalielese" on pages 254–257.) He schemed and plotted to borrow Mencken's books from the library, and when he succeeded, his career as a writer began.*

Determined to be a writer, Richard Wright worked on the Federal Writers' Project, wrote for the New Masses, *and finally won a prize from* Story *magazine for a short novel called* Uncle Tom's Children. *The following year, he was awarded a Guggenheim Fellowship, and in 1940 he published his novel* Native Son, *which has become an American classic. In 1946 he emigrated to Paris, where he lived until his death. His later novels included* The Outsider *(1953) and* The Long Dream *(1958). In 1977, his publisher issued the second half of* Black Boy, *entitled* American Hunger.

81

RICHARD WRIGHT

The Library Card

1   One morning I arrived early at work and went into the bank lobby where the Negro porter was mopping. I stood at a counter and picked up the Memphis *Commercial Appeal* and began my free reading of the press. I came finally to the editorial page and saw an article dealing with one H. L. Mencken. I knew by hearsay that he was the editor of the *American Mercury*, but aside from that I knew nothing about him. The article was a furious denunciation of Mencken, concluding with one, hot, short sentence: Mencken is a fool.

2   I wondered what on earth this Mencken had done to call down upon him the scorn of the South. The only people I had ever heard denounced in the South were Negroes, and this man was not a Negro. Then what ideas did Mencken hold that made a newspaper like the *Commercial Appeal* castigate him publicly? Undoubtedly he must be advocating ideas that the South did not like. Were there, then, people other than Negroes who criticized the South? I knew that during the Civil War the South had hated northern whites, but I had not encountered such hate during my life. Knowing no more of Mencken than I did at that moment, I felt a vague sympathy for him. Had not the South, which had assigned me the role of a non-man, cast at him its hardest words?

3   Now, how could I find out about this Mencken? There was a huge library near the riverfront, but I knew that Negroes were not allowed to patronize its shelves any more than they were the parks and playgrounds of the city. I had gone into the library several times to get books for the white men on the job. Which of them would now

help me to get books? And how could I read them without causing concern to the white men with whom I worked? I had so far been successful in hiding my thoughts and feelings from them, but I knew that I would create hostility if I went about the business of reading in a clumsy way.

    I weighed the personalities of the men on the job. There was 4 Don, a Jew; but I distrusted him. His position was not much better than mine and I knew that he was uneasy and insecure; he had always treated me in an offhand, bantering way that barely concealed his contempt. I was afraid to ask him to help me get books; his frantic desire to demonstrate a racial solidarity with the whites against Negroes might make him betray me.

    Then how about the boss? No, he was a Baptist and I had the 5 suspicion that he would not be quite able to comprehend why a black boy would want to read Mencken. There were other white men on the job whose attitudes showed clearly that they were Kluxers or sympathizers, and they were out of the question.

    There remained only one man whose attitude did not fit into an 6 anti-Negro category, for I had heard the white men refer to him as a "Pope lover." He was an Irish Catholic and was hated by the white Southerners. I knew that he read books, because I had got him volumes from the library several times. Since he, too, was an object of hatred, I felt that he might refuse me but would hardly betray me. I hesitated, weighing and balancing the imponderable realities.

    One morning I paused before the Catholic fellow's desk. 7

    "I want to ask you a favor," I whispered to him. 8

    "What is it?" 9

    "I want to read. I can't get books from the library. I wonder if 10 you'd let me use your card?"

    He looked at me suspiciously. 11

    "My card is full most of the time," he said. 12

    "I see," I said and waited, posing my question silently. 13

    "You're not trying to get me into trouble, are you, boy?" he 14 asked, staring at me.

    "Oh, no, sir." 15

    "What book do you want?" 16

    "A book by H. L. Mencken." 17

    "Which one?" 18

    "I don't know. Has he written more than one?" 19

    "He has written several." 20

    "I didn't know that." 21

22   "What makes you want to read Mencken?"

23   "Oh, I just saw his name in the newspaper," I said.

24   "It's good of you to want to read," he said. "But you ought to read the right things."

25   I said nothing. Would he want to supervise my reading?

26   "Let me think," he said. "I'll figure out something."

27   I turned from him and he called me back. He stared at me quizzically.

28   "Richard, don't mention this to the other white men," he said.

29   "I understand," I said. "I won't say a word."

30   A few days later he called me to him.

31   "I've got a card in my wife's name," he said. "Here's mine."

32   "Thank you, sir."

33   "Do you think you can manage it?"

34   "I'll manage fine," I said.

35   "If they suspect you, you'll get in trouble," he said.

36   "I'll write the same kind of notes to the library that you wrote when you sent me for books," I told him. "I'll sign your name."

37   He laughed.

38   "Go ahead. Let me see what you get," he said.

39   That afternoon I addressed myself to forging a note. Now, what were the names of books written by H. L. Mencken? I did not know any of them. I finally wrote what I thought would be a foolproof note: *Dear Madam: Will you please let this nigger boy —* I used the word "nigger" to make the librarian feel that I could not possibly be the author of the note — *have some books by H. L. Mencken?* I forged the white man's name.

40   I entered the library as I had always done when on errands for whites, but I felt that I would somehow slip up and betray myself. I doffed my hat, stood a respectful distance from the desk, looked as unbookish as possible, and waited for the white patrons to be taken care of. When the desk was clear of people, I still waited. The white librarian looked at me.

41   "What do you want, boy?"

42   As though I did not possess the power of speech, I stepped forward and simply handed her the forged note, not parting my lips.

43   "What books by Mencken does he want?" she asked.

44   "I don't know, ma'am," I said, avoiding her eyes.

45   "Who gave you this card?"

46   "Mr. Falk," I said.

47   "Where is he?"

"He's at work, at the M—— Optical Company," I said. "I've 48
been in here for him before."

"I remember," the woman said. "But he never wrote notes like 49
this."

Oh, God, she's suspicious. Perhaps she would not let me have 50
the books? If she had turned her back at that moment, I would have
ducked out the door and never gone back. Then I thought of a bold
idea.

"You can call him up, ma'am," I said, my heart pounding. 51

"You're not using these books, are you?" she asked pointedly. 52

"Oh, no, ma'am. I can't read." 53

"I don't know what he wants by Mencken," she said under her 54
breath.

I knew now that I had won; she was thinking of other things and 55
the race question had gone out of her mind. She went to the shelves.
Once or twice she looked over her shoulder at me, as though she was
still doubtful. Finally she came forward with two books in her hand.

"I'm sending him two books," she said. "But tell Mr. Falk to 56
come in next time, or send me the names of the books he wants. I
don't know what he wants to read."

I said nothing. She stamped the card and handed me the books. 57
Not daring to glance at them, I went out of the library, fearing that the
woman would call me back for further questioning. A block away
from the library I opened one of the books and read a title: *A Book of
Prefaces*. I was nearing my nineteenth birthday and I did not know
how to pronounce the word "preface." I thumbed the pages and saw
strange words and strange names. I shook my head, disappointed. I
looked at the other book; it was called *Prejudices*. I knew what that
word meant; I had heard it all my life. And right off I was on guard
against Mencken's books. Why would a man want to call a book *Prejudices*? The word was so stained with all my memories of racial hate
that I could not conceive of anybody using it for a title. Perhaps I had
made a mistake about Mencken? A man who had prejudices must be
wrong.

When I showed the books to Mr. Falk, he looked at me and 58
frowned.

"That librarian might telephone you," I warned him. 59

"That's all right," he said. "But when you're through reading 60
those books, I want you to tell me what you get out of them."

That night in my rented room, while letting the hot water run 61
over my can of pork and beans in the sink, I opened *A Book of Prefaces*

and began to read. I was jarred and shocked by the style, the clear, clean, sweeping sentences. Why did he write like that? And how did one write like that? I pictured the man as a raging demon, slashing with his pen, consumed with hate, denouncing everything American, extolling everything European or German, laughing at the weaknesses of people, mocking God, authority. What was this? I stood up, trying to realize what reality lay behind the meaning of the words . . . Yes, this man was fighting, fighting with words. He was using words as a weapon, using them as one would use a club. Could words be weapons? Well, yes, for here they were. Then, maybe, perhaps, I could use them as a weapon? No. It frightened me. I read on and what amazed me was not what he said, but how on earth anybody had the courage to say it.

62   Occasionally I glanced up to reassure myself that I was alone in the room. Who were these men about whom Mencken was talking so passionately? Who was Anatole France? Joseph Conrad? Sinclair Lewis, Sherwood Anderson, Dostoevski, George Moore, Gustave Flaubert, Maupassant, Tolstoy, Frank Harris, Mark Twain, Thomas Hardy, Arnold Bennett, Stephen Crane, Zola, Norris, Gorky, Bergson, Ibsen, Balzac, Bernard Shaw, Dumas, Poe, Thomas Mann, O. Henry, Dreiser, H. G. Wells, Gogol, T. S. Eliot, Gide, Baudelaire, Edgar Lee Masters, Stendhal, Turgenev, Huneker, Nietzsche, and scores of others? Were these men real? Did they exist or had they existed? And how did one pronounce their names?

63   I ran across many words whose meanings I did not know, and I either looked them up in a dictionary or, before I had a chance to do that, encountered the word in a context that made its meaning clear. But what strange world was this? I concluded the book with the conviction that I had somehow overlooked something terribly important in life. I had once tried to write, had once reveled in feeling, had let my crude imagination roam, but the impulse to dream had been slowly beaten out of me by experience. Now it surged up again and I hungered for books, new ways of looking and seeing. It was not a matter of believing or disbelieving what I read, but of feeling something new, of being affected by something that made the look of the world different.

64   As dawn broke I ate my pork and beans, feeling dopey, sleepy. I went to work, but the mood of the book would not die; it lingered, coloring everything I saw, heard, did. I now felt that I knew what the white men were feeling. Merely because I had read a book that had spoken of how they lived and thought, I identified myself with that

book. I felt vaguely guilty. Would I, filled with bookish notions, act in a manner that would make the whites dislike me?

I forged more notes and my trips to the library became frequent. 65 Reading grew into a passion. My first serious novel was Sinclair Lewis's *Main Street*. It made me see my boss, Mr. Gerald, and identify him as an American type. I would smile when I saw him lugging his golf bags into the office. I had always felt a vast distance separating me from the boss, and now I felt closer to him, though still distant. I felt now that I knew him, that I could feel the very limits of his narrow life. And this had happened because I had read a novel about a mythical man called George F. Babbitt.

The plots and stories in the novels did not interest me so much 66 as the point of view revealed. I gave myself over to each novel without reserve, without trying to criticize it; it was enough for me to see and feel something different. And for me, everything was something different. Reading was like a drug, a dope. The novels created moods in which I lived for days. But I could not conquer my sense of guilt, my feeling that the white men around me knew that I was changing, that I had begun to regard them differently.

Whenever I brought a book to the job, I wrapped it in newspaper 67 — a habit that was to persist for years in other cities and under other circumstances. But some of the white men pried into my packages when I was absent and they questioned me.

"Boy, what are you reading those books for?" 68

"Oh, I don't know, sir." 69

"That's deep stuff you're reading, boy." 70

"I'm just killing time, sir." 71

"You'll addle your brains if you don't watch out." 72

I read Dreiser's *Jennie Gerhardt* and *Sister Carrie* and they re- 73 vived in me a vivid sense of my mother's suffering; I was overwhelmed. I grew silent, wondering about the life around me. It would have been impossible for me to have told anyone what I derived from these novels, for it was nothing less than a sense of life itself. All my life had shaped me for the realism, the naturalism of the modern novel, and I could not read enough of them.

Steeped in new moods and ideas, I bought a ream of paper and 74 tried to write; but nothing would come, or what did come was flat beyond telling. I discovered that more than desire and feeling were necessary to write and I dropped the idea. Yet I still wondered how it was possible to know people sufficiently to write about them? Could I ever learn about life and people? To me, with my vast ignorance, my

Jim Crow station in life, it seemed a task impossible of achievement. I now knew what being a Negro meant. I could endure the hunger. I had learned to live with hate. But to feel that there were feelings denied me, that the very breath of life itself was beyond my reach, that more than anything else hurt, wounded me. I had a new hunger.

75   In buoying me up, reading also cast me down, made me see what was possible, what I had missed. My tension returned, new, terrible, bitter, surging, almost too great to be contained. I no longer *felt* that the world about me was hostile, killing; I *knew* it. A million times I asked myself what I could do to save myself, and there were no answers. I seemed forever condemned, ringed by walls.

76   I did not discuss my reading with Mr. Falk, who had lent me his library card; it would have meant talking about myself and that would have been too painful. I smiled each day, fighting desperately to maintain my old behavior, to keep my disposition seemingly sunny. But some of the white men discerned that I had begun to brood.

77   "Wake up there, boy!" Mr. Olin said one day.

78   "Sir!" I answered for the lack of a better word.

79   "You act like you've stolen something," he said.

80   I laughed in the way I knew he expected me to laugh, but I resolved to be more conscious of myself, to watch my every act, to guard and hide the new knowledge that was dawning within me.

81   If I went north, would it be possible for me to build a new life then? But how could a man build a life upon vague, unformed yearnings? I wanted to write and I did not even know the English language. I bought English grammars and found them dull. I felt that I was getting a better sense of the language from novels than from grammars. I read hard, discarding a writer as soon as I felt that I had grasped his point of view. At night the printed page stood before my eyes in sleep.

82   Mrs. Moss, my landlady, asked me one Sunday morning:

83   "Son, what is this you keep on reading?"

84   "Oh, nothing. Just novels."

85   "What you get out of 'em?"

86   "I'm just killing time," I said.

87   "I hope you know your own mind," she said in a tone which implied that she doubted if I had a mind.

88   I knew of no Negroes who read the books I liked and I wondered if any Negroes ever thought of them. I knew that there were Negro doctors, lawyers, newspapermen, but I never saw any of them. When I read a Negro newspaper I never caught the faintest echo of my pre-

occupation in its pages. I felt trapped and occasionally, for a few days, I would stop reading. But a vague hunger would come over me for books, books that opened up new avenues of feeling and seeing, and again I would forge another note to the white librarian. Again I would read and wonder as only the naïve and unlettered can read and wonder, feeling that I carried a secret, criminal burden about with me each day.

That winter my mother and brother came and we set up house-   89
keeping, buying furniture on the installment plan, being cheated and yet knowing no way to avoid it. I began to eat warm food and to my surprise found that regular meals enabled me to read faster. I may have lived through many illnesses and survived them, never suspecting that I was ill. My brother obtained a job and we began to save toward the trip north, plotting our time, setting tentative dates for departure. I told none of the white men on the job that I was planning to go north; I knew that the moment they felt I was thinking of the North they would change toward me. It would have made them feel that I did not like the life I was living, and because my life was completely conditioned by what they said or did, it would have been tantamount to challenging them.

I could calculate my chances for life in the South as a Negro   90
fairly clearly now.

I could fight the southern whites by organizing with other Ne-   91
groes, as my grandfather had done. But I knew that I could never win that way; there were many whites and there were but few blacks. They were strong and we were weak. Outright black rebellion could never win. If I fought openly I would die and I did not want to die. News of lynchings were frequent.

I could submit and live the life of a genial slave, but that was   92
impossible. All of my life had shaped me to live by my own feelings, and thoughts. I could make up to Bess and marry her and inherit the house. But that, too, would be the life of a slave; if I did that, I would crush to death something within me, and I would hate myself as much as I knew the whites already hated those who had submitted. Neither could I ever willingly present myself to be kicked, as Shorty had done. I would rather have died than do that.

I could drain off my restlessness by fighting with Shorty and   93
Harrison. I had seen many Negroes solve the problem of being black by transferring their hatred of themselves to others with a black skin and fighting them. I would have to be cold to do that, and I was not cold and I could never be.

94   I could, of course, forget what I had read, thrust the whites out of my mind, forget them; and find release from anxiety and longing in sex and alcohol. But the memory of how my father had conducted himself made that course repugnant. If I did not want others to violate my life, how could I voluntarily violate it myself?

95   I had no hope whatever of being a professional man. Not only had I been so conditioned that I did not desire it, but the fulfillment of such an ambition was beyond my capabilities. Well-to-do Negroes lived in a world that was almost as alien to me as the world inhabited by whites.

96   What, then, was there? I held my life in my mind, in my consciousness each day, feeling at times that I would stumble and drop it, spill it forever. My reading had created a vast sense of distance between me and the world in which I lived and tried to make a living, and that sense of distance was increasing each day. My days and nights were one long, quiet, continuously contained dream of terror, tension, and anxiety. I wondered how long I could bear it.

____ CONSIDERATIONS ____

1. How do you heat a can of beans if you don't have a hot plate in your room? How is Wright's answer to this question an autobiographical fact that might affect your appreciation of his essay?

2. In Paragraph 65, Wright says of himself, "Reading grew into a passion." You don't have to look too far in the lives of other writers to find similar statements about reading. Reread the first paragraph of the Preface to this book, and think about the importance of reading to your prospects of improving as a writer.

3. Compare what Wright had to endure to use the public library with your own introduction to the same institution. How do you account for the motivation Wright needed to break the barriers between him and freedom to read?

4. The word Wright uses throughout to refer to his own race is no longer widely accepted. Why? What other words have been used at other times in American history? What difference does a name make?

5. Notice how Wright uses dialogue in this essay. How do you decide when to use dialogue? What are its purposes?

6. The authors mentioned by Wright in his essay would make a formidable reading program for anyone. If you were to lay out such a program for yourself, what titles would you include? Why?

A Rhetorical Index

The various writing patterns — argument and persuasion, description, exposition, and narration — are amply illustrated in the many essays, stories, journal entries, and poems in *A Writer's Reader*. If any classification of writing according to type is suspect — because good writers inevitably merge the types — this index offers one plausible arrangement. Anyone looking for models or examples for study and imitation may well begin here.

A word about subcategories: We index two sorts of argument — formal and implicit — because some selections are obvious attempts to defend a stated proposition, often in high style, whereas others argue indirectly, informally, or diffusely, but persuasively nonetheless. Under "Description" we index not only whole selections, but also sections within selections that primarily describe persons, places, or miscellaneous phenomena. We call "Expository" selections those which clearly show the various rhetorical patterns of development: example, classification, cause and effect, comparison and contrast, process analysis, and definition. Again, both whole selections and separate paragraphs are listed. "Narration" categorizes memoirs, essays, stories, and nonfiction nonautobiographical narratives.

We have starred short selections (under 1,200 words). Numbers in parentheses refer to paragraph numbers within selections. At the end, we list the non-essay materials in the *Reader* — journal entries, short stories, poems, and drama.

ARGUMENT AND PERSUASION

DESCRIPTION

EXPOSITION

NARRATION

JOURNALS, DIARIES, NOTEBOOKS, SHORT TAKES

SHORT STORIES

POEMS

DRAMA

A Thematic Index

BIOGRAPHY, AUTOBIOGRAPHY, TRUE STORIES

CHILDHOOD, GROWING UP, RITES OF PASSAGE

CONTESTS, STRUGGLES, WINS AND LOSSES

EDUCATION, THE GETTING OF WISDOM

EPIPHANY, IMAGINATION, VISION

FAMILIES, PARENTS AND OFFSPRING

FREEDOM AND RESTRAINT, OPPRESSORS AND OPPRESSED

INDIVIDUALITY, PRIVACY, SOLITUDE

MEN AND WOMEN, LOVE, SEXUALITY

MUTABILITY, AGING, DEATH

NATURE, ENVIRONMENT, WONDERS OF CREATION

PLAY, GAMES, SPORTING LIFE

REBELS AND CONFORMISTS

RELIGION, GOD, FAITH, SPIRITUAL LIFE

SCIENTIFIC INQUIRY AND DISCOVERY

THE SOCIAL FABRIC, GOVERNMENT, FAMILY OF MAN

WORKING

WRITING, LANGUAGE, RHETORIC, AND STYLE

To the Student

Part of our job as educational publishers is to try to improve the textbooks we publish. Thus, when revising we take into account the experience of both instructors and students with the previous edition. At some time in the future your instructor will be asked to comment extensively on *A Writer's Reader*, Third Edition, but right now we want to hear from you. After all, though your instructor assigned this book, you are the one for whom it is intended (and the one who paid for it).

Please help us by completing this questionnaire and returning it to College English Developmental Group, Little, Brown and Company, 34 Beacon Street, Boston, Mass. 02106.

School _____Course Title _____

Instructor's Name _____

Other Books Assigned _____

Tell us about the readings.

	KEEP	DROP	DID NOT READ
ADAMS, *Winter and Summer*	____	____	____
AGEE, *Knoxville, Summer 1915*	____	____	____
ALLEN, *Death Knocks*	____	____	____
ANGELOU, *Mr. Red Leg*	____	____	____
ARNOLD, *Dover Beach*	____	____	____
AUDUBON, *The Passenger Pigeon*	____	____	____
BALDWIN, *Autobiographical Notes*	____	____	____

	KEEP	DROP	DID NOT READ
BERGMANN, *Two Sides of Freedom*	——	——	——
BERNSTEIN, *The Art of Conducting*	——	——	——
BIBLE, *From Ecclesiastes*	——	——	——
BIERCE, *Some Devil's Definitions*	——	——	——
BIRD, *Where College Fails Us*	——	——	——
BLY, *Getting Tired*	——	——	——
BLYTHE, *Aging and Sexuality*	——	——	——
BOULDING, *Nature and Artifice*	——	——	——
BOURNE, *A Philosophy of Handicap*	——	——	——
CATTON, *Grant and Lee . . .*	——	——	——
CONROY, *A Yo-Yo Going Down*	——	——	——
DAVIS, *Logic and Logical Fallacies*	——	——	——
DICKINSON, *There's a certain Slant of light*	——	——	——
DIDION, *On Keeping a Notebook*	——	——	——
DILLARD, *Strangers to Darkness*	——	——	——
DOUGLASS, *Plantation Life*	——	——	——
EISELEY, *How Flowers Changed the World*	——	——	——
EPHRON, *A Few Words about Breasts*	——	——	——
FAULKNER, *A Rose for Emily*	——	——	——
FEIFFER, *Superman*	——	——	——
FITZGERALD, *Journal Entries*	——	——	——
FITZGERALD (LANAHAN), *Introduction to Letters to His Daughter*	——	——	——
FITZGERALD, *Letters to His Daughter*	——	——	——
FRANKLIN, *From Poor Richard's Almanack*	——	——	——
FROST, *The Gift Outright*	——	——	——
GANSBERG, *38 Who Saw Murder . . .*	——	——	——
HELLMAN, *Runaway*	——	——	——
HEMINGWAY, *Hills Like White Elephants*	——	——	——
HUGHES, *Salvation*	——	——	——
HUGHES, *Two Poems*	——	——	——
HUGHES, *Two Tales of Simple*	——	——	——
JEFFERSON, *The Declarations . . .*	——	——	——
LAWRENCE, *Pornography*	——	——	——
LINCOLN, *The Gettysburg Address*	——	——	——
McPHEE, *Ancestors of the Jump Shot*	——	——	——
MAILER, *A Walk on the Moon*	——	——	——

	KEEP	DROP	DID NOT READ
MARVELL, *To His Coy Mistress*	____	____	____
MENCKEN, *Gamalielese*	____	____	____
MOMADAY, *The Way to Rainy Mountain*	____	____	____
MORGAN, *Exam-Week Unrealities*	____	____	____
MORRIS, *Odd Balls*	____	____	____
NIN, *Journal Entry*	____	____	____
O'CONNOR, *The Total Effect and the Eighth Grade*	____	____	____
O'CONNOR, *A Good Man Is Hard to Find*	____	____	____
O'CONNOR, *From Flannery O'Connor's Letters*	____	____	____
ORWELL, *Politics and the English Language*	____	____	____
ORWELL, *Shooting an Elephant*	____	____	____
ORWELL, *A Hanging*	____	____	____
PARRISH, *Welcome to Vietnam*	____	____	____
PAZ, *Mexican-American Differences*	____	____	____
PIRSIG, *The Church of Reason*	____	____	____
PLATH, *Journal Entries*	____	____	____
PLATH, *The Bee Meeting*	____	____	____
PLATO, *Socrates to His Accusers*	____	____	____
RETTIE, *"But a Watch in the Night"*	____	____	____
SAGAN, *The Measure of Eratosthenes*	____	____	____
SHAKESPEARE, *That time of year . . .*	____	____	____
SHARP, *Under the Hood*	____	____	____
STAFFORD, *A Way of Writing*	____	____	____
SWIFT, *A Modest Proposal*	____	____	____
TERKEL, *Phil Stallings, Spot Welder*	____	____	____
THOMAS, *Notes on Punctuation*	____	____	____
THOREAU, *To Build My House*	____	____	____
THURBER, *Which*	____	____	____
TWAIN, *Was the World Made for Man?*	____	____	____
TYNAN, *Here's Johnny! . . .*	____	____	____
UPDIKE, *Ace in the Hole*	____	____	____
VIDAL, *Drugs*	____	____	____
WELTY, *A Worn Path*	____	____	____
WELTY, *The Point of the Story*	____	____	____
WHITE, *Once More to the Lake*	____	____	____

	KEEP	DROP	DID NOT READ
WOLFE, *Journal Entries*	——	——	——
WOOLF, *If Shakespeare Had Had a Sister*	——	——	——
WRIGHT, *The Library Card*	——	——	——

Did you use the Rhetorical and Thematic Indexes?————————

How might they be improved?————————————————

————————————————————————————————

————————————————————————————————

Were the Introductions and Considerations that accompany each selection helpful?———— How might they be improved?————

————————————————————————————————

————————————————————————————————

Should we add more stories and poems?————————————

Please add any further comments or suggestions.————————

————————————————————————————————

————————————————————————————————

————————————————————————————————

Date ———— Your Name ————————————————

————————————————————————————————

Mailing Address